Resort Destinations
Evolution, Management and Development

Resort Destinations
Evolution, Management and Development

Bruce Prideaux
Professor of Marketing and Tourism Management
James Cook University, Australia

AMSTERDAM • BOSTON • HEIDELBERG • LONDON
NEW YORK • OXFORD • PARIS • SAN DIEGO
SAN FRANCISCO • SYDNEY • TOKYO
Butterworth-Heinemann is an imprint of Elsevier

Butterworth-Heinemann is an imprint of Elsevier
Linacre House, Jordan Hill, Oxford OX2 8DP, UK
30 Corporate Drive, Suite 400, Burlington, MA 01803, USA

CRL
338. 4791068 PRI
7 day

British Library Cataloguing in Publication Data
A catalogue record for this book is available from the British Library

Library of Congress Cataloging-in-Publication Data
A catalog record for this book is available from the Library of Congress

ISBN: 978-0-7506-5753-2

For information on all Butterworth–Heinemann publications
visit our web site at www.elsevierdirect.com

Printed and bound in Great Britain
09 10 11 12   10 9 8 7 6 5 4 3 2 1

Dedication

To the very special people in my life, my dear wife Lin and our children Jillian, Benjamin, Joshua, Krystin and Jeremy.

Thank you for your support patience and encouragement without which this book would never have been possible.

Thank you to my many colleagues for their advise on this project, Alana Iles who assisted in the writing of Chapter 6, Sally North whose encouragement helped me complete the journey and the team at Elsevier who guided me through the production process.

Contents

Preface

Destinations and resorts are key building blocks in the development and operation of the global tourism system. Their viability, sustainability and long term management are critical to a healthy global tourism system. While much has been written on aspects of destinations and resorts, including their development, management, sustainability, marketing, history and so forth major gaps remain. The aim of this book is to examine some of these gaps with a specific emphasis on future sustainability in its broadest sense in a rapidly changing world where the future will be redefined in ways that are not yet obvious but which must be speculated on and planned for. Climate change and the enormous cost of providing food and shelter for a future global population that according to the UN is likely to be 50% higher in 2050 than today will present enormous challenges to the global political system and strain global markets to provide the basics of life. The most recent news on the climate front is that the IPCC's (2007) forecast of sea level changes are significantly underestimated and that a rise of 1 meter of more is now more likely than not. This has significant implications for coastal tourism and the 50% of the global population who live in coastal zones. The reordering of global markets in the wake of the Global Financial Crisis may see a fundamental shift from neo-liberal free market economics to a more regulated global economy. All of these forces and many more discussed in this book will create a new world in which tourism will continue to thrive but within constraints that take into account the impact of climate change and the need to achieve a new level of sustainability that recognizes there are limits to growth. Destinations will need to adapt to these new realities. It is my hope that this book goes at least some way to contributing to the debate we need to have on how the gathering storm of climate change and declining global sustainability will be confronted at the destination level.

Bruce Prideaux

CHAPTER 1

Introduction

When confronted by change innovation is a strategy for success

Tourism destinations are an important and intellectually fascinating component of the global tourism system. From an academic perspective destinations (and resorts) have provided a fertile ground for research. The three-decade long debate sparked by the publication of Butler's Tourism Area Life Cycle in 1980 testifies to the passion that issues related to destinations and resorts have aroused. Surprisingly, the debate has focused on specific forms of destinations and resorts and the problems they face with less emphasis on a more general discussion about the role of destinations within the overall tourism system. Moreover, there has been a dearth of research into a number of significant issues including climate change, climbing rates of urbanization and peak oil that are now beginning to have an impact on the structure and operation of destinations. The WTO (2002) and leading tourism sector firms including Airbus Industries (Airbus Industries, 2007) continue to forecast significant growth in international travel, but the reality as Becken (2008) reminds us is that the oil-dependent aviation sector will face a significant shortfall in jet fuel availability as we begin to move into an era of declining oil output but increasing demand. The implications for destinations of changes of this magnitude have yet to be assessed in detail. To begin the process of redressing this research gap this book examines destinations from a new perspective by integrating research on specific aspects of destinations (modelling, planning, transport and crisis management) with the responses of specific destination types (cities, coastal zones, mountains and islands) to these challenges. The book then moves the debate on these issues forward to focus on how destinations might respond to the significant challenges of the future.

There are dangers in this approach given that some of these areas of enquiry have already developed an extensive literature. A single book cannot hope to

1

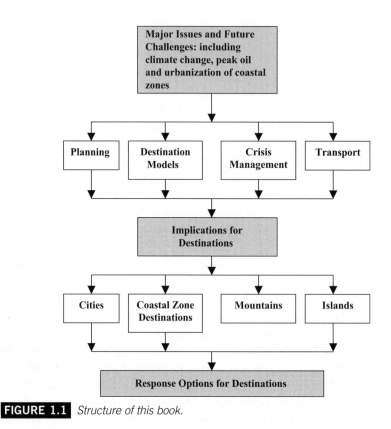

FIGURE 1.1 *Structure of this book.*

cover each area of interest in detail resulting in some issues being glossed over and others ignored. But the aim of the book is not to undertake an exhaustive analysis of specific aspects of destination research. Rather, the aim is to draw together a number of themes and apply them in a more holistic manner to stimulate a new direction in the ongoing study of the destination and resort phenomenon. The structure of the book is outlined in Figure 1.1. This chapter sets the scene for the discussion of a range of issues later in the book, commencing with the approach taken in individual chapters. The chapter concludes with a brief overview of a number of key concepts discussed in later chapters.

APPROACH TAKEN

Chapter 2 commences with a discussion on destination models, their purpose, how they are used and in some cases abused. Models are a popular method of explaining complex problems but it is apparent that models have limitations including an inability to move beyond the explanatory stage. As a consequence few models have been operationalized to the extent that they are able to be regularly used by policy makers and planners to find solutions to real-life situations. This situation reflects similar difficulties encountered by other areas of the social sciences when attempts are made to model complex, time-sensitive, multi-faceted problems. In the physical sciences computer modelling has been successfully used to build complex structures including aircraft, spacecraft, bridges and ships. The unpredictability of consumer demand has and will continue to be a major impediment to social science modelling of this type but that should not be an excuse for failing to try. Even simple measures of the nature suggested in Chapter 2 (Figure 2.8) can enrich our understanding of the operation of destinations, given that the majority of tourism models are necessarily a simplified version of a more complex reality. As a consequence, the application of a group of specialist models to problem solving in specific areas of enquiry is likely to give a more detailed and informed view than the application of a single model can hope to achieve. Of even more importance is the need to recognize that most tourism models can more properly be described as theories and should be treated as such. Models of this nature are excellent as teaching tools and for explaining the trends of the past. They are not adequate for planning the future. Just as economists seek to model national economies using complex econometric computer-based models, there is a need for tourism researchers to team with economists and other experts to build a new generation of predictive models that can assist in destination planning and management.

The fundamental requirement for effective destination governance and a sustainable future cannot be achieved without effective, thoughtful science and mindful consultative planning as highlighted in later chapters. While complex and time consuming planning should not been seen as an administrative process that is used to archive a preferred outcome but as a process that encourages multi-party dialogue, debate, acceptance that there are constraints imposed by the physical and natural environment, and recognition of the voice of all stakeholders. In the coming age of great change it is essential that the debate recognizes that the future will be different from the present. This has not always been the reality of destination planning and in their haste to develop plans administrators, planners and investors have often ignored the complexities of time and the mechanisms of change. Even a passing analysis of history reveals the dynamic nature of time and change, the difficulty of prediction and the cost of ignoring warnings. Forecasts rarely achieve a high level of accuracy, essentially because the relationships of the past are rarely mimicked in the future. Yet more than ever there is a need to identify the forces that are shaping the future and develop strategies for forward planning that will minimize disruption and maximize opportunities.

New Orleans was poorly prepared for the disaster that occurred when Hurricane Katrina struck the city on 29 August 2005. Over 1800 persons perished and the damage bill was estimated to be in excess of US$ 80 billion (Khadd *et al.*, 2006). The city and the various agencies of the state and federal governments were simply not prepared for the disaster that unfolded. Fast forward 3 years to Hurricane Gustav (which struck on 2 September 2008) and we see an entirely different situation. Evacuation of nearly 3 million residents commenced several days before the Hurricane was predicted to strike the city, and the civilian emergency authorities and the military were better equipped and trained to assist the city's administration. Before Hurricane Katrina disaster planning had largely ignored what was then regarded as a one in one hundred year chance of being struck by a hurricane of the force of Katrina. After Hurricane Katrina it was apparent that the one in one hundred year chance did not mean the event would happen in a hundred years time and repair works were undertaken to prepare for a future hurricane of this intensity. As is argued in Chapter 5 disaster planning needs to be shifted from an optional activity to be included as a necessary element of destination planning and in marketing strategies.

A central tenant of planning is to develop a future that is desirable and that is an improvement on today's situation. For many, the desirable future is viewed as a bigger and more attractive destination than the present. In reality it is of more importance to create destinations that are sustainable. Forecasts of future tourism flows used for planning investment by the private and public sectors have a poor record of accuracy over the long term and often fail to incorporate the unexpected. In Chapter 3 and later in Chapter 10 the discussion considers a number of factors that influence the future and how the future can be understood within the context of the factors of change currently observable in society, economy and nature. Scenarios are suggested as an additional planning tool that, used in conjunction with other forecasting methodologies, offer the promise of a more sophisticated glimpse into the future than can be achieved with the methods currently used. Despite their promise alternative methods of forecasting have been largely ignored, perhaps because numerical predictions of future tourism flows are easier to understand than a more conceptual version of the future that passes the onus of selection of alternatives onto the user. Given the poor track record of existing quantitative forecasting, it is apparent that other complementary or alternative methodologies should be considered. The reality is that unexpected shocks that deflect forecasts from their predicted path are normal rather than exceptional (Prideaux and Laws, 2007).

Although forecasting specific patterns of tourism flows on an annualized basis has been difficult, the aggregate pattern of flows over the last century have been upward, spurred on by increasing global GDP and assisted by a global transport system that has consistently adopted new technologies to reduce travel costs while increasing safety, comfort and reach. Surprisingly, the literature has largely ignored the role of the transport system as an agent in tourism growth leaving it to other disciplines to undertake transport-related research. As Chapter 4 argues, transport is an important element in the global tourism system and an element will come under increasing pressure in the near future from policies designed to mitigate the effects of climate change and from the anticipated global shortfall in oil supplies (Duval, 2007; Becken, 2008). It is apparent that the role of transport has been either taken as a given or ignored for so long that many researchers and destinations remain unaware of the potential dangers that lie ahead, or worse, are in denial of these dangers. The chapter seeks to place transport issues to the forefront of future research arguing that the manner in which the transport industry responds to the cost challenges of climate change mitigation policies including carbon trading, is able to adopt new technologies including third generation biofuels and other substitute fuel sources, and adapt to the pressures of rapid urbanization will be a major factor in shaping future pattern of demands for all types of destinations.

The theme of crisis management is developed in Chapter 5 and should be seen as an essential component of destination management. Crises are rarely predictable as a specific event but are common and should be incorporated into planning and management of destinations. The previous discussion on New Orleans highlights the difference between an unprepared destination (New Orleans in 2005) and a prepared destination (New Orleans 2008). It is apparent that crises are a complex phenomenon and deserve considerable attention from academics, policy makers, planners and the private sector.

As later chapters argue the genesis of some of the crises that will confront tourism and destinations in the future can be found in the present. The previous discussion on the major issues facing the global transport system is one example amongst many. We now realize that oil availability will be a significant problem and policy makers in some countries have commenced the task of looking for solutions. While the tourism literature has now elevated the study of crisis to a more mainstream position in the research agenda there remains a reflective or reactive feel about the direction of crisis research. Crises of the near past have been analysed and response frameworks suggested, but the consideration of future crises has been largely neglected. This book argues that emerging crises, some of which are now apparent, have the potential to profoundly change the structure of global tourism flows. It is now time to move the study of crisis forward to consider the future while continuing to draw on the lessons of the past.

Understanding that the past is a key requisite for developing an appreciation of how structures and relationships have developed and where institutions and individuals fit into the mosaic of the contemporary world. While concern for the present is important it is how we prepare for the future that will determine the long-term success or otherwise of destinations. If we seek to shape and direct policies and other activities to achieve a better future we need to understand how the factors that have shaped today will play out over time and where, through intervention, it is possible to create a more desirable future. Figure 1.2 highlights the concept of change that is developed in greater detail in Chapter 10. Change is constant, often not understood, usually unnoticed but often precedes a new order or state of being. Change drives society and tourism. As Chapter 10 argues, successful destinations must seek to understand change and channel the implications of change into directions that enhance the competitiveness and desirability of the destination. Successful destinations are also innovative destinations and understand the competitive advantages of being the leader in introducing new ideas.

As much as possible the various aspects of destinations considered in this book look at the past, present and future in the belief that the past informs the present and that the present informs, to some degree, the future. Figure 1.2 seeks to encapsulate this idea of time and events.

To explore how the themes of planning, modelling, crisis management, future and issues of sustainability may be understood in a destination context, four specific types of destinations were selected for analysis. Each destination type provides an opportunity to measure the impact of the preceding themes.

In the past there has been a tradition of evaluating the role of cities in a context that emphasized type, function and activity categories in preference to spatial and ecological considerations. The result is a growing literature on the

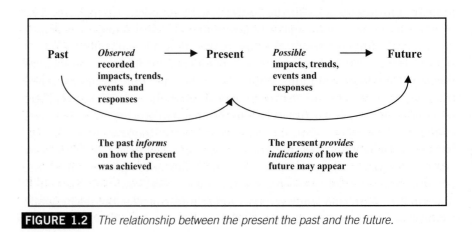

FIGURE 1.2   *The relationship between the present the past and the future.*

role of historic cities, city destinations and seaside resorts. Less emphasis has been placed on the relationship between the city and the surrounding spatial and ecological environment. For this reason coastal tourism research has focused on seaside resorts and their connection to the tourism system while largely ignoring the spatial and ecological contexts they exist within. Chapter 6 follows a traditional approach to classifying the roles and activities of cities in the tourism system before investigating how cities are able to respond to change and what form future cities may take. In Chapter 7 this book adopts a different approach to the study of coastal tourism. Coastal cities and their tourism industries are considered from the perspective of their position and role in the coastal zone rather than their evolution as a seaside tourism location. This redefining of the context of coastal tourism follows the wider social science and scientific literature which now recognizes the need to consider issues affecting coastally located cities in a broad social, ecological, economic, environmental, planning and administrative context rather than in isolation. A continuing recognition of the importance of tourism in the emerging discipline of coastal zone management should not be assumed. Tourism must compete with other industries and other land uses and must be able to demonstrate its ability to contribute to city economies. While the worth of tourism from a tourism industry perspective is apparent this view might not be shared by other actors in the coastal zone. To prove its worth and justify its inclusion in the wider debates now emerging on issues that confront coastal zone management the tourism industry must look beyond its industry and disciplinary confines, fund extensive research to become conversant with emerging trends, prove its relevancy and take its place with other actors in the coastal zone debate.

Mountains are dominating features of the landscape that have attracted huge tourism interest in recent decades. The democratization of recreational activities including skiing and the opening up of remote mountainous regions has created a new four-season playground although not without a cost to the environment. As Chapter 8 argues mountains are fascinating, challenging and despite their looming presence are places where fragile ecosystems often reel under the impact of unsympathetic development. As with the other ecosystems described in this book climate change is likely to have a significant impact on mountain communities, ecosystems and the future sustainability of tourism use of some mountain landscapes. The ability of mountain destinations to recognize emerging threats, develop planning approaches that encourage adaptation and adopt innovative approaches to product development will determine their future place in the global order of destinations.

Islands have a charm and mystique that has long been the playground for novelists, filmmakers and marketers. The images they create have become incorporated into a more general view of islands as desirable places for play, escape and carefreeness. Numerous island communities have seized on this view and embraced tourism as a path to economic development but in the process have exposed their social, economic, cultural and natural environments to change that in some cases has not been managed well. Chapter 9 examines a range of issues that are now beginning to have an impact on the future viability of island destinations. How island destinations respond to the issues of globalization, social change, climate change, peak oil, etc. and to the local issues of sustainability and the plethora of other issues that daily confront island tourism industries will determine their future success and place in the global tourism industry.

This book aims to place the study of destinations within two contexts, the tourism context where destinations are a major component of the tourism system, and in a wider global context where tourism is one of a large number of industries that have benefited from global economic growth but that will also experience problems in the future as new global issues arise and solutions are developed. To ignore this larger external environment in which tourism is only one of many competing actors, is to ignore events that shape tourism demand and the ability of destinations to satisfy that demand. The issue of climate change is increasingly being recognized as a major factor that will impact on tourism in the near future. However, a number of other factors must also be recognized including changing consumer demand patterns, the changing nature of family composition, challengers from other areas of consumer demand, peak oil, growing world population, rapid urbanization on a global scale, new technologies, the quest for sustainability, food security, political conflict, insurgency and the fight by some groups for political voice, water security and pandemics. Many of these issues have been ignored or given little priority by tourism researchers; however, the impact of events such as the Asian Financial Crisis of 1997–1998, SARS in 2003, and the 9/11 attack on the United States have shown that ignoring the issues associated with crisis will not make them go away and in many cases, as demonstrated by the volcanic eruption in Rabaul (the 20th century version of Pompeii), failure to recognize crisis will compound losses and delay recovery.

INNOVATION

From a tourism perspective innovation is central to achieving tourism development that is sustainable, adaptive and competitive (Carson and Jacobsen, 2005). The process of innovation describes the recognition, adaption and successful adoption of new ideas and techniques in a specific setting (Rogers, 1995). Lee *et al.* (2000) describe systemic innovation as a continuous process of generating and applying new ideas to the creation and upgrading of products, processes and services. In the tourism industry, innovation involves identifying multiple approaches to using existing resources while engaging in a search of new ideas (Macbeth and Carson, 2005).

From a destination perspective Jacobsen (2005) identified a number of factors that may be necessary to develop innovative tourism destinations:

- A sense of leadership that recognizes the need to take calculated risks which lead to change and the skills to identify and acquire necessary resources for this process;
- An ability to form effective collaborations and partnerships with other stakeholders in the system;
- An ability to obtain and share knowledge about the market;
- Effective interactions between the public and private sectors and consumers;
- A willingness to adopt new ideas and technologies;
- A sufficient amount of resources, including financial resources, infrastructure and knowledge to test new ideas and to allow for failures;
- Points of focus including natural and cultural assets which inspire alternative views about their use and lead to multiple options for development.

Roger's (1995) well-known model of innovation (see Figure 1.3) explains innovation as a process that occurs over time where innovators seek out and take up new ideas later followed by others variously described as early and later adopters and a final group who never adopt. Innovation gives early adopters a time advantage allowing them to introduce new products and in the process increase profits. Late adopters enter the market when it is becoming increasingly competitive and may find it difficult to generate adequate profits.

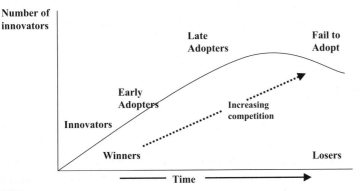

FIGURE 1.3   *Rogers' Model of Innovation.*
Source: adapted from Rogers (1995)

As will be argued later in this book innovation is a key strategy for successfully responding to the dangers that are now beginning to confront many destinations. The literature on innovation as an area of research is large and growing although sadly tourism specific research remains in its infancy.

PROBLEMS WITH DEFINITIONS

When approaching the study of destinations from a global perspective it becomes apparent that there remain definitional issues over the appropriate use of the terms 'resort' and 'destination'. In part, this is a result of the use of these terms by the industry and policy makers and the context in which the terms were originally applied. Resorts can be defined in a number of ways and from a number of perspectives, depending upon the purpose of the definition. In the Australian context, the term 'resort' is sometimes used interchangeably with the term 'destination'. The term is also used to describe individual properties, resulting in some confusion as to the precise meaning of the term. King (1994) notes that apart from using the word resort as a noun or verb it has also been used as an adverb, is poorly defined and can be used to describe localities that range from the highly specific to the highly nebulous. Craik (1991) used the word resort as a term of abuse or rebuke. Tourism, according to Craik, is 'resorted to' because of the absence of viable alternatives to the mass tourism experiences available at many coastal resorts.

In the earliest use of the word, resort was used to describe a seaside holiday locality or a mountain ski town. In the European context the term 'resort' describes a spatial entity where tourism is a major activity. Seaside and mountain resorts are examples of this usage of the term. In the same context the term 'destination' is used to describe larger spatial areas that may range in size from a province (examples include Tasmania, Rhode Island, Jersey, Rajasthan, Wales) to a nation or even several nations. The European view of the resort-destination continuum is illustrated in the south of England where Cornish coastal towns including Torquay and Padstow may be classified as resorts while Cornwell may be classified as a destination. In Asia, Kuta on the island of Bali may be classed as a resort while Bali is classed as a destination. It is inevitable, given the lack of precision prevalent in tourism research, as in other social sciences, that matters of definition are imprecise and the subject of continuing debate.

It is not possible, given the existing state of debate, to identify a global definition of resort, nor is it necessarily desirable to do so. In this book the term 'destination' is used in preference to the term resort to achieve consistency although resort is used to a limited extent in Chapter 7 in recognition to the traditional use of the term as applied to seaside areas where tourism is a major economic activity and in Chapter 8 for similar reasons.

THE FUTURE GLOBAL ECONOMY

In the future issues that include globalization, changing consumer trends, climate change, peak oil, water security, food security, and global population growth will test the ability of global society to adapt and meet these challenges in a way that secures not only the future of current generations but also of future generations. One issue that has yet to attract significant attention is the shape of the future global economy. The demise of communism and before it fascism in the 20th century has left capitalism as the dominate model for economic organization. In its current form, the capitalist model is based on the neo-liberal philosophy of continuing growth. Given that many non-renewable resources are likely to be exhausted at some time in the future growth in its current form sustainable or even desirable? At the time this book was written there was an emerging debate on the failure of Laissez-faire neo-liberalism capitalism and speculation on the need for a revamped social democratic capitalism where a resurrected state was prepared to actively intervene to regulate markets.

If growth of the nature we know today and have experienced for many centuries ceases to be an option for the future because of exhaustion of raw materials it becomes critical to understand how the global economy will respond. Unfortunately this issue has yet to emerge as an area of research interest in much the same way that the first IPCC (1990) report on climate change failed to generate wide debate then and even two decades later continues to be largely ignored in the tourism literature. Yet this is a fundamental issue that will at some point in the future demand the attention of policy makers while raising the anger of leaders of developing nations that face being shut off from the type of growth currently enjoyed by citizens of the developed nations. In a post-capitalist global economy how will resources be allocated, will losers be compensated and to what extend will tourism be allowed to participate in the new economy? As difficult as these questions are, they do need to be considered.

Using the Ecological Footprint approach to estimating the Earth's carrying capacity Krebs (2008:533) observed 'By this measure, the Earth is already at its full carrying capacity, and many countries have exceeded their available ecological resources and are thus in deficit'. Some might claim that the measurement of carrying capacity using the Ecological Footprint argument is a Malthusian approach and overly alarmist. As with Malthus's gloomy prediction in his treatise (*An Essay on the Principle of Population* published as six editions between 1798 and 1826) that exponential population growth would overwhelm the Earth's resources, the anti-growth lobby's prediction of growing disruption and forecasts of ecological disaster echoes earlier fears expressed by Y2K proponents who predicted widespread economic and social disruption. The pro-growth lobby point to technology and innovation as the keys to sustaining growth or least as the mechanism for averting the doomsday scenarios offered by some extreme no-growth proponents. This approach has succeeded in the past allowing global population numbers to far exceed the point at which Malthus felt that the global population was sustainable. The alternative views on future growth are: growth is desirable and achievable provided new technological fixes continue to provide solutions; or we have now exceeded global carrying capacity and further growth is unsustainable. The resolution of this fundamental question awaits the passing of time, the impact of events and the reaction of the international political processes. At the destination level the impact will be some time away. Preparation for change of this magnitude is exceedingly difficult but must commence with recognition that the problem exists and be followed by the adoption of innovation as a core value for planning, product development and marketing.

THE ROLE OF SCIENCE

In a number of chapters this book argues that it is essential to recognize that science can perform a useful role in informing the tourism community of the options that are available for the use of particular natural resources. All too often the interests of the developer or the economy in general are put ahead of the environment in the belief that nature can be dominated and made to do what is required of it. It is now obvious that in many circumstance, the domination approach leads to degradation and lost of ecological integrity. Climate change is an example of our collective ability to ignore the environmental implications of our actions and our continuing inability to change despite the obvious perils of failing to change. Domination, a theme that has been central to the manner in which tourism has often approached development and its use of nature is closer to destruction than coexistence.

For many years the literature has called for environmental responsibility and recognition of the need for sustainability but the tourism industry in general has been slow to listen. A better grounding in science is one avenue for demonstrating the positives of sustainability and for highlighting the costs of unsustainable practices. Case Study 8.2 highlights how science can contribute to our understanding of change giving those who recognize the threat time to respond and develop new experiences and activities. Part of the solution might be to recruit collaborators from within the ranks of the scientific community and develop new paradigms for transdiscipline research blending the power of scientific enquiry and measurement with the social sciences understanding of human society.

CASE STUDIES

A number of authors (Parkhe, 1993; Yin, 1989, 1993, 1994) have highlighted the usefulness of case studies as a research method. Robson (1993:52) defined case studies as a research strategy *'which involves an empirical investigation of a particular phenomenon within its real life context using multiple evidences'*. In practice, many investigations into tourism development had adopted this approach to research. Yin (1989:23; 1994:13) identified the four core components of case study research as:

- investigation of a contemporary phenomenon within its real-life context; when
- boundaries between phenomenon and context are not clearly evident,
- multiple sources of evidence are used and
- research should be part of a comprehensive research strategy, not just a data collection tactic or a design feature.

According to Yin (1994) case studies also enable the integration of patterns of behaviour for understanding phenomenon of interest. For these reasons this book presents a number of case studies to highlight specific aspects of the topics under discussion.

SUMMARY

This chapter has outlined the approach to the study of destinations that lies at the core of this book. Given that the aim of the discussion is to build a holistic view of the destination phenomenon many issues are introduced but not discussed in depth, a task that must be left to other authors or for the future. Many of the issues raised should be incorporated into future research agendas including:

- Innovation will be one of the keys to successful adaptation to change in the future.
- Climate change will not go away and must be moved into a more prominent position in destination research.
- The world will at some time in the future enter a new stage of history where the prevailing capitalist model of economic organization will be challenged and must change from a philosophy of encouraging growth based on gaining access to new resources to a new form of economic organization that ensures demand is within the limits of the global environment to deliver. How this will be achieved will have significant implications for the tourism industry and all other industries.

- Further growth of existing and new destinations will need to be achieved within the resources available on a global basis. There is likely to be a scramble for control of resources with winners (those who can pay) and losers (those who cannot pay) and the potential for conflict in this process.
- What impact will globalization and the seemingly inexhaustible passion for war on a grand scale have on tourism and destinations? We can only speculate and hope for peaceful resolution hoping that as many argue, tourism is a force for promoting peace.

CHAPTER 2

Modelling Destination Development

Models simplify understanding but in this process there is a danger that simplicity will replace complexity in our understanding of the phenomena

INTRODUCTION

Attempts to identify and model the forces and processes that collectively shape the rate of growth and in some circumstances the decline of destinations have occupied the attention of tourism researchers for decades, commencing as early as 1939 when Gilbert examined the growth of inland and seaside health resorts in England. Since that time the topic has become an enduring area of research and debate in the tourism literature and continues to be a popular area of research. To explain the forces that operate within destinations a number of typologies (for example, Plog, 1973; Peck and Leipie, 1977; Smith, 1977; Soane, 1993) and models (for example, Gilbert, 1939; Lavery, 1974; Miossec, 1976; Butler, 1980; Gormsen, 1981; Young, 1983; Keller, 1987; Smith, 1992; Kermath and Thomas, 1992; Burton, 1994; Russell and Faulkner, 1998; Weaver, 2000) have been proposed. Only the destination life cycle model proposed by Butler (1980) has been extensively tested in the literature. The paradox of the ongoing debate over the destination life cycle model is that while it has been extensively tested, refined, modified, updated and extended (for example, see Oglethorpe, 1984; Wilkinson, 1987; Strapp, 1988; Cooper and Jackson, 1989; Weaver, 1993; Morgan, 1991; Choy, 1992; Getz, 1992; Williams, 1993; Bianchi, 1994; Harrison, 1995; Digance, 1997; Tooman, 1997; Hovinon 2002; Weaver, 2000; Agarwal, 2002; Russo, 2002) the model still lacks the ability to be used as an operational planning tool, a role it was

15

never intended to undertake. This chapter examines the use of models and considers how they may be applied individually and collectively to understand the destination phenomenon and provide guidance to destination managers and planners. Before considering how models may be used it is useful to consider the aims of modelling and limitations on how they may be used.

Essentially, a model is an attempt to:

- identify a number of core relationships and the variables that drive them, and
- explain relationships that are identified in a simplified manner that can be used for understanding or in a more complex form, for planning.

However, in the process of identifying relationships and encoding them into symbolic forms that may then be presented as a two-dimensional drawing in a print form of a model or as a series of mathematical equations in a computer version of a model, assumptions have to be made with the result that many of the complex relationships that occur may not be adequately represented. In other disciplines, manufacturing for example, where the relationships between variables can be identified and quantified mathematically, it is possible to develop quite complex and very accurate predictive mathematical models. In aircraft design, the various relationships that occur between aircraft components and aerodynamic forces are well known and computer modelling has evolved to the stage where a significant proportion of the prototype testing of new aircraft designs such as the Boeing 787 is able to be preformed in a computer laboratory. In the human world however, the views and tastes of consumers are constantly changing in response to a range of stimuli such as advertising, changes in personal financial capacity, national economic factors and education. Modelling how humans respond to their environment is therefore much more difficult than in the scientific environment where relationships are more stable, able to be tested and most importantly replicated with a knowledge that responses to changes in the environment are known and predicable. In the social sciences, models are essentially simplified expressions of a more complex reality. Social science models thus seek to find connections that can be standardized and in this way show relationships between a number of variables to allow comparisons and in some cases prediction.

As knowledge of the tourism phenomenon increases, and the relationships between many of the variables that together create and sustain this phenomenon become clearer, existing knowledge will need to be reviewed and previously accepted concepts and models revised or even dispensed with. In tourism, as in other fields, there has been criticism that academics are loath to dispense with the old familiar paradigms and models and treat new ideas and models with suspicion. In the business world and in politics, where survival requires innovation and rapid change, old paradigms and ways of thinking are continually revised and dispensed with following patterns of idea adoption and innovation that is best described by the innovation model discussed in Chapter 1. The challenge for academics is to adopt a similar perspective to theory and while not chasing every new idea that emerges, look for innovation and more effective explanation. There also remains the need to exercise caution over elevating models from an explanatory role to a post-theory stage where the model is accepted as reality rather than a theory.

In tourism research, as in many other areas of social science, models are most commonly displayed in a two-dimensional format in a printed form. Given the complexity of the world this approach usually leads to gross over-simplification, often because this format precludes the complexity that mathematical models (where dozens if not hundreds of variables are included) are able to achieve. Another problem with many models is that the variables shown are the visible part of very complex and unseen interactions that ideally should be included but because of the limitations of two-dimensional model formats may need to be ignored or be modelled separately. In one sense the forging of simplicity out of complexity allows for more rapid understanding by the reader but often at the cost of a deeper understanding of the complexity that is the true reality of the relationship being described. This leads to a conundrum: two-dimensional models are useful teaching tools and are able to offer a simplified understanding to quite complex problems but the process of simplification reduces their utility as an operationalizable planning tool. One solution to this conundrum is to take a different approach and use a group of linked models to explain specific aspects of the phenomenon being investigated. The Resort Development Spectrum (RDS) discussed later in this chapter demonstrates an attempt to use three linked models to explain some of the factors that affect destination development.

Before commencing a detailed discussion of the role that models play in assisting in the understanding of the processes that create, sustain or even extinguish destinations, it is worth considering where destinations fit into the wider perspective of the tourism phenomenon. There have been a number of attempts to model the tourism system (for example Mill and Morrison, 1985; Leiper, 1990; Cooper *et al.*, 2005). A major problem encountered in model construction of this nature is the representation of complexity in a medium that requires simplicity. The multi-dimensional reality of time and space is difficult to represent in a diagrammatic two-dimensional format meaning that much of the complexity of reality is lost. For example, in the well-known Mill and Morrison (1985) model of the tourism system (Figure 2.1), the

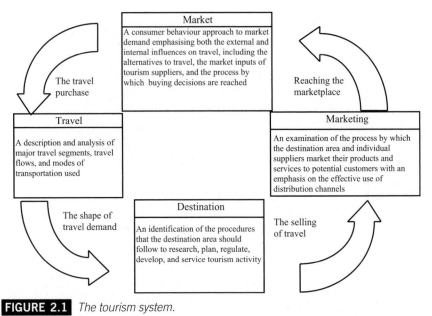

FIGURE 2.1 *The tourism system.*
Source: Redrawn from Mill and Morrison (1985).

tourism phenomenon is shown as a four quadrant model with each quadrant connecting only to the one immediately before or after it. While useful as an introduction to the concept of a system approach, the model has no capability to predict. At an industry level there are hundreds if not thousands of relationships that can be identified. A similar observation may be made about destinations. Showing the relationship between elements, even as a static system, is not achievable leaving models with a largely illustrative role. Jafari and Ritchie (1981) remind us of a different element of complexity that is related to the use of models, in this instance from a disciplinary perspective. The tourism phenomenon is also studied by other disciplines each of which have their own views on the role of models.

It is useful to consider several other models that can be used to contextualize the position occupied by destinations within the overall tourism system. The push–pull model (Figure 2.2), the distance decay model (Figure 2.3) and the Core Periphery Model (Figure 2.4) explain some, but certainly not all, aspects of the forces that collectively influence decisions by tourists to visit specific destinations.

The push–pull model illustrated in Figure 2.2 illustrates the travel motivations that encourage tourists to select a particular destination. Push factors are generally agreed to be a range of socio-psychological motives that influence individuals to travel. Push factors are internal (Usal and Jurowski, 1994) while

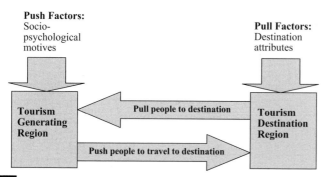

FIGURE 2.2 *The destination – origin push–pull model.*
Source: Adapted from Leiper (1990).

pull factors are external to the person. Numerous push motivates have been identified including escape, rest and relaxation, learning, status and prestige and social interaction (Dann, 1977; Crompton, 1979; Ryan, 2003). Pull factors (Uysal and Jurowski, 1994) attract tourists and include easy access, tourism attractions, natural environment, history, low cost and so on. While some authors state that push and pull factors do not operate synonymously because push factors are the primary influence on a person to travel, other authors see them working in parallel (Yuan and McDonald, 1990; Usal and Jurowski, 1994; Jang and Cai, 2002). If combined with other models, the push–pull

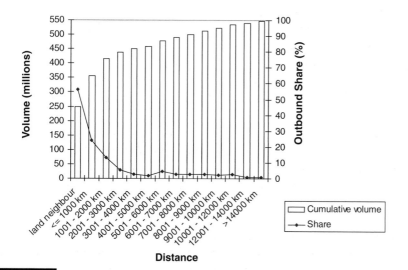

FIGURE 2.3 *McKercher's distance decay model of international travel.*
Source: McKercher et al. (2008).

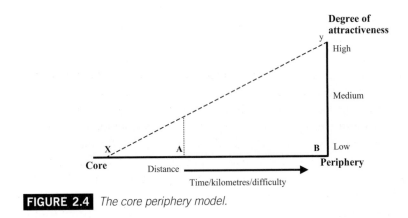

FIGURE 2.4   *The core periphery model.*

model provides a useful and quantifiable measure of the motives that attract tourists to a specific destination and provides the destination with a useful measure of the type of destination features that must be developed to attract specific tourism markets.

A recent paper by McKercher *et al.* (2008) provides a particularly useful demonstration of the distance decay model. Based on an investigation of 2002 outbound figures for 41 major outbound markets visiting 146 destinations McKercher *et al.* found that demand declines sharply for destinations over 1000 km from the source market with absolute aggregate demand falling by 50% with each additional 1000 km of added distance. Eighty percent of all international tourism occurs within 1000 km of home and with a few exceptions, distant destinations have great difficulty attracting more than 1% or 2% of departures from distant source markets.

The Core Periphery Model illustrated in Figure 2.4 builds on earlier work by Weaver (1998), Oppermann (1993), Wall (2000) and the concept of distance-decay (see Duval, 2007; McKercher *et al.*, 2008). The Core Periphery Model highlights the inverse relationship between the attractiveness of place and its distance from an origin and postulates that destinations located some distance from a core or a tourism generating region will experience difficulty in attracting visitors because of the increased time and cost it takes to visit the periphery compared to destinations that may lie closer to the core. Prideaux (2008) noted that the degrees of peripherality would effect investment decisions, management practices and marketing strategies. As remoteness or peripherality increases, the scale of uniqueness or 'differentness' of the attractions offered by these destinations must increase in proportion to the increased distance travelled otherwise visitors will travel to destinations closer to their origin. In the language of the push–pull model outlined previously, a destination located on the periphery must undertake actions to increase its pull factor, assuming that it has the requisite uniqueness qualities.

In Figure 2.4 the line XY represents a measure of distance, time and cost while the vertical line is a measure of attractiveness. As a tourist travels further from the core the cost of travel and the time taken will increase. Thus a hypothetical destination located at B will only attract visitors if it is able to offer a level of uniqueness that adequately offsets the additional cost in money and time incurred by travel to the destination. If B is only able to offer a medium level of attractiveness it will receive fewer visitors than it would receive if its level of attractiveness was at the upper level, near Y. If however another destination located at A is able to offer the same type of experiences offered at B but at a lower time and money cost, A is likely to attract visitors who would otherwise have travelled to B. From a core-periphery perspective destinations located on the periphery will always find it difficult to compete with destinations located near to the core unless they can offer a unique or differentiated product.

DESTINATION MODELS

In discussing the conceptual validity of models as a means for explaining the process of development Oppermann and Chon (1997) observed that many tourism models were developed from the positivist tradition of geography and were designed to provide researchers with an analytical framework. Further, Oppermann and Chon (1997:35) stated that within the geographical literature the concept of 'model' remains contested with Unwin (1992:215) arguing that a model is 'a structure used to interpret the operation of a formula system; a structured representation of the real' while Johnson (1991:1) asserts that models are 'a theory, a law, a hypothesis or any other form of a structured idea'.

The tourism literature recognizes two major classes of models, those relying on graphical or diagrammatic representations of the data, and those employing mathematical equations (Getz, 1986). Mathematical equations are most commonly used to forecast tourism demand. However, even in mathematical models where there is scope to include numerous and complex relationships, some significant factors maybe overlooked or ignored. For example, in a metanalysis of international tourism demand models Lim (1997) identified 100 studies that had identified a range of factors that underpinned growth. Surprisingly, and given the discussion on the fundamental role of transport in destination development in Chapter 4, she found that transport cost variables had been omitted for 54 of the studies. Mathematical models also have limitations and while useful as forecasting tools, models of the type identified by Lim (1997) and those used by tourism forecasters have limited applicability to modelling the factors that collectively create the synergies that stimulate destination growth.

According to Getz (1986) non-mathematical models can be grouped into two classes, 'theoretical' and 'process'. Theoretical models attempt to explain some functional elements of the tourism industry while process models describe the management/planning process. Theoretical models can be further grouped according to the manner in which they model the tourism system and are described as: descriptive, explanatory and finally predictive. Process models can be subclassified as: subjective; traditional models based on problem solving and those based on systems theory. In summing up the role of models Getz (1986:23) stated that, '*Models – first descriptive, then explanatory and finally predictive in nature – are the building blocks of theory*'. The relationship between theory and process models is illustrated in Figure 2.5. The key outcome of the process described by Getz is that prediction based on application of models is possible. Many tourism models including those reviewed in this chapter fail to move beyond the predictive stage in theory models or the planning stage in process models.

Oppermann and Chon (1997) take a different path in categorizing models, observing that there are two basic approaches to developing models that can be used to explain aspects of the tourism phenomenon. The first group follows

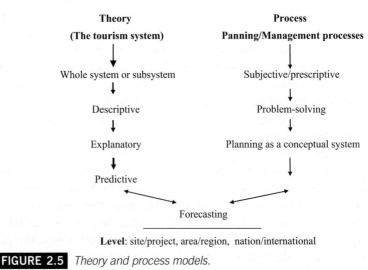

Level: site/project, area/region, nation/international

FIGURE 2.5 *Theory and process models.*
Source: Redrawn from Getz (1986:22).

the inductive route and derives generalizations out of observations. The preferred approach according to Oppermann and Chon is the alternative positivist route where testing can be used to validate hypothesis and thereafter be used as a platform for constructing explanation.

A number of the models postulated by tourism researchers have drawn heavily on the theory of development stages suggested by economists including Rostow (1960) who proposed a six-stage process of growth in national economies. The concept of tourism growth occurring in discernible stages was adopted by a number of tourism researchers including Thurot (1973) who theorised three phases, Miossec (1976) proposed five stages, Butler (1980) postulated six stages and Burton (1994) who postulated four stages. Most models confine their analysis to the volume of tourism and changes in the type of visitors (Oppermann, 1993:537). Butler (1980) extended the concept of development stages by combining development theory with the theory of the product life cycle to produce a model that is claimed to identify an evolutionary resort life cycle of six stages.

USE OF MODELS TO EXPLAIN TOURISM DEVELOPMENT

A number of authors (Quade, 1979; Dunn, 1981) have commented on the process of model building and testing. In the following discussion it is suggested that models can be built for a specific purpose using a formula that is based on a simplified six-stage development sequence. This approach is able to be used for models that emulate from either a deductive or inductive approach to modelling building where induction is the process of discovering explanation to produce a previously unknown proposition and deduction is a process that relies on developing conclusions from theory that is based on existing accepted principles (Parkle, 1993) often using a positivist approach. Importantly, the suggested structure includes sequencing through a number of stages, recognizing the need to test predictions and finally including a feedback loop that allows revision of the initial stages of the model development process.

The process of model building entails a number of stages that should commence with problem definition and conclude with a method of prediction or forecasting. The purpose for which a model is intended will determine how it will be constructed. For example, forecasting models require the identification of a number of variables that can be represented in a series of mathematical equations that simulate observed trends. Running these models allows qualified predictions to be made of future demand based on changes to the

Stage	Action
Stage 1	Identification of the problem or problems to be studied.
Stage 2	Systematic observation which includes identification of stakeholders and classification of dependent and independent variables followed by data collection.
Stage 3	Generalisation of relationships observed in step 2.
Stage 4	Explanation of observed relationships.
Stage 5	Prediction of likely outcomes.
Stage 6	Testing of predictions and if necessary alteration of elements in stages 1 to 5.

FIGURE 2.6 *Six-stage process of model development.*
Source: Modified from Dunn (1987) and Quade (1979).

variables inputted. According to Quade (1979) and Dunn (1981) the development of models is a six-stage process as illustrated in Figure 2.6.

Existing models of destination development generally fail to progress beyond stage four of the six stages outlined above. While providing comfortable frameworks for comparative studies of tourism development, models that do not progress beyond stage four are not able to be operationalized, that is, used for prediction at the level required by destination managers and planners. Most research into destination development has taken a deductive approach using theory testing and relying on qualitative data for evidence.

In stages five and six, models may require the development of computerized models to test the relationships between a range of variables with the aim of predicting likely outcomes. However, a tourism model that includes stage five and six characteristics will have a tendency to rely on generalizations rather than on quantifiable, econometric predictive capabilities. The number of processes and relationships between factors such as price, demand, supply, management, policy and competition between the tourism industry and other industries within the destination is enormous and the relationships between variables are constantly changing. Overlaying all of these relationships is the unpredictable nature of consumer preference or consumer taste and unanticipated crises or disasters. A product (or destination) that may be desirable one year may experience a significant fall in popularity almost overnight, illustrating the difficulty in applying econometric modelling to the process of destination model development. An alternative method to econometric modelling is the use of scenarios which are able to combine econometric modelling with the use of generalization of likely courses of events based on observed of past trends (van Doorn, 1986). This approach is discussed in more detail in Chapter 3 of this book.

Getz (1986) notes that models usually rely on identifying correlations between variables and assuming casual factors. These limiting characteristics usually prevent a full evaluation of cause and effect. As a consequence, little progress has been made in developing non-mathematical destination models that are able to identify future demand or predict the impact of tourism growth on infrastructure requirements. For similar reasons there has been little progress in developing mathematical models except for the more specific task of forecasting demand. As a result, models currently in use have limited capability for forward planning but may have some use as remedial planning tools. Before examining several development models in more detail the following discussion examines a number of issues relating to the role of models and typologies in explaining development.

Most contemporary models exhibit a weakness in their ability to predict how growth will affect infrastructure including transport, accommodation types, shopping and the provision of services such as water, electricity and communications. While the Resort Development Spectrum (Prideaux 2000a, 2004) illustrated later in this chapter goes some way to redressing these deficiencies it still requires additional work to identify the roles of relationships such as capacity, sustainability, demand, elasticity and equilibrium. The shortcomings in contemporary destination models have been noted in existing tourism research and although an extensive literature has emerged about the merits of various models used to explain the growth patterns of destinations, fundamental issues such as the role of the market (expressed as price, demand and supply forces) and the importance of infrastructure development have been largely ignored by both model designers and reviewers. It should be noted however that many of the earlier models of destination development were not designed to incorporate an action, or planning element and were more concerned with interpretation and explanation of the tourism phenomenon.

RESEARCH INTO DESTINATION DEVELOPMENT

Gilbert (1939) and Barrett (1958) drew attention to the types of development often observed at coastal resorts in the United Kingdom. Later, Christaller (1963) drew attention to an evolutionary cycle that appeared to be operating in tourism areas, offering one of the first limited theoretical explanations of the forces at work. In subsequent decades, a number of typologies and models have been developed to explain the process of destination development. Existing typologies and models generally examine the issue from either the perspective of tourist motivation or an examination of the factors that influence the development process. Rather less emphasis has been given to the significance of demand and supply factors.

Use of typologies and models to explain resort growth

Researchers have attempted to conceptualize the process of destination growth by developing a range of explanatory typologies and models (Mo *et al.*, 1993). Although clearly different in their purpose and intent, there is some confusion in the literature regarding the definition of the terms typologies and models. Gordon and Goodall (1992) compared a number of models and typologies to identify similarities and differences in the alternative approaches using the product life cycle and the environmental quality cycle as benchmarks. Table 2.1 builds on Gordon and Goodall's original table by adding several additional models. From the table it is apparent that models and typologies explore the same processes but from different perspectives.

In general, models aim to predict whereas typologies aim to classify. Considerable differences exist between these two approaches, particularly when applied in a tourism context. Models are often used to identify basic relationships, identify the principle variables involved and formulate these relationships into either mathematical equations or graphical representations. These relationships can then be used for explanation and prediction.

The role occupied by models and typologies in the tourism literature is influenced by the concept of tourism adopted by individual researchers. There remains some dispute on what actually constitutes the phenomenon of tourism (Tribe, 1997:2006). Tourists can be segmented by a number of variables including income, taste, race, social class, religion and age or, on a microscale, by attributes such as predisposition to food styles, shopping, entertainment and attractions. The way in which tourism is viewed at this level can have a significant bearing on the way in which the phenomenon is understood and analysed. Attempts made by researchers within and from outside of the discipline of tourism, accepting that tourism is a discipline, to explain the roles of these variables and their outcomes have provided the basis for the development of the existing range of tourism typologies and models. The difficulty faced in developing typologies and models is that the concept of tourism may have different meanings to different people or even groups of people. As a consequence, there is a tendency for individuals to fail to comprehend the perspectives of others (Wall, 1993). This is reflected in the research literature that in many instances refers to similar aspects of the tourism system but from different perspectives. One newly evident example of this is the use of the term

TABLE 2.1 Integration of Resort Cycles, Product Cycles, Economic Cycles and Tourism Models and Typologies

Interrelated Typologies Cycles and Models

Resort models						Product life cycle	Typologies					Environment quality cycle	General, for example Rostow (1960)	Tourism related, for example Keller
Miossec (1976)	Original Butler model (1980)	Butler model modified	Smith (1992)	Christaller (1963)	Prideaux (1996)		Cohen (1972)	Plog (1973)	Cohen (1979)	Doxey (1976)	Smith (1977)			
Pioneer resort	Exploration	Discovery	Local settlement	Exploration of forgotten places	Local tourism	Introduction	Existential experimental		Explorer	Euphoria	Explorer	Natural attraction	Pre-condition for take off	Local control
	Involvement		First tourism; first hotel				Experiential	Allocentric	Drifter		Elite off-beat	Identity		Regional involvement
Multiplication of resorts	Development	Growth	More hotels	Development	Regional tourism	Growth	Diversionary	Mid-centric	Individual mass	Apathy	Incipient mass	Development	Take-off	National control
			More lodging											
Hierarchy and stagnation	Consolidation	Maturity	More hotels	Mass tourism	Mass tourism	Maturity (saturation)	Recreational	Psychocentric	Organized mass	Irritation antagonism	Mass charter	Degradation	Drive to maturity	International control
	Stagnation				Image degradation							Crowding	Age of high mass consumption	
Hierarchy specialization saturation	Decline	Decline	Resort government rails	Decline	Decline	Decline						Decline		Local involvement
	Rejuvenation	Rejuvenation	Fully urbanize											

'sustainability' to describe development that is designed to restrict the level of development to a level that does not lead to long-term degradation of the resource. However, in the new era of rapid climate change many ecosystems will undergo rapid and in some cases radical change (Hunter, 2007) requiring a redefining of the meaning of sustainable at least from a tourism perspective.

Typologies

Typologies do not employ the same form of analytical approach used in models and are used primarily for classification and comparison (Mo *et al.*, 1993; Pearce, 1981). Patton (2002:457) observed that typologies are '*classification systems made up of categories that divide some aspect of the world into parts along a continuum*'. According to Patton (2002:457) typologies are built on 'ideal types' or 'illustrative endpoints' while Grey *et al.* (2007:23) argue that a typology should show all possible combinations of two or more variables. As a consequence, empirical testing of typologies is rare (Mo *et al.*, 1993). Emphasis is placed on observing factors such as psychological, social, cultural and geographic relationships. Based on the results of these observations, classifications are developed. Primarily descriptive in nature, typologies provide a framework for description, understanding and interpretation but have limited predictive capability. Some researchers go as far as stating that typologies of tourist roles are of little value in understanding tourism motives and for the analysis of supply (Lowyck *et al.*, 1992). In the literature, the distinction between models and typologies is often unclear. For example, Stabler (1991) refers to Plog's (1973) discussion on Psychocentric–Allocentric personality types as a model while Lowych *et al.* (1992) classify Plog's theory as a typology. In another example, Burton (1994) incorporated elements of typologies developed by Cohen (1972) and Plog (1973) along with elements of models developed by Butler (1980) and Leiper (1990) to develop a model based on changing spatial patterns.

Typologies can be grouped into those based on observed morphological characteristics of destinations (for example, Smith, 1992; Lavery, 1974; Gormsen, 1981) and those that investigate the factors that influence the individual's decision to travel (Plog, 1973; Smith, 1977). Typologies provide a convenient method of classifying the processes that can be observed occurring in destinations. These processes are generally morphological or psychological in nature. In their overall application typologies can be used to indicate potential phases of destination growth by visitor types or even styles of the built environment. Typologies, however, are of little use in predicting factors such as destination infrastructure requirements or potential visitor flows.

Models

Models are commonly employed to identify basic relationships, identify the principle variables involved and formulate these relationships into either mathematical equations or graphic representations. These relationships are then available for explanation and prediction. Tourism models that have been used to explain destination development are able to be grouped into three major categories:

- geographical models based on spatial factors;
- economic models;
- management and marketing models.

Geographical models, incorporating an element of spatial relationships and time, constitute the largest group of models developed to explain destination development. Little attention has been given to economic models or management and marketing models. Butler's model is the recognized orthodoxy of destination development studies although it has been criticised for its lack of a predictive capability and there are continuing debates over the shape and direction of the development curve. Developing a satisfactory mathematical model of destination development has proved to be an almost impossible task and no satisfactory model has been published.

A review of the models and typologies cited in this chapter indicates that research into destination development exhibits a number of characteristics including: a deductive rather than inductive approach has been the preferred approach to research; researchers use a mix of quantitative and qualitative methods with a preference for qualitative research; extensive use is made of case studies to test existing models and explain theories of destination development; and there has been a focus on geographic and psychological aspects of development while investigations into economic factors such as specific supply side factors have been limited.

LIMITATIONS OF MODELS USED TO EXPLAIN DESTINATION DEVELOPMENT

Surprisingly, a number of issues have not been addressed to any real extent in the development and testing of destination models (Prideaux, 2004). These are summarized as follows:

- The role of economic relationships (for example the price mechanism) has been largely ignored.
- Many models offer only a descriptive analysis, limiting their ability to be used as a planning tool.

- Because of over reliance on qualitative data, empirical analysis (Agarwal, 1997:67) is often difficult.
- Apart from the extensive testing and modification of Butler's (1980) model most other models have either not been tested or have been tested on only one or two occasions.
- Where testing has occurred it has usually been in a single destination, not over a number of sites that allow results to be compared and contrasted.
- The possibility that the phenomenon involved in destination development may be explained by a series of models has not been explored in detail.
- Many models have ignored the issue of environmental capacity. In the near future as climate change begins to impact many ecosystems will undergo change altering current concepts of sustainability.
- Little attention has been given to the role of consumer preferences and the impact that marketing can exert on consumer purchasing patterns.
- Although Russell and Faulkner (1999) identified the role of individual entrepreneurs in the development process little additional work has been undertaken in this area.
- In general, little attention has been paid to competitive forces either nationally or internationally.

While a large number of destination models have been developed, the literature has focused on Butler's destination lifecycle model and largely ignored the others. This is a serious weakness in the literature. It is obvious however, that no one model will ever entirely describe the processes at work and that a more useful approach may be to adopt the approach taken in Figure 2.7 where a number of models may collectively be able to more effectively describe the range of processes at work. After briefly examining how a number of models have been applied to the Gold Coast Australia the

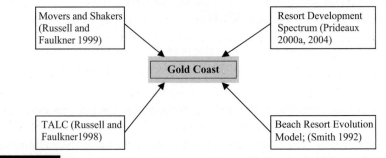

FIGURE 2.7 *Examples of development models applied to the Gold Coast, Australia.*

discussion in this book will narrow its focus to the destination life cycle model (Butler, 1980) and the more recent Resort Development Spectrum (Prideaux, 2000a, 2004).

Case Study 2.1 The Gold Coast, Australia

The Gold Coast is a major domestic and international tourism destination located in South East Queensland. The destination attracted 3.6 million domestic and 830,000 international visitors in 2006 and had a residential population of 466,000. Measuring approximately 42 km in length the destination contains a number of urban foci that combine to form one continuous urbanised strip paralleling the beach. Located on a narrow coastal plain bounded by the Pacific Ocean to the east and the Great Dividing Range to the west the destination had its origins as a coastal beach resort. In recent decades the Gold Coast has evolved into an international leisure, shopping, recreation and entertainment destination. Because of its significance in Australia's tourism industry and because it is located near a number of Universities there has been extensive examination of the destination by academic researchers who have sought to explain its growth from a number of perspectives. One of the first attempts to model development was undertaken by Russell Smith (1992) who cited the Gold Coast as a case study in his Beach Resort Evolution Model.

As illustrated in Figure 2.7, a number of models have been applied to the Gold Coast. Each application of a model has identified part of the complex matrix of forces that collectively encourage growth. At the same time, while each model in isolation appears to offer a satisfactory explanation for the destination's development, other factors that were not identified also offer valid explanation. While Smith's analysis of spatial changes is observable he did not question the cause of these changes in the manner undertaken by Russell and Faulkner (1999) who found that the destination's entrepreneurial class were the instigators of the development observed by Smith. A more robust examination of this technique is likely to add a new level of understanding to the destination development processes. Unfortunately, except for the discussion accompanying Figure 2.8 the limitations of space prevent exploration of this technique in detail but it is a research avenue that should be explored in more depth in a different context.

Figure 2.8 suggests an approach to destination research based on assembling the findings from a number of models to enable a more holistic view of the development process to be undertaken. The advantage of this technique is its ability to allow comparisons of the range of forces at work within a destination over a time scale that connects the past to the present and extends to the future.

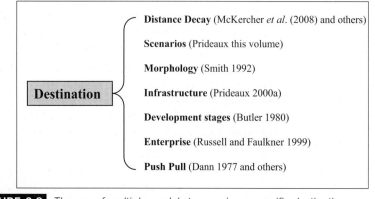

FIGURE 2.8 *The use of multiple models to examine a specific destination.*

Butler's destination life cycle theory

In a seminal paper on destination development that was to set the agenda for research into destination development for nearly three decades Butler (1980) refined the idea of evolutionary change by proposing a destination life cycle model. The model fused the concept of development stages with the theory of the product life cycle first proposed by Vernon in 1966 (Debbage, 1990). In a historical sense the destination life cycle model builds on earlier work by Defert (1954 cited in Oppermann and Chon, 1997), Christaller (1963) and Stansfield (1978) who suggested that there might be a cycle of development occurring in tourism destinations. Some similarities can be observed between Butler's model and typologies, for example, the Destination Life Cycle's 'exploration stage' has similarities with Plog's 'allocentrics', Cohen's 'drifters' and 'explorers' and Smith's explorers (1977). Butler (1980:6) noted that in the product development cycle '*sales of a product proceed slowly at first, experience a rapid rate of growth, stabilise, and subsequently decline; in other words, a large basic asymptotic curve is followed*'.

Drawing on the concept of the product life cycle, Butler postulated that a similar trend was evident in tourist destinations where development moves through a series of stages, commencing with 'discovery' of the area by a small group of adventurous tourists. Movement from one stage to the next depends on a number of variables that exist both inside and outside the destination. Typically, these variables include accessibility, the attitude of local authorities, resource availability, competitors, political will and visitor preferences. Development is decomposed into a series of stages that commence with exploration, and move through involvement, to development followed by consolidation to a point where stagnation, decline or rejuvenation occurs. The model is based on the product life cycle theory that postulates that products evolve through a series of stages following an S-shaped pattern of introduction, growth, maturity and decline. The ability of the product life cycle to be used as a forecasting tool has been the subject of intense debate and refinement and its applicability to destination growth patterns remains contentious. While a number of scholars have attempted to refine and modify Butler's original model (for example Keller, 1987; Haywood, 1986; Kermath and Thomas, 1992; Strapp, 1988; Kermath and Thomas, 1992; di Benedetto and Bojanic, 1993; Baum, 1998) the modifications have not been widely accepted.

The model has been extensively tested in a diverse number of locations including Malta (Oglethorpe, 1984), Louisiana (Meyer-Arendt, 1985), small island nations (Wilkinson, 1987), The Isle of Man (Cooper and Jackson, 1989), the Caribbean (Weaver, 1990), Majorca (Morgan, 1991), Nigeria Falls (Getz, 1992), Dominican Republic (Kermath and Thomas, 1992), Cyprus (Ioannides, 1992), Minorca (Williams, 1993), Alpine areas of Australia (Digance, 1997), Portugal (Gonclaves and Aguas, 1997), British seaside resorts (Cooper, 1997), Pennsylvania (Houvinen, 2002). Priestly and Mundet (1998) used the model to compare the development of three Spanish resorts.

The simplicity of the model is both a strength and a weakness: it explains the process of growth but it cannot be operationalized as a planning tool because it fails to provide sufficient detail for the development of planning and policy in tourism areas. Results of many of the applications of the model appear to support the general theory of development cycles but many deviations from the idealized model have been noted (Cooper, 1992a; Kermath and Thomas, 1992).

Problems identified with the model fall into eight general areas (Prideaux, 2000a): scepticism over the ability of one model to explain tourism development (Choy, 1992; Bianchi, 1994; Prosser, 1995), problems with the concept of the product life cycle (Hart *et al.*, 1984; Kotler, 1988), conceptual limitations of carrying capacity (Getz, 1992; Haywood, 1986), the use of the cycle concept in tourism planning (Cooper and Jackson, 1989; Haywood, 1986; Getz, 1992), a lack of empirical evidence to substantiate the concept (Prosser, 1995), calibration of the life cycle model particularly in respect to identifying turning points and identifying stages (Cooper, 1992a) and problems in applying the life cycle concept in tourism destinations areas (Bianchi, 1994; Shaw and Williams, 1994). To these general areas of concern should be added the failure to take into account the operation of the economic market in destination areas (Prideaux, 1998).

In a discussion of the model, Liper (2004:133) echoed the views of other researchers (Lundtrop and Wanhill, 2001; Hovinon, 2002) when he observed that '*Despite its popularity, the theory is seriously flawed. In many, possibly most instances where it has been applied, the theory has been either useless or misleading'*. Importantly, Leaper observed that the destination life cycle model is unable to explain fluctuations in visitor numbers and has no capacity to predict them. In this regard Hovinon (2002) found that in Pennsylvania, signs of growth, stagnation, decline and rejuvenation could all be found occurring concurrently, a pattern that is not explained by the model.

In summing up, the destination life cycle model has a number of limitations that preclude it from being able to be used as a planning tool. However, the model has provided useful insights into the processes that destinations undergo and the points a destination will move through when growth is occurring. In the following discussion of the Resort Development Spectrum a different approach has been taken and rather than using a single model the growth process is modelled through three interlinking models, each illustrating a different element of the process.

Before examining the Resort Development Spectrum which was developed to explain growth patterns in tourism destinations it is useful to consider the arguments advanced in Chapter 7 that most of the coastal tourism does not take place in the classical beach resorts that to date have largely defined the extent of coastal tourism research. In reality it is the rapidly expanding coastal zone cities that are the new powerhouses of coastal tourism. Houston (USA), New York, Tel Aviv and Hong Kong are not regarded as beach destinations but are located on the coast and receive enormous numbers of tourists. In these cities tourism is usually only one of a large number of industries that compete for recognition from city and state administers. Unfortunately, the literature has yet to give full recognition to the role of these cities as a legitimate component of coastal tourism.

The Resort Development Spectrum

The Resort Development Spectrum was developed as a framework that integrates three interconnected models that collectively explain the operation of the destination microeconomy, the form that tourism growth takes and the patterns of infrastructure construction that are required to support growth. The model observes how changes in the patterns of interaction between buyers (the demand side) and sellers (the supply side) create a multi-dimensional view of development that includes: changes in destination infrastructure composition as growth occurs and in the structure of the infrastructure that supports growth; the implications of changing patterns of demand; and the economic relationships that result as growth occurs. As originally conceived the RDS applies to the development patterns observed in many European and other developed nations where a suitable undeveloped locality was 'discovered' and developed, with development based on expanding the geographic market that first focused on the local area before and later expanding to encompass regional, national and in some cases international markets. This form of development can best be described as *evolutionary* where change is incremental and cumulative.

Not all destinations grow in such predictable patterns and in some instances development occurs as the result of a major development being parachuted into a relatively undeveloped area creating a catalyst effect that encourages other investors to invest in the destination in a pattern that may be the reverse of the pattern outlined above. This form of development can be termed the *big bang* pattern of development. Cancun in Mexico is an example of this form of development. The underlying principles of the model are sufficiently robust to explain both types of destination development. The following discussion will first outline the published version of the model that examined growth following an evolutionary path that commenced with an undeveloped but tourism resource rich locality that over time evolved into an international mass tourism destination. The application of the model in this form was demonstrated in two destinations, Cairns (Prideaux, 2000a) and Gold Coast (Prideaux, 2004). Case Study 2.2 examines an example of the *big bang* form of development.

From an economic perspective, the RDS illustrates the growth path as a series of partial equilibrium points that occur at specific phases during the growth process, on a continuum that commences with an undeveloped locality that possesses a range of potential tourism asserts and concludes when that destination has evolved into an international destination. Growth is not automatic nor is it likely that all destinations will grow into mass international tourism destinations. While the published version of the model shows (Prideaux, 2000a, 2004) growth as a four phased process with a possible fifth phase of either decline, stagnation or rejuvenation a different growth path can be envisaged where the initial phase of growth is based on the development of the destination as an enclave for the wealthy. This path will be demonstrated later in the chapter. Each phase of growth is based on a specific visitor group whose demand and supply side characteristics determine the composition of the destination's visitor market at any point on the scale that begins with local tourism and concludes with mass international tourism. Capacity at any point on the growth curve is determined by a combination of forces including the ability of the environment to support development, land supply, community aspirations, perceptual (psychological) components (Wall, 1982), government policy, levels of sustainability, tourism demand, supply, availability of infrastructure services and transport access (Prideaux, 2000b). As originally published, the factors of capacity, sustainability, demand, elasticity and equilibrium are considered in a collective sense and their individual contributions are not specified or quantified. The model does however recognize that demand is a reflection of the perceived uniqueness of the destination and depends on three factors:

1. The uniqueness of the destination's natural, built and cultural attractions in local, national and international markets,
2. The level of interest that is able to be aroused in individual tourists by the destination's combined natural, built and cultural attractions and how these are marketed,
3. The reputation of the destination in local, national and international markets in terms of price, quality and accessibility.

Price mechanism

A major failing of many previous destination models has been the lack of analysis of the economic factors that underpin growth. Given that destinations are a significant component of the tourism landscape, the paucity of research in this area is surprising given that tourism is very much a product of the ability of the economy to fund tourism consumption after other needs have been met. The following discussion outlines a number of basic criteria that underpin the destination economy. Assumptions made about the development of destinations, based on the operation of the price mechanism are outlined below.

- The price system operates in a manner that matches the demand for goods and services with the quantity suppliers are willing to produce (Samuelson, 1992).
- Demand is a function of tourist's income and the price of the services they consume (Crouch, 1992).
- Supply forces create the conditions necessary to stimulate development based on investment. Governments may play a role in encouraging the supply side.
- Demand forces can be manipulated by factors such as advertising to create demand for the services provided by the supply side.
- Demand can be elastic based on the tourist's income and price (see Chapter 4 for further discussion). Thus if prices increase, demand may fall or if prices fall, demand may increase. Alternatively, if the tourist's income increases, demand may increase, however if tourist's income declines, demand can be expected to fall.
- No assessment is made as to which is necessarily first, demand or supply.

- No assessment is made of the role of the individual who champions development; however, this is an important aspect of the development process (see Russell and Faulkner, 1999 for a more discussion).
- The hypothetical model used in the following discussion of the interaction of demand and supply represents a small coastal town that is heavily dependent on tourism. In this case development is evolutionary and does not follow the big bang approach discussed earlier.
- Demand conditions relate to the reaction of tourists faced with a decision in selecting a holiday destination. Tourists are assumed to be normal consumers who wish to maximize available resources of time and money when selecting a destination.
- Supply forces are assumed to constitute both the public and private sectors. Private sector suppliers are assumed to be profit maximizers.
- Price refers to the standard of the holiday experience and access price. A high price may indicate upmarket accommodation and the additional cost of transport, while low price is an indicator of more modest accommodation such as a motel or caravan park and a lower transport access price.
- Access cost refers to the cost of transport from tourism generating regions to the destination. The key factors relating to the distance between generating regions and destinations are: as distance increases the cost of travel will rise (see Figure 4.3) and as the distance between generating regions and the destination increases the impact of the distance decay model comes into play (see Figure 2.3).

Equilibrium

In economic theory an equilibrium occurs when the quantity of goods and services producers are willing to produce at a given price equals the amount of those goods and services that consumers are willing to purchase at the given price. If prices rise, demand may fall creating a disequilibrium condition. Similarly, if prices fall demand will increase causing a shortage again creating disequilibrium. Theoretically, it is possible for each product to achieve a unique equilibrium point referred to as a partial equilibrium in the aggregate economy. In the aggregate economy the sum of all partial equilibrium equates to overall equilibrium.

Equilibrium points will occur in the life of a destination. Changes to the demand or supply profiles of a destination previously in equilibrium will cause disequilibrium to occur. For example, this may occur if demand for travel to the destination increases leading the accommodation sector to increase price. In turn the increase in price and demand will encourage investors to construct new accommodation facilities some of which will charge higher prices. Equilibrium will be re-established when demand and supply are again in balance. At this new equilibrium point there may be a number of price levels as accommodation facilities match quality of supply (type of rooms) with the level of price individual customers are willing to pay. In this case there may be a range of partial equilibrium points within the accommodation sector that together constitute the equilibrium point for the destination accommodation sector. Assumptions made about the development of destinations, based on the operation of destination equilibrium, are outlined below.

- Disequilibrium may occur if supply lags behind demand or demand lags behind supply.
- If supply lags behind demand new suppliers are encouraged to enter the market. New entrants may either replicate existing price levels if attempting to attract additional customers prepared to pay existing prices or increase prices (and the quality of the service provided) if attempting to attract a new group of customers prepared to pay a higher price. If new entrants are able to attract new tourism sectors (for example, interstate or international sectors) prices may rise crating a new and higher destination price level thus moving the destination to a new higher equilibrium level.
- Demand for destination goods and services is not homogenous and there may be a range of demands based on the price tourists are willing to pay. These may, for example, range from affluent tourists staying in 5 star accommodation to tourists only able to afford Backpacker style accommodation. As a consequence there may be a number of partial equilibrium points for accommodation and other services within the same destination. On this basis it is conceivable that some accommodation sectors may be in equilibrium while others are in disequilibrium in the same destination at the same time. The importance of this observation will become apparent in the following discussion.
- In some circumstances the introduction of external economies of scale such as cheaper transport or other supply side inputs may generate an increase in demand as real prices fall resulting in a fall in equilibrium price. In the longer term the initial fall in real prices may be absorbed as the destination's business sector engages in profit taking and increase prices until the point where demand and supply are again in equilibrium.

The RDS model demonstrates how growth will create a demand for a range of infrastructure that will develop along predictable patterns (illustrated in

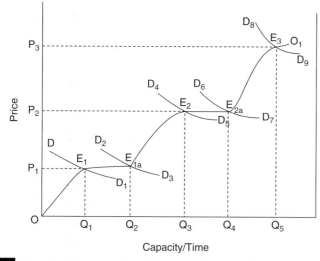

FIGURE 2.9 *Growth path caused by shifts in equilibrium points.*
Source: Prideaux (1998).

Table 2.3). The identification of the relationship that exists between growth in visitor who are identified by their origin and the types of experiences they require and the type of infrastructure that is required to support each phase of development allows planners to identify at what point in time new facilities are required. Table 2.3, for example, identifies the changes that will occur in accommodation types and transport systems as new visitor sectors are attracted. Because of the limitations of using a single diagrammatic model the processes described by the RDS are illustrated in three complementary models. Figure 2.9 shows a range of demand and supply relationships that occur in the destination microeconomy based on price factors while Figure 2.10 illustrates growth according to market sectors based on distance from the generating region. Table 2.3 outlines the sequential development of infrastructure over time based on changes in market sectors. The growth path illustrated in Figures 2.9 and 2.10 show the growth process from two perspectives but with the same overall outcomes. Thus Figure 2.9 includes a discussion on price, while Figure 2.10 illustrates the process of growth using market segments without indicating a price element.

The RDS recognizes that as destinations grow, spatial changes appear in the built environment caused by the construction of shopping facilities, apartments for destination residents, new attractions, recreational facilities for residents as well as visitors, additional hotels and so on. These changes reflect changing patterns of demand in the destination. Smith's (1992) Tentative Beach Resort Model provides a useful commentary on the type of

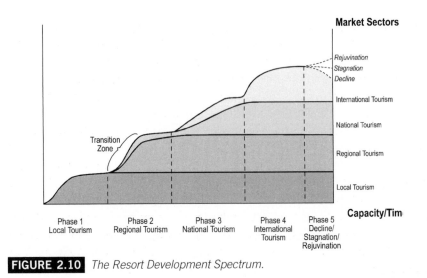

Market Sectors

- Rejuvination
- Stagnation
- Decline
- International Tourism
- National Tourism
- Regional Tourism
- Local Tourism

Transition Zone

Capacity/Time

| Phase 1 Local Tourism | Phase 2 Regional Tourism | Phase 3 National Tourism | Phase 4 International Tourism | Phase 5 Decline/ Stagnation/ Rejuvination |

FIGURE 2.10 *The Resort Development Spectrum.*

spatial changes that may occur. One of the reasons previous models have not been able to develop a predictive capacity is that they have largely ignored the role of the destination's economy. The RDS argues that the destination's economy exercises a significant influence on the investment decisions made by suppliers, and through their decisions, the path and format that growth will take.

Much of the following discussion relating to the theory underlying the RDS has previously been published in Prideaux (2000a, 2004). The following discussion draws heavily on those sources. Compared to the destination life cycle model the RDS is relatively untested except for two case studies (Cairns and Gold Coast) in Australia. Its ability to be used to describe growth in non-coastal areas will require revision to change the market parameters; however, the economic theory of changing equilibrium points outlined in Figure 2.9 are not likely to require revision. It can be expected that testing the model in other contexts will produce revisions of the model as well as criticisms and suggestions for improvement.

The RDS argues that the pattern of growth can be traced through a series of equilibrium or partial equilibrium points which occur during the life of a destination. In Figure 2.9 the line OO_1 represents both the long-run supply line of the destination as well as the long-run growth path. The growth path reflects changes in the equilibrium points that occur over time. This is illustrated in Figure 2.9 where growth is assumed to commence at point O and continues until the maximum price level within the destination reaches P_1. Price in this case is a de facto indicator of the type of accommodation, shopping and other services that are offered. An increase in price indicates an upward shift in the type of services and products that are offered. In the first phase growth levels out because equilibrium (E_1) is reached between the demand (DD_1) for holidays at P_1 and the supply of facilities at P_1. The actual number of tourist arrivals may continue to increase, attracted by the relatively low-price level of the destination. This is reflected by the new demand curve D_2D_3 that creates a new equilibrium point at E_{1a}. Growth between Q_1 and Q_2 is based on the expansion of facilities that remain roughly within the budget line imposed by P_1. If the highest price commanded by commercial establishments in the destination rises to P_2 a new equilibrium point emerges at E_2. An increase in price will only be possible if a new visitor sector is attracted to the destination and is prepared to pay a higher price that stimulates the supply side to enhance the quality of services and products. In turn this allows the destination to increase the scope of its target market. Part of the increase in price between P_1 and P_2 will include the cost of transport, as well as upgrading of destination facilities including more expensive accommodation and restaurants. Growth between O and OQ_4 will occur at price level P_2 while growth beyond point OQ_4 will only occur if additional infrastructure including hotels, transport access and new attractions is constructed and the destination is able to attract new groups of tourists prepared to pay the higher price P_3. Following a further period of expansion a new equilibrium point E_3 will be reached. The emergence of multiple visitor markets will create a destination economy that has a number of price segments each with its own unique price elasticity profile. If the destination is able to attract additional investment it is likely that growth will continue beyond E_3 until a point is reached where the destination has reached spatial and ecological capacity.

The rate of growth between equilibrium points E_1, E_2 and E_3 will vary depending on the ability of the destination to satisfy 14 key criteria of development outlined in Table 2.2.

Together, these factors (Table 2.2) reflect the constraints to growth at any point along the destination growth path. These factors will also determine the shape of the growth path, the capacity of the destination and its ability to achieve long-term social and economic sustainability. Ecological sustainability is desirable but in coming decades when climate change will cause rapid change in many ecosystems, the current assumptions regarding sustainability become questionable. Climate change will create new or modified ecosystems that will force a rethink about current concepts of sustainability with the result that for some time there will be no clear clues as to what the final level of sustainability of the modifying ecosystem might be. Table 2.2 may also be used for comparison and evaluation between competing destinations. If one or more criteria are violated or cannot be

TABLE 2.2 Key Destination Development Criteria

1. The main tourist attractions of the destination (these usually, but not always, include both natural and built attractions)
2. Ability to develop an effective and representative destination marketing authority with appropriate distribution channels
3. Success in developing new tourism generating regions and new tourism sectors through marketing
4. The support given by local authorities and local residents for tourism development.
5. The time that a particular destination takes to expand its supply side capacity (hotels for example) to meet demand
6. Carrying capacity and sustainability expressed as land available for development, availability of natural resources to absorb visitor flows without sustaining damage, availability of resources such as water, environmental factors and political factors
7. Ability to attract new investment and the composition of that investment.
8. The level of support given by regional, state and national governments (this may include support for marketing, building infrastructure and tax concessions)
9. Impact of competing destinations
10. Changes over time in the national and international economies and the production systems that underlie them
11. Investment in new transport infrastructure
12. The distance between the destination and its major generating regions
13. The ability of the destination to adapt to climate change which might include increasing sea levels and changing weather patterns based on increased occurrences of droughts, floods and fire
14. The potential threats that many destinations face from natural forces including earthquakes, windstorms and volcanoes. New Orleans for example is subject to periodic hurricanes that can be very destructive

supported, criteria 6 for example which states that there must be sufficient land available, it is likely that growth will either cease at that point or require significant policy action by the authorities.

Figure 2.10, the Resort Development Spectrum, illustrates changes in visitor segments over time on the basis of the visitor's origin. Visitor segments identified are local, regional, national and international tourists. Figure 2.10 does not illustrate the price effect outlined in Figure 2.9 because tourists from any visitor segment may choose to purchase destination experiences, including accommodation, anywhere between the lowest price and the highest price. Growth will occur when new visitor segments are added creating a destination market that may be divided into multiple visitor segments based on visitor origin. Each phase of development is based on a well-defined visitor market. Growth will only occur if new visitor segments are attracted including those from more distant generating regions. Price is only one of the factors that influence growth. Irrespective of their origin however, visitors are free to purchase destination services including accommodation, leisure activities and shopping at any price level between the cheapest and most expensive price levels. The impact of the freedom to adjust personal budgets is illustrated in more detail in Figure 4.3 in Chapter 4. In Prideaux (2000a) price was incorrectly included in the vertical axis of the Resort Development Spectrum model. This problem is corrected in Figure 2.10.

In the hypothetical destination illustrated in Figure 2.10 a small undeveloped but tourism attractive destination that meets the criteria outlined in Table 2.2 develops over time into an international destination. This path of growth is not possible for every potential destination for reasons outlined in Table 2.2. Moreover, growth is not automatic and can cease or even decline at any time in response to changes in internal and/or external factors. Internal factors include changed local government priorities, residence resistance to increasing tourism or constraints imposed by land, natural resources and water availability. External factors include competition, national economic conditions and amendments to national priorities. If disequilibrium occurs as a result of internal or external factors, growth will cease and the destination may even decline. While decline and stagnation are shown to occur after the destination has achieved international status, this process may have begun much earlier. If remedial action, including new product offerings, refurbishment of commercial facilities and destination rebranding, is undertaken once decline has been identified growth may be rekindled. If however the decline in demand extends for a lengthy period the destination may be forced to reduce its overall price level until a new lower equilibrium point is achieved.

The model also demonstrates that there are a number of market segments within a destination. While shown as a smoothed trend line in Figure 2.10 market sectors will often exhibit different rates of growth and levels of demand. For example in the case of the Gold Coast (Prideaux, 2004) the destination experienced growth in its international market while the domestic market fell in the later 1990s. The heterogenic nature of the market sectors illustrated in Figure 2.10 adds to the level of complexity in the operation of destination markets. The RDS also illustrates a transition zone where the first groups of visitors from more distant generating regions begin arriving in advance of the destination moving from one phase to the next phase of development.

Table 2.3 illustrates the changes that occur in infrastructure as this process occurs on a phase-by-phase basis that correlates with Figure 2.10. Table 2.3 traces development in a number of key areas including accommodation, transport and marketing as resorts move from one phase of growth to the next. The framework illustrated is not exhaustive and many other elements may be added including retailing, service sectors, government policy, sustainability, distribution, investment, social policy and other infrastructure. Together, Figures 2.9 and 2.10 and Table 2.3 demonstrate the multi-dimensional perspective of the processes of destination (price, markets and infrastructure) growth that is lacking in earlier models.

Figure 2.7 illustrated the application of a number of destination models to the Gold Coast, including the RDS (Prideaux, 2004). Figure 2.11 illustrates

TABLE 2.3 Infrastructure Development Progression			
Major Characteristics	**Phase 1** **Local Tourism**	**Phase 2** **Regional Tourism**	**Phase 3** **National Tourism**	**Phase 4** **International Tourism**
Tourist types	* Locals * People from nearby towns	As per phase 1 plus * Tourists travelling from areas within the state or region * Possibly limited interstate tourist traffic passing through the area on route to a larger resort	As per phase 2 plus * Tourist who travel long distances from all parts of the nation * State capital cities become primary Markets	As per phase 3 plus * Emphasis on international tourism
Accommodation	* Beach houses * Caravan parks *Licensed hotels (not resorts) *Inexpensive motels *Backpackers Hostels	*Unit and apartment development occurs * 2–3 star resort motels appear * Caravan parks still important * Outside investment commences in hotels	* 3–4 star hotels * Integrated resorts * Internationally known hotel chains commence hotel development i.e. Hilton, Ramada	* International hotel chains establish resort hotels * Numerous 5 star hotels which may incorporate golf courses, casinos and stage shows
Promotion	* Local area and surrounding towns * Undertaken by local progress and/ or tourist associations * Limited funds * Limited professionalism	* State wide * May attract government funds * Businesses operating in the resort advertise on an individual basis * Increasing professionalism of advertising campaigns	* Establish professionally staffed promotion body * Joint campaigns with state & local government and local businesses * Hotels and major attractions fund significant campaigns in national media	* Very professional approach * May attract significant government funds * Corporate advertising very significant
Attractions (Major attractions may be natural and/or built)	Limited to beach and nearby areas of scenic beauty such as National Parks	* First man-made attractions built, generally on a small scale.	* Large theme Parks or similar attractions will be constructed. These attractions will feature active rather than passive participation	* The focus of attention will shift from the beach to non-beach activities such as theme parks and up market shopping

TABLE 2.3 *(Continued)*

Major Characteristics	Phase 1 Local Tourism	Phase 2 Regional Tourism	Phase 3 National Tourism	Phase 4 International Tourism
		*Animal parks may be constructed		
		*At the end of the phase larger theme park type attractions will be planned		
Transport	* Very limited in scope	* Road access is significantly enhanced	* Scheduled interstate air services commenced by national operators or affiliates	* International air services commence
	* Main mode is road	* Other modes may be assisted by infrastructure development	* Road access continue to be improved, i.e. Freeways.	* Other modes continue to be developed
	* Possibly some traffic from rail if the resort is located close to rail services	* Limited (if any) scheduled air services operated by local airlines	* Other modes may be significantly redeveloped, i. e. sea terminals & rail services	* Depending on distance to source markets; air may become the dominant mode.
	* No scheduled air services			

the shape of the development path of the Gold Coast based on the application of the RDS. Space precludes a detailed outline of the historical trends illustrated but interested readers are referred to Prideaux (2004) for a more detailed analysis. Similarly, Prideaux (2000a) contains a similar application of the model in Cairns, Australia.

USING THE RDS AS A PLANNING MODEL

While aspects of planning are discussed in considerable detail in Chapter 3 it is worth considering how the RDS may be used as a planning tool. One method might be to use the model as a basis for developing scenarios of growth over time. Another might be to further develop the matrix outlined in Table 2.3 to assist planners determine at what point in the development process new infrastructure including airports and hotels, etc. are required. The RDS may be used at any point in the growth path of a destination to identify the potential for further growth and what form that growth may

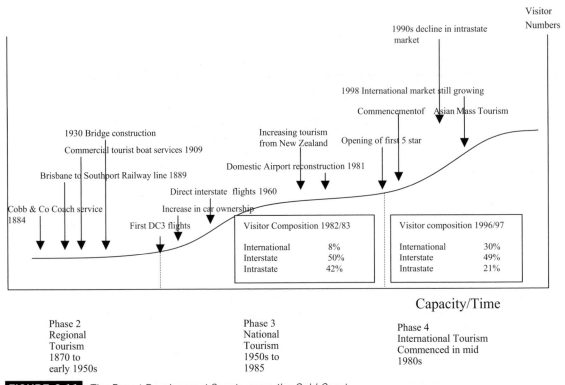

FIGURE 2.11 *The Resort Development Spectrum on the Gold Coast.*
Source: Prideaux (2004:90).

take. To demonstrate this capability two destinations are examined. Case Study 2.2 examines the situation where a small coastal community moved along a development path that was significantly different from that outlined in Figure 2.10 but adhered to the general economic principles outlined in Figure 2.9 while Case Study 2.3 examines a coastal destination that has suffered a disaster and while having the tourism resources to attract international tourists is unlikely to reach its full potential without a major shift in Government policy.

Case Study 2.2 Port Douglas – An Example of the Big Bang Growth Path

Before the tourism boom that fundamentally altered its morphology, Port Douglas could be described as the archetypical fishing village that focused on fishing and tolerated a small tourism sector based on caravan parks, second homes and several cheap motels. Tourism was not an industry that the residents contemplated. However, a visit to the region by Christopher Skase, a colourful Gold Coast (Australia) based entrepreneur, and one of the movers and shakers described by Russell and Faulkner (1999) lead to the purchase of a large area of land that was quickly developed into a Sheriden resort hotel and international standard golf course. Prior to Skase's investment in Port Douglas it was not regarded as a tourism destination however once his development began to attract international interest other entrepreneurs moved into the area forcing the local municipal authorities to adopt a planning process. Change occurred rapidly following a path that leapt from a Phase 1 and Phase 2 destination illustrated in Figure 2.10 to a Phase 4 destination in a very short period of time. Phase 3 growth followed a little later when additional accommodation was built to attract the Australian interstate (Phase 3) market. The growth path followed by Port Douglas paralleled similar destinations in Asia and Mexico where international tourism became a major sector in the first significant phase of growth.

Table 2.4 illustrates the growth in rooms by categories between 1983 and 2000. It is apparent that the opening of the Sheraton resort in 1989 signalled the start of a period of intense development over the next 10 years. During this period the number of rooms of all types and excluding caravan parks, increased from 262 to 2107.

TABLE 2.4 The Growth in Number of Accommodation Units in Port Douglas by Star Classification

Year	5 Star	4 Star	3 Star	2 Star/motel	Holiday Apartment	Caravan Park
1983				49	39	225
1984			17	46	41	225
1985			17	46	47	225
1986			17	46	74	225
1987			17	52	186	274
1988			17	49	198	274
1989	300		17	56	198	184
1990	300	50	22	81	517	220
1991	300	50	22	41	517	229
1992	300	353	42	53	529	311
1993	385	353	39	47	583	328
1994	400	353	39	47	583	277
1995	400	353	58	22	590	277
1996	400	356	538	32	590	187
1997	400	406	499	22	600	211
1998	400	448	499	26	748	162
1999	400	818	19	22	848	229

Case Study 2.3 Rabaul

In 1994 two volcanoes, Tavurvur and Vulcan, erupted destroying much of the town of Rabaul in Papua New Guinea. Figure 5.1 shows a general view of the ruins of the pre-1994 eruption town of Rabaul. Prior to 1994 the town had a reputation as a high quality dive site and was popular with international tourists despite its remoteness. In the years following the eruption the town's tourism industry failed to regain its pre-eruption visitor market, not because of ongoing fear of another eruption, but rather from a collective failure by the private and public sectors to mount an effective marketing campaign to regain market share. By 2007 the inventory of available quality properties had dwindled to one or perhaps two that offered diving and one dive shop. Other prosperities that once serviced the dive industry had either been abandoned or were used for other purposes. In terms of the RDS the destination had almost reached the bottom of the decline stage but based on the criteria outlined in Table 2.2, it has the potential to develop into a major international destination in future. However, the path to this form of development will lie in a modified *Big bang* version of the model outlined in Case Study 2.2, not through the evolutionary path illustrated in the hypothetical model outlined in Figure 2.10.

CONCLUSION

Models are useful tools for teaching and planning; however, they have a number of limitations the most significant of which is that they are simplified versions of a much more complex reality and that for complex situations there may be a need for two or more models to explain aspects of the phenomenon under investigation. As Figure 2.7 highlights, the use of four models to understand the underlying forces responsible for the development of the Gold Coast gives a more complete picture than is possible with one model. To date application of analytical processes at this level of sophistication is lacking and its absence has hindered the development of a more holistic understanding of the processes at work.

It is also apparent that current models including the RDS are useful for explaining some aspects of coastal tourism and in some circumstances may be useful for examining the behaviour of the tourism sector in coastal zone cities. It is also apparent that with suitable modifications the RDS and other models may be useful in explaining development patterns in mountain areas.

KEY ISSUES

- Models identify core relationships and the variables that drive them and explain these in a simplified manner.

- A major limitation of tourism models is that in reducing complexity into simplicity many of the underlying relationships are not identified.
- Models are useful tools for understanding development but have been misused.
- There is an urgent need to re-evaluate the models currently used for studying destination development.
- In many cases an effective approach to understand the complex nature of destination development is the use of two or more models.
- There is a need to develop a new range of models that are capable of being operationalized and which follow the principles outlined in Figure 2.8.
- The Resort Development Spectrum is a useful addition to the understanding of the processes of destination development.
- Further research into coastal tourism should occur within the context of Coastal Zone Management.

CHAPTER 3

Planning for the Future:
A New Approach

Going forward in time to ensure sustainability for the future

Planning is a key element in the life of any destination and occurs at many levels ranging from the planning decisions made by individual firms to collective planning involving all stakeholders in the destination (Gunn, 1988). Inadequate planning may place limitations on the destination's ability to grow or reduce long-term sustainability. In the past there has been a tendency to develop long-term projections of the possible growth course of destinations using quantitive methods such as forecasting and to a smaller extent, qualitative methods including Delphi studies and expert opinion. The results have not always been satisfactory and alternative planning approaches are needed that can compliment both existing methods and offer new insights into what is possible in the future. One possible approach using scenarios is discussed later in this chapter.

As discussed in Chapter 2 no single model or planning tool can adequately represent the multitude of cross sector and cross government links and drivers that operate in a destination. Destinations are complicated structures, built from a fusion of natural resources, the intellectual capacity of its residents, investors, the workforce, political structures, governance arrangements, residents and the visitors they receive. In simple terms destinations use physical, intellectual and financial resources within a particular governance model to create a tourism product that must then be sold via a distribution system in a competitive market that is subject to regulation by the public sector. Competition includes other destinations as well as other goods and services which vie for the consumer's disposable income. Destinations function most effectively when demand and supply forces are in a state of equilibrium. If growth occurs or the destination experiences a shock in the form of a crisis event,

51

disequilibrium will emerge, and it may take some time for the return of equilibrium and stability. The new equilibrium point may be the same, greater or lower than the original point. The concept of equilibrium is a significant underlying force in shaping the economic operation of destinations and was discussed in Chapter 2. Proactive planning is able to assist in addressing gaps that occur when the demand and supply sides are in a state of imbalance or disequilibrium and where the destination wishes to move to a new equilibrium point.

CONTEMPORARY PLANNING

In many destinations, planning has an underlying assumption that growth is a desirable outcome. Growth should however become an end in itself. In some instances further growth will create new environmental problems that will reduce the overall attractiveness of the destination. However, where capacity exists and there is a desire for growth, planning is the key process required to ensure that growth is sustainable and that benefits are able to be shared by all sectors of the community. Figure 3.1 demonstrates the relationships that exist between destination capacity, growth over time, policy, marketing and the

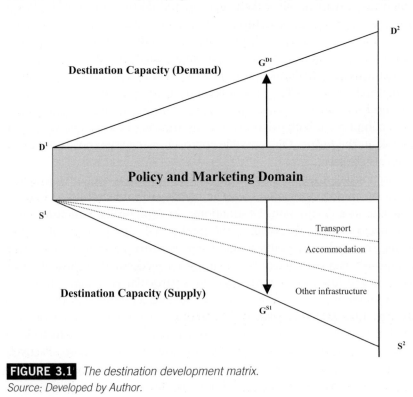

FIGURE 3.1 *The destination development matrix.*
Source: Developed by Author.

response of the demand and supply sides to growth. Economic growth is the outcome of increased demand built on increased supply. The path of growth can be traced through changes in the demand and supply sides that create a series of equilibrium points. This concept was previously discussed in Chapter 2 and illustrated in Figure 2.9.

In the development matrix shown in Figure 3.1, demand (D) and supply (S) are shown as mirror sectors where growth in one sector is mirrored by growth in the other. D^1D^2 represents the destination demand curve, which in theory may continue to grow until destination capacity is reached at point D^2. Beyond this point the destination ceases to have the capacity to maintain long-term sustainability. S^1S^2 represents the destination supply curve that must mirror growth in the demand side at the rate indicated by the curve D^1D^2. Point S^2 represents the maximum capacity of the destination's supply side to provide capacity to meet maximum demand. At any point along the demand curve, demand should match supply. For example, growth to point G^{D1} must be mirrored by growth in supply to point G^{S1} on the destination supply curve $S^1 S^2$. In the hypothetical destination illustrated, growth is shown by the curve D^1D^2. If a bottleneck occurs at the supply line and inhibits the expansion of infrastructure (illustrated here as transport, accommodation and attractions) beyond capacity G^{S1}, growth beyond point GD^1 will not be achievable. While not shown in Figure 3.1, the demand element of the model may be subdivided into specific market sectors including domestic and international. The Policy and Marketing Domain that lies between the demand and supply sides is the source of policy that determines the rate and form of growth and the marketing efforts that will be required to be implemented to translate the desired level of growth into reality. One of the key outcomes of the policy element of this domain should be effective planning and is discussed later in the chapter. Concurrently, effective marketing is required to maintain visitor interest in the destination.

Authors including Gunn (1988, 1994), Inskeep (1991) and Cooper *et al.* (2005) advocate a relatively standard model of tourism planning which incorporates a number of feedback loops. In this chapter a modified seven-stage planning model tailored to the needs of destinations is advocated. The planning process occurs within larger regional and national political, financial and social contexts that individually and collectively influence the operation and growth potential of individual destinations.

A SEVEN-STAGE PLANNING MODEL

Planning is not as straightforward a process as the seven-stage model outlined in Figure 3.2 appears to indicate. Within each destination there may be a multitude of industries, agencies, companies and other organizations

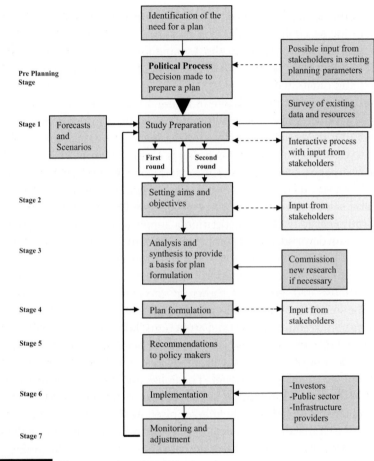

FIGURE 3.2   *The seven-step planning process.*
Source: Developed by Author.

each with its own specific planning objectives, some of which may not be sympatric to the objectives of the tourism sector. In such circumstances conflicts may occur. In many destinations it is not uncommon for the objectives of the tourism industry to differ from the objectives of other industries. In a number of nations, including Saudi Arabia and Iran, the planning process operates within a religious context that adds a further level of complexity to the operation of destinations in those nations. The first step in successful destination planning is to recognize that there are multiple planning agencies with multiple and often conflicting objectives interacting at numerous levels within any destination. Achieving consensus between the various planning bodies is often difficult. There-fore, before engaging with other sectors the objectives of the tourism in-dustry require articulation and prioritization, a process that usually requires negotiation and consensus between key stakeholders. The consen-sus position may then be used as a platform to inform the overall planning process, the best outcome of which is a tourism plan that coexists with other plans that may be operating within the destination.

One example of a tourism plan having to coexist with another planning scheme is found in the area of transport. Transport planning in a destination context has several passenger tasks: meeting the needs of residents; meeting the needs of tourists; and ensuring freight distribution is efficient. These passenger tasks may not be compatible, as tourists will often wish to travel to activities and places that differ from those that residents travel to. In this case transport planners and tourism planners will need to work cooperatively to build an effective transport network. These issues are discussed in great detail in Chapter 4.

The discussion in this chapter focuses on Stages 1 and 2 of the planning framework outlined in Figure 3.2. Prior to commencing the actual planning process decisions must be made to embark on planning, the scope of the planning to be undertaken, the funding to be allocated and how a planning team is to be selected. This preplanning stage is important because it sets the parameters for the following planning process. The preplanning stage is likely to be overtly political particularly if planning is on a substantial scale. The success of the ensuing planning process will largely depend on the terms of reference set in this per stage, the budget allocated and the selection of the planning team.

The first stage in the planning process should commence within the political process because it is this process that will ultimately determine the overall parameters of the plan and its desired outcomes. In the context used here the destination is defined as a discrete geographic region which in most cases will comprise a central urban area and surrounding hinterland. In the widest application of the term, a destination can refer to much larger areas ranging from a region through to a nation or even to multi-national regions typified by the group of countries that the Mekong River flows through. This region, referred to as the Greater Mekong SubRegion (GMS) encompasses China, Myanmar, Laos PDR, Thailand, Cambodia and Vietnam and in recent years has become the focus for cooperative tourism planning.

The outcome of the initial stage of planning is very much a reflection of the objectives of the policy makers involved in the process and what they hope to achieve. This initial stage should include a detailed assessment of the direction that the destination is anticipated to follow in the future. Considerations at this stage of planning might include:

- The intensity, rate and style of development
- Issues dealing with sustainability
- Welfare of residents
- Governance issues including boundary issues between adjoining jurisdictions and between different levels of government
- Infrastructure development and responsibilities
- Education of the workforce
- The type of tourist and form of development desired
- Development versus preservation
- Development of nearby destinations
- Issues of future size and attraction mix
- Zoning for competing land uses
- Objectives of complimentary and competing industries
- Incorporation of a capacity to respond to crisis events
- Identification of issues that affect long-term sustainability
- The role of the public sector visa a vie the private sector and the destination community
- Impact of climate change
- Adoption of suitable development models
- Identification of emerging trends that will influence the future path of development.

The significance of Stage 1 (Figure 3.2) is that the agendas and boundaries that will govern the remainder of the process are established. This process should seek stakeholder input and have a capacity to allow adjustment of the resulting aims and goals (Stage 2) through an interactive process as illustrated by the two rounds of consultation outlined in Figure 3.2. An important component of Stage 1 is collection and assessment of information that is able to be used to guide decision makers in their setting of aims and objectives. In this part of the planning process consideration should be given to previous research and new research commissioned when required. Consideration should also be given to adopting appropriate development models of the type previously discussed in Chapter 2. At this point in the planning process, which is after all an exercise that looks to the future, consideration should also be given to developing planning scenarios. Scenarios are able to provide policy makers with options for future development that might otherwise be overlooked. Scenarios also give policy makers the chance to glimpse into possible future and facilitate informed decisions on the selection of policy objectives. Apart from scenarios a range of other tools may be used to set agendas and boundaries including public consultation, discussions with lobby groups, the views of residents, previous research and expert opinion. In other sectors of the economy policy makers have found scenarios to be a useful tool during this stage of planning. Surprisingly, the tourism sector has been slow to adopt this technique with one notable exception being the VisitScotland organization, which developed four scenarios to explore possible futures. Each scenario was developed around a number of themes: Economic and Political Environment, Scottish Tourism Products, Markets and Tourist Attributes. The exercise was found to be beneficial and has been supported as an on going function of the organization (Hay and Yoeman, 2007). If care is not taken during Stage 1 of the planning process suboptimal results may emerge.

An important component of the setting of objectives is recognition that stakeholder input is required and that aims and objectives may need to be revised on the basis of that input. One important group of stakeholders who should not be overlooked is the destination community. Input from this group is vital for they are the hosts to the visitors who travel to their community. This process may take several rounds as illustrated in Stages 1 and 2. Where community input is not sought planning may fail because the community has little ownership or interest in the success or otherwise of the plan.

Given the limitations of space of this chapter Stages 3–7 are only discussed briefly. Stage 5 is an important element in the process because the success of later stages relies on how policy makers respond to recommendations by assigning appropriate resources and authorising required policy initiatives for Stage 6 implementation to occur.

Planning, as in many other aspects of tourism, has a significant scale component. The seven-step planning process is a generic process that should be applied at all levels of the industry commencing at a local level and continuing through to the national or even the international level. The administration of the planning process will largely be determined by the issues it needs to address, its sponsors, stakeholder participation, time periods and the resources available. In many cases the process will be controlled by a Steering Committee comprised of major stakeholders. The success of the overall planning process will depend on: the level of ownership of the local community and business sector have towards the plan; to what extent it is adopted by policy makers; how implementation of recommendations is undertaken; how compensation is allocated to stakeholders who suffer negative impacts; the technical competence of the planners and if the process has been designed to be dynamic rather than static.

In the past, approaches to destination planning have followed two broad paths. The first approach based on detailed centralized planning by the public sector is synonymous with socialist countries where the public sector has considerable power and is the major source of investment. Detailed planning is also possible in a market-based economy particularly when specific areas have been set aside for destination development. Planning of this nature may be undertaken by a consortium or by the public sector. For example, in Indonesia the Nusa Dau region of southern Bali was declared a development zone and the region was master planned but with individual properties built by investors (Inskeep, 1991).

The second approach to planning is that found in most developed market economies where the public sector passes considerable responsibility to the private sector by allowing the market to determine the structure and rate of progress of investment in the destination. In reality, approaches taken in market-based economies rely on some input from the public sector particularly in the setting of standards and land zoning while the market is given the opportunity to determine the best mix of attractions, accommodation, source markets and in some instances the opportunity to provide some or most of the infrastructure required. In a number of developed economies, the public sector has retreated from active involvement in many areas of infrastructure provision and has passed responsibility for ownership of airports, ports, railways and some roads to the private sector. In a number of nations including the United Kingdom and New Zealand, publicly owned airports have been sold to the private sector, which then assumes responsibility for airport operations and investment. In other countries highways and railways have also been sold to the private sector.

Both the planning approaches have limitations. Centralized planning either by a government agency or a private consortium often suffers from inflexibility and an inability to respond to changing market forces. The Mt Gumgang resort project in North Korea is an example of a public/private sector planned destination that has experienced considerable financial difficulties. The project partners, the Hyundai Corporation of South Korea and the North Korean Government, based investment in facilities on an overly optimistic forecast of visitor numbers. Visitor projections were not met and revenue never met projections causing severe financial problems for Hyundai even with substantial South Korean Government financial assistance (Kim and Prideaux, 2003). A major problem with this project was that its primary purpose was political and the needs of the North and South to demonstrate their ability to work cooperatively overshadowed market realities. As a consequence inadequate consumer research was undertaken and visitor demand was overestimated.

Abdicating responsibility for aspects of destination development to the private sector can also produce inadequate outcomes. If the profit motive and the need to recoup investment in the short term outweigh other considerations, such as the need to achieve long-term sustainability, the destination is likely to develop in a suboptimal manner. One example where resistance to promoting short-term gains has yielded substantial long-term gains is demonstrated at Noosa, a coastal destination in southeast Queensland, Australia. Efforts by developers to convert parts of Noosa township into a large integrated resort with high-rise and canal developments were thwarted when a pro-conservationist local council was elected in 1982 (Gloster, 1997) and parts of the shire that had been designated for development were declared a national park. Subsequent local councils have limited the height of buildings and actively promoted the expansion of the shire's national parks. In 1997 the Noosa Strategic Town Plan incorporated a population cap based on the shire's environmental carrying capacity. As a consequence the town has developed a village atmosphere centred on the Hastings Street shopping and accommodation precinct. This amenity, combined with the town's adjacent national parks, has underpinned the town's emergence as one of the state's premier tourism destinations. In this case the willingness of the public sector to listen to stakeholders during Stages 1 and 2 resulted in a change in the planning aims and objectives that emerged at the conclusion of Stage 2. Ongoing monitoring in Stage 7 has been fed back into ongoing Stage 1 discussions which has allowed the destination to create a unique blend of development and conservation.

One of the major criticisms of tourism plans has been the failure to include mechanisms for regular reviews. For plans to operate effectively over a long time period they need to be dynamic, have the capacity to evolve as unforeseen changes occur and importantly be designed to cope with crisis when it occurs. Steering committees or the bodies given responsibility for managing the plan should not see their task as time limited but as an ongoing process. The feedback mechanism that operates between Stages 7 and 1 in Figure 3.2 as well as the feedback process that captures the views of stakeholders therefore become vital components of successful planning.

In capitalist economies the norm for high-level planning is to outline broad overall social and economic objectives and allow the market to operate within these broad guidelines. Planning in this context has a political element that produces the overall legal and administrative framework within which the market is encouraged to operate to maximize returns. Intervention usually occurs only to correct market failure or ensure that other social, economic and equity objectives are obtained. The United States for example does not have a national tourism master plan leaving issues of this nature to individual states. New Zealand, as with many other countries, has a more detailed plan that outlines national objectives in aspects of tourism such investment strategies, environmental policies and marketing (NZ Ministry of Tourism, 2007).

Initiating the development process is a complicated task and the planning process suggested in Figure 3.2 may not always occur. The process of growth is complex and may be sparked by a number of factors that may emanate from the public sector, the private sector or both. In a typical capitalist economic model, the public sector usually restricts involvement in economic development to legislative initiatives designed to assist the growth process as well as various forms of financial assistance. Direct investment in commercial ventures is becoming rare because the private sector is now seen as more efficient at making successful investment decisions than the public sector. In the tourism sector, governments at all levels have increasingly adopted a position of guidance through policy and regulation and investment in strategic infrastructure such as transport while leaving other investment such as accommodation to the private sector. The one area where the public sector retains an ability to manage development is by controlling development through strategies including zoning, licensing and environmental impact assessment. The result is that the public sector in most cases has to wait until investment initiatives emanate from the private sector.

Driven by the profit motivate, the private sector will normally only invest in projects when profit opportunities are identified. As a consequence, tourism plans are able to set goals but of themselves cannot initiate development, being able only to guide it when it does occur. If sufficient consultation has not occurred and the needs of the entrepreneur and the wider commercial sector including corporations and other investment bodies differ from the strategies suggested by planners development may not occur. Understanding this process is a key factor in initiating a successful growth strategy. To date the planning literature has not given a great deal of attention to the role of investors and entrepreneurs as growth initiators although this is starting to change. Russell and Faulkner (1999) highlighted the role of leading entrepreneurs in their study of the expansion of the tourism industry on the Gold Coast Australia. According to Russell and Faulkner (1999) constructs such as the Destination Life Cycle Model overlook the role of entrepreneurs to whom they ascribe a more fundamental position in the processes of destination development. Development initiated by entrepreneurs is described as unpredictable, even chaotic. The behaviour of developers according to Russell and Faulkner (1999:411) *"is a creative process where entrepreneurs play a primary role both as chaos-makers and as initiators of adaptive responses to chaos induced by external events"*. Case Study 2.2 illustrates the role of the entrepreneur described by Russell and Faulkner (1999).

Development may also be a function of the rate of adoption of new innovation or ideas. Successful innovations, described by Rogers (1983:11) as *'an idea, practice or object that is perceived as new by an individual or other unit of adoption*' capture the attention of markets and the first destination to introduce a new innovation is able to create a short-term market advantage. In the planning process new ideas should be explored and where possible introduced to secure a market advantage. In some destinations innovation may be as simple as a new form of attraction or activity introduced by an innovator entrepreneur that attracts the attention of other entrepreneurs thereby creating a momentum for growth.

Rogers (1983) described an innovation-decision process that commences with knowledge of the innovation followed by persuasion (understanding of the innovation), decision, implementation and confirmation of the decision. Once introduced by the first adopter other investors assess the innovation and decide if they will follow in a process that Rogers describes as an S-shaped curve of adoption. The first adopter (or innovator) is followed in turn by early adopters, early majority, late majority and finally by laggards in a pattern that in most cases reflects a bell-shaped curve over time as illustrated in Figure 1.3.

In the near future it is likely that many destinations will respond to growing consumer concern over climate change and introduce carbon offset schemes. While it might seem cynical to use concerns about climate change as a marketing tool destinations that do not respond to growing public concern over the issue are likely to be seen as laggards in the sense used by Rogers and face the prospect of loosing market share to destinations that exhibit positive responses. A parallel to this situation can be found in the rapid adoption of the term, if not the practice, of ecotourism in the mid-1980s. Within a space of several years many businesses then operating in the nature tourism area rebadged their products as ecotourism experiences, often ignoring the operational practices that were required to make the transition. It may be anticipated that a similar failure to go beyond the rhetoric of climate change adaption will occur as destinations begin to market climate change friendly experiences.

USING SCENARIOS

A major consideration that confronts policy makers, planners and investors is estimating future demand for the experiences and activities that individual destinations provide. If planners and investors miscalculate there may be severe consequences for the destination in the future. Bood and Postma (1997) observed that standard forecasting methods are based on an extrapolation of the past and as a consequence forecasts tend to view the world as essentially stable and linear. Recent experience with terrorism, disease, stock market corrections of the nature of the 2008–2009 Global Financial Crisis and natural disasters indicate that stability cannot be assumed to be the norm and an allowance for instability needs to be included as a planning parameter. In some parts of the physical world where systems are stable mathematical models are used to predict physical processes such as short-term changes in day-to-day weather patterns. A number of authors (Wack, 1985; Schwartz, 1988; Prideaux *et al.*, 2003) have demonstrated the limited effectiveness of forecasting particularly when the time frames stretch beyond 1 or 2 years or when unpredicted events occur.

On a larger scale, which may extend beyond the next year or two, the vast majority of future events are unpredictable. For example, the oil price spike of early 2008 caught many airlines by surprise forcing them to revise predictions of future traffic growth. Fearing that increased fuel prices would sharply reduce demand for travel many airlines retired older aircraft, cut unprofitable routes and cancelled or deferred aircraft orders. By January 2009 oil prices had fallen to 2006 levels because of the Global Financial Crisis. Given the shortcomings of current forecasting methods, there is a need to employ other methods as supplements or alternatives. The range of techniques and methods used by futurologists (discussed in detail in Chapter 10) provide planners with alternative views of how the future may develop. This however raises an interesting question about the future, does it occur in linear fashion of the nature that underpins current forecasting models or are there alternative futures that can be predicted, or even created, based on our current state of knowledge.

To overcome the inadequacies of existing forecasting models Bood and Postma (1997) suggested the use of multiple scenarios because they present managers with a set of fundamentally different views on the future. Used in this sense, scenarios have two time elements, the *contemporary world* measured by the interaction between the known and the unknown and a *future world* where the measurable relationships of the future world may assume entirely different patterns and structures depending on the assumptions used. Although not widely used in tourism settings or discussed in the tourism literature, other disciplines including management and disaster planning made extensive use of scenarios for investigating the possible course of the future (Fink, 1986; Haimes *et al.*, 2002). In some circumstances scenario analysis is able to provide an effective alternative to forecasting as will be demonstrated in the extended case study on Papua New Guinea discussed later in this chapter. In other circumstances, scenarios may be used in conjunction with standard forecasting techniques.

While this chapter will focus on scenarios as a tool for planning there are a range of other techniques that are available to planners. In this chapter we review only scenarios however in the literature that discusses futurology and future studies, broadly defined as the art, practice and science of postulating the future, a range of techniques have been advocated including Delphi method, Future history, Futures wheel, trend analysis, technology forecasting, Environmental scanning and Causal layered analysis (CLA).

According to van der Heijden (1996) scenario planning is a useful method for assessing the future for strategic purposes. In its basic form, scenario planning is based on the understanding that a wide range of possible futures exist and that the future is not predetermined. Scenarios may be described as a method of understanding the dynamics that will shape the future. The use of scenarios as a planning tool has been criticised on the grounds that their construction lacks the mathematical rigor that is a characteristic of statistical forecasting tools. However, the inability of standard forecasting methods to achieve long run accuracy has created the need for other methods such as scenarios.

In a strategic planning environment, scenarios provide a useful tool for preparing organizations (and destinations) for changes in the business environment (Godet, 2000; Porter, 1985; van der Heijden, 1996). The construction of scenarios requires the development of a number of credible alternative possible futures, an assessment of the probability that these futures may occur and finally an evaluation of the desirability of each scenario (Niiniluoto, 2001). A number of large corporations including Royal Dutch/Shell, Levi-Strauss, the Electrolux Group, British Airways, Pacific Gas and Electric, Motorola, and Global Business Network (Ringland, 1998; Schwartz, 1998) have successfully employed scenarios as management tools.

The functions for which scenarios are used, outlined in Figure 3.3, depend on the needs of their users. Scenarios can be used to test new policies, to reduce risk and test how policies may behave in the future (see Figure 3.8). Scale is an important consideration that has at least two elements: size and time. Scale may range from an individual firm to the nation, and time can be measured as the near future to the distant future. At the destination level scenarios are useful for investigating how a mix of private and public sector policies may be used to achieve a desired future or on a smaller scale to test how consumers will respond to new products.

While it is not possible to predict the future with even a small degree of certainty, a glimpse of the type of futures that may occur is possible by using scenarios. Of course care must be taken to employ realistic assumptions to illustrate the possible outcomes of a range of combinations of policy and planning initiatives (Singer and Prideaux, 2005). The need for destinations to be able to explore a range of potential futures to determine which best suits the needs of its stakeholders (residents, investors, visitors, the private sector and government) provides a strong justification for using scenarios.

1. Testing alternative futures by assessing the future impacts of changes made to contemporary policies and strategies

2. Reducing risk by assessing dangers that may emerge in the future

3. Examining how the future might change if factors that govern current systems of government or other social and cultural structures undergo change

4. Testing how a specific policy initiative may behave in the future

5. Identifying how relationships between factors (related or independent) will evolve over time

6. As a means of identifying desirable futures and working towards achieving them.

7. Triggering or accelerating policy initiatives

FIGURE 3.3 *Functions of scenarios.*
Source: Developed by Author.

Scenarios allow destination stakeholders to explore how markets might behave if new products are introduced and to develop an understanding of the likely impact of new government planning policies in the short, medium and long terms. In a recent demonstration of the employment of scenarios in this manner Singer and Prideaux (2004) examined the possible impacts of Norfolk Island's tourism industry failing to introduce new products to attract the emerging babyboomer seniors market (See Case Study10.1). It was apparent that a continued failure by the Island's tourism industry to develop new products and services for this new visitor sector would lead to declining yields and visitor numbers.

To test risk, destinations and firms are able to develop scenarios of possible future events such as market downturns triggered by a major crisis (a major terrorist attack for example) (Ayres, 2000) or natural events such as floods and earthquakes and explore how their current market mix would react. Given that events of this nature have occurred in the recent past and that there is an increasing volume of research in the area of disasters assessment (Hall *et al.*, 2003; Ayres, 2000), firms and destinations now have credible research to assist with the development of realistic scenarios. Scenario planning used in this manner is able to provide a method for reducing risk and avoiding the consequences of adopting suboptimal risk management strategies. Scenarios may also be used to test the future impacts and outcomes of policy changes (Wilson, 2000). However, in using scenarios for this purpose Wilson (2000) warned that implementation and execution of

1. Identification of trends and other factors that are known to be operating in the present and that will influence the future to create probable futures.

2. Developing versions of the future that are seen as desirable and which may be able to be achieved if conditions and policies in the present and near future are altered to actively work towards achieving that future

3. Testing 'what if' factors. This class of scenario investigates futures that might occur if specific shocks or stimuli are applied.

4. Specific courses of action are tested to gauge reactions to specific outcome

5. Gaming. For example, War gaming is used by the military to test the possible outcomes of battlefield strategies on their own forces as well as enemy forces

FIGURE 3.4 *Classes of scenarios.*
Source: Developed by Author.

policy based on scenario analysis may be difficult. Scenarios therefore provide a picture of the future that traditional forecasting methods find difficult to provide. Moreover, they are a useful tool for predicting the outcomes of policy changes and identifying the possible outcomes of fundamental shifts in occurring in market relationships.

At least five classes of scenarios may be constructed to meet the needs of users (see Figure 3.4). Three of these classes can be used to create pictures of the future and are referred to as future scenarios (classes 1, 2 and 3 in Figure 3.4). The first class of scenarios, demonstrated later in this chapter, involves the identification of trends, drivers and other factors that are known to be operating in the contemporary environment and that will influence the future. These trends and other factors can then be projected into the future using a range of scenarios that represent the spectrum of futures that lie between the best case and the worst case. In Figure 3.5 these futures are identified as probable futures. A probable future is underpinned with data that has been identified as realistic and can be interpreted by expert opinion. Case Study 5.1 was developed using this approach.

The second class of scenarios is based on developing versions of the future that are seen as desirable and which may be achieved if conditions and policies in the present and near future are altered to actively work towards achieving specific future outcomes. Unlike probable futures, this class of scenarios may be used to illustrate how changes to policy may play out over time. In this sense, scenarios of this type allow users to create the future they desire using targeted policy changes rather than allowing the future to unfold without any

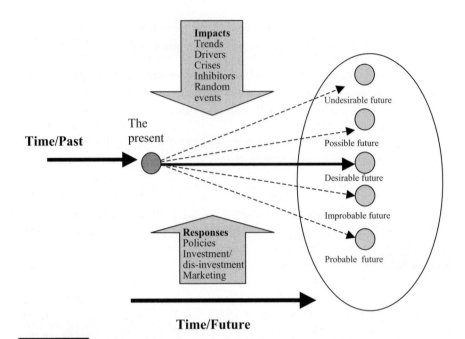

FIGURE 3.5 *A range of futures showing the effect of impacts (trend, random events, crises, drivers and inhibitors) and responses (policies, investment and marketing). Source: Developed by Author.*

attempt to change the factors that shape the future. In Figure 3.5 this class of scenario is represented by desirable futures and possible futures.

The third class of scenarios refers to 'what if' factors occurring. Included in this class of scenario are futures that do not currently appear plausible given the current state of knowledge about trends that alter history. For example, an extreme scenario of this nature is an invasion by alien beings. Apart from friction writers and movie directors there is no verified indication of an occurrence of this nature. However, as Prideaux *et al.* (2003) point out, until 2001 an incident of the nature of the September 11, 2001 attack on the United States was not considered plausible but today, terrorism attacks on an even bigger scale must be factored into forecasts of the near future. In Figure 3.5 this class of scenario is represented by improbable and undesirable futures.

A fourth class of scenarios not illustrated in Figure 3.5 because they operate at sub destination levels describes circumstances where specific courses of action are embarked upon to gauge specific outcomes. In the hospitality industry, secret shopper programs use this form of scenario. The secret shopper is given sets of scenarios they must play out and then evaluate the response of the hotel staff. Another example of the use of this class of scenario is to test consumer reactions to change such as the imposition of an entrance fee to a previously free-entry national park. The outcome of the scenario may be used to predict changes in visitor patterns generated at various levels of fees.

The final class of scenario is based on gaming theory. Masini and Vasquez (2000) noted that the concept of scenarios was based on war gaming exercises used by the US Defence Department and developed during the 1950s. Strategies are tested and based on the outcomes, new strategies are developed.

The process of scenario development is determined by the purpose that it is to be used for. In developing scenarios, a number of stages are used in the analysis commencing with problem identification and are followed by an analysis of the current *drivers* of the situation or policy being analysed (Medina and Vasquez, 2000). Drivers are defined as factors that influence the future course of events (see Chapter 10 for a more comprehensive discussion). Climate change is an emerging driver that will significantly influence government policy making and investment in future decades. Similarly, rapid growth in GDP is a key driver in the recent growth of outbound tourism from both China and India. Once key drivers have been determined, the elements that relate to the situation that the scenario is being used to investigate may be identified and classified. Thus, in a global scenario numerous factors and their relationships will need to be considered whereas in a regional setting the factors and their relationships will be much smaller in scale and number. Following the construction of a number of scenarios that reflect the future possibilities of the situation or policy under examination, policy makers or other scenario users are able to develop policy responses that allow them to achieve better future outcomes. Not all scenario construction follows these steps (Masini and Medina Vasquez, 2000). Godet (2000) developed an approach based on the construction of probability and operations research, while the SKI-Shell method is orientated towards the occurrence of specific events (Masini and Medina Vasquez, 2000).

Singer and Prideaux (2004) noted that scenarios are not developed to pinpoint the future in specific terms but to understand the key factors that push the future in various directions. These forces are made visible through the development of scenarios. Scenarios can be used to identify undesirable as well as desirable trends and facilitate corrective actions if required. The construction of scenarios utilizes a range of techniques and should not be confused with forecasting which employs a range of quantitative methods to achieve a different type of outcome. Scenarios also have the capacity to include evaluation of drivers and trends that are not usually included in econometric forecasting. These include the impact of new technology and unforeseen crisis events.

When used as part of the destination planning process, scenarios may be used to: predict the impact of specific changes such as changing entry fee for parks or the increase in visitors that may be expected if a new large capacity airport is constructed; testing the response to specific policy changes such as imposing limits on the size of the accommodation sector or visitor numbers in a specific destination; or on a larger scale predicting a range of futures for a destination based on significant changes in the public sector planning environment.

By seeking to understand the potential shape of the future based on an analysis of the known, there is some scope to exercise limited control over a specific future by introducing a mix of policies and strategies to achieve a desired outcome.

Figure 3.5 illustrates how the relationship between *impacts* (including crises, trends, drivers, random events and inhibitors) and *responses* (policy, investment, disinvestment and marketing) over time can produce a range of futures. As impacts occur, the destination responds and in the process has some potential to push the destination towards a future state that is more desirable than might otherwise be the case. Chapter 10 discusses these concepts more extensively. The role of time is significant and the further forward in time a scenario is projected the less certain one can be of its ability to incorporate the unknowns of the future. The scenarios identified in Figure 3.5 are classified as:

- Possible futures
- Probable futures
- Undesirable futures
- Improbable futures
- Desirable futures

Other authors explain the future with different classifications. For example, Lindgren and Bandhold (2003) postulated three types of futures (possible, probable and desired) but did not consider the influence of trends or random events.

Possible future

A possible future describes two conditions: a future that may occur as a result of changes in government policy, private sector investment policy or changes in the direction of prevailing trends in the contemporary era. One example of a trend that is subject to change is concerns over declining fertility rates that in many countries have raised concerns about the ability of future generations to bear the cost of an ageing society (Fleischer and Pizam, 2002). This trend is reversible but will require a new policy agenda by government. The second condition concerns a change in the general direction of growth that occurs through an unanticipated change. A change of this nature occurred when in early 2008 The Global Credit Crunch together with rapidly rising oil prices forced many airlines to retire older aircraft, reduce frequencies and raise tariffs. Possible futures may be viewed as either good or bad depending on the viewpoint of those affected by the future course of events.

Probably future

A probable future is one that is likely to occur when current trends are allowed to continue into the future without intervention by government. In these circumstances forecasting tools may be a useful indicator of the future course of events.

Undesirable future

An undesirable future is one that will be seen by the participants in that future as undesirable. For example, the threat of a global Avian Flu pandemic (Garrett, 2005) on a scale similar to the 1918–1919 Spanish Flu aroused considerable concern in 2005. If a pandemic of this nature were to occur the global economy would undergo considerable disruption, slowing if not stalling economic growth, and both domestic and international tourism would suffer a substantial decline. At the destination level one example of an undesirable future is where demand declines to the extent that firms are bankrupted and rising unemployment forces an out-migration of the labour force.

Improbable future

An improbable future is one that describes a future that does not appear possible with the current understanding of science, the underlying forces that govern the economy or the state of civil society. An extreme example of this type of future is a new ice age occurring in the next few decades. An event of this type appears highly improbable given the current understanding of global weather patterns but cannot be totally excluded because of our lack of knowledge of long-term forces that control global climatic patterns.

Desirable future

Finally, a desirable future is one that society or in this case a destination deems to be worth achieving but only if new policies are implemented to actively work towards this future. A desirable future may not be attainable if the destination lacks the resources to achieve the future it deems to be desirable. Developing a scenario of this nature relies on identification and extensive analysis of the variables that govern the operation of a particular destination. This should normally be a function of Stages 1 and 3 of the destination planning process described in Figure 3.2.

SCENARIO CONSTRUCTION

The construction of scenarios is a rigorous process that occurs sequentially using a wide range of data sources. Commencing with the problem or issue of interest and paralleling the considerations made during Stage 1 of the seven-stage planning model outlined in Figure 3.2, identification of the core issue of interest moves through a series of steps (outlined in Figure 3.6) to develop a policy response. The incorporation of an evaluation stage with associated feedback loops as suggested in Figure 3.2 develops a 'living' or dynamic scenario development process that can be regularly updated to reflect changes in the external environment. Problem identification is often the most difficult part of the exercise because problems are not always straightforward and able to be identified (Dunn, 1981). In many circumstances the symptoms of the problem have higher visibility than the cause of the problem resulting in inaccurate scenario construction. At this point some consensus should emerge as to the vision that is to be achieved. A number of techniques have

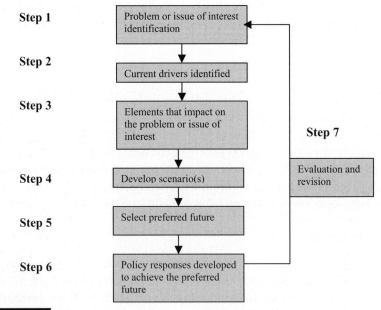

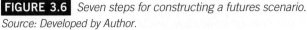

FIGURE 3.6 *Seven steps for constructing a futures scenario.*
Source: Developed by Author.

been developed to identify future issues including 'hexagons' (Hodgson, 1992) and 'futurescoping' (Future Foundation, 2004). At a destination level the problem is commonly crouched in terms such as achieving long-term sustainability, identifying preferable growth strategies, identifying future markets and servicing new markets. Consideration of these issues involves a process described as environmental scanning where information is sought and a decision is made on which information is to be observed and followed (Yeoman and McMahon-Beattie, 2005). Wide consultation with all stakeholders is a necessary condition during this step in scenario construction. Once the problem or problems have been identified and an agreement on desirable ways forward struck, the actual process of scenario development can commence with identification of current drivers.

Identification of all major drivers and their relationship to the key variables governing the operation of the destination is important as illustrated in Step 2. How the drivers react to change in their operating environment must also be identified (see Case Study 3.1). Drivers are defined as factors that unpin change and cause it to occur. Not all drivers will have specific impacts on the destination and in this stage some assumptions may need to be made because of the imperfect state of knowledge. Out of the debates that are a feature of this stage, planners will develop a number of scenarios that are based on possible (most likely to occur) and probable (could occur based on current trends and relationships) futures. Each of these should be justifiable and based on current knowledge, observed relationships and the probability of various events occurring that will deflect the future path of development.

Case Study 3.1 Fluctuations in Exchange Rates Causing Unexpected Outcomes

Fluctuations in currency rates provide one example of how observed relationships can be deflected by changes in the economic and political environment. In the years following the Asian Financial Crisis of 1997–1998 Indonesia experienced a significant devaluation of its currency making travel to Indonesia much cheaper than it had been previously. In normal circumstance, demand for travel should have increased as tourists substituted Indonesia for other destinations. However, serious internal problems emerged as a reaction to the Asian Financial Crisis causing widespread civil disruption culminating in the mass evacuation of foreign residents from Jakarta by air when rioting threatened their lives (Prideaux *et al.*, 2003). In the normal course of events this evacuation was an improbable event but observers who had some knowledge of Indonesian politics and history could have identified these events as possible and developed an appropriate scenario. The result was that rather than stimulating tourism through lower prices, devaluation fermented civil disruption deterring visitors.

The planning model illustrated in Figure 3.2 refers to the use of scenarios as a tool that can be used to inform decision makers on what futures (using the terminology outlined in Figure 3.5) they prefer. Unfortunately, this rarely occurs and little thought is given to looking at alternative futures and the pathways that need to be pursued to achieve those futures. While there is a strong case for advocating the use of scenarios as an input that is able to assist policy makers determine optimum development aims this method should be seen as only one of a number of planning tools that should be utilized in the planning process. Ideally, scenarios, or other such methods, should be used together with forecasting in Steps 1 and 2 in the planning model. The final outcome of the planning process should be a future vision for the destination that enjoys wide community and industry support and is in turn supportable given the destination's particular mix of resources. Having a vision of the desired future aided by planning tools that include scenarios empowers policy makers to determine which group of policies need to be implemented to achieve the particular future that is judged to be the most appropriate. On implementation, there is a strong possibility that there will be winners and losers and if losers are not compensated their reactions may force policy adjustment. In such circumstances second best policy solutions may become necessary to placate the stakeholders involved but in the long-term may produce suboptimal results.

To demonstrate how scenarios may be used in destination planning the following case study is used to evaluate measures to stimulate tourism in Papua New Guinea (PNG). PNG was selected because despite having significant resources able to support tourism the nation has failed to develop a strong tourism industry.

Case Study 3.2 Papua New Guinea

Papua New Guinea (PNG), an island nation located in the South Pacific, has largely failed to capture the interest of the global tourism industry in spite of the nation's rich culture and largely unspoilt marine and terrestrial ecosystems. Since independence in 1975, the national government has supported the concept of tourism development but has been unable to provide many of the basic assurances that investors require and has experienced difficulty providing a secure physical environment for tourists. The consequence has been that the PNG tourism industry has been unable to achieve the level of visitation achieved by many of its competitors in the South Pacific. Between 1999 and 2006 tourism arrivals declined from 100,000 to less than 75,000 (PNGTPA, 2007) only 18,000 of whom were leisure visitors. Fiji by comparison had over 500,000 visitors in 2005. While PNG occupies a peripheral locality relative to most major international outbound markets, the nearby Australian market is close and accessible but has not been developed despite Australia being a major generating region for many other South Pacific nations including Fiji and Vanuatu.

PNG faces a range of problems that have hampered national growth and tourism development. Tourism development cannot occur in a vacuum and in parallel with other industries relies on government for political leadership and stability and for the provision of a range of infrastructure services including transport, education, financial institutions and an amenable law and order environment. Some commentators (Holden Bale and Holden, 2003; Windybank and Manning, 2003; Basu, 2000; Koczberski *et al.*, 2001) have questioned the PNG government's ability to provide a stable political, administrative and economic environment and even its ability to survive as a viable nation because of a stagnant economy, rising crime and lawlessness, systematic corruption, recurrent government deficit spending and a decline in public health.

PNGs reputation for lawlessness has attracted considerable attention in the Australian media which has reduced the attractiveness of the nation as a potential vacation location. Security, including the absence of serious crime is a key element in destination development (Pizam *et al.*, 1997; Pizam, 1999), but cannot be guaranteed in many parts of the country. Further, persistent media coverage of government corruption, the Bougainville Succession War (1989–1997) and narrowly averted Army lead coup attempts in 1997 and 2001 (Windybank and Manning, 2003) have consistently painted PNG as a faltering nation where personal security cannot be guaranteed.

In common with many of its Pacific Ocean neighbours, PNG has a wide variety of attractive landscapes ranging from tropical beaches and adjacent coral reefs through to lofty jungle clad mountains, large numbers of unique birds and animal species and a rich tapestry of indigenous cultures. Figure 3.7, taken in Rabaul illustrates the types of natural resource that can be found in the coastal regions in numerous parts of the nation. Many of the nation's 800 tribal groups are separated by high, often impenetrable, mountain ranges resulting in the emergence of unique cultural traditions that are expressed in a rich and diverse pattern of dance, ritual and

FIGURE 3.7 *A typical example of the type of landscapes available for tourism development in PNG. In this location coral reefs are located a few meters off the beach.*

art. Together with its marine ecosystem, rugged landscape, tropical ecosystem and cultural heritage, PNG has significant potential for ecotourism and marine tourism.

Although its tourism potential has been recognized by the national government for many decades, past attempts to encourage the growth of a national tourism industry have been unsuccessful. A five-year tourism planning document published in 1987 (DCATC, 1987) established a target of 60,000 international visitors by 1992 however 15 years after the release of the report this target has never been achieved. Even as early as 1991 law and order issues were identified as an impediment to tourism development (Milne, 1991). Other factors identified by Milne that continue to impede tourism development include: high-domestic airfares, limited road network, relatively expensive domestic airfares, high-accommodation tariffs, and lack of investment in tourism accommodation by overseas investors.

A review of the most recent plan (Papua New Guinea Tourism Promotion Authority, 2007) indicates continuing failure to recognize the key issues that have to date hindered tourism development. Crime, a sensitive issue in PNG, was largely ignored and the report failed to undertake a rigorous analysis of potential markets and ignored competitors, instead calling for significant investment by the public sector in subsidies for marketing and administration. A significant problem with the plan was its failure to undertake an exhaustive study of inbound visitors. Data of this nature is vital for planning and if collected on an annual basis can be used to measure success or otherwise of the planning and marketing processes. Another deficiency was noted in the failure to collect extensive information about nearby competitors in the Pacific Ocean. Information that could be gained from research of this nature should highlight the types of products that Australian and New Zealand outbound tourists are seeking.

In this case study three future scenarios were selected to test possible paths for tourism development in PNG. The future scenarios selected were based on the generic futures illustrated in Figure 3.5 and were labelled: possible future, desirable future and undesirable future. Probable and improbable futures were not considered in this analysis because they would require very detailed assessment of factors that are beyond the scope of this chapter. The scenarios were based on the current situation in PNG and assume that the government has the capability to implement plausible policy changes to stimulate tourism including authorising new air routes, achieving acceptable security in regions of high-visitor interest and investing in infrastructure to support tourism development. In building the scenarios using the process outlined in Figure 3.6 the current situation in PNG was considered and an assessment made of the government's capability to either leave policy arrangements as they are or to introduce new policies that may hinder or promote tourism development. Outcomes are based either on an extrapolation of the likely impacts of current patterns supported by findings of probably tourist behaviour patterns based on previous literature or on research findings used to test possible outcomes of changes made to policy. The conditions described in each scenario in Step 4 (Figure 3.8) are realistic and based on trends that are identified in PNG in 2007. The process used to build the scenarios relevant to PNG is illustrated in Figure 3.8 and aligns with Steps 1–6 outlined previously in Figure 3.6. Step 7 (re-evaluation) advocated in Figure 3.6 is not shown because this example is a planning exercise for the purposes of this book. As a substitute, Step 7 is shown as possible outcomes if Scenario 2 is adopted.

Steps	Factor
1. Problem Identification	Lack of international tourists, lack of knowledge about PNG in major potential markets, ineffective government leadership
2. Current drivers	Crime, lack of infrastructure, lack of investment by private and public sectors, lack of direct air access to potential tourism regions, corruption, governance issues
3. Elements that impact on problem	Lack of personal security for travellers, high cost of travel to PNG, difficulty of travel to some regions, government policy deficiencies
4. Develop scenarios	*Scenario 1* Possible: no increase in tourism if policies remain the same *Scenario 2* Desirable: development of new tourism sectors, such as backpackers and nature tourism *Scenario 3* Undesirable: overall reduction in visitor numbers
5. Select preferred scenario	As the aim is to develop tourism, scenario 2 was selected
6. Policy responses	• Introduce direct air services to regional destinations • Reduce crime in designated areas by allocating greater law enforcement resources • Encourage investment by the private sector • More effective policy environment • Provide required infrastructure • Develop appropriate marketing campaigns
7 Possible outcomes of Scenario 2	• Increased visitor numbers • Backpackers and nature tourists could become lead sectors for an expansion of overall tourism • Increase in employment and taxation revenue

FIGURE 3.8 *Constructing scenarios of potential tourism development in PNG.*

Scenario 1: probable future

This scenario assumes a steady-state situation under which the PNG government makes no major changes to the present suite of government policies; there is no change in the current law and order situation; and no new policies are introduced to encourage the growth of new segments such as nature tourists, divers and backpackers. Under this scenario tourism is unlikely to grow substantially beyond the level that it has currently achieved and standard forecasting tools can be used to predict future growth patterns. Based on past policy performance and without new infrastructure this scenario is the most likely view of the future.

Scenario 2: desirable future

This scenario is based on: an improvement in the law and order situation; introduction of policies to develop new markets such as the backpackers market; encouragement of local enterprises to invest in tourism-related facilities; and introduction of new international aviation services to regional areas. The ability of the nation to achieve a sustained increase in visitor arrivals will depend on its ability to successfully implement these initiatives. If implemented the nation should be able to emulate the development path that other South Pacific Islands have followed.

Scenario 3: undesirable future

This scenario is based on increased lawlessness and political instability in the future leading to a reduction in the ability of the central government to control outlying provinces, thus increasing the possibility for the emergence of new secessionist movements. This scenario has parallels to the collapse of the central government in the Solomon Islands in 2003 which caused a cessation of tourism. In this future, tourism will decline in parallel to the decline in law and order and the ability of the central government to govern the outer provinces.

On the information presented in this case study 'Scenario 2: desirable future', is the preferred future but it may only be achieved if the public sector at national and provincial levels makes a conscientious decision to work towards achieving the outcomes that appear to be possible in this future. If the government does not actively attempt to achieve this future the futures represented by Scenarios 1 and 3 become the probable trajectory of future events. Because of the failure to develop a viable tourism industry to date, Government intervention will be required to achieve the form of tourism development envisioned by Scenario 2. In terms of the foregoing scenario analysis, the policies required to achieve this future include new marketing strategies that build on further infrastructure development and successful outcomes for strategies to restore public safety and reduce crime.

Scenarios were selected as the primary predictive methodology in this case study because there was no data available that could be used to support quantitative linear forecasting of new visitor sectors. The construction of alternative forms of the future enables the authorities to glimpse at what might happen if a particular suite of policies is introduced. In this case, current policy allied with the impact of the contemporary law and order situation indicated that without a substantial change in the direction of tourism policy to encourage specific tourism groups such as backpackers, Scuba divers and nature tourists the PNG tourism industry has little potential for growth.

By generating specific forms of futures based on current trends and policies, policy makers are able to investigate, in a limited way, what might occur in the future. These futures are however a product of the present and changes in present policies can therefore be used to develop more acceptable futures. In the group of futures illustrated in Figure 3.8. Scenario 1 illustrated that the current policy for tourism development was not working. From the perspective of the PNG Government Scenario 2 describes a more desirable long-term outcome. Introduction of policies to achieve this long-term outcome is therefore an action that should be considered.

CONCLUSION

The aim of this chapter was to review the role of planning in the management of destinations and discuss scenarios as a planning tool that may be used to augment existing planning approaches. The major role that scenarios may be used for is to provide a rich source of information on how the future may unfold. Based on this knowledge policy makers have an increased but certainly not perfect ability to make informed decisions on policy matters including possible growth and its management. If used as an integral part of the planning process together with forecasts, scenarios are able to make a useful contribution to developing new perspectives of the future. If the forecasts made by the IPCC (2007) are correct most destinations will experience some adverse impacts from climate change which may be more effectively modelled by using scenarios than forecasting.

Currently, scenarios are largely ignored as a tourism planning tool however as Hay and Yoeman's (2007) Scottish study has shown there is a place for this methodology. As has been demonstrated by the case study in this chapter Yeoman's scenarios are able to inform the political sector and planners by developing an expanded range of possible futures. There is a case for scenarios to be used more extensively in planning particularly at destination level.

In the future there is every possibility that new factors will arise that will impact on global tourism demand and tourism flows. Any change to the current system will impact at destination level. Scenarios are able to provide policy makers with a powerful tool for analysing the effect of climate change, emerging markets and the introduction of new technologies. In an era of increasing change, even volatility, the relationships that govern the current structure of tourism will change and if destinations are to survive let alone prosper, their must be a significant allocation of intellectual effort and physical resources allocated to identifying these issues, their impacts and how they can be accommodated through an interactive planning process.

The planning process is difficult, complicated and often conducted in a climate of uncertainty: uncertainty if current demand conditions will exist in the future; uncertainty about unanticipated shocks; uncertainty about how stakeholders will respond and so on. The process outlined in Figure 3.2 is relatively comprehensive but to succeed must be well informed as possible. The use of scenarios is one mechanism to enhance the flow of ideas to the planner. There is also a need for planners to draw on development theories of the nature outlined in Chapter 2. The processes described by destination development models are not static and new relationships will emerge that require modifications to existing models or even their deletion. The challenge for planners is to understand the processes that create destinations, as they now exist, to identify the forces of change, and to incorporate these elements in future planning exercises.

KEY ISSUES

- Planning is not a straightforward process and requires considerable attention in the preplanning stage to achieve satisfactory outcomes
- Planning needs to include regular reference to stakeholders and should be dynamic rather than static.
- Despite repeated failures existing forecasting models continue to enjoy wide support from tourism academics, industry and government.
- Scenarios are a useful addition to planning techniques.
- Understanding the drivers that cause change is an import element in planning.
- Scenarios can be used to identify desirable futures which may be achievable with judicious application of policy.

CHAPTER 4

Transport – A Key Element in Destination Development and Operations

Mobility, a neglected element of the touristic experience

INTRODUCTION

A recent Singapore Airlines advertisement boasted '*Unwind in unrivalled space, Singapore Airlines new business class, most spacious the World has ever seen*' (The Economist, 2008:32). At the other end of the airline spectrum, Low Cost Carrier (LCC) Air Asia.com tempted readers with the slogan "*I need a break!*" and advertised flights from Macau to Kuala Lumpa (one way) from Mop 132 (US$ 19) with an extension to Singapore for Mop 24 (US$ 4) (The Macau Daily, 3 April 2008, p. 3). On the ground, high-speed rail systems and high-capacity freeways facilitate rapid travel from home to nearby destinations in Europe, Japan and Korea.

Transport is innovative, a global economic sector, an integral part of the tourism system and a sector that is facing increasing economic pressure from peak oil and from environmentalists and legislators striving to reduce global carbon emissions. How the global transport system responds to these challenges will determine the future ability of the global transport system to sustain tourism at the levels it now operates.

Although access to global transport networks is an essential prerequisite for destination development, analysis of transport systems and services from a destination perspective has been largely ignored in the tourism literature. This chapter will explore a number of transport issues that underpin the operation of destinations. The chapter is organized into five sections that commence with a discussion of the changing role of transport over the past two millennia

79

FIGURE 4.1 *Water transport.*
This photo taken in Sydney harbour illustrates two major forms of water transport. The Sydney harbour ferry seen to the centre of the photo operates scheduled passenger services within the harbour area while ocean cruise ships of the type illustrate on the left operate pleasure cruises in the South Pacific. In the background, the Sydney Harbour Bridge illustrates the role of roads in urban transport systems.

before examining a number of conceptual models that are able to assist managers and planners in identifying the role of transport in the operation of destinations. The third section of the chapter examines issues that govern the development and operation of tourism transport systems with a specific emphasis on city destinations. The fourth section examines developments within specific transport modes including air, road and rail. The chapter concludes with a brief discussion on the implications of a number of economic and environmental issues that will determine the capacity of the transport system to support the tourism industry in coming decades. In the following discussion transport modes are as defined as road (motorized land transport including automobiles and buses), rail, water, air and space (Figure 4.1).

HISTORICAL PERSPECTIVES

In the contemporary era domestic and international travel is comfortable, safe, fast and relatively inexpensive. There is now a routineness about travel where the travail of travel, described as the discomfort of the journey that characterized travel in earlier times, has been replaced by a sense of complacency where the major complaints are now about the quality of the food service and entertainment or the comfort of seats rather than attacks by bandits or the danger of sinking or crashing.

There appears to be an innate human urge to travel which is today satisfied by the global tourism industry. New evidence uncovered by geneticists (Stix, 2008) has tracked the course of human migration over the last 60,000 years by examining genetic markers contained in the Y chromosomes of males. These markers identify the linage of males and where the linage originated. The evolutionary tree that has been constructed using this research indicates that modern humans first arrived in South America about 10,000 years ago, in Australia about 50,000 years ago and in Spain about 30,000 years ago. More recent migrations have occurred in the South Pacific as sea faring technologies evolved to the extent that the Māoris were able to settle remote New Zealand possibly over 1000 years ago. It is little wonder that humans of the 21st century continue to exhibit a thirst for travel but now aided by highly efficient transport systems.

Travel was not always safe, fast, comfortable and inexpensive. History records many accounts of the dangers and difficulties encountered by travellers in earlier eras. Herodotus, the first recorded travel writer, provided fascinating insights into the culture and daily life of the fifth century BC world of the Mediterranean and Middle East (Casson, 1994). Two centuries later an unknown scholar compiled the must see sites of the third century BC. These Seven Wonders, which usually include the Great Pyramid of Giza, the Hanging Gardens of Babylon, the Statue of Zeus at Olympia, the Temple of Artemis at Ephesus, the Mausoleum of Maussollos at Halicarnassus, the Colossus of Rhodes and the Lighthouse of Alexandria, constituted the iconic sites of the time, similar to the contemporary list of places that are described as variations on the theme of 'places I should visit before I die'. For example Steve Davey and Marc Schlossman's (2007) compilation of *Unforgettable Islands to Escape to Before You Die*, the fourth in the series of recommended activities to do before you die, was the product of 11 months of travel and designed to highlight unique island destinations. In a similar exercise Schultz (2003) recommended 1000 places to visit while Watkins and Jones (2006) recommended a series of unforgettable things to do before you die.

It is worth briefly considering just a few histories of earlier journeys to provide context to the role of transport in destination development. In Classical Greece the pre-Trojan War story of the quest of Jason and the Argonauts to find the Golden Fleece inspired readers for millennia. The Christian Old Testament contains many accounts of harrowing journeys in the Middle East while the New Testament journeys of St Paul the Apostle give a revealing account of life in Imperial Rome in the first century AD. During the Roman period a vast network of roads 85,000 km in length was built for trade, administration, defence and travel.

In Asia, the thousand years between 500 AD and 1500 AD was an astonishing period for commerce, art, learning, religion and trade. Asia had the largest cities in the world during this time (Stewart, 2008) while in Europe the overthrow of the last Western Roman Emperor (AD 476) lead to a decline in commerce and trade for the following 500 years. In that period, usually known as the Dark Ages, learning art and commerce was stifled, as was travel with the exceptions of pilgrimages and participation in the Crusades in Palestine. As the opportunities for travel in Europe declined the opportunities for travel in Asia expanded. Trade routes emerged and were conduits for travellers who engaged in trade, learning and spreading the great Asian faiths of Buddhism and Islam. Although largely ignored by Eurocentric scholars, a number of accounts of travel in Asia have emerged which rival the accounts of Marco Polo. Stewart (2008) describes a number of such journeys in his scholarly and fascinating account of Asian travellers between 600 AD and 1500 AD. Perhaps the most famous Islamic traveller of this period was Abu Abdullah Muhammad Battuta, a Berber scholar who undertook a series of journeys that covered an estimated 117,000 km during a 30-year period in the 14th century. His travels covered almost all the known Islamic world as well as South East Asia, China, the Indian subcontinent and Europe, and were recorded in a series of journals titled the *A Gift to Those Who Contemplate the Wonders of Cities and Marvels of Travelling* or in the shortened form, *Rihla*. While parts of his account appear fanciful they do provide a picture of society in the 14th century. In a modern celebration of his achievements the Ibn Battuta Shopping Mall has been opened in Dubai and is themed around many of the countries Ibn Battuta described in his book (Mackintosh-Smith, 2003). Extensive road networks were also built by pre-Columbian civilizations in South America. Unfortunately, few records of their achievements remain and we know almost nothing of the journeys of travellers from that period of history.

In the West, as the nations of Europe emerged from the Dark Ages and shook off the introspection that had denied travel beyond regional borders for many centuries, the tales of travellers like Marco Polo and the exploits of Portuguese and Spanish mariners awoke interest in trade and travel. Marco Polo, a Venetian trader, undertook a journey along the Silk Road to the Great Kahn of the Mogul Empire in Khanbaliq, present day Beijing. His journeys in the latter part of the 13th century were recorded while he was in prison following a clash between Venice and Genoa and were later published in Old French in a book titled *Le Divisament dou monde* ('The Description of the

World'). The book became an instant success although copies had to be hand written as the printing press was still two hundred years away from being invented (Larner, 1999).

In the preceding discussion of the pre-industrial revolution transport system it is apparent that the large-scale movement of people was hindered by the ability of the transport system to move large numbers of people as well as the level of economic development. In the modern era, efficient transport networks provide the preconditions necessary for the development of a truly global tourism industry (Abeyratne, 1993; Chew, 1987; Page, 1999; Prideaux, 2000b) and have a central role in the development of domestic and international tourism (Teye, 1992). Surprisingly, the relationship between tourism and transport, and between transport and destination growth, has been largely ignored except for a small group of researchers including Page (1999), Prideaux (2000b) and Duval (2007). One reason for this is that the transport system is often taken as a given part of the larger tourism system. In reality the structure and operational aspects of the transport system have a significant role in shaping and sustaining destinations.

The 19th century witnessed the rapid expansion of British seaside resorts as a direct result of the building of rail networks. These networks connected the growing industrial centres to the coast offering the leisure classes the opportunity to holiday by the seaside. Before the construction of railways, travellers endured bone-shaking travel by horse drawn carriages, a form of travel that discouraged most thoughts of all but essential travel. Railways ushered in the era of mass travel that for the first time allowed passengers to enjoy the journey, was affordable, fast and comfortable (Gilbert, 1939; Kaiser and Helber, 1978). Later, the mobility that is a characteristic of the automobile and the aeroplane laid the foundations for extensive growth in domestic and international tourism during the 20th century. According to Chew (1987) the railway, cars and planes were the three transport revolutions that shaped tourism. In the model of the tourism system proposed by Cooper *et al.* (2005), transport has been assigned a centrality lacking in other models.

Even a cursory reading of the histories of many of today's major destinations reveals the importance of the transport system. Prior to the introduction of long-range passenger jet aircraft, Hawaii was an isolated destination relying on passenger shipping supplemented to a limited extent by high-cost airline services. The introduction of jet passenger aircraft underpinned Hawaii's growth as a major domestic and international destination. Bali, Phuket and many similar destinations in Asia could never have emerged as major international destinations without the massive expansion in aviation capacity that followed the introduction of the Boeing 747 airliner.

The structure and capacity of the transport system influences destination development in a number of ways including: the ability to connect destinations with generating regions; the number of visitors that can be transported to the destination and at what cost; the ability of the system to transport tourists to attractions within the destination and to nearby areas; and the capacity to carry freight and fuel. The distance between the generating region and the destination is a significant factor previously highlighted in Figure 2.3. This relationship can be viewed from the perspective of peripherality which is defined by Cooper *et al.* (2005:795) as areas away from the core. As the degree of peripherality increases the cost of travel rises.

THE ORIGIN PERSPECTIVE

In its most basic form tourism is about a journey and includes places visited, activities undertaken and the people encountered during the period between leaving home and returning home. Leiper (1990) encapsulated this relationship in a simple yet elegant model illustrated as Figure 4.2. In the model, the transport system is shown as a transit zone. While simplistic the model is widely used to demonstrate the role of transport within the larger tourism system.

A more detailed explanation of the central role that transport occupies in the tourism industry is encapsulated in a series of updated postulates originally proposed by Kaul (1985:502–503) and illustrated in Table 4.1.

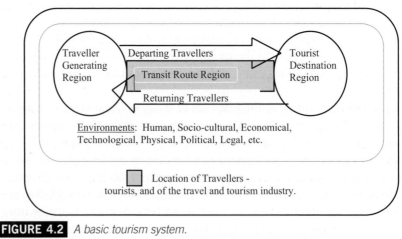

FIGURE 4.2 *A basic tourism system.*
Source: Leiper (1990).

TABLE 4.1 Kaul's Postulates in the Role of Transport in Tourism Development	
One:	The evolution of tourism is greatly influenced by and is a function of the development of the transport system.
Two:	Tourism is a mass phenomenon as well as an individual activity, which requires facilities and technology that are suitable for each category of activity.
Three:	Transport facilities are an initial and integral need for tourism and operate both as an expanding and a delimiting factor for traffic flows; the quality of transport services offered also influences the types of tourist flows.
Four:	The planned development, maintenance and operation of transport infrastructure under a well-conceived integrated transport policy able to meet the present and future technology and demand requirements, is the key to the success of the transport system contributing to the growth of tourism.
Five:	Transport prices influence elasticity of demand for traffic and diversification of the price structure. Competition has encouraged price reduction and qualitative improvements amongst modes of transport to the benefit of tourism.
Six:	The integration of domestic and international transport systems and parallel co-ordination with other countries contributes to the ease of domestic and international tourism flows and the growth of domestic and international tourism.
Seven:	Transport technological developments exercise a deep influence on the means and patterns of transportation in both developing and developed societies. The results of a more efficient, faster and safer transport system are beneficial to the growth and expansion of tourism.
Eight:	Accommodation, as an essential ingredient of tourism development and success, must maintain comparative growth to meet the increasing and diverse demands of tourism and transport expansion.
Nine:	The satisfactory development and equipping of terminals and en-route facilities, the systematic improvement in infrastructure, the absorption and adoption of new technology and appropriate mass marketing techniques in transport will have a pervasive impact on the continued growth of future world tourism.

Source: Adapted from Kaul (1985).

TRANSPORT COST MODEL

The economic significance of transport as a factor in tourism demand has been acknowledged by a number of researchers (Martin and Witt, 1988; Taplin, 1980; Witt, 1980; Duval, 2007). In a study of the demand elasticities of short and long haul tourists Crouch (1994) found evidence that the sensitivity of demand for long haul travel was significantly different from that of short haul travel due to the increase in transport costs as distances become greater. Martin and Witt (1988) noted that the cost of travel to substitute destinations was a factor in destination selection. More recently Duval (2007) observed the value of gravity models in understanding the scale of size and distance impacts in transport patterns between origins and destination. Scale impacts result in cities with larger populations generating more activity than smaller cities while distance affects the level of interaction between cities which declines the further they are apart. Distance–decay models of this nature demonstrate that the power of a place such as a city is inversely proportional to its distance from an origin. Other studies have focused on the value of travel time

(Ankomah and Crompton, 1992; Cherlow, 1981; Chevas *et al.*, 1989; Walsh *et al.*, 1990), mode characteristics (Barff *et al.*, 1982) and the opportunity cost of various modes of transport (Morrison and Winston, 1985). The consensus of researchers is that there is evidence of a direct relationship between the value of time spent travelling and estimates of consumer surplus (Walsh *et al.*, 1990). While the measurement of travel characteristics including time, cost and choice of mode and their impact on travel decisions has been a fertile area of research in the transport and engineering literature (Coto-Millan *et al.*, 1997; Hensher, 1993; Mayeres *et al.*, 1996), the issue has not been perused to a great extent in the tourism literature.

The Resort Development Spectrum (Figure 2.10) illustrates some aspects of the contribution of the transport system to destination growth. The significance of the structure and capability of the transport system becomes evident at the point where the transition from one phase of growth to the next commences. At this point, expansion of transport infrastructure becomes a critical factor in allowing the destination to gain access to more distant markets. The transport cost model (Prideaux, 2000b) illustrated in Figure 4.3 demonstrates the impact that changes in transport costs have on demand for travel to competing destinations.

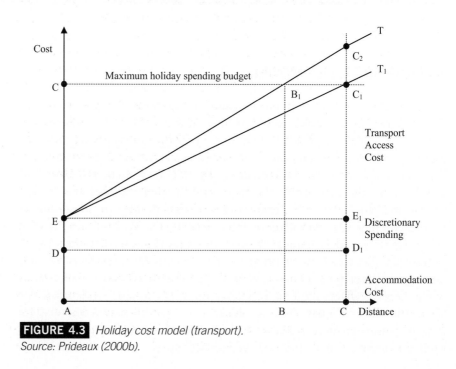

FIGURE 4.3 *Holiday cost model (transport).*
Source: Prideaux (2000b).

From an economic perspective, the cost structure of travel to a destination is determined by the interactions that occur between demand and supply (see Figure 3.1). Demand side costs refer to those costs directly incurred by the tourist and must be paid for from the tourist's personal holiday budget. Supply side costs refer to those costs incurred when establishing and operating a destination and include the cost of building hotels, educating the workforce, providing security and developing and maintaining transport networks. Costs of this nature are relatively fixed and incorporated in the general destination price structure. From the perspective of the tourist, holiday travel entails a range of personal costs that may be grouped together into three broad cost categories: *accommodation cost*; *discretionary spending and transport access cost*. While accommodation cost is largely self-explanatory, the other cost categories can be further subdivided into specific subcategories. The discretionary spending category can be subdivided into pre-travel expenditure and destination expenditure. Pre-travel expenditure includes the cost of visas and passports, prepaid airport taxes, vaccinations, purchase of new clothing, travel insurance and purchase of other travel accessories such as cameras and luggage. Once at the destination discretionary spending includes entrances to attractions, dining, gift purchase, tours, entertainment, in-destination travel and souvenir purchase. Tourists have the ability to substitute expenditure within their discretionary spending category to maximize their utility. For example, a tourist may elect to pay for an expensive day trip by eating at low-cost restaurants for several nights.

Transport access costs refer to costs associated with the transport component of travel described as the journey from the point of origin to the destination and the return journey at the end of the holiday. Transport costs within the destination are included in the discretionary expenditure category because these costs are separate from the cost of travel to and from the destination.

Transport access costs comprise three broad subcategories: actual fares paid for travel; an indicative value on the time taken for the journey; and the cost of the comfort level of travel required. Although not discussed in detail in this chapter, time may be a significant cost especially for time-sensitive travellers and is an area requiring additional research. Similarly, the premium paid for comfort is also a significant factor but is not considered in detail. Time is a significant variable and transport modes offer a range of travel times. Travel by road is comparatively slow and time consuming while air travel is faster. Travel by air therefore gives the tourist more time in the destination compared to travel by road particularly over long distances. If a tourist has limited time, the time cost may be more important than the actual monetary cost of travel. Time is significant because of its finite nature (Feldman and Hornik, 1981). The time poor status of some groups of tourists including professionals results in the choice of travel being made on the basis of perceived time utility rather than on the basis of cost. The comfort of travel is also a significant transport cost variable and can be measured in actual costs, the cost of first class airfares being one example. While some tourists are prepared to pay a premium for first class travel, others place a lower value on comfort and are satisfied with lower price economy travel. For this reason, the growth of low cost airlines, discussed later in this chapter, has recently become a significant factor in some tourism markets.

In a manner similar to the ability of tourists to substitute within each of the major cost categories it is also possible to substitute between cost categories. For example, a tourist may reduce their accommodation budget to allow for additional expenditure on discretionary spending such as souvenirs and gifts or to travel by air rather than rail.

The theoretical relationship between demand for travel (expressed as transport access cost to a destination) and the components of transport cost can be expressed in general terms as:

$$TAC_i = f(PF_i, TJ_i, CT_i, TIC_i)$$

where THC: is total holiday cost; i: unique destination; TAC_i: transport access cost to destination i; PF_i: price of fares to destination i; TJ_i: time of journey to destination i; CT_i: comfort of travel to destination i; TIC_i: transport infrastructure costs at destination i; and f: denotes some function.

Similarly, the theoretical demand function for transport can be expressed as a relationship between total holiday expenditure and the various categories of expenditure and can be expressed in general terms as:

$$THC_i = f(DS_i, AC_i, TAC_i)$$

where i: unique destination; DS_i: discretionary spending at destination i, AC_i: accommodation costs at destination i; TAC_i: transport access costs to destination i; and f: denotes some function.

Figure 4.3 illustrates the relationship between the three categories of holiday costs and the selection of a holiday destination based on factors that include a personal travel budget. The model assumes that tourists have a personal holiday spending budget and will make destination choices based on the amount of money they wish to spend for a holiday experience, the type of experiences they seek, time availability and the level of satisfaction that they hope to derive from choices made about the accommodation standards selected, level of discretionary expenditure and transport access cost.

In Figure 4.3, the vertical axis represents holiday costs by category while the horizontal axis represents distance from the tourist's origin point A. In the model, the proportion of total holiday expenditure incurred on accommodation and discretionary expenditure is assumed to be fixed. In reality, tourists may select cheaper accommodation to allow for greater spending on tours, entertainment and dining. Backpacking is a classic example of the trade-off between cheap accommodation and expenditure on other holiday activities. For the purposes of this discussion the premium paid for more comfortable travel (first class, for example) will not be discussed. Accordingly, the components of transport access cost considered are the actual monetary value of fares paid for the transport used and the time component of the journey.

Assuming that holiday budgets are fixed and that expenditure on accommodation is discretionary and determined by the tourist's accommodation preferences as well as the general destination price level for accommodation, transport access cost will be a significant factor in destination selection. In Figure 4.3, A represents the tourists' origin point, B represents a nearby destination while C represents a distant destination. Lines ET and ET_1 represent two transport cost scenarios, with ET being the higher cost scenario. If the cost of travel from the origin point is E_1T_1 the tourist may select destination C as it falls within the predetermined holiday budget CC_1. If, however, the transport access cost for travel to destination C rises to E_1T the total holiday cost will exceed the tourist's holiday budget and force the tourist to seek an alternative holiday destination such as destination B, unless the tourist is prepared to forego some other component of holiday expenditure and reduced costs in that part of the overall holiday budget. For destination C to regain its previous market at origin A, total destination costs must be reduced to a level equal to the tourist's maximum holiday budget. This may be achieved in a number of ways including: reducing infrastructure costs; introducing new technology that will reduce transport fares; or through packaging of holidays.

The impact of the 2008 oil spike on tourism travel can be explained by the model. In the case of destination C assume that the cost of travel rises from E_1T_1 to E_1T. Travel to destination C now exceeds the tourist's holiday budget and they have to decide to either increase their travel budget, reduce spending in other holiday expenditure categories or select an alternative destination such as B. If the price of fuel falls the destination again becomes cost competitive. In the future the introduction of carbon trading and declining oil supplies are likely to add to the cost of air travel with the strongest impact being felt by long haul destinations. It is highly likely that the net combined effect will increase long haul travel costs to the extent that consumers will switch to cheaper short haul destination creating difficulties for many destinations. Another externality that might emerge in the future is consumer concerns over the size of their carbon footprint. If the level of concern increases there may be a shift in demand from long haul carbon expensive destinations to lower carbon cost short haul destinations.

In recent decades the development of inclusive holiday packages has stimulated the development of mass travel particularly to foreign destinations. The importance of transport access cost as a factor in determining destination selection depends on the percentage of the total holiday budget consumed by the transport component. Thus the distance of the destination from the tourist's point of origin is a significant variable. If other categories of holiday expenditure are considerably higher than transport access costs, the significance of transport access cost is substantially reduced. To some extent this is seen in Europe where the success of low cost airlines including Ryanair, Germanwings and SkyEurope has reduced the cost of air travel to such an extent that the airfare component of a significant proportion of intra-Europe leisure travel is no longer a major factor in destination selection. A similar trend is emerging in Asia led by Low Cost Carriers including Air Macau, Air Asia.com (Malaysia), Jestar (Australia) and Oasis (Hone Kong).

The model may also be used to illustrate how transport access costs are affected by substituting one mode of transport for another. As the distance between the origin and destination increases, the relative costs of modes change. Over short distances for example, travel by car may be cheaper than travel by air but as distance and the time of travel increase air tends to become cheaper than car travel given that overnight car travel incurs the cost of meals and accommodation (Prideaux, 2000b).

Martin and Witt (1988) noted that travel costs to substitute destinations may be a factor in destination selection. Figure 4.3 demonstrates in broad terms the impact of transport access cost on the ability of a destination to attract tourists from a specified origin market. In its current form the transport model (Figure 4.3) does not attempt to quantify the relationship between transport access costs and destination selection. One method of quantifying the relationship may be to estimate the price elasticity of demand between destinations competing in the same origin market base. The simplest elasticity equations test changes in consumption brought about by changes in price (Beaman *et al.*, 1991). However, the existence of numerous exogenous factors including individual preferences for transport modes, seasonality, ethical travel considerations and destination attractions requires the construction of an elasticity equation that incorporates a wide range of factors (see Rolle (1997) for a discussion on computation of transport elasticities and Crouch (1994) for a discussion on demand elasticities for short haul and long haul tourists).

Price elasticity is a useful concept and apart from being a measure of transport demand may also be used to understand a range of relationships described in this book including the selection of one destination over other alternatives and the selection of a particular activity over other possible expenditures such as an expensive meal or purchase of a costly souvenir. Elasticity can be described as a measure of the extent to which tourists (or any consumer) responds to changes in prices. Thus a change in the price of goods and services leads to a change in the demand for those goods and services (Li, 2008). For example, as airfares fall because of low-cost air travel offered by Low Cost Carriers the demand for air travel increases. Conversely, as fuel prices rise demand for air travel may fall. As a formula, elasticity is expressed as:

$$\text{Price elasticity} = \frac{\%\ \text{change in quantity}}{\%\ \text{change in price}}$$

The relationship between the price of a good and the quantity demanded is described as being either elastic or inelastic. If demand is elastic a small increase in price will generate a larger shift in demand (resulting in a positive elasticity coefficient). If demand is inelastic a shift in price will not generate a large shift in demand. One example of price elasticity may be demonstrated where a change in exchange rates makes a destination cheaper to visit resulting in a large increase in tourists. The fall in the value of the US dollar during the credit crunch of early 2008 made travel to the United States cheaper for Europeans but conversely travel became more expensive for US citizens intending to travel to Europe. In both cases the elasticity of demand was a significant factor. The terms of trade, measured by the value of currencies between countries, exercise a powerful effect on travel elasticities particularly in the leisure sector. In the business sector, where travel is an essential component of doing business, travel tends to be less elastic although during business downturns there may be a migration of demand from first class to business, business class to economy and economy on full service airlines to Low Cost Carriers.

Not all products have a uniform low level of elasticity, petroleum being one example (Duval, 2007). In the period 2000–2007, the price of crude oil increased by 400% but this did not result in a corresponding decrease in demand for either motor vehicles or petroleum in the major automobile owing nations of the west. There is evidence however that automobile demand profiles have changed from large powerful vehicles to smaller more fuel-efficient vehicles.

The significance of the transport access component of destination selection has generally been overlooked in past tourism research. The model demonstrates, in a simplistic manner, the dynamic relationship between the three major categories of holiday expenditure and the tourists' point of origin. Increased distance generally leads to increased transport access costs and represents a significant factor in total holiday cost. Applied in conjunction with the Resort Development Spectrum, (Figure 2.10) it is apparent that transport access cost is an important factor in destination growth. If destinations can increase accessibility, through reductions in transport access times or enhanced efficiency of transport infrastructure they can expect to gain access to a wider market with the caveat that future increases in oil prices will introduce a new cost burden that has been absent in the past. This is highlighted later in the chapter when the impact of LCCs is discussed. As destinations grow and develop a wider range of facilities including hotels and attractions, they are better placed to attract customers with holiday budgets that range from the economy end of the scale to the luxury end of the scale.

THE DESTINATION PERSPECTIVE

The mix and significance of individual modes that provide transport to and within destinations is governed by the needs of the destination's residents as well as the needs of its visitors. The pattern of resident use of public transport is dominated by periods of peak demand including morning and afternoon commuting between home and work, school children going to and from school and smaller flows of shoppers, evening diners and residents participating in evening entertainment. Visitor demand patterns are determined by the range of attractions and activities they are engaged in.

The specific structure of the transport system that develops in each destination must be capable of servicing the needs of both residents and tourists and may be operated by the private sector, the public sector or a mix of the two. Supply side factors that influence the structure of destination transport systems include:

- *The nation in which the destination is located*. Destinations in developed nations have a greater capacity to invest in mass public transport and road networks than nations in developing countries. In parts of India, for example, it is not uncommon to see rail passengers sitting on top of rail carriages simply because of the high demand for public transport and the inability of many people to pay the fare. A similar situation could not be imagined in Japan or the United States.
- *The destination's size including population and physical area*. Large destinations usually dominated by a major city are more likely to have extensive dedicated mass public transport networks than smaller destinations. In the United States, for example, New York has an extensive underground rail network while other major but small destinations such as Flagstaff (Arizona) have a much smaller public transport network, partly because of low demand by residents for public transport.

- *The pattern of destination development*. Cities have developed in a spectrum of density patterns from compact high-density urban areas to sprawling low-density semi urban settlements. In city destinations that have high-population densities it is relatively easy, although still expensive, to develop high-capacity underground rail networks that together with bus, and in the case of Hong Kong, tram and ferry services, operate frequent services. In Tokyo, New York, London, Paris and Hong Kong, subways services operate every few minutes. In the highly suburbanized cities of North America and Australia low-population densities make it uneconomic to build extensive rail networks or provide profitable bus services outside the CBD area. Where suburban rail systems exist they generally have low-service frequencies. In rural areas public transport is often poor, forcing visitors to find alternatives including rental vehicles and commercial tours or miss the area entirely.
- *The location of tourism attractions*. As illustrated in Figures 4.6 and 4.7 the location of attractions within the destination and in nearby areas will determine if tourists are able to use existing transport systems or require a dedicated tourism system.
- *Dispersal patterns*. In large cities typified by Hong Kong, Paris, Moscow, London, Singapore and Tokyo the central urban transport system is organized around public transport. Tourists visiting these destinations quickly become accustomed to using of public transport even if they are private car owners in their home country. In other large city destinations such as Phoenix, USA public transport, except in down town areas, is relatively poor because private vehicles undertake most of the transport task. Car orientated cities occupy large areas of land while public transport oriented cities are relatively compact.
- *Ownership structure of transport networks*. Ownership is an important issue for several reasons. Transport systems operated by the public sector are less responsive to changes in demand and may have to operate services for political rather than demand reasons. Efficiency may also be an issue and inefficient systems often require substantial subsidies. On the other hand, private systems will usually seek to gain the maximum return for capital invested and will not operate loss making services for the public good unless the government is prepared to pay a subsidy of uneconomic services.

Collectively, these factors govern the structure of transport networks within destinations. The ability of a city destination to provide adequate public transport will depend on the size of its domestic transport task and demand patterns of its visitors. If tourists use their own private transport, as is the case in many European, North American and Australian destinations, the provision of efficient road networks and supporting parking areas becomes critical. In the alternative case where visitors use public transport as the primary means to travel, there is the expectation that the destination will develop a public transport system capable of meeting visitor needs.

The significance of the primary mode or modes of travel to a destination and dispersal once in a destination becomes apparent when the percentage of car ownership used for intraurban and interurban travel is analysed. In the United States, Kenworthy and Laube (2001) noted that 88% of all journeys in US cities were by motorized private vehicles compared to 79% in Australia, 42% in higher income Asian cities and 50% in Western European cities. The number of parking spaces per 1000 CBD jobs also indicated the relative importance of private motor vehicles between nations with the United States having 555, Australia 505, West European nations 261 and higher income Asian cities having 105 parking spaces. These figures indicate that motorized city destinations need to allocate a high proportion of total landmass to support private motor vehicle use.

TOURISM TRANSPORT SYSTEMS WITHIN CITY DESTINATIONS

Throughout history cities and other urbanized areas have attracted visitors for purposes that range from commerce through religious observances to governance and recreation. In the modern era cities and towns have also become significant tourism destinations. It is useful to examine the specific capabilities that urban transport systems must develop to support the needs of the tourism industry in addition to the capabilities that are required to support the destination's resident population. The following discussion examines the various tasks that the transport system must provide to support the tourism industry.

The transport tasks in cities may be subdivided into four components:

1. Passenger travel into and out of the city;
2. Passenger transport within the city (this will include both residents and tourists);
3. Passenger transport from the city to hinterland attractions;
4. The transport of freight, in this case to support the tourism industry.

The mix of and significance of specific transport modes used in these tasks are governed by the following factors:

- *The distance between the generating region and destination.* If the distance is relatively short private cars, local train services and, where they operate, ferry services may be popular. However, as the distance increases the model demand will shift from cars to mass transport systems such as air transport or in some cases to rail. In Europe for example travel between France and the United Kingdom may be undertaken by air, ferry and fast train via the Channel Tunnel.

- *Modes of transport available for travel within the city.* Depending on the size and prosperity of the city, the transport system will usually consist of private transport (cars) using the city's road network and one or more public mass transport modes including bus, rail and in some cases watercraft. There may be significant traffic conflict between private cars and other forms of transport as illustrated in Figure 4.4 unless planning is in place to allow multiple modes of transport with designated route networks.
- *Information technology and level of integration between modes.* Public transport systems by their nature are rarely able to offer the single-mode, door-to-door convenience of the private car, hence the popularity of the car as the preferred urban transport mode. However, the use of information technology to create smart integrated transport systems that reduce travel times and increase convenience can increase the passenger friendliness of public transport. Multi-modal ticketing using

FIGURE 4.4   *This photo illustrates the type of conflict that can occur when inadequate road space is available for pedestrians and cars. This photo was taken in the tourist town of Yufin in Japan.*
Source: Photo courtesy of Bruce Prideaux.

electronic recharge cards is at the forefront of this type of technology along with more efficient network wide scheduling and accessible information that enables passengers to plan the optimal route for their trip. In Hong Kong, for example the Octopus recharge card can be used to travel on any transport mode within the overall transport network as well as allowing the passenger to use the card as a debit card at an increasingly large number of retail outlets.

- *Transport networks.* In many cities multi-modal transport networks radiate out from the city's core often requiring passengers to change mode or route during a journey.
- *The types of freight that must be carried to support the tourism sector.* Freight is often overlooked but the daily task of supplying food and bottled beverages for tourism consumption as well as petroleum and other goods consumed in the support of the tourism industry is a significant task. Without proper planning supply bottlenecks may occur.
- *The time and money that tourists have available to fund a specific tourism journey.* In some destinations where public transport is inadequate or non-existent tourists will turn to other forms of transport including taxis and tour buses. In Bali, the lack of an efficient urban public transport system has encouraged the growth of a large fleet of private taxis and tour buses. Figure 4.5 illustrates a typical response to

FIGURE 4.5 *Privately owned Public Transport in Papua New Guinea.*

inadequate public transport and poor road networks in Papua New Guinea. In this example a privately owned converted truck is used for public transport because of its ability to carry passengers, farm produce, passenger's freight and traverse badly maintained roads.

■ *The position of the city within the tourist's itinerary* The structure of the journey and the number and locality of places included in the itinerary are significant. For example a passenger arriving at New York by air from Europe and who wishes to include a trip to Washington has a number of options for the New York–Washington sector of the journey. They may travel by air, motor coach, Amtrac (rail) or rent a vehicle. The selection of a specific mode or even a number of modes will depend on factors that include cost, convenience, time availability and the type of experience required. If experiencing the countryside between the two cities is not important, air travel is an obvious option.

In motorized cities the structure of the tourism transport system will be governed by: the proportion of total visitors who either drive their own vehicle to the destination or rent a vehicle on arrival; the cost of public transport; the structure and operational characteristics of the city's public transport system; the quality of the road system; and the location of attractions. Visitors arriving via their own car will be largely indistinguishable from residents however visitors arriving by public transport will need access to public transport either in the form of mass transport networks such as rail or bus or provided by coaches, taxis, etc.

The structure of the tourism component of the transport system will be determined by the location of the city's major attractions. In Figure 4.6 many attractions are located outside the city. If public transport services are not provided the private sector will respond with tour coaches. Where attractions are located within easy access of a public transport system (Figure 4.7) there will be a reduced requirement for tour coaches.

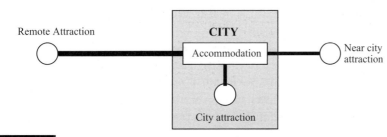

FIGURE 4.6 *Attractions located mainly outside of the city.*

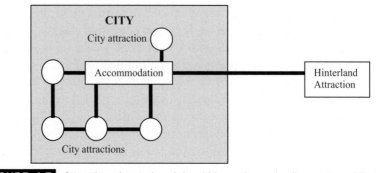

FIGURE 4.7 *Attractions located mainly within a city and adjacent to public transport networks.*

THE ROLE OF RAIL, ROAD AND AIR IN TOURISM TRANSPORT

This section of the chapter highlights how some modes have responded to specific needs generated by the tourism industry. Commencing with rail the discussion also examines drive tourism and the impact of Low Cost Carriers.

Rail Tourism

Since the introduction of the first commercial rail passenger services in 1841, railways have played a key role in the development of the global tourism industry. Today rail continues to occupy an important role in urban public transport and in many countries remains the major form of intercity passenger transport. In the past the development of passenger railway services underpinned the development of the first coastal resorts in the United Kingdom, Europe and the East Coast of the United States. In the contemporary era, rail continues to be a primary form of transport for domestic travellers in many developing countries and in parts of Europe. The significance of long distance passenger rail for holiday travel rail was graphically demonstrated in 2008 when unexpected cold weather caused significant delays in Golden Week travel in China stranding tens of millions of travellers and creating considerable security concerns about possible rioting. The most recent innovation in high-speed rail technology is the Maglev. This technology uses magnetic levitation to raise and propel a train above a track. Current test models have reached speeds of up to 580 km/h with higher speeds anticipated in the future. Commercial operations using Maglev technology include a low-speed version at Birmingham International Airport, a high-speed operation in Shanghai China and the Linimo JR Line in Japan.

The primary purpose of rail passenger transport is to transport large numbers of passengers between origins and destinations. The distance between the origin and destination may be short or intradestination as in the case of urban rail or much longer in the case of interdestination travel. In nations where high-speed rail networks have been built, rail is a feasible substitute for air over medium length journeys. In South Korea the high-speed rail network running from Seoul to Busan offers a faster service than air when the time taken to travel between the CBD and airports and airport check-in times are taken into account. A similar situation exists in many parts of Europe that have access to Very Fast Trains

Aside from its task of providing point-to-point travel rail, there is a growing interest in the heritage value of rail (Prideaux, 1999b). Adam-Smith (1983:10) wrote of rail that 'There was a romance about railways in the days of steam that caused the trains and the men who ran them to appear larger than life, to become legends'. Fascination with rail has underpinned the growth of heritage rail and long distance rail journeys as significant niche transport attractions. In Africa Rovos Rail's Edwardian operates a Train Safari that is advertised as offering its passengers a 'unique steam safari through some of the most spectacular scenery in Africa. ... reliving the romance and the adventure of the pioneers, slave traders, ivory hunters and gold prospectors who dared to conquer the region over a century ago' (Rovos Rail, 1996:2). As Prideaux (1999:74) noted 'the notion of train travel, as distinct from commuting by rail, tends to conjure up images of the nostalgic past with wood panelled carriages, the clack of steel rails and the billowing smoke of the steam engine'.

The nostalgic value of rail has created a growing niche market for heritage rail travel as illustrated in Figure 4.8 which shows a small volunteer operated heritage railway. Figure 4.8 illustrates a steam locomotive that is being readied to be connected to heritage railway passenger carriages.

Speculating on the growing interest in rail travel Dann (1994) suggested that a number of themes in rail nostalgia can be observed:

- *Land of hope and glory: the imperial quest.* Train travel allows passengers to immerse themselves in the glorious days of long past Empire.
- *Travelling first class: living above one's situation.* Some trains such as the 'Orient Express' allow passengers to become a King or Queen for a day.
- *The pain of the train; travel by rail.* Building on the original term for travel, 'travail', train travel can be a task filled with discomfort yet providing a journey of discovery.
- *Tracking back to childhood: playing at trains.* Evoking an adventurous past, train travel might recall childhood memories and fantasies.
- *Window gazing: the voyage of voyeurism.* Travelling by train allows one to come face to face with a variety of harsh environments whilst cocooned in relatively comfort of rail carriage.

FIGURE 4.8 *Interest in heritage railways is growing as shown by a steam locomotive being readied for a heritage passenger train service.*
Source: Photo courtesy of Bruce Prideaux.

Taking a more pragmatic view Taylor (1983) suggested that trains were attractive because they offered travel that was fast, smooth, comfortable, offered attractive amenities, was sociable and safe, offered views from the train and was cheap. From a different perspective Kosters (1992) suggested that although trains are an interesting alternative form of travel they are not relevant for most holidaymakers.

In the future there is a strong possibility that intracity and intercity rail will increase in popularity as fossil fuel prices increase and concern about people's personal carbon footprint from holiday travel increases. Any switching between modes for long distance travel will be a function of the success of new rail technologies such as the Maglev, the ability of aircraft engine makers to develop aircraft engines that use of renewable fuel and the level of concern that individual travellers have over the environmental cost of their travel, both for work and for holiday.

Drive Tourism

High auto ownership levels in many developed countries have resulted in a substantial shift of the passenger transport task from public mass transport to private cars. During holidays there is a correspondence preference for self-drive travel either through travel by a private car or the use of hire cars once at a destination. Drive tourism, described as holiday travel using a car in preference to any other transport mode, is now a major sector in many countries and in a number of countries including the United States, United Kingdom and Canada and is the main form of transport used for domestic holidaying. Dive tourism can be divided into three specific forms: day tourism where the journey does not involve overnight accommodation; transit where the self-drive car is the primary means of transport used to travel from home to a destination; and drive routes which become the destination as is the case with some caravan journeys.

Day tripping using a car is a popular form of tourism and in many areas has stimulated the development of small subdestinations located in close proximity to major cities. In Chapter 8 the Blue Mountains is described as a day trip destination located west of Sydney. Similar examples can be found in other destinations. The Great Wall of China is an increasingly popular day trip for many of Beijing's car owners while the wine growing area of Martinborough is a popular day trip location for residents of Wellington, New Zealand wishing to engage in culinary tourism and purchasing wine.

Transit is possibly the most significant component of the drive tourism sector and describes the use of a car to convey the visitor from home to the destination. This area of research has attracted increasing interest with a number of models and theories of spatial mobility (see Zillinger, 2007 for a review of theoretical perspectives on tourist routes) being proposed. The use of a car as the main mode of transport between an origin and a destination allows the visitor to include visits to attractions along the transit route within the overall holiday experience (see Figure 4.9). In terms of dispersal, transit travel provides regional and rural areas with significant opportunities to develop on-route attractions provided they can attract the attention of transiting travel parties. A further attraction of this form of transport is that the visitor does not have to rely on public transport once at the destination. The growing popularity of Low Cost Carriers, described later in the chapter, is beginning to attract visitors away from self-drive travel with the result that many businesses in transit zones are suffering a decline in visitor numbers.

The flexibility of the private car as the primary means of travel has resulted in the emergence of the drive route as a destination in its own right. In the United States, Route 66 has become both a destination in its own right and a coast-to-coast transit route for drive tourists. The highway, towns, cities, attractions and landscapes along the route collectively form the destination which they travel through rather than to. The route destination can be a designated route such as Route 66 or a unique route determined by the traveller. In Australia this form of travel has become popular with retired seniors who travel around the nation towing a caravan for months at a time. Known as Grey Nomads, this group has emerged as a specific tourism sector that has attracted considerable interest from regional tourism organizations. In the United States a similar phenomenon has emerged with the Snow Birders who often travel long distances in Motor Homes that range from very basic to grandiose.

Table 4.2 illustrates a typology of drive routes presented as a hierarchy commencing at the national level with national highways. In this typology national highways constitute the main transit routes connecting origins with destinations but also have secondary roles as themed routes where the emphasis is on attracting visitors to extend their trip to visit regional areas. Touring routes are described as less trafficked routes and typically attract tourists who are more interested in visiting regional and rural areas for extended periods of time. Finally, local tourist routes describe those regions close to major urban centres that are frequented by day-trippers.

Drive tourism often involves travel to multiple destinations. Lue *et al.* (1993) proposed a model of multi-destination trips based on trip patterns and destinations. The patterns illustrated in Figure 4.9 include single destination, regional tour, base camp, en route and trip chaining patterns. The last four categories involve multiple stops in various destinations. For example the base camp pattern of touring describes the drive from home to a base destination from where multiple trips commencing and ending at the base destination are made. Actual trip patterns are likely to incorporate variations of these patterns.

Hardy (2003) suggested that tourists use three main types of travel patterns when they follow iconic touring routes: A to B; A to B with stops; and touring. The A to B group do not spend time visiting locations along the route preferring to travel between the origin and destination as quickly as possible. Once in the destination this group may undertake limited day or even overnight trips from the destination. In Table 4.2 this group travel along national highways ignoring other themed routers. The second group, A to B with stops, are more interested in breaking their journey with short stops and are more likely to seek out experiences along themed routes. The journey from home to A2 in Figure 4.9 is an example of this pattern of travel. Touring describes a meandering pattern, where tourists stop when they please and experience local points of interest usually seeking out themed routes as well as touring routes. Other factors that govern travel patterns include the condition of the road, the range of facilities that are available, distance between the origin and destination, level of family disposable income and the cost of fuel (Olsen, 2002). Weather is also important. Drive tourists tend to avoid seasons where rain or snow may cause delays or at times of the year when there are extremes of temperature.

TABLE 4.2 Types of Tourism Drive Routes

Route Type	Characteristics	Challenges	Examples
National highways	■ Major interstate highways connecting major cities ■ Typically, have better quality highway infrastructure ■ Have high-traffic volumes ■ Are marked as main transit routes on most maps	■ Need to focus on visitor awareness of the product and experiences that are available along the highway ■ If well marketed they provide attractive opportunities for stopovers boosting local economies ■ Maintaining the interest of stakeholders to commit resources for promotion.	Route 66 in the United States
Themed routes (may be based on national highways with some diversions to include significant on-route attractions)	■ Are linked by a common theme or experience with a logo and brand ■ Usually parallel major national highways with some loops to include places of significant interest such as a major historical site or a major national park ■ Usually promoted at a national level often with public funding	■ Require considerable effort to engage and retain the interest of the tourism industry ■ While they can present a critical mass of product to attract visitors, one bad experience can affect the entire route	Goldfields Highway in Western Australia
Touring routes	■ Typically less trafficked highways outside the national highway network ■ Present visitors with attractive options for increasing the length of stay in the area serviced by the themed route	■ Gaining recognition from tourists during their trip planning phase ■ Having sufficient product and experiences to develop an attractive touring experience ■ Maintaining local support for infrastructure provision and maintenance	State Road A1A in Florida, USA is designated as the A1A scenic and Historical Coastal Highway
Local tourist drives	■ Comprised of the road networks that connect points of interest in the vicinity of large urban areas ■ Structured around sites within one day's travel of an urban area ■ Little opportunity to develop overnight stays	■ Identifying suitable points of interest ■ Provision and maintenance of infrastructure including signs, promotional material and parking ■ Gaining support of local stakeholders particularly in raising funds for marketing	The Talimena Scenic Drive in Southeastern Oklahoma; The Great Tropical Way in North Queensland, Australia

Source: Adapted from Tourism Queensland 2004

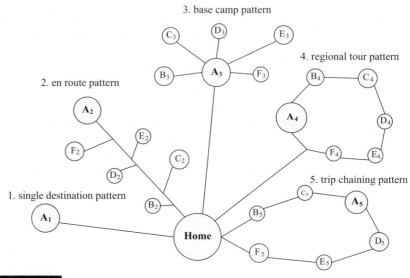

FIGURE 4.9 *Multi-destination trip patterns*
Source: Adapted from Lue et al. (1993).

According to Prideaux *et al.* (2001) the main elements of drive tourism are:

- The road and all associated activities required to build and maintain it
- The travel pattern adopted in terms of Figure 4.9
- Accommodation
- Refuelling facilities
- Supplies – food and beverage
- Information – signage, information centres, brochures
- Enforcement of road rules and regulations by police
- Vehicle repairs and recovery
- Attractions
- Promotion of on-route attractions

Collectively, opportunities to visit on-route attractions, the scenery along the route and the tour infrastructure of hotels, service stations and so on constitute the essential experience of the drive tour.

In countries with high levels of private car ownership drive tourism is an important segment particularly in the regions surrounding major urban areas. As distances increase there is a propensity for tourists to migrate from their car to mass public transport. In developing nations such as China rapid increases in car ownership paralleled by major upgrading of the nation's highway infrastructure have seen a significant growth in drive tourism. The recent announcement by Tata Motors in India that it has commenced production of the Nano, claimed to be the world's cheapest car at a cost of US$ 2500, is likely to promote not only drive tourism in India but will also generate a substantial cost burden in the form of environmental costs, infrastructure development and carbon emissions. If there is a shift away from car ownership towards public transport as a result of high-fuel costs and concern over carbon footprints the popularity of drive tourism may decline.

In the future, intraurban and intercity rail are likely to become more important as the era of cheap oil draws to a close and carbon-trading forces fuel prices even higher. Even the promised introduction of fuel cells may not be sufficient to prevent new urban spaces being built to accommodate higher population densities and mass urban transport networks as a substitute for cars.

Low Cost Carriers

Low Cost Carriers (LCC) are airlines that have developed business models designed to minimize all areas of cost to provide low airfares. Commencing in the United States with the introduction of the Airline Deregulation Act in 1978, the LCC model spreads first to Europe and later to Asia and Australia (Chang *et al.*, 2008). Table 4.3 summarizes the strategies adopted by LCCs to reduce costs. From the passenger perspective the most obvious strategies are

TABLE 4.3	Examples of the Competitive Strategies Adopted by Low Cost Airlines
Markets/routes	Prefer highly volume routes where market penetration strategies based on low-cost can be applied
	Alternatively, they develop niche markets by targeting leisure markets using secondary airports
Equipment	Generally operate one type of aircraft to save on inventory, spares and training
Airport Terminals	A preference for basic passenger facilities and fast aircraft turnarounds, for example Southwest Airlines aims for a 20 min turnaround of aircraft
Utilization	Aim is to achieve 11 h flying time or more per aircraft per day
In-flight service	No complementary in-flight service. Passengers are usually able to purchase snack food and a limited range of beverages. This eliminates on-board kitchens and associated overheads
Labour costs	Employ pilots and cabin staff at pay rates below those of full service airlines
	Try to avoid overnight stays for crews
	Use higher numbers of contract and casual employees
	Maintain a small head office and locate themselves near airport or in a lower priced rental area.
Distribution	Use direct business and Web bookings and do not pay commissions to travel agents
Pricing strategy	Keep fares below the full-service airlines
	Simplified fare structures
	Advertise special offers to stimulate demand and maintain customer interest
	All one-class travel.
	May charge an additional fee for luggage

Source: Adapted from Whyte and Prideaux (2008).

Internet only sales, elimination of most of the in-flight services offered by Full Service Carriers (FSC) and reduced seat pitch (Whyte and Prideaux, 2008). LCCs prefer to operate short haul flights to gain more operating cycles and achieve a higher number of flying hours per day than most full service airlines are able to achieve (Frawley, 2004).

LCCs have been most successful where they target the leisure and other cost-sensitive markets with many business travellers preferring to retain the benefits of in-flight service, frequent flyer points and airline lounges offered by FSCs. In Europe, Ryanair set the benchmark for LCC travel and has enabled many destinations to benefit from the growing interest in short stay holidays. In Asia a number of LCC operators have emerged and again have stimulated considerable growth in short haul international travel. In a new trend a number of Asian LCCs have moved into medium haul routes with AsiaX, Jetstar and Tiger flying between Asian ports and Australia. An analysis of the impact of LCCs on tourist visits to Cairns in Australia (Whyte and Prideaux, 2008) found that demand for leisure travel by air increased as a result of lower airfares. The same study also found that part of the increase came from mode substation as drive visitors switched to LCCs.

FUTURE TRANSPORT TRENDS

This chapter has examined a range of issues associated with the provision of transport to support the global tourism industry. In the future it is apparent that concern about climate change, the upward trend in oil prices, growing consumer demand and future trends in urban design will exercise significant influences on the structure and operation of the transport system. The response of the transport system with new technologies and strategies to reduce its carbon output and increase efficiency will be important. How soon and in what form these changes will occur is unclear and the impact that changes will have on the tourism industry is also uncertain. What is clear however is that in the future all industries including tourism will be required to reduce their ecological footprint in tandem with reduction in carbon production.

Consumer reaction to climate change and the adaptation and mitigation agendas adopted by governments will also be important. If consumer concern about personal carbon emissions becomes a factor in destination selection, the carbon cost of long haul flights is likely to result in a shift in demand from long haul travel to short haul travel. Carbon trading schemes will produce upward cost pressures on transport particularly aviation which is likely to remain dependent on current fossil fuel sources for some time. A more detailed discussion on climate change can be found in Chapter 10.

The impact of rising fuel prices (as a result of changed global demand and supply conditions and/or carbon trading schemes) on tourism demand will have a significant role in shaping future tourism demand patterns (Yeoman *et al.*, 2007). Transport is energy intensive (Gossling *et al.*, 2005) and uses 50% of global oil output (Becken, 2008). As Susanne Becken (2008) notes in her timely paper on peak oil, defined as that point at which oil extraction has reached 50% of all known global oil reserves, current tourism forecasts do not include the challenge of oil availability resulting in overly optimistic forecasts of the future. In a discussion on peak oil that should be read by all forecasters Busby (2006) found that if peak oil was reached in 2007 there would be sufficient jet fuel to satisfy only 60% of the forecast passenger volumes leading up to 2030. As Becken points out there is little evidence that the tourism sector is aware of peak oil and its implications for future travel patterns. Given that oil supplies are likely to peak at some point in the near future alternative energy sources and propulsion systems will have to be identified, developed and commercialized. Given the lead times required by researchers to make the breakthroughs required and the time that it will take to convert breakthrough science into commercial products, some disruption is inevitable.

Peak oil is a serious issue compounded by the lack of transparency in estimations of remaining oil reserves published by governments and oil companies. Compared to the first 50% of oil reserves, remaining reserves will be harder to access, will cost more to produce and are subject to increasing demand. Given the laws of demand and supply, increasing demand for remaining supplies will drive up global oil prices, something already witnessed with the increase in crude oil prices from US$ 23 per barrel in 2003 to US$ 110 per barrel in March 2008 and US$ 145 in July 2008 before dramatically falling later in the year as a result of the 2008–2009 Global Financial Crisis. Except for short-term reductions that occur in all markets there is unlikely to be any final ceiling to oil prices particularly if demand from newly developing economics including India and China continues to increase along with increasing demand for transport including that generated by the tourism industry. Perhaps the success of the oil-based increase in global tourism flows of the past will be the author of the demise of mass long haul tourism in the future.

The timing of peak oil is disputed with estimates ranging from 2008 to the 2020s or even the 2030s (Bentley, 2002). The potential for production of non-conventional oil from bituminous sands (oil sands), oil shales, coal liquefaction and gas-to-liquids may defer the onset of peak oil for some time but at the added cost of further large increases in greenhouse emissions driven by the extraction methods these processes require. As demand escalates higher oil prices will stimulate development of new technologies including fuel cells and oil drilling methods that will enable the recovery of remaining 'difficult to get' oil in existing fields. Many existing fields still have significant reserves that in the past were difficult to recover due to technical issues. In the automobile industry the successful introduction of low-cost fuel cells or other low-carbon power sources will underpin the continued health of the drive tourism market.

The impact of rising oil prices was demonstrated in 2008 when many airlines trimmed routes and decommissioned older fuel inefficient aircraft. While aircraft and aircraft engine manufactures are addressing this problem with new aircraft designs including the Boeing 787 Dreamliner and Airbus 380, future demand in a period of increasing fuel prices will be determined by the elasticity of demand for travel in general and by the desire to visit specific iconic destinations. If alternative propulsion systems become viable, the impact on travel patterns may not be as great as indicated earlier in this discussion.

In their rush to find easy solutions to difficult solutions the European Union (*The Directive on the Promotion of the use of Biofuels and Other Renewable Fuels For transport 2003/30/EC*) mandated that by 2010 biofuels will supply 5.75% of fuel used for transport in Europe, rising to 10% by 2020. Because planners failed to think through the long-term implications of this policy or fund research into alternative sources of biofuels including third generation sources using algae, there have been growing unanticipated consequences and the policy is currently under review. As farming lands in Europe and in many other parts of the world have been converted from food production to biofuel production, the world supply of many grains such as rape and corn has declined forcing up food prices not only in Europe but also in Africa and the Middle East. In effect the policy has created considerable hardships for people who can least afford to compete with oil companies for the purchase of grain and vegetable oil. Another unanticipated consequence has been the rapid conversion of pristine rainforest in Indonesia and other countries into oil palm plantations to cash in on the increasing EU demand for biofuel. The lessons from this poor application of policy include: there are no easy solutions to replacing fossil fuels; unanticipated consequences may be large and costly and need to be thoroughly investigated prior to policy implementation; the potential of science to identity new solutions, in this case into third generation biofuels, should be considered before policy is implemented: and consideration should be given to assisting losers if any groups of this nature are identified.

The impact of peak oil will include a transition to a less oil intensive tourism industry where fewer people will fly to long haul destinations and short haul tourism journeys will become a necessary alternative. Island tourism will be disproportionately affected (Tol, 2007). The main implication for destinations is that they will need to reassess their markets, product mix and the structure of the transport systems that services the destination. A worst-case scenario might see oil being guaranteed for essential transport and life-supporting industries only (Kilsby, 2004). Given the implications of peak oil and climate change destinations should invest in research to produce new scenarios of the future and from these develop new markets and infrastructure to meet the challenge. It is equally apparent that many destinations will fail to do this and fight a rearguard action to keep existing markets.

QUESTIONS ABOUT MASS TOURISM

Looking forward, will the transport system of the future continue to sustain current levels of mass tourism? In the short run it is apparent that more efficient engines and other design efficiencies will improve the fuel efficiencies of all forms of transport. For cars and coaches the possibility that hydrogen fuel cell technology will achieve the necessary technology breakthroughs is high and in the future, automobiles and coaches will increasingly rely on hydrogen-based fuel cells. Fuel cells convert external fuel including hydrogen and oxygen to produce electricity. While the basic physics and chemistry have been known for many decades the engineering and chemical processes involved still require considerable development before they are commercially competitive with fossil fuel energy (Duval, 2007). Use of biomass, described as material derived from recently living organisms including algae, woody plants and animal by-products, also offers some opportunities for alternative renewable fuel sources if it can be converted to energy production that is carbon neutral. Third generation biofuels produced from algae have the potential to produce low-input but high-yield feedstocks that can be used to manufacture biofuels. The productivity of this form of biofuel is such that it produces many times more energy per hectare than land-based biofuel crops such as rape and corn. In the near future there is also considerable scope to produce electric cars as battery technology improves.

The rail sector is increasingly moving away from diesel to electric power and, providing environmental clean electricity can be produced, it is probable that rail will become increasingly popular for both short and long distance travels. In the great suburbanized cities of the developed world, rail is unlikely to gain increasing market share of the total transport task unless fuel cell technology fails to achieve the desired breakthroughs or there is a move to rebuild these cities. In the latter case, increase in population densities will make the provision of mass public transport more economic than continuing to support current road and parking structures. Given the strong probability that future sea level rises will force many coastal cities to relocate at least part of their populations to higher ground there is a strong case for rebuilding these low-density cities to achieve higher population densities that will support mass transit systems. As part of any rebuilding process, either through urban renewal or rebuilding on a larger scale, the potential for incorporating green transport systems will need to be evaluated. Green transport includes bicycles and walking.

In the future, it is apparent that there will be increasing pressure to develop more fuel efficient and lower polluting transport systems. Given the current state of technology and anticipated advances it is very likely that efficiencies of the scale required will be achieved with one possible exception. Unless unforeseen technologies are developed aviation will remain oil-dependent into the foreseeable future. As global oil stocks dwindle there will be a point at which it becomes impossible for aircraft engine manufactures and airframe builders to achieve additional efficiencies and air travel will rise in price in parallel with rising fuel costs. The implications for long haul international travel are obvious and long haul destinations such as Australia and New Zealand may be the first to suffer followed by the mass tourism markets between Europe, Asia and the Americas. The timing for changes of this nature cannot be forecast at this point of time but will depend on a function of the elasticity of demand for long haul travel, the ability to introduce new environmentally clean engine technologies and the level of concern individual travellers have for their personal carbon footprint.

CONCLUSION

It is apparent from the discussion in this chapter that transport is an important element within the tourism system and an essential element of the long-term economic sustainability of destinations. To argue that transport is more or less important than other elements of the system serves little purpose. As this chapter has shown destinations need transport networks that provide efficient and cost-effective transport between origins and destinations. If this is not achieved tourists will look elsewhere for their holiday experiences. In the future, transport systems in general will come under increasing pressure to become more fuel-efficient and produce less carbon outputs. As this chapter has argued this appears possible but the cost, timing and scale remain uncertain.

KEY ISSUES

- Transport is a key though often unrecognized element of destination development.

- Relatively little research has been undertaken into the role of transport in determining how and to what extent destinations develop and function.
- A key characteristic of the transport system has been its ability to innovate and create new opportunities for tourism development.
- The emergence of LCCs has created significant opportunities for growth in many destinations.
- In the near future the ability of the transport industry to respond to climate change and rising oil prices will have a significant impact on tourism demand patterns.
- There are a number of promising transport technologies that may assist the sector in successfully responding to the challenges of climate change and rising fuel prices.
- In the future, as in the past, the ability of the transport system to sustain many destinations will rest on the level of consumer elasticity of demand for travel, the price they are prepared to pay for the transport component of travel and possibly concerns over non-monetary issues including concern about the impact of person travel on global carbon emission levels.

CHAPTER 5

Responding to Crisis – The Destination Perspective

Preparing for future crises by reducing the risks

INTRODUCTION

Crisis and disaster are humanities' fellow time travellers often colliding, sometimes interrupting but never halting the journey of progress. The fear of disaster constantly stalks the individual as it does society. As individuals we fear, at least in times of quite reflection or periods of impending disaster, the disruption that loss of possessions, personal injury or death of loved ones will cause. The literature and media have found in this innate fear a rich playground of themes, images and storylines for movies, poetry, songs and writing. Rarely can we turn on the television and not see murder, medical emergency or personal catharsis. As individuals we fear disaster yet disaster lies at the heart of the human experience, visiting in the form of death, injury and in a multitude of other guises. Yet rather than succumbing to its fears humanity constantly rises to the challenge and progresses forward. On a destination level crises and disasters are part of the fabric of the norm, not something that can be gazed upon from afar. Responding to the challenge of crisis is a key to ensuring long-term economic sustainability and is the subject of the discussion in this chapter.

In recent years crises have affected tourism destinations on every continent. Each crisis is unique but at its core there are three distinct time periods: the period prior to the crisis, the period of the crisis and the period after the crisis. How destinations respond to each period of a crisis situation will vary depending on their level of preparedness, the severity of the crisis and the time

113

period that the crisis occupies. It is becoming increasingly clear that while the actions undertaken in the post-crisis period will determine how a destination recovers it is the policies that are implemented in the pre-crisis stage that will ultimately determine the rate of recovery of the destination. This chapter will examine a range of issues that are related to crisis response by the private and public sectors in the destination context. The following scenario of a cyclone striking a Pacific island destination is based on actual events and illustrates the three broad time periods/stages of a crisis. The case study is used to highlight aspects of the discussion later in this chapter.

Case Study 5.1 A Crisis Scenario: Struck by Cyclone

Immediate Pre-Crisis Stage

Setting: A small independent developing island state located in the Pacific Ocean. The island is remote, tourism-dependent and suffers from high levels of unemployment.

Time: 0200 h, Day 1

The weather forecast shows the impending arrival of severe tropical Cyclone Tribulation with wind speeds of up to 240 km/h. The system is expected to cross the coast near the nation's primary concentration of coastal tourism resorts sometime in the next 20 h. Because it is peak tourist season resort properties are running at near full capacity and there are an estimated 2000 guests on the path of the cyclone. The forecast indicates that the cyclone is likely to cross the coast at high tide creating a severe storm surge and that the heavy rains preceding the cyclone will cause major flooding in all the coastal areas. Further flooding is expected to close the island's international airport in 6–10 h.

Crisis Stage

Time: 1400 h, Day 1

The airport has closed and coastal flooding has prevented the evacuation of most tourists in the coastal resort centres. Roads that remain open are jammed with anxious locals seeking to flee the cyclone in an uncontrolled and unplanned exodus. The Head of the newly established National Disaster Commission, a retired politician, drowned when his vehicle was washed off the main highway while travelling in the coastal area to make an on the spot assessment. Local police have failed to establish an operational command/control and communications structure to deal with the situation and no attempt has been made to rescue the remaining tourists.

Time: 0200 h, Day 2

Severe Tropical Cyclone Tribulation passed through the nation's major resort region destroying or heavily damaging most properties. Several hundred tourists and locals are feared to have drowned trying to escape the tidal surge that preceded the cyclone. The international airport will remain closed for up to a week because of damage to the air traffic control system and the nation's major hospital was destroyed by the cyclone. An operational command/control and communications structure has yet to be established.

Post-Crisis Stage

Time: 1400 h Friday Day 10

With the assistance of foreign military forces, all surviving international tourists have been evacuated and most of the dead identified. The nation's tourism infrastructure is devastated and even with extensive foreign aid it will not be functioning for at least 18 months. International media reports have been highly critical of the failure of the government to prevent such a large loss of life. The nation's government and tourism industry leaders meet to consider how to repair the damage caused to the tourism industry and in what form marketing should occur in the interim period. No post-crisis media recovery response has been put in place.

Time: 1400 h Day 30

Lessons Learnt

An analysis of the nation's crisis response mechanisms found a number of serious deficiencies including:

- Pre-crisis planning was ineffective
- A resilient command/control and communications structure able to deal with the death or injury of key personnel had not been established in the period prior to the crisis
- Evacuation routes had not been established and the movement of refugees away from the coast was not controlled. Most deaths can be attributed to the failure to develop and control escape routes.
- Backup arrangements had not been developed to maintain operations at the airport
- A post-disaster recovery plan had not been developed
- Media planning had been deficient
- Tourism has ceased with the only income from visitors now being generated by foreign military and aid workers assisting in post-crisis recovery and reconstruction

THE IMPACT OF CRISES ON TOURISM

Successfully dealing with crisis events is crucial to the long-term viability of the tourism industry. In the example outlined above, as has been the case in many of the more recent crises that have affected national tourism industries and individual destinations, there had been inadequate pre-planning which resulted in significant loss of life and extensive damage to infrastructure. In some crisis situations such as the 2004 Tsunami in Asia it was inevitable that lives would be lost given the scale of the event and its level of unpredictability. However, the impact of crisis events may be substantially reduced if effective planning is in place. If warning systems had been developed in the pre-crisis period and plans made for evacuation of coastal areas the death toll from the 2004 Tsunami may have been substantially lower. In many crises a significant loss of life will become a major factor inhibiting successful post-crisis recovery.

The following discussion examines aspects of crisis as it pertains to tourism destinations.

Until recently, tourism crisis planning has not been regarded as a priority although following a large number of crises that have affected destinations in recent decades this situation is beginning to change (Prideaux and Lawes, 2007). The impact of crisis events on the tourism industry depends on a range of factors including the scale of the event, its cost, funding for recovery, the ability of victims to recover and the length of the recovery/rebuilding phase. One tangible impact on tourism flows is a reduction in visitor numbers. In events such as the 2004 Tsunami rapid rebuilding and effective post disaster rebuilding in the Thai destination of Phuket resulted in a speedy recovery in visitor numbers. However, in other forms of crisis the impact may be different.

When the first draft of this chapter was written in May 2007 large parts of the global economy had enjoyed over a decade of continuous growth and economic forecasters were predicted continuing economic prosperity based on the resources boom generated by the rapid growth of the Chinese and more recently the Indian economy as well as strong consumer demand in many countries. There were also early signs that a global financial crisis was possible, a consequence of poor home lending practices in the United States. Climate change was emerging as an issue and there were growing concerns about *peak oil* and the possibility of a global Avian Flu pandemic. Oil prices were seen as high reaching around $70 per barrel.

By July 2008, barely a year later, oil had risen to $145 a barrel and then fallen to US$ 120 per barrel, the Dow Jones Industrial Average Stock Index in the United States had fallen from a high of around 13,700 points in June 2007 to below 11,000 points in July 2008, a global credit crunch had emerged as a direct consequence of the US subprime home loan crisis and the United States appeared to be in a recession. As a result of the oil price spike many airlines cut back on services, retired older planes, cut staff, dramatically increased their fuel surcharges and predicted large falls in profits. In July 2007 even the pessimists were not predicting the magnitude of change that occurred in the period June 2007–July 2008. By the end of 2008 the US credit crunch had grown into the most serious global recession since the great depression of 1929.

The global financial crisis had a different set of impacts to those that emanate from crises that cause physical damage. The most significant impact on consumers in most countries was a substantial reduction in personal wealth as assert values of homes and shares declined. Many consumers respond by reducing spending in other areas including holiday travel. By the beginning of 2009, the global outlook for travel in 2009 looked uncertain. Destinations and firms that failed to recognize the dangers that a crisis of this nature could have on their business are at risk. A catalogue of major crises that have adversely affected destinations in recent years is outlined in Table 5.1.

In the first decade of the 21st century there have been numerous crises and disasters that have had an impact on tourism. The new millennium commenced with global fears of a global economic melt down caused by the YK2 Bug (Prideaux, 1999a). Fortunately, early recognition of the problem resulted in enormous investment in upgrading computer networks to eliminate the problem. Later in the decade other crises affected the tourism industry including the 9/11 attack on the United States, the SARS emergency, The Madrid train bombing in Spain in 2004 (which killed 191 and wounding 2050 persons), extensive flooding in parts of Europe over a number of years in the decade and on a smaller scale, numerous aircraft crashes, ferry disasters, train crashes, night club fires, foot and mouth disease in the United Kingdom, forest fires in the United States and Europe and so on. It is also apparent that there are, in addition to these short sharp shocks to the tourism system, a number of lower profile but long running crises that are now beginning to or will shortly begin to impact on the global tourism industry. These include increasing oil prices and global climate change. Each of the crises referred to in Table 5.1 had an impact on the tourism industry in the regions they occurred in and many had much wider effects as the ripple of impact moved into surrounding regions, countries and even globally. Thus while the Bali bombings of 2002 and 2005 caused a serious decline in inbound tourism to Indonesia, the wider regional tourism industry did not suffer. At the other end of the scale the September 11 attack on the United States had both national and international impacts that continued to be felt years after the physical damage of the attack was cleared away.

As history so graphically tells us, if we take time to listen, disasters and crises are as much a part of the human condition as growth. Indeed, the rhythm of human history is one of the waves of growth and prosperity followed by decline and disaster which in turn is followed by a new phase of growth and prosperity. The 20th century is an excellent example of this pattern. Emerging from a depression in the late 1890s the world was embroiled in World War One (1914–1918), enjoyed prosperity in the early years of the 1920s, suffered depression from 1929 to the mid-1930s and endured a further World War between 1939 and 1945. Although overshadowed by the Cold War between 1946 and 1991 the global economy grew rapidly, decolonization gathered pace and globalization became a dominant theme in international affairs. Apart from a number of regional crises including the Asian Financial Crisis of 1997, the Dot.com stock market crash of 2000–2001 and September 11, 2001 the world economy expanded rapidly until the emergence of the unexpected global

TABLE 5.1	Examples of major Crises in the Period 2000–2008 from regional to Global Impacts		
Date	**Event**	**Area Affected**	**Impact on Tourism**
February–September 2001	UK Foot and Mouth	The United Kingdom	National impact: to prevent the spread of the disease large parts of the countryside were effectively sealed and tourism in those areas creased. In Scotland the loss to the tourism industry was esteemed to be between 200 and 250 million pounds. (Hall, 2007)
11 September 2001	September 11	New York at first then global	Global impact: global disruptions to air travel in the short-term. In the long-term a dramatic increase in airport security levels leads to substantial increases in air travel costs (Litvin and Crotts, 2007)
November 2002–July 2003	Severe Acute Respiratory Syndrome (SARS)	Commenced in Peoples Republic of China and spread to Hong Kong, Singapore, Canada, Thailand and Taiwan	International impacts: a total of 774 deaths occurred (mortality rate of 9.6%). Fear of a Spanish Flu like pandemic resulted in the isolation of Hong Kong for a short period and severe disruptions to travel in the affected countries (Henderson, 2007)
12 October 2002 and 1 October 2005	Bali bombings	Bali as well as Indonesia	National impact: a steep decline in visitors after the first bombing of a night club by members of the Jemaah Islamiyah terrorist group. 202 persons were killed and 209 injured. A second terrorist attack by the same group in 2005 killed fewer people (23 including 3 terrorists) but reinforced a negative image about safety in Bali (Gurtner, 2007)
11 March 2004	Madrid Train bombing	Madrid	National impact: reduction in visitor numbers for a short period (Laws et al., 2007)
26 December 2004	Tsunami	The main countries affected were Indonesia (Sumatra), Thailand (Phuket), India, Sri Lanka	International impact: an estimated 230,000 causalities occurred around the Indian Ocean rim. There was significant damage to tourism infrastructure and an immediate downturn in tourism. By 2007 many of the affected regions had reported recovery to pre-Tsunami visitor levels (Gurtner, 2007)
29 August 2005	Hurricane Katrina	New Orleans and Louisiana	Regional impact: hurricane Katrina flooded about 80% of New Orleans, killed 1836 people and caused in excess of US$ 90 billion damage. Tourist were slow to return to New Orleans and by 2007 numbers had not returned to pre-Hurricane levels (Prideaux and Laws, 2007)
2008	Global oil price spike	Global	Increased price of transport, particularly air
2008–2009?	Global Financial Crisis	Global	At the time of writing the global financial crisis had spread worldwide

financial crisis of 2008–2009. It is obvious that crises are as much a part of the life of destinations as growth and need to be understood by all stakeholders within the destination community. This chapter explores some of these issues as they pertain to destination planning and response to crisis.

Collectively, humanity has a wonderful ability to move beyond crises and rebuild on the ashes of past disaster. Out of the ruins of World War Two (1939–1945) both the victors and vanquished emerged stronger and wealthier and are now significant tourism generating and receiving regions. Later, the unanticipated collapse of the USSR in 1991 paved the way for the emergence of a stronger, wealthier Russian Federation. One significant growth of tourism is into and out of the nations that previously formed the Warsaw Pact group of nations during the Cold War era. Destinations also experience similar patterns of decline and rebirth (Butler, 1980; Prideaux, 2000a) but as with national economic growth, the process is not automatic and must be carefully managed by all sectors within the destination. In destinations where management of this nature is absent growth may falter or decline. In the wake of the 2004 Tsunami, Thailand was able to rebuild its tourism industry through collaboration between the public and private sectors and the international distribution chain. However, in Rabaul, a dive destination located in Papua New Guinea, the public and private sectors failed to manage the aftermath of the 1994 volcanic eruption that destroyed much of the town (see Figure 5.1) and

FIGURE 5.1 *This photo taken in 2006 illustrates how a volcanic eruption buried much of the original town of Rabaul with volcanic ash in 1994. The haze in the centre of the photo was caused by volcanic fumes.*
Source: Photo courtesy of Bruce Prideaux.

by 2007 tourism was largely irrelevant as an economic sector despite the high quality of the former destination's marine resources.

Crises are a common, if unwelcome, phenomenon and as such there is a need for crisis planning to be an integral part of destination management, marketing and forward planning (Prideaux 2003). To fail to acknowledge that crises are possible or even probable reduces a destination's ability to use the pre-crisis stage to prepare for possible crisis events and to respond rapidly and effectively by implementing long-term recovery planning based on infrastructure repair and/or enhancement and marketing. After briefly reviewing the growing research into destination crisis and recovery this chapter will examine strategies for disaster planning. Readers are referred to the literature for a more detailed discussion on crisis management in edited collections of case studies such as Laws *et al.* (2007), Laws and Prideaux (2005) and detailed assessment of crisis response by Beirman (2003) and Santana (2007). After a discussion on the possible impacts of future crises the chapter will conclude with several case studies that highlight aspects of how destinations have successfully responded to crises.

As the preceding discussion demonstrates, crises are as much a part of destination life as growth and need to be considered as a significant factor in management and development planning. Surprisingly, most of the tourism and destination planning literature fails to acknowledge the need for crisis planning although this is beginning to change as a brief survey of the literature will indicate. The first serious attempt to advocate the need for crisis planning can be traced back to Bill Faulkner who's often cited disaster model (Faulkner, 2001) has become a primary model for academic research into crisis planning within the tourism sector. The World Tourism Organization (WTO) (1996, 1998) and PATA (Pacific Asia Tourism Association, 1991) were also amongst the early contributors to the development of tools that could be employed to assist the industry plan and cope with crises. The global impact of the September 11 attack created a great deal of interest in the need for crisis research reflected in a growing number of special issues (Journal of Tourism and Travel Marketing, 2005, 2007), books (Glaesser, 2003) and papers (see for example Prideaux *et al.*, 2003; Blake and Sinclair 2003; Hall *et al.*, 2003; McKercher, 1999; Peters and Pikkemaat 2005; McKercher and Pine, 2005; Sonmez *et al.*, 1999; Drabek, 1995; Barton, 1994; Gee and Gain 1986; Steene 1999; Huan *et al.*, 2004; Mansfield, 1999; Faulkner, 2001; Faulkner and Vikulov, 2001; Pizam and Fleischer, 2002; Pizam *et al.*, 1997; Ritchie, 2004). Within the literature there are a growing number of case studies discussing the response of destinations to crises.

UNDERSTANDING CRISIS

The terms 'crisis' and 'disaster' are commonly used to describe a range of events that are created by an external shock and include national crisis, personal crisis, business crisis, political crisis, military crisis, marketing crisis and so on. In the following discussion all events that generate a shock to the tourism system are referred to as 'crisis' or 'crises'. However, the use of the term 'crisis' in this manner lacks precision and in the context in which it is usually used has a utility quality where it may mean many things to many people. According to Santana (2003) the word crisis is derived from the Greek 'Krisis' which means a decision or turning point. Santana (2003) further observed that there is no accepted agreement on the causes of crisis. One group of scholars (Mitroff *et al.*, 1992) view crises as normal accidents while other scholars see crises as the result of 'wrong' decisions. Despite the lack of precision it is apparent that the term is widely used to describe an incident or event that disrupts and it is in this broad context that the term is used in this discussion. In this context the term may be used to describe an event of any magnitude that disrupts the orderly operation of the tourism industry (Prideaux and Laws, 2006).

Crises can occur at any level of tourism operation ranging from individual businesses through to a destination, regional, national and in some cases global level. In destinations, a crisis is usually characterized by an event or sequence of events that result in falling visitor numbers. As arrivals fall the destination will experience a decline in employment paralleled by a decline in private sector profits. Further outcomes may include: a reduction in government revenue which in turn has implications for reinvestment in public sector infrastructure; falling business revenue which will force businesses to defer further investment and cause some businesses to fold; and loss of confidence in the destination by the travel distribution system. The origin of crisis events ranges from internal, as in the case of poor business practices within a firm, to external including natural disasters or political turmoil. Further, crises may be unanticipated or anticipated and be able to be mitigated by prior action (such as construction of higher sea walls) or at worst be totally uncontrollable as occurs when an earthquake strikes.

A large-scale crisis generates complex movements away from the previous business relationships within the destination leading to a shift away from stability and equilibrium to instability and disequilibrium for both firms and the destination. Equilibrium of the nature outlined in the Resort Development Spectrum (Prideaux, 2000a) in Chapter 2 is an essential element of destination stability and is a platform for continuing growth. A crisis may generate multiple events, the follow-on effects of which may prolong the period of disequilibrium unless a new equilibrium situation can be quickly achieved. Russell and Faulkner (1999) and Mc Kercher (1999) state that chaos theory is able to provide a paradigm for the investigation of changing complex situations where multiple influences impact on non-equilibrium systems. In situations of uncertainty of this nature, strategy development and destination management must be able to incorporate contingencies for the unexpected. The application of Chaos theory to crisis management in a tourism setting demonstrates that some elements of system behaviour are intrinsically unstable and as a consequence they are not amenable to formal forecasting. In a tourism setting, crises are often unpredictable and when they occur usually invalidate tourist forecasting. In circumstances of this nature a new approach to forecasting is required. One such approach based on scenarios was discussed in Chapter 3.

In his 2001 paper Faulkner synthesized research by Fink (1986:20), Keown-McMullan (1997:9) and Weiner and Kahn (1972:21) to identify a number of key factors that are related to crisis:

■ A triggering event that is of such magnitude that it challenges the existing structure, routine operations or survival of the organization. Trigger events may include economic decline, terrorism activity, political crises, religious or ethnic tensions, and more recently climate change;

■ Crisis is characterized by 'fluid, unstable, dynamic' situations (Fink, 1986:20);

■ A crisis will produce situations where there are a high threat level, short decision time and an element of surprise and urgency;

■ There is a perception of an inability to cope among those directly affected;

■ A turning point occurs where decisive change, which may have both positive and negative connotations, is imminent. Keown-McMullan (1997) observed that organizations and in the case here destinations, will undergo significant change even when a crisis situation is successfully managed.

From the previous discussion it is apparent that a clear understanding of the terminology used to describe many elements of crisis is desirable to reduce confusion and to build a base for further debate and planning particularly where there are multi-disciplinary issues involved. Prideaux and Laws (2005) developed a suggested set of definitions that can perform such a function and are outlined in Table 5.2.

The impact of crisis events creates a shock which disrupts the flow of visitors between origins and destinations. Figure 5.2 builds on the push–pull model discussed in Figure 5.2 to illustrate the factors that disrupt flows between an origin and a destination and are classed as inhibiting factors and repellents. Competing factors such as other destinations and activities that

TABLE 5.2 Suggested Definitions of Terms Associated with the Study of Crisis Events

Term	Meaning
Crisis	An unexpected problem seriously disrupting the functioning of an organization, sector or nation; a general term for such problems
Trends	Those sequences of events that can be identified in the present and which, unless remedial action is taken, will cause some magnitude of disruption in the future
Disaster	Unpredictable catastrophic change that can normally only be responded to after the event, either by deploying contingency plans already in place or through reactive response
Triggering event	The origin of a crisis. May be of human origin, the result of natural forces or a combination of the two
Crisis episode	The period during which the crisis occurs
Crisis pre-planning	Managerial planning to ensure the best possible responses to a crisis including training, role play, and the acquisition and storing of appropriate resources
Crisis management	Management strategies that commence with pre-crisis planning are activated to respond to the crisis as it unfolds and are implemented to recover from the crisis
Crisis reporting	A mechanism to facilitate learning from crisis episodes to further improve crisis pre-planning
Knowledge sharing	Organizational, industry or regional mechanisms to analyse and share knowledge with relevant individuals and bodies
Turning point	When decisive change, which may have both positive and negative connotations, is imminent
Crisis scenario	Scenario based planning that may lead to better responses during actual crises
Organizational learning	Organizations acquire new management strategies and systems to deal with crisis
Risk	The level of probability of an undesirable event or incident occurring
Event	A situation which may lead to crisis if not contained
Incident	Similar to even a situation which may lead to crisis if not contained
Trend	Sequences of events that can be identified in the present and which, unless remedial action is taken, will cause some magnitude of change (positive or negative) in the future
Crisis communications	The development and implementation of communications strategies: prior to a crisis; during a crisis; and in the post-crisis recovery period
Command, control and communications	A command structure that has the capacity to withstand loss of personal and equipment during a crisis but is resilient enough to continue exercising control through a command structure that has a comprehensive and hardened communications network
Shock	Refers to the event or events that caused the crisis to occur
Recovery	The process of repairing physical damage and restoring visitor flows to pre-crisis levels

Source: Modified from Prideaux and Laws (2005).

may make calls on consumer's free time and savings may also affect the magnitude of the pull and rush factors that operate between destinations and generating regions. When flows between specific origin and destination pairs are interrupted because of a crisis, tourists are repelled from the specific destination and the pull factors operating in competing destinations may cause a substitution effect to occur. If the destination is to later regain its market share it will need to increase its pull power. This might occur through

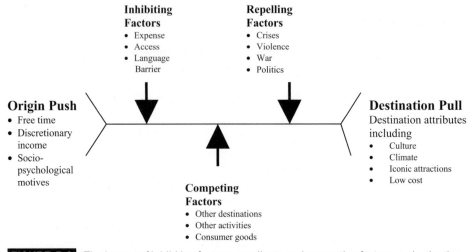

Inhibiting Factors
- Expense
- Access
- Language Barrier

Repelling Factors
- Crises
- Violence
- War
- Politics

Origin Push
- Free time
- Discretionary income
- Socio-psychological motives

Destination Pull
Destination attributes including
- Culture
- Climate
- Iconic attractions
- Low cost

Competing Factors
- Other destinations
- Other activities
- Consumer goods

FIGURE 5.2   *The impact of inhibiting factors, repellents and competing factors on destination – origin push–pull forces.*
Source: After Laws (1995:22).

post-crisis marketing as an initial step and later by investing in new attractions and developing new markets.

The form the crisis takes and how it impacts on policy formulation, investor response and consumer demand is important. Figure 5.3 illustrates how various types of responses can shape the course of destination development. Where recovery is rapid, growth resumes on its previous trajectory. Where recovery is slow, it takes time for the previous trajectory to be resumed. In the final trajectory recovery does not occur, as demonstrated by the decline of tourism in Rabaul (see Figure 5.1).

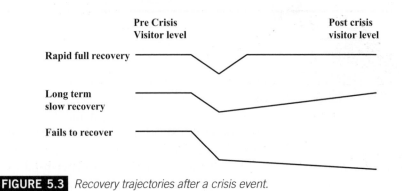

Pre Crisis Visitor level

Post crisis visitor level

Rapid full recovery

Long term slow recovery

Fails to recover

FIGURE 5.3   *Recovery trajectories after a crisis event.*

SCALES OF IMPACT

The impacts of crises may be classed as direct, indirect and cumulative. The scales that these impacts occur on can be classified as:

- *size*, measured in terms that include the extent of damage, the cost of damage, loss of historic places and ecosystems, and loss of visitors;
- *time* taken for recovery (defined as a return to pre-crisis visitor numbers) to occur;
- *geographic extent* the size of the area affected by the crisis event,
- *Level of recognition of danger.* This scale refers to crises that are evident but have yet to impact on tourism flows.

Time can be subdivided into specific periods including: short-term, medium-term and long-term. In the case of the Bali bombing of 2002 the impacts of the crisis may be examined in the short terms using a range of indicators including: number of people killed and injured, the cost of physical repairs to buildings, the cost of medical support for victims and the decline in visitor numbers. In the long-term, key indicators include the length of time taken for visitor numbers to return to pre-incident levels and changes in market share.

Figure 5.4 based on Prideaux and Laws (2007:385) illustrates one method of comparing the impact of multiple crises using two scales. The vertical scale

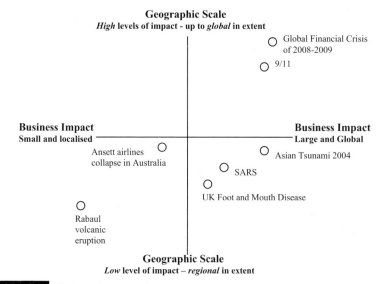

FIGURE 5.4   *Scale estimation of crisis impact based on business impact and geographic reach.*

Source: Adapted from Prideaux and Laws (2007:385)

measures impact on a geographic scale while the horizontal axis is a measure of business impact. Specific examples of recent crises are given.

While often ignored, time scales are critical indicators of success in restoring destinations to normality in the post-crisis period. Indicators of success include the restoration of company profits and government revenue. While destinations understand the need to react to a crisis event that has occurred there is often less recognition of the need to respond to emerging crises that may not begin to cause problems until some point in the future. In some circumstances destinations do not respond until a point is reached where urgent action becomes essential. Climate change has a scale of this nature. It has been apparent for some time that global weather patterns are changing and that probable consequences will include changes in sea levels, changes in the biosphere and changes in weather patterns (IPCC, 2007; Stern, 2006). While there is increasing recognition that change of this nature is beginning to occur inappropriate coastal development continues to be approved with little thought being given to the future impacts of rising sea levels. In the recent geological past sea levels have fluctuated extensively as demonstrated by the rise in sea levels during the most recent interglacial period, the Holocene epoch which commenced about 11,000 years ago. 2007.

From this perspective it is not inappropriate to consider medium-, long- and very long-term impacts of sea level fluctuations. The 2007 IPCC report on climate change indicated that contemporary best estimates of sea level rises over the remaining years of the 21st century range between 0.18 and 0.59 m but exclude future rapid dynamic changes to ice flows. These may lead to even greater increases if melting of the polar ice caps continues to increase. Rises of this nature will have significant impacts on coastal destinations and will be more extensively discussed in Chapter 10. In the worst case scenarios low lying coral atoll islands including the Maldives in the Indian Ocean and Kiribati in the Pacific Ocean will be submerged and the populations will be forced to migrate elsewhere.

The danger for the tourism industry of failing to incorporate probable changes in sea levels into coastal planning was demonstrated in part by the flooding that occurred in New Orleans during September 2005 when Hurricane Katrina breached sea walls and levees inundating large areas of the city. In that incident there were systemic problems that included a failure to maintain existing levees, failure to build new levees to meet the probable storm surges and planning failures that allowed the loss of protective wetlands that might have absorbed part of the impact of the hurricane. Moreover, there was very little coordination between emergency organizations and evacuation plans were inadequate leading to a substantial loss of life. Surprisingly, and in spite of the IPCC (2007) warnings and the obvious extent of damage that occurred

FIGURE 5.5 *An example of a marina development that will be exposed to flooding if sea levels rise in the 21st century.*
Source: Photograph courtesy of Bruce Prideaux.

during Hurricane Katrina, coastal development such as marinas continues to occur with no apparent allowance included for projected sea level increases. Figure 5.5 illustrates the construction of a coastal marine with no apparent provision for future sea level rises.

Geographic extent of the impact is an important scale for analysing the extent of crises. The impact of Hurricane Katrina in 2005 was localised to the states affected. However, the earlier September 11, 2001 attack on the United States had an impact that was global in nature and in the short-term caused a sharp decline in international air travel. The long-term impacts included the cost of upgrading airport and aircraft security to prevent attacks. In the September 11 crisis, the direct costs related to replacement or repairs to buildings and aircraft and the cost of medical services for victims were far outweighed by the ongoing cost of security that has been incurred globally, including by countries that were remote from the country where the attack occurred.

Level of recognition of danger. There are a number of ongoing problems that can be identified in the present but which are largely ignored because they are perceived as having little effect on tourism. Examples of these include Malaria which killed an estimated 1 million persons in 2006 (www.who.int/entily/mediacentre/factsheet/Fs094/en/ visited 20 August 2007) and Tuberculosis (www.who.int/mediacentre/factsheets/Fs104/en/index html visited 20 August 2007) which killed an estimated 1.5 million persons in 2006. These and other diseases, while acknowledged as major health problems in many tropical countries, are either ignored because they currently have little impact on most tourism markets or are located in areas far removed from the main areas of current activity. One possible impact of climate change will be an increase in the range of the malaria carrying *anopheles* mosquito into tourism destinations presently free of malaria. In areas identified as being at risk in the future, planning will need to incorporate mitigation policies designed to minimize risk and deal with crises once they occur. Where coastal areas are at risk from sea level rises, construction standards should incorporate measures designed to protect against anticipated increases in water levels. In some regions where earthquakes are common or anticipated, many planning authorities including those in Japan, New Zealand and earthquake prone parts of the United States already incorporate design requirements into buildings to protect them from earthquake damage. When planning of this nature does not occur or where the planning is ineffective the cost in lives may be significant as demonstrated by the Sichuan Earthquake in China on 12 May 2008 which killed an estimated 69,000 people with 18,000 listed as missing. Other possible crises of this nature include peak oil, growing scarcity of fresh water and concerns over world food production.

MANAGING CRISIS

Developing a successful strategy to cope with crisis in both the pre- and post-crisis periods was recognized by Faulkner (2001) as an essential first step towards successfully dealing with crisis. While this model has been adapted by a number of authors its essential framework has withstood the test of time and provides a useful crisis-planning framework. Faulkner (2001:44) postulated a six-phase process for crisis management (see Figure 5.6), which in this book is telescoped into three stages: pre-crisis, crisis and post-crisis.

An important element in crisis planning is recognizing that national cultures should be regarded as a frame against which the responses to crises may be studied. According to Schmidt and Berrell (2007), the study of how national culture influences human behaviour is now at a post-theory stage, that is the field of study is well developed and accepted as a reality rather than a theory. In Western countries societies can be classed as low-context while a number of Asian countries can be classed as high-context, where context refers to values, views on long-term relationships and dealing with insiders. In a high-context nation significant value is placed on long-term relationships while in low-context countries greater value is placed on universal principles and short-term relationships. Members of each type of society think differently about causality, space and cosmology (Schmidt and Berrell, 2007) and as a consequence can be expected to respond to crises differently. In high-context countries decision-

Tourism disaster management framework

Phase in disaster process	Elements of the disaster management responses	Principal ingredients of the disaster management strategies
1. *Pre-event* When action can be taken to prevent or mitigate the effect of potential disasters	*Precursors* • Appoint a disaster management team (DMT) leader and establish DMT • Identify relevant public/private sector agencies/organisations • Establish coordination/consulative framework and communication systems • Develop, document and communicate disaster management strategy • Education of industry stakeholders, employees, custimers and community • Agreement on, and commitment to, activation protocols	*Risk assessment* • Assessment of potential sisasters and their probability of occurrence • Development of scenarios on the genesis and impacts of potential disasters • Develop disaster contingency plans

2. *Pre-event*
When it is apparent that a disaster is imminent
	Mobilisation
	• Warning systems (including general mass media)
	• Establish disaster management command centre
	• Secure facilities
		Disaster contingency plans
		• Identify likely impacts and groups at risk
		• Assess community and visitor capabilities to cope with impacts
		• Articulate the objectives of individual (disaster specific) contingency plans
		• Identify actions necessary to avoid or minimise impacts at each stage
		• Devise strategic priority (action) profiles for each phase
		  ○ *Prodromal*
		  ○ *Emergency*
		  ○ *Intermediate*
		  ○ *Long-term reocovery*
		• On-going review and revision in the light of
		  ○ *Experience*
		  ○ *Changes in organisational structures and personnel*
		  ○ *Changes in the environment*

3. *Emergency* The effect of the disaster is felt and action is necessary to protect people and property	*Action* • Rescue/evacuation procedures • Emergency accommodation and food supplies • Medical/health services • Monitoring and communication systems	
4. *Intermediate* A point where the short-term needs of people have been addressed and the main focus of activity is to restore services and the community to normal	*Recovery* • Damage audit/monitoring system • Clean-up and restoration • Media communication strategy	
5. *Long-term (recovery)* Continuation of previous phase, but items that could not be attended to quickly are attended to at this stage, Post-mortem, self-analysis, healing	*Reconstruction and ressessment* • Repair of damaged infrastructure • Rehabilitation of environmentally damaged areas • Counselling victims • Restoration of business/consumer confidene and development of investment plans • Debridfing to promote input to revisions of disaster strategies	
6. *Resolution* Routine restored or new improved state establishment	*Review*	

FIGURE 5.6 *Tourism management framework.*
Source: Faulkner (2001:144).

making is usually hierarchical and based on seniority creating barriers to rapid independent responses by junior officials in the filed. In low-context countries there is greater opportunity for flexibility particularly by junior officials who have greater latitude to respond without first seeking directions from senior authority.

In this chapter a simplified version of Faulkner's framework is used to illustrate aspects of crisis response and management. The *pre-crisis* stage parallels Faulkner's Phase One, the *crisis* stage combines Faulkner's Phases Two and Three and the *crisis recovery* stage incorporates Faulkner's Phases Four to Six. Faulkner model illustrated in Figure 5.6 has been extensively debated, but the essence of the model showing the move from a pre-crisis time period to a recovery period has been retained.

PRE-CRISIS STAGE

As the scenario at the beginning of the chapter illustrates, a crisis can occur rapidly and in most circumstances is unexpected. In the absence of crisis contingency planning, responses by the public and private sectors are likely to be ill-informed and uncoordinated. In the absence of planning there is scope for high-causality levels as demonstrated by the 2004 Boxing Day Tsunami and Hurricane Katrina. Where there is adequate planning in place the likelihood of causalities is greatly reduced. In April 2006 severe Cyclone Larry with winds speeds of up to 240 km/h struck the coast of North Queensland, Australia damaging or destroying up to 70% of the buildings in its path (Falco-Mammone *et al.*, 2006). The civil defence authorities had planned for and practised such an event and were able to evacuate all residents at risk with the result that there were no deaths although the damage bill exceeded AUD$1 billion. The success of the emergency services in dealing with Cyclone Larry illustrates the importance of retaining organizational learning in the post-resolution stage of Faulkner's model. Lessons learnt from Cyclone Winifred which struck the same region 20 years before (Falco-Mammone *et al.*, 2006) had been used to develop a detailed response plan and to inform local government disaster planning.

In destinations including Wellington, Tokyo and San Francisco where there are known risks of earthquakes, considerable thought has been given to building designs, escape routes, causality handling and post-event crisis management. However, in many other destinations the level of preparedness for crisis is much lower, if present at all, leaving these destinations and their visitors vulnerable to the effects of crisis. It is therefore critical for all destinations and the businesses in each destination to be aware of the need for crisis planning and to actively support such planning. Undertaking action of this nature is a significant first step towards minimizing the impact of a crisis when it does occur. The following diagram (Figure 5.7) adapted from Lyon and Worton (2007) illustrates a suggested series of steps that should be taken in the pre-crisis period.

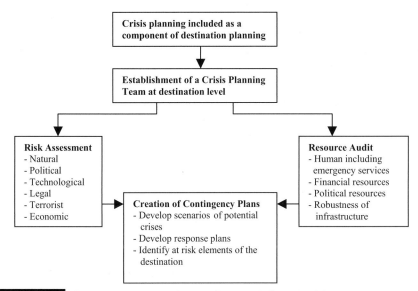

FIGURE 5.7 *Crisis management planning framework for pre-crisis stage.*
Source: Adapted from Lyon and Worton (2007).

The success of this process will be determined by the ability of the destination to develop and practise an effective command, control, communications and recovery structure that will be able to take overall responsibility for crisis planning and coordination. While command, control and communications is a well-defined military concept, it is not widely used by civilian agencies. In its military application a 3CI (command, control, communications and intelligence) organization has a capacity to withstand loss of personal and resources while continuing to exercise effective command and gather intelligence about the surrounding threat. In a civilian adaptation a 3CR organization (command, control, communications and recovery) is an appropriate model that can exercise command and control during the crisis stage and move into a recovery phase in the post-crisis stage.

If lines of command and control are ambiguous or divided between a number of organizations, there is ample scope for mistakes to occur. This was demonstrated during Hurricane Katrina when the Commanding Officer of the 920th Rescue Wing of the Air Force Reserve Command spent the first 24 h after the hurricane attempting to obtain authority to commence rescue flights (Prideaux and Laws, 2007). Because The US Federal Emergency Management Authority was not authorized to task military units confusion arose in both civilian and military chains of command over who was authorized to respond to requests for military assistance by civilian agencies. While this confusion was being sorted out hundreds of people were being injured or were dying.

Disaster planning should be an integral part of the planning process commencing within the debates that occur in the formulation of the aims and objective stage. Inclusion of crisis planning in its broadest sense (short- to long-term perspectives) will assist the destination developed appropriate criteria in responding to crises including the important post-crisis recovery period (Stages 5 and 6 in Faulkner's model).

CRISIS STAGE

A crisis event can be difficult to respond to because it is often unpredictable and in many circumstances normal structures of governance and communications are disrupted. In their discussion on the management tasks required immediately after the crisis event, Laws *et al.* (2006:3) identified four tasks:

- *Dealing with the crisis itself*. This may include measures to enhance the safety and well being of visitors and residents perhaps by evacuation. Other measures may include actions to protect property and infrastructure such as moving equipment to safer ground, relocating art works and closing down infrastructure that might cause environmental problems if damaged.
- *Responding to concerns and needs of people directly affected*. Actions that might need to occur including treating injuries, restoring communications networks to allow contact with concerned relatives and friends and external rescue authorities, ensuring an adequate flow of information from the authorities, arranging safe accommodation and caring for the injured.
- *Minimizing the damage which might result directly from adverse publicity*. Action taken here will largely depend on the extent of damage. If the damage is relatively minor the destination may undertake an advertising campaign to inform prospective visitors that the destination is still functioning.
- *Resolve difficulties with suppliers and other business partners*. This is an important consideration because of the potential for these organizations to incur a substantial decline in revenue. This tactic has been used successfully by Fiji in the past. After cyclone strikes, the nation's tourism authorities rapidly inform the global distribution system which resort properties remain open.

Damage can be expected to occur to the environment as illustrated in Figure 5.8 and buildings as illustrated in Figure 5.9. While there is an obvious need to restore buildings extensive remedial work may also be required to

FIGURE 5.8 *An uprooted tree cause by Cyclone Larry demonstrates the impact of a cyclone on the natural environment.*
Source: Photo Courtesy of Bruce Prideaux.

FIGURE 5.9 *Impact of Cyclone Larry on a hotel. (See colour insert.)*
Source: Photo Courtesy of Bruce Prideaux.

assist the natural environment to recover. Unlike buildings (Figure 5.9) restoring the natural environment is a task that may take a long period of time and in some sensitive environments may take decades or even centuries.

While the actions that should occur in the crisis period are only discussed briefly in this chapter the manner in which the destination reacts during the crisis period is critical and will have significant implications for future recovery.

CRISIS RECOVERY STAGE

The growing number of international destinations and the increasing ease of cross border travel have created a global tourism industry that is competitive, able to readily offer substitute destinations for those affected by crisis and comprised of tourists who have few loyalties to previously visited destinations. The danger for destinations affected by disaster is that without a well resourced and managed post-disaster recovery strategy, demand will contract and take a long period to return to pre-crisis levels. This has been the case in Bali where even in 2007 the international market had not recovered to the level that existed prior to first bombing in 2002. Despite reduced prices and increased publicity many tourists have switched to other low-cost beach destinations largely because of continuing uncertainty about personal safety. In the post-crisis period, assurances that the destination remains open for business, is safe and continues to be attractive will result in a smaller decline in visitor numbers over a shorter period of time. The successful post-recovery phase of marketing undertaken in North Queensland, after it was struck by Cyclone Larry in 2006, resulted in only a slight fall in visitor numbers in the month after the event and full recovery by the end of the year.

Case Study 5.2 Singapore's Response to the SARS Epidemic of 2002/2003

The difficulty of dealing with an unanticipated crisis event is discussed in the following case study that traces the response of Singapore's tourism industry to the SARS crisis of 2002/2003. In her description of the impact of SARS on Singapore Henderson (2007) noted how disease has the capacity to seriously disrupt international tourism. First appearing in Guangdong China in late 2002, SARS spread to Hong Kong and other parts of Asia, creating a wave of hysteria that seriously disrupted regional tourism flows. In May 2003 international arrivals to Singapore fell by 70% compared to the year before and for the calendar year of 2003 fell by 19.1%.

The SARS crisis developed with little pre-warning forcing the government to manage the crisis using a containment and damage limitation strategy. The World Health

Organization (WHO) recommended a number of measures to affected countries designed to contain the epidemic and prevent it escalating into a pandemic. One measure recommended by the WHO was warning international visitors to cancel travel to affected areas and for affected countries to implement health checks for those visitors who continued to undertake travel. Intergovernmental meetings were arranged to coordinate containment and management strategies and data sharing protocols were established. The tourism industry met regularly with representatives of the Pacific Asia Tourism Association (PATA), Asia Pacific Economic Cooperation (APEC) Tourism Working Group and the World Travel and Tourism Council (WTTC) to share information and work on post-crisis recovery strategies.

To assist the tourism industry a Director of Emergency Planning and a 'Cool Team' were appointed (Henderson, 2007). The Singapore Tourism Board (STB), a government appointed body, was supported by the Singapore Government which made available a S$ 230 million relief package to be distributed to the worst affected businesses. While the recovery of the tourism industry was an important priority, bringing SARS under control had the highest priority. In the hospitality industry considerable attention was paid to infection control to prevent the further spread of the disease.

After being declared free of the disease by the WHO, the Singapore tourism industry shifted from a defensive mode to an offensive mode. The Singapore Tourism Board initiated a broad range of marketing measures to both restore confidence and kickstart the nation's inbound sector. Measures included worldwide marketing, promotional packages and hosting of trade and media personnel. The STB also established a new Emergency Planning Division to undertake emergency planning for future crises. By June 2003 the first signs that recovery was occurring became evident.

CRISIS AS A TOURISM ATTRACTION

The aftermath of a crisis may leave places that in time become tourist attractions attracting the gaze of revulsion, fascination or curiosity (Lennon and Foley, 2000). The City of Pompeii in Italy was buried in a severe volcanic eruption in August AD 79 and today is a major international tourist attraction. In Hawaii, the USS Arizona which was sunk by the Japanese Imperial Navy in the 24 December 1941 attack on Pearl Harbour, has become a major tourism attraction managed by the US Parks service. In an edited collection on aspects of Dark Tourism, Ashworth and Hartmann (2005) wrote that atrocity has become an attraction that is able to be packaged and promoted for touristic purposes. In this manner the seriousness of the events remembered is introduced into the fun of tourism, sometimes leading to trivialization. There are many other sites that remember disaster including the Death Camps (including Auschwitz, Trebinka and Belzec) of the Holocaust period in Nazi Germany, numerous Civil War battlefields in the United

States, the concentration camps of Soviet era, the Cambodian killing fields of the Pol Pot era (1975–1978) and the 1994 genocide of the Tutsi tribe in Rwanda.

FUTURE CRISES

As discussed earlier, there is a need for destination managers in both the private and public sectors to be alert to the range of factors that may precipitate future crises. The possible impact of climate change has been canvassed as one such future crisis. The impact of *peak oil* on the ability of the transport system to continue to sustain the current levels of international travel let alone the growth predicted by the UNWTO (2003) will also become an increasingly important issue in the future. There are many other potential candidates some of which are listed in the following discussion. From a destination perspective it is necessary to identify potential candidates for future crises so that some preparatory planning can be undertaken. There is, of course, no certainty that all potential threats are identified or adequately prepared for, however it is apparent that some level of pre-event planning will enable participants to better cope with the crisis when it does occur. Failure to undertake action of this nature may lead to undesirable futures of the type discussed in Figure 3.5.

It is apparent that climate change will generate a range of associated crises including changing rainfall and temperature patterns. Evidence of events directly related to changing climatic patterns is already starting to emerge and governments and businesses are beginning to respond. Some firms have positioned themselves to turn fears of climate change into a positive by offering consumers opportunities to offset their carbon footprint. For example, Virgin Blue (Australia) along with an increasing number of other airlines offers passengers the opportunity to offset the carbon generated by their travel. Sensing that there is a commercial advantage to be seen in responding positively to the threat of climate change Sir Richard Branson's Virgin Airline group has established Virgin Fuels with a mandate to develop clean fuels. One of the first projects that the company has undertaken is to develop biofuels for aircraft in conjunction with Boeing Company and aircraft engine maker, GE Aviation (Yoon, 2007).

Climate change will have a great influence on future tourism flows, most of which can be modelled by using scenario analysis based on current and projected trends. Some of these threats have been discussed in this and other chapters of this book. Given the dire nature of the predictions contained in the 2007 IPCC report and the 2006 Stern Report, it is imperative that destination authorities consider the likely impact of climate change on their destination in a time frame that extends far beyond the normal time frames used by managers and even planners. The imperative of this recommendation can be demonstrated by research (Prideaux, 2006) that found that 40% of backpackers visiting Cairns in Australia would seek alternative destinations if the Great Barrier Reef, the region's major tourism attraction, was severely damaged by climate change, an event that is predicted by the IPCC (2007) to occur within the next 30 years. To mitigate such a crisis the destination will need to consider strategies that might help preserve parts of the reef as well as develop new alternative iconic attractions.

While associated with climate change, increasing demand for fresh water has the potential to create significant political tension particularly in the Middle East and in parts of Asia as well as disrupt established urban settlement patterns. Change can occur quickly as demonstrated by the overuse of Lake Chad in Africa for irrigation and grazing. In a period of a little over 40 years the area of the lake was reduced by about 70% causing severe disruption to both regional and national economies dependent on the lake (Pearce, 2006). Lack of fresh water may become a major issue for some destinations in the future, particularly if political tensions are generated.

Throughout history plague and other pandemics have wrought havoc on human populations. Hollister and Bennett (2006) reported that the Bubonic plague and possibly other diseases killed an estimated 20 million Europeans, or one third of the population during the Black Death of 1347–1351. The plague had struck many times earlier and struck again later. For example, the Great Plague of London (1665/1666) is estimated to have killed up to 100,000 persons. In 1918 an influenza pandemic (the Spanish Flu) appeared and by the time it had run its course in 1919 an estimated 40–50 million persons had died. The SARS epidemic of 2002/2003 highlighted the potential damage that a pandemic of the nature of the Spanish Flu could cause to global tourism. The Asian Development Bank estimated that an Avian flu pandemic could collectively cost Asia almost US$ 282 billion or 6.5% of its Gross Domestic Product (Mc Donald, 2005). The World Bank estimated that the global economy could incur losses of the order of US$ 800 billion. Influenza is just one of a large number of diseases that could create crises for the tourism industry. Other candidates include a spread of malaria into new areas as regional climatic patterns change, AIDS/HIV and tuberculosis.

There are numerous other trends that have the potential to cause future crises. This chapter has examined a number of these but to this list must be added terrorism, technological changes, wars on scales that range from local to global, financial crises ranging from recession to depression, the impending peaking of global oil reserves, ageing of some large population groups and threats from disease to global food stocks. It is obviously difficult for destinations to keep abreast of developments in wide and diverse categories of risks.

This should be the task of government and/or industry associations. It is important however for destinations to be aware of risk and that crises may occur with short or no warning period and take a form that had not been previously anticipated. Developing a managerial capability to deal with the unexpected is an imperative that must be incorporated within destination management and planning by each of the firms, individuals and agencies that collectively constitute the destination. To avoid or mitigate the type of events described in the scenario at the beginning of this chapter planning for crisis needs to be incorporated in every aspect of destination planning and needs to be regularly updated. To fail to plan will hamper recovery when a crisis does occur. Humanity has faced and will continue to face new crises perhaps even on the scale of the Black Death. Planning assisted by science and the support of the community is the bedrock on which destination survival in the long-term will be built.

KEY ISSUE

- Crises and disasters occur regularly, often with little or no warning.
- Destination planning should include crisis planning and recovery as key elements.
- Future crises may include climate change, the impact of *peak oil* and further economic disruptions.
- Scale is a useful mechanism for assessing the possible impacts of crisis events.

CHAPTER 6

City Destinations – The New Focus of Tourism Activity

Celebrating the city – exploring the tapestry of urban form, shape and lifestyle
(with Alana Iles)

A recent in-flight magazine advised readers that '*Midtown Manhattan uses some heavy – hitter retail chrismal to come up trumps again*' (Peasley, 2008). Shift to Asia where Hong Kong, Malaysia and Singapore vie for the title of the region's best shopping destination. '*Shop till you drop in Kuala Lumpa!*' proclaimed a recent advertisement by Malaysian Airlines (Vacations and Travel, 2008:154). Advertising of city life makes extensive use of images depicting glamour and self-indulgence. Nature, aside from the occasional glimpses of famous parks, is largely absent. In natures' place are the temples of post-modern life, glitzy shopping arcades, day spas, entertainment venues and fine dining. Cities appeal to people on many levels: as avenues for escape, opportunities to participate in the exotic and the erotic, indulgence, and ostentatious exhibitions of wealth. For some it is escape from the mundane into another world, where the boundaries of everyday life disappear for a time replaced by less rigorous and non-judgemental boundaries. For others it is the desire to be for a while immersed in another world, to associate with power and, as long as funds permit, to be the 'other person' of their inner most fantasies: maybe a high-roller at the gambling tables of Monacco; a member of high-society viewing the latest production of Pyotr Tchaikovshy's Swan Lake at the West End in London; or a star indulging in the latest fashions in Paris. For whatever their reasons, people find cities attractive and cities for their part find visitors important sources of employment and wealth generation.

As society moves into the 21st century we find a world that is increasingly dominated by cities. In the past the Earth was an enormous place where

Resort Destinations: Evolution, Management and Development

humans made little impact. Today the reverse is true. Cities dominate the landscape and use an ever-growing volume of resources. The Earth's wild places are shrinking and worrying new trends including climate change, food shortages, declining reserves of fresh water, pollution and urbanization present new threats to cities and the welfare of their human populations. In the future the dominance of cities over the landscape is likely to grow (Table 6.1) as cities increase in size and numbers.

From a tourism perspective cities have an important role as generating regions and destinations. Cities are attractive spaces for visitors, the repository of commercial and national wealth and power, the creators and leaders of culture and fashion and the incubators of intellectual ferment. Cities also embody national spirit exhibited through the tapestry of public and private buildings that testify to national origins and contemporary political and business power. They act as the custodians of national history and culture through institutions such as the church or other religious organizations, museums, art galleries and theatres. Popular culture is fermented in the creative precincts of city life and radiated out via the electronic media to the world. Fashion is

TABLE 6.1 The Size of the Resident Population of the Worlds' 20 Largest Cities

Rank	City	Population	Year
1	Mumbai (Bombay), India	11,914,398	2001
2	São Paulo, Brazil	11,016,703	2006
3	Shanghai, China	10,928,800	2006
4	Moscow, Russia	10,126,424	2006
5	Seoul, South Korea	9,820,171	2005
6	Delhi, India	9,817,439	2001
7	Karachi, Pakistan	9,339,023	1998
8	Istanbul, Turkey	8,831,805	2000
9	Jakarta, Indonesia	8,699,600	2005
10	Beijing, China	8,689,000	2001
11	Mexico City, Mexico	8,591,309	2000
12	Tokyo, Japan	8,483,050	2005
13	Shenzhen, China	8,277,500	2005
14	New York City, USA	8,143,197	2005
15	Tehran, Iran	7,796,257	2004
16	Cairo, Egypt	7,786,640	2006
17	London, UK	7,429,200	2004
18	Bogotá, Colombia	7,050,133	2007
19	Lima, Peru	6,954,517	2005
20	Dhaka, Bangladesh	6,479,751	2006

Source: Fact Monster/Information Please® Database, © 2007.

created, celebrated, modified and eventually superseded by the next trend. Cities by their nature occupy a central role in the tourism experience and as Law (1993:3) observed are '... *arguably the most important type of tourism destination in the world*'.

This chapter discusses a range of issues associated with the development and maintenance of city destinations. The chapter commences with a brief examination of the role of cities in the past and is followed by a discussion on contemporary urban landscapes as places of tourist interest. The chapter then considers aspects of supply and demand for city tourism. The chapter concludes with a discussion of the threats to cities and offers some suggestions for how future cities can respond to future challenges.

In a review of urban tourism research Page and Hall (2003) stated that while there has been some progress there is not yet a strong case for suggesting that urban tourism exists as a distinct form of tourism inquiry. This is surprising given the role of cities as attractions and generating regions. Research remains fragmented, even ad hoc resulting in under representation of tourism interests in city planning and governance. Law (2002) attributed this to the 'invisibility' of tourism as an industry and past methodological approaches that tended to ignore the contribution made to city economies by tourists. Recent interest in city tourism has been reflected in a small number of books that examine aspects of city tourism including Page and Hall (2003), Law (2002) and Ashworth and Tunbridge (2000).

One of the problems faced by urban tourism researchers is access to statistical data sets which extends beyond standard socio demographic nature (see Law, 2002; Shaw and Williams, 2002). Many official data sets classify visitors into specific and exclusive categories precluding a more detailed analysis of the factors that may influence decision-making. Motivations for example are not easily captured in officially data sets. As a result there has been a shift towards qualitative methodologies. Qualitative research is able to offer a range of methods that assist in addressing some of the complexities unique to urban tourism research. Case studies are one qualitative method that is often used because it can draw on a range of data to investigate complex multi-discipline issues. Examples include Cape Coast, Ghana (Agyei-Mensah, 2006), Dublin, Ireland (Dunne *et al.*, 2007), New Orleans, USA (Dimanche and Lepetic, 1999) and Vaasa, Finland (Laaksonen *et al.*, 2006).

Content analysis is also emerging as a useful research tool. Travel magazines and their writers act as trend setters and provide a useful indicator of emerging trends. In the April 2008 edition of *The Sunday Times Travel* magazine, for example, a feature identified what the editors believed to be the world's 18 hippest cities. Themes that emerged in the article include shopping, fashion, nightlife and architecture, perhaps pointing to the type of activities and attractions that are of most interest to the demographic at which the magazine is aimed at. Of Valencia the article says *'Admire the results of a sexy urban makeover: A mix of gothic and galactic that's out of this world'* (The Times, 2008:118), of Buenos Aires it remarks *'Flash new buildings, hot fashion and boutique hotels ... Buenos Aires tangoes (sic) to a fabulous beat'* (The Times, 2008:122) and Chicago is described as *'For a decadent no-sleep-til-check-out weekend, Chicago beats New York and LA hands down'* (The Times, 2008:109). Before examining aspects of the contemporary city and its appeal as a destination it is useful to examine the role of cities and their visitors in the past.

THE LUE OF THE CITY – FROM THE PAST TO THE PRESENT

The first urbanized settlements probably emerged in the Middle East during the Neolithic period. Jericho, a city still inhabited today, was amongst the earliest of these cities with a history dating back to 9000 BC (Gates, 2003) while others such as Ur and Eridu emerged on the fertile river plains of the Tigris and Euphrates Rivers. The sequence of events that resulted in the emergence of these early cities is lost in antiquity, but it is apparent that trade and the need for defence (O'Flatery and Brendan, 2005) are likely candidates for the conditions that nurtured their development. The ability of farmers living in the fertile river plains to produce surplus grain and other agricultural outputs underpinned the rise of an urban population who traded their output of manufactured goods such as cloth, pottery and other household goods for the farmer's grains, animal products and other food stuffs (Bernstein, 2008).

The unique aspect of early cities is that they usually emerged where the surrounding agricultural hinterlands could produce sufficient surplus to maintain non-food producing urban populations. These cities grew when they engaged in trade. Although cities appear to have first emerged in the Middle East (examples include Ur, Babylon and Uruk) they soon emerged in India (the Mohenjo-daro civilization in the Indus Valley), China (Chang'au now Xi'an) and later in Africa (Awdaghust and Kumbi-Saleh in Ghana), Europe (Rome, Athens and Corinth) and Teotihuacanin in Mexico. Many of these cities were very large even by contemporary standards and it is estimated that at the end of the first century BC Rome had a population in excess of 1,000,000 persons. In all cases trade between the city and its surrounding hinterland and between the city and other cities and regions beyond their borders was the key to sustaining urban life.

Cities began as multi-functional places, a role they continue to fulfil in the present and will continue to fulfil in the future. In the past, visits by ordinary folk to town and cities were for practical purposes such as trade, for religious observances and for festivals or to discharge obligations for military service. The daily grind of life and meagre surplus of agriculture (after the payment of taxes and other levees which has been part of the human condition since structured society first emerged) prevented travel to towns and cities except for the most important of reasons and then only for a limited time. Even so early towns and cities did offer many of the services that are considered as essentials by contemporary tourists: lodgings, food, drink, places of worship, places that were viewed with awe, entertainment and red light districts. Today, many of the great cities of antiquity lie in ruins (e.g. Ephesus, Ur and Babylon) but still continue to attract visitors, many who come simply to stand in awe at the magnificence of the past accomplishments of our ancestors.

Millennia later as Europe emerged from the Dark Ages (about 500–1000 AD , also referred to as the Early Middle Ages) cities again flourished as trade energized national economies and cities assumed new responsibilities as centres of culture, scientific discovery, commerce and learning (Bernstein, 2008). Later, in those periods where war was not the national preoccupation and national borders were open for non-commercial travel, the 'Grand Tour' described as an educational rite of passage for the sons of the British elite, emerged as a travel phenomenon (Buzard, 2002). The daughters meanwhile were kept at home to preserve their virtue and to prepare for marriage into the 'correct' families to enhance their family's social or economic position in society. Europe's cultural centres became the new stamping ground for the sons of the wealthy who were schooled in the arts, commerce, religion and from accounts of the time (Carson, 1994) in the 'joys of the flesh'. The opportunity to benefit from this travel sector and emerging domestic interest in travel encouraged the commodification of national culture and significant places as attractions for tourist in what Judd and Fainstein (1999) label the 'empire city' circuit which still remains popular with the mass tourist and backpackers of today. The contemporary trend in the United Kingdom and other nations of travelling abroad in the 'gap year' prior to commencing tertiary studies has parallels with the grand tour, without its gender bias.

The growing power and wealth of 19th century European and US cities funded by the massive wave of urbanization that was created and sustained by the industrial revolution found expression in the Expo movement (Law, 1993) where the host city demonstrated its greatness and progressiveness through the construction of magnificent buildings, monuments and parks and the provision of spaces for fun and for marketing the cities' industrial output. London's Crystal Palace built as the centrepiece of the Great Exhibition of 1851 was at the cutting edge of contemporary architecture and building methods of the time though sadly a 1933 fire destroyed this fine example of 19th century architecture. The Philadelphia Exhibition of 1876 held to commemorate 100 years of US independence attracted 10 million visitors and introduced Bell's telephone and Remington's typewriter to the world. In Paris the 1889 Exposition Universelle was held to celebrate the 100th anniversary of the storming of the Bastille and is remembered for its engineering marvel of the time, the Eiffel Tower that even today continues to enchant its visitors. Between them these three Expos attracted 44 million visitors. In the 20th century, Expos have been used for similar purposes: to profile host cities, to revitalize decaying urban areas and to make a statement that the host city is open for visitors.

On an even grander scale the new Olympics movement has been used to profile host cities and the host nation in addition to the primary role of providing a venue for international sports at the highest levels of competition. Commencing with the first modern Olympic games at Athens in 1896, the Games have been increasingly used as a platform to showcase national achievement and to profile the host city as a place where tourists are welcome. The Beijing Olympics of 2008 followed this pattern of duality by offering what are claimed to be the most modern and spectacular sports venues in existence and at the same time making a statement to the international community industry that the city is open of business, 'so come visit us'.

Contemporary urban landscapes

Built urban landscapes reflect the role of specific cities in the economic, social, cultural and political life of nations. While the skylines of commercial cities are dominated by the impressive headquarters of national companies and financial institutions the skylines (see Figure 7.8 for an example) of capital cities are crowed with buildings symbolizing the power of government. Older cities often display a patchwork of urban landscapes reflecting the past and present positions as centres of economic, social and economic power. In Beijing the Forbidden City, the seat of power for Chinese Emperors from 1420 to 1912, today shares prominence with the new icons of the 2008 Olympics, the Bird's Nest athletics stadium and the Water Cube swimming stadium. Both buildings cleverly expand the ordinary from a micro- to a macroscale. The Bird's Nest stadium takes the traditional Chinese cuisine of bird's nest soup from the local to the global scale, while the Water Cube expands the shape of the soap bubble to macroproportions (Allchin, 2008). Dubai, once an economic backwater has shot to international prominence with stunning architecture including the seven star Burj Al Arab hotel, the Palm Islands, Burj Dubai (the world's tallest building) and the World, an artificial archipelago of 300 islands built to represent a map of the world. In other cities urban landscapes have been transformed and rejuvenated creating new forms, shapes and spaces.

In other cities older precincts have been preserved and opened for new uses including tourism. The old city of Warsaw is one such example as is the Rocks waterfront area in Sydney.

The industrial revolution (beginning in the United Kingdom and lasting from the late 18th century to the mid-19th century) and the parallel development of European colonial empires nurtured the growth of large scale international trade (Bernstein, 2008) and encouraged the emergence of business travel followed closely by the construction of the associated support system of hotels, restaurants and so on. Travel for pleasure became an increasingly important part of life and underpinned the emergence of the first seaside resorts in the United Kingdom in the late 18th century closely followed by the construction of winter resorts in mountain regions. In the early 20th century the development of more efficient and low-cost transport and communications systems facilitated new trends in manufacturing and distribution and importantly in the latter part of the century, the emergence of a new service and information-based economy that was free of the old restraints imposed by the traditional requirements for access to raw materials, ports and freight networks. Twenty-first century cities have greater freedoms to specialize in the service sector including e-commerce and the information sector creating new demands for business travel, visiting friends and relatives and where opportunities exist, for pleasure travellers.

The Brazilian city of Belem located near the mouth of the Amazon River typifies the blending of old and new urban landscapes. In Figure 6.1 centuries old buildings representing the city's maritime history are overshadowed by the more recent, and far less elegant, structures of the present. As Ashworth and Tunbridge (2000) observed cities are often a blend of the old and the new with the preservation of the old often being a function of chance rather than good planning. Much of what is left to preserve is the result of escape from fires, war, earthquakes and redevelopment. Conservation of what remains relies on value judgements about restoration to conform to a particular time and function in the building's history of use, conservation, funding and uniqueness. Authenticity in this case is a moving target. As Ashworth and Tunbridge (2000:15) note '... *the world stock of preserved buildings is not an authentic representation reflective of world history of urban architecture and civic design*'.

There is a growing body of research in other literatures which has examined the emergence of the post-modern city as a new urban form. In their analysis of the post-modern city, which according to Mansfeld dates from about the 1970s onwards, the post-modern city is described as an architectural style that has moved from homogenous to heterogeneous with new building described by Page and Hall (2003:35) as '... *a patchwork of symbols and opportunities for*

FIGURE 6.1 *The Belem waterfront. (See colour insert.)*

consumption'. Dear and Flusty (1998) proposed four broad and at times over-lapping themes for cities:

- The *world city* concept that has emerged from globalization.
- The *dual city* where social polarization is a dominant element.
- *Altered spaces* where urban change and the reconfiguration of communities and space new cultural spaces emerge in cities.
- The *cybercity*.

Later in this chapter the *Ecocity* concept is briefly discussed and proposed as a fifth theme to those outlined above.

In 1900 urban populations accounted for 13% of the globe's population. By 1950 this had grown to 29%. By 2008 over 50% of the world's population were living in urban areas (Cohen, 1995). This trend shows no sign of abating with predications that the urban population will swell to 8.3 billion by 2030 according to projections released by the US Census Bureau (http://www.factmonster.com/ipka/A0762181.html accessed 08 August 2008). The transformation of the global population from rural to urban dwellers was a feature of the 20th century and has given rise to the supercities of today. These new urban forms are so large that scholars (Gottmann, 1961) have created new terms such as megalopolis and megacity to describe them. Typically, these super urban areas have consolidated into conurbations that spread in some cases for hundreds of kilometres with little open space separating previously quite distinct cities. In the United States the continuous urban strip that stretches along the Eastern seaboard from Boston to New York and Washington DC demonstrates the concept of megalopolis, a term first suggested in 1961 by Jean Gottmann. The term BosWash has been used to describe the Boston–New York–Washington DC megalopolis. Other urban forms of this nature include the Quebec City–Windsor Corridor, the Taiheiyo Belt in Japan (running from Fukuoka Prefecture in the south to Ibaraki Prefecture in the north and home for 82.9 million people) and the Beijing–Tianjin–Tangshan corridor in China (23 million people). In each of these supercities, interlinked ground transportation corridors, efficient distribution systems and high-speed, high-capacity communications provide the backbone on which these structures operate.

Despite the views of poverty, slums and social disharmony often associated with mass urbanization, the shift to massive urbanization has become a prerequisite for economic growth. In China and India, the move from the countryside to the city has been rapid and a part of the economic growth process of those nations. A recent report by the McKinsey Global Institute (2008) suggested that to boost per capita output, improve energy efficiency and reduce the loss of arable land to urbanization China should build either 15 supercities with average populations of 25 million people each or alternatively 11 clusters of cities each with a combined population of 60 million people. Driven by a forecast influx of an additional 240 million rural residents China's urbanization rate is anticipated to climb from 44% in 2005 to 66% in 2025. On current rates of urbanization China is expected to have 219 cities with populations over 1 million persons by 2025 compared with 35 European cities of over 1 million in 2008 (McKinsey Global Institute, 2008).

In some nations cities (Kabul and Colombo for example) have been seen as havens from warfare and insurgency that has been waged in rural areas between competing political factions. In other cases cities are viewed as centres for opportunity that offer hope for a better life, particularity for rural populations. It is not unusual for waves of rural poor to flock to cities in search of opportunities and services not available in the hinterland giving rise to cities such as Mumbai (India), Jakarta (Indonesia), Mexico City (Mexico) and numerous cities in China, Africa and the Middle East. San Paulo (Figure 6.2), South America's largest city, is an example of the ability of large cities to attract new immigrants, some of whom end up in slums.

As the move to urbanization on a global scale gathers pace smaller towns and cities will also grow and in many cases look to tourism as an addition to the city's economic base. This trend is illustrated by the Chinese city of Shenzhen located immediately across the border from Hong Kong. Before

FIGURE 6.2 *The San Paulo skyline from a downtown vantage point.*
Source: Photo courtesy of Bruce Prideaux.

its declaration as a Special Economic Zone (SEZ) in 1980 the city could best be described as a sleepy fishing village with no buildings higher than four stories. The declaration of the city as a SEZ and the discovery of consumerism by the Chinese masses propelled development and by 2007 the population had grown to over 8 million and was ranked 13th in the list of the world's largest cities. In the Lonely Planet *Hong Kong and Macau City Guide* (Stone *et al.*, 2008:234), Shenzhen is described as an '*extended shopping mall and a good place for a massage (legitimate and otherwise) and dim sum*'. To the west of the city a collection of theme parks has emerged '*filled to the brim with snap-happy Chinese tourists*' visiting theme parks that offer commodified collections of replicas of world famous monuments. The rapid growth of Shenzhen and other Chinese cities in Guangdong province adjacent to the Pearl Delta is creating a new megalopolis that also incorporates Hong Kong and Macau.

Functions of cities

The shift in the emphasis of the global economy from agriculture to manufacturing and more recently to services and information has changed the functionality of cities. Figure 6.3 highlights the changing nature of global competition in recent decades. Not surprisingly, many cities and towns have

Decade	Factor	Threatened national industries
1960s	Labour intensity	Textiles, shoes, simple assembly
1970s	Capital intensity	Automobiles, machinery, chemicals
1980s	Technology	Consumer electronics, telecommunications
1990s	Information	Financial services, media, 'systems' businesses
2000s	Entertainment, e-shopping and e-business	Tradition shopping spaces, traditional entertainment spaces

FIGURE 6.3   *The changing nature of global competition.*
Source: Adapted from Stopford and Strange (1991).

restructured and repositioned themselves in the service sectors including finance, business headquarters, government bureaucracy (Meethan, 1996) and more recently in the new e-commerce and e-entertainment industries.

The rapid emergence of post-industrial, globally competitive e-industries has been underpinned by the development of abundant and cheap energy, efficient transport and mass high-volume communications. The implications for city tourism of this rush to global urbanization are significant. Cities are able to generate as well as attract greater numbers of visitors but in doing so must create additional infrastructure to service the needs of these visitors including accommodation, food supply and transport. Away from the optimism of new markets, growing cities also generate considerable waste and pollution as well as absorb nearby land, which in many areas consists of good quality farmland. From a touristic perspective, an understanding of the interplay between the city and visitor, and the impact that this has on the environment, is essential to ensure efficient and effective planning, to achieve economic growth and meet competitive challenges from other cities. As Ashworth and Tunbridge (2000) observed urban tourism is based on a variety of holiday experiences, which collectively is a key element of their attractiveness. Moreover, tourists share these activities with residents leading to the multi-functional city servicing multi-motivated users.

Defining urban tourism is an issue that has occupied scholars for some time and remains a subject for debate. Small towns, often located in the hinterland of larger cities, have little in common with large metropolitan cities either in form, function or service richness (Law, 2002). Several typologies of cities based on function have been suggested in the literature. Judd and Fainstein (1999) identified three basic types of tourist cities;

- Resort cities – places created expressly for consumption by visitors,
- Tourist-historic cities – where the historic and cultural identity (whether conserved or constructed) is the key,
- Converted cities – where infrastructure is built for the purpose of attracting visitors. Sites that had been abandoned or were decaying undergo renewal and conversion into tourism zones.

Case Study 6.1 York, a Heritage City in the United Kingdom

In 1911 (p. 5) Benson, writing about York as a heritage tourism experience described the city in the following terms '*It would seem that if there is one thing which can be done at York better than anywhere else in the kingdom, that thing is the realizing of history. It is in this, above all, that the charm lies*'. On the next page the power of the tourist gaze is described in the following terms. '*The stranger, as he walks out of the railway station, is agreeably surprised to find these ancient fortifications immediately presented to his gaze. This surprising view enchants the lover of the picturesque, he is captivated by the beauty of the scene: and York adds another to her numerous admirers*'. Later in the book Benson bemoans the fact that the Shambles is the only street that preserves its narrow mediaeval characters, many other such building having been pulled down. Today, The Shambles is one of York's major tourism attractions.

A century later, York is still a major tourism centre with its historic core being designated as a conservation area in 1968. In 2007, the city was voted as European Tourism City of the Year by European Cities Marketing.

In a more detailed classification of the touristic functions of cities Page (1995) suggested typologies (Figure 6.4) based on purpose. From a different perspective Hall (2000) encapsulated the administrative functions performed by cities into a typology based on function (Figure 6.5).

Preceding classifications focused on purpose but neglected the importance of appeal. To redress this gap a further typology (Figure 6.6) is suggested which incorporates the attractiveness of size and the diversity of activities and experiences this generates. The following activity centric typology is not exclusive and can be juxtapositioned on any of the proceeding typologies to give a richer interpretation of city functionality and attractiveness to form the multi-function typology illustrated as Figure 6.7. So diverse are the opportunities for cities to generate attractions that any list is likely to be incomplete, overlapping and in constant need of updating.

Amsterda .

- Capital cities (eg. London, Paris, New York) and cultural capitals (eg Rome)
- Metropolitan centres and walled historic cities (eg. Cantebury and York)
- Large historic cities (Oxford, Vienna)
- Inner city areas (eg. Manchester)
- Revitalised waterfront areas (eg Sydney's Darling Harbour)
- Industrial cities (eg. Bradford)
- Seaside resorts and winter sports centres (eg. Lillehammer)
- Purpose built integrated resorts (eg. Cancun)
- Tourist-entertainment complexes (eg. Las Vegas, Disneyland)
- Specialised tourist service centres (eg. Spas and pilgrimage destinations)
- Cultural art cities (eg Florence)

FIGURE 6.4 *Page's 1995 typology of cities according to purpose.*

• *Multifunction Capitals*	Combining most of the highest national-level functions (London, Stockholm)
• *Global Capitals*	Representing supernational roles in politics and/or commerce (New York, Tokyo)
• *Political Capitals*	Created as seats of government where the political function is the primary purpose (Canberra, Ottawa, Brasilia)
• *Former Capitals*	No longer fulfil the role of government but retain historical significance (St. Petersburg, Philadelphia)
• *Ex-imperial Capitals*	Cities which have lost their empires but may function as a national capital or retain other functions (Madrid, Vienna, Budapest)
• *Provincial/ State Capitals*	Phoenix, Vancouver, Cardiff
• *Super-Capitals*	Functioning as centres for international organisations (Brussels, New York)
• *Cultural Capitals*	Particularly in Europe where a declaration of Cultural Capitals has been formalised through the EU process (Krakow)
• *Brand Capital*	Where a place describes itself as a capital in terms of a particular product (eg. Detroit)

FIGURE 6.5 *Hall's (2000) typology of cities according to function.*
Source: Hall (2000).

Type	Function
Visiting Friends and Relatives	Increasing mobility has scattered families and generated increasing demand for this form of travel.
Activity	This category refers to a broad range of activities that may be organised and include group participation or individual activity such as photography. The range of activities is large and growing.
Sport	A diverse range of iconic events that include the Olympics and World series sports find their home in major cities while local sporting events are found in even the smallest of towns.
Entertainment	Experiencing activities in music, concerts, stage shows, festivals, nightlife and other events.
Health	The search for health underlies much of the modern wellness movement and finds outlet in day spas, gyms, cosmetic surgery and in spa destinations such as Beppu in Japan.
Business	The fascination of financial districts (Wall Street and the City in London) and the power of skyscrapers to signify success and wealth (eg Petronas Twin Towers in Kula Lumpa, once the world's tallest buildings now surpassed by Burj Dubai in Daubi.)
Active learning	The recognition of education as a prerequisite for personal and national wealth is a major attraction.
Implicit learning	Informal learning is a process described as 'Come, see and understand'.
Pilgrimage	Rome, Jerusalem and Mecca are three of the great cities of faith that annually draw millions of pilgrimages.
Symbolism	Capital cities and their grand buildings are symbols of power ie Naypyidaw in the Union of Myanmar, Brasilia in Brazil.
Nature	Nature is packaged and sold as tourism products within cities (zoos) and in hinterlands (national parks).
Heritage and culture	The opportunities to connect with the past can take form in visiting old buildings and national museums as well as participating as an onlooker or participant in dance, festivals and celebrations of cultures past.
Shopping	The size of cities creates opportunities for unique shopping experiences from farmers markets through night markets and super malls to shopping districts such as New York's gold district.
Culinary opportunities	Experiencing tastes and flavours that are unique to a particular region.
Form and fabric of urban landscapes-	Experiencing unique building styles and urban settings.
Erotic	Becoming a voyeur as participant or observer.
Exotic	Experiencing shapes, forms and activities that contrast to the seemingly ordinariness of home.
Gambling	Chancing a win by engaging in risk. Examples range from poker machines in a sports club to casino destinations including Atlantic City and Monaco.

 FIGURE 6.6 *A typology of the attractions of cities based on activity.*

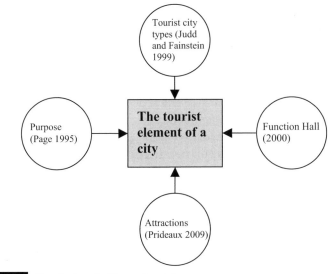

FIGURE 6.7 *Typologies of cities as touristic spaces.*

While discrete classifications allow for a systematic approach to research the variety of functions performed by cities coupled with their unique attributes will invariably challenge and perhaps even undermine any typology. In his study of capital city tourism Pearce (2007) noted the difficulty of isolating the 'capital' dimension from other aspects of tourism in the city. This could well be said of any classification.

In isolation, none of the preceding typologies effectively encapsulates the experiences sought by tourists who visit cities. To redress this deficiency Figure 6.7 illustrates how each of the factors identified in the typologies previously discussed combines to attract the interest of the tourist in cities as touristic spaces.

GROWTH OF CITY TOURISM

The increasing ease of travel has made towns and cities more accessible facilitating the growth of inter-urban as well as intra-urban and rural–urban travel for purposes that include business, pleasure, visiting friends and relatives, other personal needs and, in those parts of the world where secularism has been held at bay, for religious observances. More recently, the affordable nature of modern transport networks both in cost and importantly in time has generated the short city break as a new form of tourism activity. A Berlin resident can board a plane on Friday night, play golf for two days in southern Spain and be back home by Sunday night. Alternatively, a resident of Madrid may fly to Berlin for the weekend, attend a concert on Saturday and be home on Sunday evening. These patterns of travel illustrate the twin themes of 'escapism' and 'enrichment' made possible by travel of this nature (Ashworth and Tunbridge, 2000). Commenting on recent trends in European cities Dunne *et al.* (2007) observed that in 2005, city tourism arrivals grew by 20% compared to 3% growth in sun and beach holidays.

The factors driving the interest in city tourism are as much a reflection of economic growth, power, the function of cities as centres for the creation and expression of fashion as they are of the fascination that people have always had about cities. These include:

Cities as home. As the global rate of urbanization passes the 50% level and as urban residents become increasingly mobile in the search for employment, education and entertainment there is a growing VFR segment travelling between city and city and city and the countryside reconnecting with friends and family left behind in the transitory lifestyle that is becoming more common with city dwellers.

Cities are fun places. Cities offer the opportunity to participate in a multitude of activities and pleasures. Figure 7.7 encapsulates many of the attractions of cities that include dining, shopping, casinos, entertainment and nightlife districts, cultural districts, the pairing up of people on the prowl and the 'naughty' side of city life.

Increased holiday and leave entitlements. Increasing levels of paid recreation leave, particularly in the developed world, and the abutting of public holidays to weekends allow for more frequent, short trips. Cities attuned to this development have the opportunity to create a variety of experiences in a relatively short period of time.

Rise in personal disposable income. General increases in disposable income allow tourists to consider cities where cost (particularly accommodation and meals) may have been a deterrent in the past. The increasing trend towards dual income couples and the ability to afford indulgence has led to greater disposable income. Dunne *et al.* (2007) found in their study of Dublin that most visitors were partners and rarely involved families with children. The DINKs (double income, no kids) findings of their study support this notion of higher disposable income leading to greater short break travel.

Development of transport infrastructure and transport technology. Significant improvements in transport infrastructure have supported the growth of tourism in general and city tourism in particular. Cities have been able to metamorphose from transport and manufacturing hubs to places of tourism interest. The ease of access has made cities appealing destinations. In Europe, Japan, Korea (and in the near future in China), high-speed trains (the Japanese *Shinkansen* and Germany's Inter City Express) are able to move large numbers of tourists over large distances very quickly. In Europe Low Cost Carriers are also playing an increasingly important role in this form of holiday. Dunne *et al.* (2007:107) cite the following example of a Glaswegian tourist to Dublin; '*It was cheaper to come here than what it is to go to my work, and it was quicker. I mean it takes me an hour and a half to go to my work, whereas I mean I couldn't believe it, it was 50 minutes. We left home at 7.00 o'clock in the morning and arrived here at 7.52 ... I couldn't believe it for 70 p each way – I mean that's much less than I pay going to work*'.

Improved access to communication technology. Communications technology has increased awareness of cultures, heritage and experiential opportunities on offer around the globe. Beginning about the mid-1990s the Internet has increasingly democratized travel planning and purchase. Tourism providers use the Internet as a low-cost distribution tool and consumers scour the Web for travel information, travel bargains and entertainment opportunities in other cities. The simplicity of booking the main components of a city break (accommodation and transport) on-line eliminates much of the risk associated with the purchase of tourism products. Tourists can 'shop around' at their leisure, conduct research and, if they chose, make a decision at very short notice.

Increased marketing activity and competitiveness between city destinations. Most cities now realise the value of tourism and actively promote themselves as destinations. Major events including sporting events, conferences and celebrations are courted and used in promotion of cities. Collectively, the scale and volume of activities has generated a new interest in cities as destinations instead of or perhaps beside the other destination forms such as beach resorts, mountains and islands.

Services available in cities. Cities by their size are able to generate significant economies of scale and as a consequence offer a diversity of specialized services that may not be available in smaller areas including medical care, tertiary education and elite schools, commercial services offered by the financial sector, justice and entertainment including classic and contemporary forms of expression.

Intellectual fervour. Cities have long provided a point of convergence between artistic interpretation of life and culture, the youthful passion of students, the wisdom of scholars engaging in intellectual debate and at times the fervour of political dissent.

Fascination with power. Cities are places of power where the grand buildings of the corporate world and the government vie for dominance of the urban landscape using structures as symbols of power.

A TYPOLOGY OF CITY TOURISTS

From a marketing perspective it is important to develop profiles of city visitors so that products and attractions may be developed for specific market sectors that capitalize on the cities' existing tourism resource base. Page (1995) suggested a typology of nine categories of city visitors, however the speed of change now necessitates an update with an expanded, though most likely not fully inclusive, list of tourist types. The following example illustrates the changing nature of city tourism. In recent years the escalation of tensions in many regions has seen the deployment of large numbers of troops and aid workers by the United Nations, other international groups and Non Government Organizations (NGO) to nations in conflict including Bosnia, Kosovo, Iraqi, Afghanistan, Lebanon and East Timor. While serving in these countries, armed force members and aid workers spend rest periods as local tourists adding another category of visitor type. The categories illustrated in Figure 6.8 are not exclusive and in many circumstances visitors will demonstrate behaviours of two or more of these categories. An example is the business traveller who attends a play one evening, spends the next morning shopping and before returning home visits a religious shrine.

Page's Original Typology	Additional Visitor Types
• Visiting friends and relatives	• Shopping visitors
• Business travellers	• Entertainment seekers
• Conference and exhibition visitors	• UN Peacekeepers
• Education tourists	• Visitors on government business
• Cultural and heritage tourists	• Occupying military forces
• Religious travellers (eg. Pilgrims)	• MICE
• Hallmark event visitors	• Health visitors
• Leisure shoppers	• Fly and Flop – tourists on extended stays
• Day visitors	• Sporting visitors
	• Emergency and aid workers
	• Favourable weather seekers
	• Short break

FIGURE 6.8 *Revised typology of city tourists.*
Source: Adapted from Page (1995).

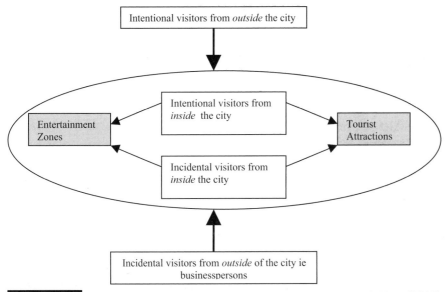

FIGURE 6.9 *Classes of city visitors based on Ashworth and Tunbridge (2000) classification of tourist and resident use of a city's attractions.*
Source: Constructed by author based on a discussion in Ashworth and Tunbridge (2000).

From a different perspective Ashworth and Tunbridge (2000) distinguished the tourist use and resident use of a city's resources in the following manner:

■ Intentional users from outside the city region who may be holiday makers staying in the city or outside it, using the city for excursions (tourists),
■ Intentional users from inside the city region making use of the city's recreation/ entertainment facilities or enjoying its character while engaging with others (recreating residents),
■ Incidental users from outside the city region, which includes business and congress visitors and those on family visits (non-recreating visitors),
■ Incidental users from inside the city region, the most numerous group being ordinary residents going about the ordinary affairs (non-recreating residents).

These visitor groups and their relationship to entertainment zones and tourist attractions are illustrated in Figure 6.9.

Ashworth and Tunbridge's (2000) analysis captures the complex patterns of the use of city facilities by residents and visitors and the multi-dimensional motivations that create the need for travel. A further method of describing city tourism is illustrated in Figure 6.10 which illustrates the continuum that

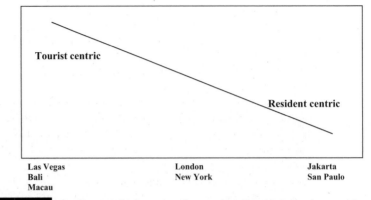

FIGURE 6.10 *Continuum of urban areas from resident centric to tourism centric purposes.*

exists between urban areas that remain resident centric and do not specifically seek to nurture tourism as an economic sector, and touristic centric cities that promote tourism. Cities that are not generally promoted as leisure destinations may attract visitors but for reasons that may not include leisure. Between the two ends of the continuum are a large number of cities that include tourism as a part of their overall portfolio of economic activity.

DEVELOPING CITIES AS A TOURISM PRODUCT

Globalization has generated substantial change in the shape, form and activities of cities. In response many cities have been compelled to shift their focus to attract business and citizens. Kolb (2006) noted that some cities in decline because of outdated industries or business moving elsewhere have identified urban tourism as an alternative industry. This trend of capitalizing on tourism has been recognized by a number of researchers including Meethan (1996), Kolb (2006) and Griffin and Hayllar (2007). Judd (1999), for example, noted that because there are few barriers of entry into the tourism industry even unlikely places may be tempted to invest in tourism.

The process of change can be accomplished through at least six processes:

1. Urban regeneration – waterfront areas, disused railway marshalling yards and special districts.
2. Development of existing product – ethnic quarters, shopping, heritage.
3. Attracting new products including conventions, Expos and shopping malls.
4. Themeing, including heritage, city of the future, shopping cities, cultural cities.
5. Creating entertainment zones, including theme parks.

Plate 1 (Figure 5.9 on page 133 of this volume)

Plate 2 (Figure 6.1 on page 146 of this volume)

Plate 3 (Figure 6.11 on page 160 of this volume)

Plate 4 (Figure 7.3 on page 185 of this volume)

Plate 5 (Figure 7.5 on page 187 of this volume)

Plate 6 (Figure 7.8 on page 191 of this volume)

Plate 7 (Figure 8.1 on page 206 of this volume)

Plate 8 (Figure 8.3 on page 210 of this volume)

Plate 9 (Figure 8.4 on page 211 of this volume)

Plate 10 (Figure 9.2 on page 249 of this volume)

6. By collectiveness through including the city in a circuit where each member city destination supports the other members of the circuit creating an experience that in sum, is greater than the sum of its individual parts.

As cities undergo urban regeneration and are redeveloped a new emphasis has been placed on leisure space, entertainment zones, parks and open spaces and new forms of inner city residential areas. Redevelopment of this nature injects economic life into cities attracting both city residents and visitors. Rejuvenation has gained momentum as cities embark on social and economic renewal, however from the tourist perspective there is a limit to the number of cultural centres, museums and other tourism infrastructure that can be built before the market is saturated. The key to transforming urban landscapes into successful tourism centres lies in the ability of the city to innovate creating uniqueness that enables it to stand apart from competitors. Uniqueness in this sense refers to the ability of the city to create spaces, styles, zones, activities and other features that differentiate from competitors. Dubai's Burj Al Arab hotel and Palm Islands are examples of strategies to create urban uniqueness. Uniqueness may be regional, national or international in scale.

Fremantle, in Western Australia is an example of a city that has identified an element of uniqueness that it uses to compete successfully on regional and national scales. According to Griffin and Hayllar (2007:6) Fremantle is 'an area with a rich history and diverse cultural mix where tourism has been superimposed on, but not replaced, the commercial maritime fabric (of its past)'. After a long period of decline the port city was rejuvenated as the host city for the 1987 defence of the America's Cup yachting race. Since then it has maintained its position as a tourism centre that has a focus on maritime heritage. On a regional scale the city has no equals but on a national scale competes with Geelong (Victoria) and Sydney (New South Wales). Internationally there are many competitors including Wellington and St Petersburg. Figure 6.11 illustrates a section of Freemantle's waterfront that has been saved from redevelopment and is now used as a university campus.

For the process of change to be successful a specific city identity must be created to give it appeal and uniqueness. Image develops identity that may be based on place, occasion, form or use. Identity is a critical element in all tourism destinations and in city embodies the experiences they are able to provide. Identity can be categorized into:

- *the broad sense*, which refers to the way and manner in which cities are generally viewed in terms that range from vivant to dull and boring,
- *the specific sense*, the perception of particular cities that may be negative or positive for the participant.

FIGURE 6.11 *Restored building in Freemantle's Waterfront District. (See colour insert.) Source: Photo courtesy of Bruce Prideaux.*

In the broad sense cities are identified as places that offer variety and in some cases uniqueness. Los Vegas is the sin city of the United States, a haven for hedonism while further south Rio de Janeino has a reputation as a carnival city. Detroit has a reputation as the auto capital of the world while in Europe, Basil is associated with watches due to its annual watch fair and Milan is promoted as the World's fashion centre. Incorporated within the context of the broad sense of image are negative and positive perceptions that colour visitor views.

Translating the broad image of cities into a specific image for a particular city requires identification of the elements of the city that are appealing and building on those positives to create an image that is competitive in the particular market places that the city is aiming for. In the previous example of Fremantle this was achieved by emphasizing its maritime history. Miami emphasizes its climate, beaches and hedonistic life style with great success. Similarly, Cairo and Rome emphasize heritage. As part of the imaging process there is a need to recognize negative perceptions and rather than seeking to paper them over with slick advertising, efforts are required to solve the problem. This may be difficult because negative images include views of cities as dirty, crowded, congested, ugly, noisy, polluted, unhealthy and unsafe; places that are immoral, anonymous, lonely, places full of busy, dismissive residents; and as Mules *et al.* (2007) noted cities that are just plain boring, stuffy or dull.

The selection of a specific city destination over other destinations is the first level in the process of city selection followed by a second level selection process that entails ranking cities against the specific attributes that are sought by visitors. A visitor to Las Vegas, for example, may be interested in the glamour of the city at the general level and the opportunities it has for gambling at the specific level. Similarly, tourists interested in heritage as a general theme may find Paris appealing while at the specific level the opportunity to visit the Louvre is attractive.

Aspects of supply – what tourists come to experience

The sum of the activities suggested in Figure 6.6 and the functions outlined in Figure 6.5 create an overall city image. This image along with the essentials of hotels, communications, government services, public security, transport and other services constitute the core of the cities' tourism supply. From the perspective of the push–pull theory of tourism activity (see Figure 2.2), the pull factor of cities operates at the two levels discussed in the previous section. On the *broad level* the positive image that cities seek to create is one of an exciting touristic space. On the *specific level* the pull factor refers to the ability of a particular city to convert general positive images of cities into a visit.

Viewed from another perspective, the supply of experiences has two major elements, the *fabric*, which is tangible and indicates what is possible, and the *individual experience*, which is intangible and real only in the sense that it expresses the uniqueness of the experience that a city is able to create for individual visitors. Understanding the need for both forms of experience, their differences and the conversion process from general interest into a visit to a specific city lies at the heart of how cities must develop their destination. The following discussion gives a brief overview of the role of some of the numerous elements that constitute the fabric of the city experience and how these can be used to create unique individual experiences.

Heritage and culture

The elements of culture and heritage are very strongly linked and have been acknowledged by a number of scholars (Ashworth and Tunbridge, 2000) as being an important element in the fabric of cities that generates tourism interest. Transmission of the form and values of the past into the contemporary world is a process that underlies heritage tourism. Some older cities do this reasonably well. Rome, Cairo, London and Athens retain many of the globally recognized icons of their built past, while suffering from the bulldozer mentality of urban renewal in some older precincts. In other cities heritage has become a causality of modernity. In their haste to modernize, cities including

Singapore and Hong Kong and to some extent pre-2008 Olympics Beijing have torn down the old to make way for the next phase of city function, often in ignorance of the value of the past as a tourism resource. However, it must be acknowledged that the process of regenerating lies at the heart of urban function as old uses give way to new uses which in time become new additions to the future cities' heritage. Achieving a balance between preserving the past and meeting the needs of the present creates ongoing tension for city administrators because to mindlessly preserve the past for its own sake fails to recognize the changing needs that cities have for space, form and function. Tourism provides a useful excuse for preserving at least the best and most representative elements of the past by providing it with commercial value.

Expression of creativity has long been associated with urban forms. The wealth of cities and their capacity to produce large numbers of domestic participants are essential to support concert halls, art galleries and other venues for the expression of culture from classical music to pop, opera to rap and the great masters to graffiti. Tourists provide a 'top up' to the resident base and in doing so help support culture. Commenting on the role of culture Page and Hall (2003) suggested that there is an overlap between the contemporary and classic and suggestion culture can be classified as:

- High-culture (performing arts, heritage attractions such as galleries).
- Folk and popular culture (gastronomy, sport, architecture, rock, pop, rap, etc.).
- Multi-culturalism (racial diversity of culture and language).

Collectively, these elements of culture contribute to the appeal of cities in terms of their attractiveness and 'vibe'.

Ethnic quarters

Ethnic quarters or enclaves have often been viewed with suspicion and a degree of mistrust and in many cities are the living evidence of past migrations of ethnic minorities and their treatment as aliens (Collins, 2007). The foundation of the Armenian Quarter, one of the four quarters of the Old City of Jerusalem, can be traced back to AD 451 when the Armenian Church separated from the established church. The Armenian Quarter has endured despite numerous political changes that have swept through Palestine and remains as a separate urban precinct in contemporary Jerusalem.

Inclusion of ethnic precincts in the modern tourist city adds to the richness the city experiences by providing opportunities to 'dip' into other cultures through unique food and beverage experiences, shopping, participation in ethnic festivals and generally engaging with these precincts at the level that suits their interests. Ethnic populations and their unique expressions of culture, rituals, customs, dress and cuisine help build a cosmopolitan image that can be consumed by tourists (Gotham, 2007). San Francisco's Chinatown was once viewed as a slum but at the same time challenged visitors with the allure of participation in the 'other' and the opportunity to gaze on the foreign from the security of the familiar. In recent decades the sights, sounds, tastes and smells of the Orient have been used to redevelop Chinatowns across the United States into significant attractions (Santos *et al.*, 2008). As in many other areas of tourism ethnically distinct enclaves have been commodified to sell 'the other' to visitors. Recognition of slums as a unique urban environment has allowed other slum areas including Rio de Janeiro's favelas to become tourism attractions.

EVENTS

Cities use events as a means of attracting visitors, branding and generally raising the profile of the city. From a marketing perspective events can be used to:

- construct a positive image,
- fill a void in the low-season,
- promote city administrations for political purposes,
- form the basis of a marketing strategy.

Events may be: held regularly at the same locality (e.g. the Edinburgh Tattoo or Oktoberfest in Munich); special events which move between cities (e.g. Commonwealth Games); events which occur simultaneously across a number of cities (New Year's Eve celebrations, Football World Cup); or one-off events (bi-centennial celebrations, ordination of a King or Queen). Events can be small scale (a travelling exhibition of Andy Worhol, a rock concert or a regional sporting carnival) which will draw visitors within a limited catchment to large scale hallmark events that raise the awareness and appeal of a city. The impact of the Olympic Games on Tokyo and Seoul was significant in terms of international recognition and Beijing is hoping that the 2008 Olympic Games will not only draw visitors but also elevate the image of the city in the global market place.

Quinn's (2005) discussion of arts festivals could easily be applied to events in the broader sense. She notes there that '*its connotations of sociability, playfulness, joviality and community provides a ready-made set of positive images on which to base a reconstruction of a less than perfect city image*' adding that many cities have seen festivals as a 'quick fix' to their image problems. Other cities draw on their cultural precincts to create tourism attractions, New York's Broadway and London's West End for example.

Shopping

Shopping is a major attraction for tourists and opportunities for uniqueness, exclusiveness, superior quality and low-cost are often used in marketing that includes a shopping message. Cities are able to offer unique shopping districts (Tokyo's Ginza) and cultural shopping experiences (Turkish carpets in the Grand Bizarre of Istanbul, delft china in Amsterdam and silk in Bangkok). The retail landscape presents itself in a number of forms for consumption by the tourist as illustrated in Figure 6.12.

Places to play

Cities have a long tradition of providing places for play through providing nightlife that may range from the halls of high-culture featuring ballet, opera and symphony orchestras to nightclub districts, gaming districts and red light areas. As with ethnic quarters, nightlife and entertainment are often clustered in specific distinct districts but for different reasons. The transport and regulation within such areas usually dictate that they are limited to particular spatial boundaries. Often these areas include restaurants, bars, nightclubs, clubs, venues and sometimes include casinos and/or adult entertainment venues. Examples of nightlife and entertainment districts include Bangkok's Patpong district, Kings Cross in Sydney, Broadway in New York and Soho in London.

SIZE	Retail Shopping		FORM
Large	District	Ginza	Clustered
	Mega-malls	West Edmonton Mall (Alberta, Canada)	
	Streets	Rodeo Drive (Los Angeles) Oxford St (Sydney)	
	Markets	Stanley Markets (Hong Kong)	Scattered
	Airports	Duty free at most international airports	
	Department stores	Harrods (London), Bloomingdales (New York)	
Small	Specialist Retail	Women's fashion in Milan	Discrete

FIGURE 6.12 *Elements of the shopping experience based on size and form.*

MARKETING THE CITY

Marketing is an essential factor in developing a successful tourism industry and needs to be undertaken with care. Kolb (2006) identified uniqueness as a major factor in successful city marketing while Griffin and Hayllar (2007) found that 'general ambience' rather than particular sites or features motivated visitors. Image, discussed earlier contributes an important element to the marketing message. Dunne *et al*. (2007) identified the 'vibe' of the city as important citing the vibe emanating from the youth of Dublin as a basis for the city's image as a 'fashionable' destination. Other authors see the urban environment as a commodity to be bought and sold to consumers (Judd and Fainstein, 1999; Meethan, 1996; Shaw and Williams, 2002), however this view needs to be tempered against the intangible aspects of fabric discussed earlier. In reality and as Holcomb (Judd and Feinstein, 1999:55) argue the previous views need to be balanced against the realization that cities have limited control over the character and quality of their image as a consequence of inherited characteristics included as climate, geography, topography, history, culture, religion and traditions.

Innovation as a key to future city tourism

It is apparent from the previous discussion that cities in the future will be different from those of today, as those of today are different from those of the past. Elsewhere in this book a number of the emerging challenges that will help shape future cities are discussed. How cities will respond depends on their function, the views of citizens, visitor needs, public and private sector leadership, the tax base, policy, engineering capability and importantly their ability to innovate. It is apparent that as they have in the past, future cities will continue to adapt to changes in their physical environment, society and production systems and develop new attractions. At the heart of this process lies innovation.

FUTURE CHALLENGES TO CITIES

As in the past contemporary cities face a number of serious challenges. The following discussion is framed in the context that cities in their current form are unlikely to be sustainable in the distant future, an arbitrary time that may be as far away as the 22nd century or as close as mid-21st century. The context of this view is that as new technologies have shaped cities in the past, new technologies and urban forms will need to be developed to assist future cities in mitigating as well as in adapting to climate change, meeting the challenge of declining fossil fuel reserves and finding the additional food needed to feed an estimated 2.8 billion extra people by 2050 (Krebs, 2008).

In the future cities will be forced to evolve into new forms beyond contemporary post-modern patterns and in this process decide if they are to adopt policies of co-existence with nature, adapt to nature as it changes through climate change or alternatively seek to dominate nature. To retain their capacity to support their inhabitants, cities will continue to need to be sustained by surrounding natural systems. This is an enormous challenge and one that will take many decades to achieve primarily because of the enormous economic costs involved and uncertainty over the rate, direction and intensity of change. One concept that has emerged as a possible solution for developing future cities that are able to co-exist in harmony with nature is the Ecocity. While the Ecocity concept is relatively new and not yet widely accepted as a guiding philosophy for city planning it is used as the basis of the following discussion because it is one concept that holds some promise for adapting to the significant environmental problems that will be faced by all cities. The Ecocity concept also offers the promise of an attractive environment for tourism in the future.

The idea of building ecological cities originated in the 1980s and is based on earlier debates in the 1960s about ecological responsibility. Initial ecological concepts focused on the urban metabolism, or the cycles of energy, water, waste, emissions, and the protection of the environment within urban structures. More recently, a worldwide Ecocity movement has developed, where an emphasis has been placed on creating sustainability in urban settings.

The Ecocity concept

The concept of the Ecocity is based on urban ecology, which studies 'the relationship between cities and natural systems, and is based on the reality that cities are a part of – not separate from – the "natural" environment' (Downton, 1997). This view forms the underlying ideology in the following discussion of Ecocities. Urban ecology foundered in Berkeley in 1975 was transformed into the Ecocity Builders, whose mission was to rebuild cities in balance with nature. The Ecocity is seen as a place where inhabitants are able to live, work, shop and recreate in amenities that are all within short distances. According to this philosophy cities should be built with all the amenities people require gathered together with the places where people want to be. Hence, transportation becomes something you do to get where you want to be, either by walking, bicycle, public transport or finally automobile. Building on the concept of urban ecology, Register (1997) conceptualized Ecocities as living systems or organisms in their own right that should become part of the natural environment, subject to the rules of ecology.

The reality is that cities in the future will need to perform the same range of functions that they presently undertake. These include providing employment, offering security, supplying the essentials of life, offering opportunities for recreation and entertainment and educating the young. How these functions will be preformed is the central issue of any discussion of the future. From the Ecocity perspective future cities need to be rebuilt to improve their environmental performance and long-term sustainability. A number of principles have been suggested for defining an Ecocity (Graedel, 1999):

- The city must be sustainable over the long term.
- The city must utilize a systems approach to evaluating its environmental interactions.
- The city design must be flexible enough to evolve gracefully as the city grows and changes.
- The open space of an Ecocity must serve multiple functions.
- The city must be part of regional and global economies.
- The city must be attractive and workable.

The European Union (EU, 2004) has published a list of similar principles which are designed to identify the key elements for sustainable human settlements:

- Resource budgeting.
- Energy conservation and efficiency.
- Renewable energy technology.
- Long lasting built structures.
- Proximity between home and work.
- Efficient public transport systems.
- Waste reduction and recycling.
- Organic waste composting.
- A circular city metabolism.
- A supply of staple foods from local sources.

Surprisingly, in both these concepts (Graedel, 1999 and EU, 2004) tourism was ignored but given the demand for travel that cities generate, a tourism function must be incorporated as a key element in a future Ecocity design. Yang (2004) noted that the four most common terms used to indicate Ecocities were: a city that is green, environmentally friendly, is sustainable and is based on natural ecology. Further, Yang (2004) identified six South Korean cities that were working towards establishing themselves as Ecocities but noted that these cities had yet to adopt holistic ecological systems and functions and therefore could not be defined as true Ecocities.

Downton (1997) cited in Prideaux (2005) states that Ecocities should create and maintain a balance, not only within human society, but also between humans and nature. In his opinion '*an Ecocity is a brand, a package of ethics and programs for making cities that are places of ecological restoration. It goes beyond 'sustainability' – sustaining what we now have would be like embalming a patient with a terminal illness. An ecocity is about healing*'. This idealistic view of an Ecocity is appealing but probably unrealistic. Cities in the future, as in the past, will organize around the need to generate economic activity with the needs of its citizens being accommodated within this business paradigm. While the market model of economic organization prevails the needs of the city economy will continue to govern city form and function but increasingly within the context of declining resources.

One of the first attempts to build an Ecocity commenced in 2007 at Dongtan near Shanghai in China. Dongtan aims to minimize pollution by only permitting bikes and electric cars, recycle as much as possible including wastewater, utilize renewable energy sources including solar and wind and produce its own food grown locally in environmentally sensitive farms. Unfortunately, the site is in a wetland area formerly used for small-scale agriculture and a site used by migrating water birds. Given China's reputation for pollution and waste, the development of Dongtan is an ambitious project. In terms of city tourism it may provide a blueprint for the future of cities and even if it does not, it will almost certainly attract visitors who increasingly have an interest in the balance of sustainability and city life.

The actual ability to create and sustain an Ecocity awaits the future. The more cynical observer will note that at the heart of western capitalism is the view that profit drives all decisions and without profit a concept such as Ecocities is doomed. A more realistic view might be that without some movement towards the concept of sustainable cities human populations face extreme peril from failing ecosystems and that, based on the price mechanism, Ecocities might be able to provide the range of services required to continue to sustain a high standard of living within a sustainable ecosystem.

Within this context, tourism will need to adopt new approaches where the use of resources will be more constrained than in the contemporary world. However, short of a new economic system emerging to replace capitalism with a new economic model, the demand for tourism experiences in cities will remain, and for their part cities will continue to seek tourists. Adaptations will have to be made which conform to the constraints of the future world and what these will be largely depends on the success of global mitigation strategies to reduce atmospheric levels of green house gases levels, the new technologies that will be developed to sustain the low-carbon economy of the future and possibly the emergence of new city forms based on the Ecocity concept.

CONCLUSION

This chapter has examined a large number of issues concerning urban tourism. Many of the issues are complex and multi-disciplinary and because of the constraints of space are not examined in detail. What is apparent is that cities have a central role in the touristic experience.

This chapter has sought to encapsulate key elements of the city as a tourism destination. Two new typologies were developed (Figures 6.6 and 6.7) and an existing typology revised (Figure 6.8) although they remain to be tested. It is also clear that cities will continue in their role as places of significant tourist interest, they will continue to evolve as their key industries evolve or metamorphose into new functions, be amenable to innovation and that as in the past, cities in the future will face new sets of pressures. Of all the pressures discussed growing urbanization and climate change appear to be the greatest challenges facing city destinations in the near future.

One of the greatest challenges for cities that are engaged in urban tourism will be to balance the needs of residents and other industry and service sectors with the needs of visitors. As Ashworth and Tunbridge (2000) had reminded us cities are multi-functional and service multi-motivated users.

KEY ISSUES

- The rate of urbanization is increasing on a global scale. As part of this trend new cities without any past are emerging while existing cities are growing so rapidly that their past is in danger of being submerged.
- Cities are evolving as they respond to new challenges and assume new responsibilities.
- Cites are attractive places for visitors but to maximize the potential of this market cities need to identify their particular blend of experiences to create and promote a unique image.
- In the future cities will face a range of new challenges including climate change and the need to find a balance between their use of resources and the sustainability of the resources they draw upon. One response may be the development of Ecocities.
- The literature has yet to grapple with the changes that may be anticipated as cities seek to respond to the challenges of mitigation and adaptation. One of these challenges is likely to be increased sea water levels.

CHAPTER 7

Coastal Tourism

Where the sensuousness of sand and water and the glitter and excitement
of city life combine in a new form of tourism

Coastal tourism is an enduring topic of research; a reflection of the pre-eminent position holiday resorts has been assumed to hold in the past and present holiday making patterns of tourists. Of all the models and typologies developed to explain aspects of the tourism experience, those relating to holidaying by the sea are the most numerous. However, research of this nature has remained almost entirely focused on traditional forms of coastal tourism activity that are beach and water centric while largely ignoring the rapidly growing coastal and near coastal cities that are now emerging as major centres of economic activity and new powerhouses of tourism interest. This has not been the case in other disciplines where researchers have been quick to grasp the implications of change and are now well advanced in their analysis of the forces that are driving development in coastal areas. In the broader literature the emphasis has shifted from the area immediately adjacent to the shoreline to take a more encompassing perspective that is referred to as the coastal zone and which may be described as the interconnected ecological, economic, human and physical systems that extend from the shore line to the outer edge of the continental margin and landward to adjacent watersheds.

The extent of tourism activity that occurs in coastal settings is much larger than the literature on coastal tourism resort development would suggest. Rapid urbanization in the coastal zone and the problems that this has caused have created a new context for the study of tourism in coastal settings. Coastal cities are now emerging as larger and more significant centres for tourism activity than traditional seaside resorts. This chapter is concerned with the structure and operation of tourism in the coastal zone from the

171

perspective of tourism being one of many competing industries located in this zone. Following a examination of issues that are increasingly defining the parameters of coastal zone research in the broader academic literature, this chapter reviews the well-ploughed field of research into coastal resorts in the traditional context of a largely tourist exclusive space before examining the aspects of tourism development in the coastal zone. The chapter concludes with a discussion that examines threats to coastal zone tourism in the long-term.

THE COASTAL ZONE

Academic interest in coastal zone management (CZM) emerged in the 1970s for a number of reasons: the data provided by the first generation of satellites indicated that development requiring land clearing in the coastal zone was beginning to have a negative effect on coastal ecosystems; the same imagery also hinted at changes in the climate that could effect the vast number of Biogeochemical cycles that occur in coastal zones (Vallega, 2003); the adoption of Coastal Zone Management by the United States in the early 1970s; and growth of urban populations in the coastal zone. In the United States alone, the coastal zone occupies 17% of the nation's land area and is home to 53% of the US population (NOAA Economics accessed 12 May 2008 www.ncdc.gov). The US Coastal Zone Management legislation demonstrated how individual nations could shape a coherent approach to coastal zone management. Interest in protecting the coastal zone over the next decade lead to the development of Chapter 17 of Agenda 21 of the 1992 Earth Summit of Rio de Janeiro (http://www.un.org.esa/sustdev/agenda21.htm) which addressed a number of issues associated with coastal planning. Ultimately Agenda 21 became an influential document in the preparation of the 2002 World Summit on Sustainable Development (WSSD). The result has been that coastal areas are increasingly seen as a spatial system extending seawards from the high water mark and landward towards spatial boundaries imposed by uplands or arbitrary distance-based boundaries (Vallega, 2003). In recent decades and paralleling the growing importance of the coastal zone as a centre for economic activity, coastal cities are now exerting an increasingly significant influence on the shape and expression of cultural, economic, spatial and social structures of the regions and nations where they are located. For this reason the need for Integrated Coastal Management (ICM), also referred to as Integrated Coastal Zone Management (ICZM), is now recognized as a key government responsibility.

Recognizing that development in coastal zones was occurring at an unprecedented rate the European Union (EU) undertook an extensive evaluation of Integrated Coastal Zone Management (ICZM) in Europe. The report, released in 1996, recommended that coastal member states develop national ICZM strategies. Following further investigation and consultation the EU requested that member states development national ICZM strategies by 2006 (Coastal Zone Policy http://ec.europa.eu/environment/iczm/home.htm accessed 5 June 2008). Tourism was one of a number of case study industries considered in the EU policy formulation on the recommended structure of ICZM. In relation to the tourism industry the European Commission (2001a) noted that when properly planned, tourism can be a major force in coastal zone economic regeneration but also noted that haphazard and unplanned tourism development had caused major social and environmental problems in Europe. To support a more integrated approach to planning a further EU report (2001b) outlined a methodological framework for adopting Tourism Carrying Capacity (TCC) as a planning measure for European tourism destinations. One outcome of the EU's ICZM policy development was the establishment of two sets of indicators, one aimed at measuring progress in ICZM and the other designed to measure the sustainability of coastal areas.

The coastal zone is an area that has attracted considerable interest from scholars in a number of disciplines including marine policy, coastal zone management, marine policy, conservation, ecology and heritage. Surprisingly, there has been little recognition of the significance of the coastal zone in the tourism literature. Examples from a range of disciplines where tourism impacts have been considered in the wider context of coastal zone management include: an examination of sustainable tourism development on the Red Sea (Shaalan, 2005); measurement of socioeconomic benefits of Integrated Coastal Management (ICM) in Xiamen, China (Peng *et al.*, 2006); analysis of aspects of coastal zone management in Egypt (Abd-Alah, 1999; Shaalan, 2005); Integrated Coastal Management in the Philippines (Christie, 2005); coastal tourism development in India (Noronha, 2004); Integrated Coastal Management in Belize (Cho, 2005); Integrated Coastal Zone Management in northwestern Africa (Snoussi *et al.*, 2000); coastal zone management of coastal tourism in Southeast Asia (Wong, 1986); estimates of socioeconomic benefits of ICM in China (Peng *et al.*, 2006); development problems for tourism in the coastal zone in Mexico (Ortiz-Lozano *et al.*, 2005); sustainable management of coastal resources in India (Damodaran, 2006); Turkish coastal tourism and urbanization (Burak *et al.*, 2004); heritage in the coastal zone of south west England (Callegari, 2003); Italian coastal heritage (Howard and Pinder, 2003); coastal heritage (Vallega, 2003); and trends in ocean and coastal tourism (Hall, 2001).

MANAGING THE COASTAL ZONE

A number of criteria can be used to delimit the coastal zone (Vallega, 2003) including:

- *Physical criteria*. From a geographic perspective the coastal zone extends landward to watersheds and seaward to the outer edge of the continental margin. This broad coverage gives policy makers and planners the opportunity to integrate management of river basins and coastal environments.
- *Ecological criteria.* The ecological components of the coastal zone include landwards, brackish and littoral subsystems, seawards and finally the neritic zone that extends out to the 200 m isobath.
- *Administrative and judicial criteria.* Given that planners and administrators have developed boundaries that serve purposes other than delineating physical and biological processes the definition of zoning in this context occurs within guidelines that reflect national and international agreements and legislation. For example, to seawards the coastal zone may be defined by the 200 m depth line which is used to identify the extent of continental shelves, the 12 nautical mile limit which identifies the extent of national territorial sea space, the 24 nautical mile line which defines the seaward extent of the contiguous zone and the 200 nautical mile line from shore which delimits nation's exclusive economic zone (EEZ).
- *Economic criteria.* Vallega (2003:9) defines economic criteria as the *'existing coastal resources and the location of structures and facilities ... embracing, (to) seawards, any offshore activity linked with local economic systems, and, (to) landwards, all coastal settlements, industry and agriculture'*.

The extensive nature of the coastal zone and its linkages to hinterland zones requires extensive policy coordination at national and regional levels in aspects that include zoning, infrastructure development, industry policy, social policy and sustainability issues. Where nations share land and/or sea borders with other sovereign states, international cooperation, coordination and management of coastal zones may be required. The previously cited EU example illustrates how a multilateral approach to ICM is able to achieve more effective policy outcomes. As a consequence, national governments are increasingly involved in the planning and administration of the coastal zone.

Given that tourism may or may not be a significant factor in a particular sector of the coastal zone, it is essential that a holistic view of the coastal

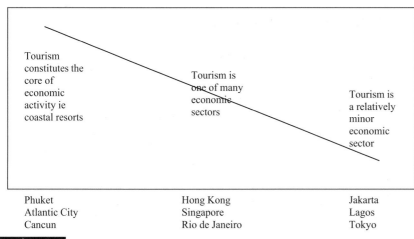

Tourism constitutes the core of economic activity ie coastal resorts

Tourism is one of many economic sectors

Tourism is a relatively minor economic sector

Phuket
Atlantic City
Cancun

Hong Kong
Singapore
Rio de Janeiro

Jakarta
Lagos
Tokyo

FIGURE 7.1 *Positioning tourism as an economic activity in the coastal zone.*

zone and its functions, operations and challenges should be the start point for attempts to understand where tourism fits into the new reality of the coastal zone economy and ICM. Figure 7.1 attempts to illustrate the range of positions that tourism may occupy in the coastal zone, commencing with a position of primacy in the traditional setting of coastal resorts and moving to a position of near irrelevancy. Because of the rapid pace of urbanization in the coastal zone, policy agendas are still fluid allowing industry sectors that include tourism to establish their place within the spectrum of stakeholders in the coastal zone economy. Where tourism has a legitimate claim for increasingly limited space in the coastal zone, it must ensure that its voice is heard at political, industrial, administrative and planning forums. For this to occur, key stakeholders in other industries competing for space need to be consulted and where possible alliances formed. Planning is a particularly sensitive issue where competing claims vie for limited space and favourable zoning. Acknowledgement as a key stakeholder is important to avoid situations where the needs of other industries are placed higher on the agenda than those of tourism. In Hong Kong the race to transform the city into a financial and business hub has been at the cost of much of the city's colonial heritage. Preservation of the city's heritage was seen to have less worth, even as a tourism attraction, than competing users in the finance, commerce and similar sectors. Conversely, in Macau the rapid development of the casino economy has not been at the expense of Macau's colonial legacy which is protected as a world heritage area.

In Turkey, where the coastal zone constitutes approximately 30% of the total land area mass and is home to 51% of the nation's population (Burak *et al.*, 2004), coastal cities have developed as industrial, commercial and tourism centres. In many coastal areas use conflict has emerged between tourism, mariculture, conservation, urbanization, industrial development, agriculture, navigation and transportation highlighting the importance of tourism industry representation in key planning forums. Tourism's contribution to land use conflict in Turkey began in the early 1980s with the growing popularity of second house cooperatives and the construction of coastal hotels. Recognition of the need to resolve disputes between various stakeholders in the nation's coastal zone leads to the introduction of coastal zone planning schemes.

Management of coastal zones requires coordination across a broad range of administrative authorities. According to GESAMP (1996:66) '*ICM is a broad and dynamic process that . . . requires the active and sustained involvement of the interested public and many stakeholders with interests in how coastal resources are allocated and conflicts are mediated. The ICM process provides a means by which concerns at local, regional and national levels are discussed and future directions are negotiated*'. Further, for an integrated approach to be effective, all aspects of the coastal zone including political and geographic borders, as well as social, economic and biological factors must be incorporated into the planning process. A planning process of this nature is difficult and involves potential conflict at many levels. Issues that may lead to conflict between various stakeholders include legal, institutional, social-cultural, bio-physical and economic factors (Christie, 2005).

In heavily populated coastal zones, Integrated Coastal Management usually focuses on a number of factors including:

- The function and scale of economic activity that is currently occurring and which may occur in the future. Examples include the potential of a coastal zone locality as a port, the site for industrial production, location of nonrenewable resources (i.e. minerals), for agricultural, aquiculture and for tourism.
- The national role of the coastal zone. This may include the extent to which areas of the zone are to be retained as protected areas, retention or change to the extent that the zone is used for farming and pastoral activities, the extent to which the zone is to be urbanized, its use for military purposes, allocation of areas for tourism purposes, allocation of space for industrial purposes and development of multi-industry and multi-function zones. If the coastal zone is central to the life of the nation in which it is located it is likely to receive significant attention from government as is the case with coastal cities including Boston, Tokyo and Anterwerp. If it sits on a periphery (either physical, social or economic) it is likely to receive less attention increasing the level of difficulty experienced in initiating and sustaining development agendas.

- The role of tourism and the space and resources it requires within the totality of the coastal zone economy.
- The coastal ecosystems including their uniqueness, fragility, complexity, sustainability and susceptibility to change, and levels of exploitation.
- Waste management including grey and black water discharge, garbage disposal and agricultural and industrial run-off.
- The social and economic aspirations of the residents of the zone, both current and future. These may include water quality, transport, employment, pollution and access to social services.
- Allocation of land for reservation as protected areas.
- Governance including political and on-the-ground coordination of ICM policies.
- Issues of the future including climate change, growing water scarcity, peak oil, changing patterns of consumption, falling fertility rates in most developed countries and completion for limited space.

These factors can be grouped into eight major domains of coastal policy problems that need to be considered at the political level before being addressed by planners, administers and the private sector. These domains include:

1. Those that relate to conflicts over resource use (Noronha, 2004),
2. Problems that relate to resource depletion (Noronha, 2004),
3. Problems that arise through pollution and/or resource degradation (Noronha, 2004),
4. Security issues including natural disasters, water security and political security,
5. The quality of life of residents of the coastal zone,
6. Long-term sustainability of industry and ecosystems,
7. Administrative responsibilities that may be divided between various levels of government and between various public and privately owned agencies and utilities, and
8. Future challenges including urbanization, globalization and climate change.

The recent growth in urban populations in coastal zones has been rapid and largely ignored by tourism researchers. According to Li (2003) the growth of mega cities, defined having populations of 8 million or more, has been spectacular. Between 1980 and 2000 the number of mega cities has grown from three (Tokyo, San Paulo and Shangri) to 20, many of which are located in the coastal zone. Growth of urban forms of this type have been generated by the role of coastal cities as: the engines for economic growth; centres for trade, investment and finance; production location; as a market place for commodities; a place for consumption; a magnet for migration from rural areas; administration; cultural attractions; and attractiveness of city lifestyles. The new mega cities are not just limited to developed nations but have emerged in developing nations including Nigeria (Lagos), India (Mumbai and Madras) and Indonesia (Jakarta). Other examples of coastal mega cities include Osaka (Japan), Metro Manila (Philippines), Istanbul (Turkey), Rio de Janeiro (Brazil), Shanghai and Tianjing (China), Bangkok (Thailand), New York and Los Angles (USA), Buenos Aires (Argentina), and Karachi (Pakistan). According to Li (2003) there were 54 coastal cities with a population of above one million in 2002. In the future the number of mega cities is expected to grow to 36 by 2015 with 22 of these located in Asia (Li, 2003).

Growth of cities in the coastal zone has intensified use conflicts between growing urban populations and farming areas, natural areas and even smaller rural communities as they become engulfed by encroaching cities. In a number of countries, including China, India and the United States growing urbanization of the coastal zone is threatening food supply as farmland is lost to encroaching cities or is used for new transport corridors and other non-farm uses. Other conflicts that have emerged include salt water intrusion in aquifers and rivers, coastal erosion, loss of open space, loss of terrestrial and marine habitats, land subsidence due to extraction of underground water supplies, loss of productivity of coastal fisheries, pollution, increased intensity of damage from natural disasters including tsunamis and wind storms, breakdown of traditional social and cultural patterns of behaviour, and climate change with possible near future sea level rises. Yet the richness of the amenities offered in cities of this size, the expanded opportunities for employment, availability of specialized medical care and variety of entertainment continue to attract fresh waves of migrants. Many of these issues are beginning to find voice through conferences such as the Rio + 10 Conference on Oceans and Coasts held in Hangzhou, China in 1999. The conference produced the Hangzhou Declaration that called for recognition of the issues associated with coastal mega cities (Li, 2003).

In many cases decisions on these issues continue to be made in a reactive manner in response to pressure groups, and other immediate needs such as development applications and the need to open new land for housing and other types of construction. As a consequence, long-term goals are often not adequately articulated and plans to attain these goals are often lacking or when developed, by-passed for a variety of reasons. Desirable policy outputs usually require specific government action that may include regulation, offering incentives or applying penalties. Measures may include (Hall, 2000):

- *Regulatory instruments.* These include regulations, permits and licences which have a legal basis and are enforceable.

- *Voluntary agreements*. Examples include developing voluntary codes of conducts for operators and visitors.
- *Expenditure*. Direct funding of parks is one method of achieving a policy aim of protecting the coastal environment.
- *Financial incentives*. Both positive (grants, low-interest loans) and negative (taxes, levies and specific charges) incentives can be used to achieve desired policy outcomes.
- *Non-intervention*. The market can be used to determine the most appropriate response.

Planning in the coastal zone is therefore complex and has the potential for conflict but also must recognize the interests of stakeholders in a framework that facilitates integration and cooperation.

While only one of a number of industries that may be operating within this policy environment, coastal tourism may create problems through resource overuse that leads to resource depletion. For example, coastal tourism has impacts on local ecosystems and water supply, requires access to sufficient land and the provision of transport corridors and may also affect the structure of communities where tourism facilities are built. These issues will be exacerbated if the impacts spread beyond the tourism sector and spill over into other sectors.

Rapid urbanization in coastal zones also has the potential to create tension between various levels of government as well as between governments within the same level. In Denmark tensions of this nature lead to the amalgamation of local governments in 2004, reducing the number of Local Governments from 274 to 100 while a parallel reform reduced the number of regional authorities (Anker *et al.*, 2004).

From a tourism perspective, it is imperative that the broader issues of coastal zone management be recognized and incorporated into the study of coastal tourism issues. In the future, as the demand for land in coastal areas intensifies and as the size and number of coastal zone cities continue to increase, the space required for tourism purposes will come under pressure from alternative users.

THE TRADITIONAL VIEW OF COASTAL TOURISM

To date, much of the discussion on coastal resorts has focused on the conversion of coastal sites into tourism enclaves, their subsequent growth, management, planning and more recently their long-term sustainability. Shaw and Agarwal (2007) traced the development of coastal resorts from their British roots to their 'export' to Europe and later North America through to the emergence of mass resorts in the period between the mid-19th century and the 20th century. This pattern of growth was driven in a large measure by the democratization of leisure in line with growing economic prosperity (Shaw and Agarwal, 2007). As part of the growth in mass tourism Urry (2002) observed the development of new forms of entertainment that in the pre-electronic age included amusement arcades typified by Coney Island in New York and Brighton Pier in the United Kingdom. King (2001) identified a growing diversification of resorts based on their characteristics and forms of specialization, including:

- Sport and beach orientated resorts.
- Theme-park and golf course resorts.
- Large-scale, water-park resorts.
- Mega-resorts.
- Boutique resorts.

To these can be added a range of other specialized resorts including:

- Nature-based resorts (Cairns, Australia).
- Heritage resorts (Dubrovnik, Croatia).
- Spa resorts (Beppu, Japan).

Gilbert (1939) was one of the first scholars to examine the resort phenomenon and observed how the 19th century belief in the curative properties of the sea and fresh air stimulated the emergence of coastal resort towns that catered for the health needs of the elite. Spearheaded at first by the elite and later boostered by the growing middle and working classes, the attractiveness of the beach and the three s' of sea, sand and sun, and in more recent times an additional S for sex and in some instances the fifth S of surf, have underpinned the growth of coastal resorts as a form of vacationing to the point where they now form coastal pleasure regions, or as Turner and Ash (1975) observed, a pleasure periphery.

Pioneering research by Gilbert (1939) and Barrett (1958) drew attention to the types of development often observed at coastal locations in the United Kingdom. Later, Christaller (1963) identified an evolutionary cycle that appeared to be operating in tourism areas, offering one of the first limited theoretical explanations of the forces at work. The process of development has attracted considerable attention from scholars who have suggested a range of models (for example, Gilbert, 1939; Lavery, 1974; Miossec, 1976; Butler 1980; Gormsen, 1981; Young, 1983; Keller, 1987; Smith, 1992; Kermath and Thomas, 1992; Burton, 1994; Russell and Faulkner, 1998; Weaver, 2000; Prideaux, 2000) and typologies (see Plog, 1973; Peck and Leipie, 1977; Smith, 1977; Soanne, 1993) to explain the process of growth. For a more detailed discussion on models of development refer to Chapter 2. Existing typologies and models generally examine the issue of tourism development in the coastal zone from either the perspective of tourist motivation or an examination of the factors that influence the development process and focus almost entirely on tourism as the primary development sector, ignoring a raft of other industries that have developed in the coastal zone.

An even larger group of scholars have tested resort development models and typologies in a variety of settings. Ioannides (1992), for example investigated how fishing villages in Cyprus underwent a change in structure as tourism stimulated the development of hotels and shopping precincts. Agarwal (1997) catalogued the rise of coastal resorts in the United Kingdom and in a later paper (Agarwal, 2002) extended her examination of seaside tourism, combining Butler's (1980) lifecycle model and the restructuring thesis (see Harvey, 1989; Soja, 1989; Urry, 1987) to provide a theoretically inter-related framework for understanding development. In other areas green field sites were designated as tourism zones and converted into resort enclaves. Inskeep (1991) provided a case study of Nusa Dua in Bali where a coastal green field site was acquired by the government and redeveloped into a tourism enclave abet with considerable investment by hotel companies. In another example of the process of resort growth Prideaux (2000a) related how the desire for a beach holiday provided the impetus for a chain of events that saw a number of small scattered beach hamlets evolve into the Gold Coast, one of Australia's major international resorts. The forms that coastal resort development may take range from small seaside settlements where second homes predominate to coastal resorts that attract large numbers of visitors, many of whom may be international tourists. In the latest phase of coastal resort development Shaw and Agarwal (2007) observed that coastal resorts are a component of globalization and subject to the interrelated processes of the globalization of tourism and the impacts of globalization on the development of coastal resorts.

While a range of issues related to coastal tourism development have been the subject of ongoing debates in the literature (King, 1994; Agarwal, 1994; Gordon and Goodall, 1992; Cooper, 1992; Cooper and Jackson, 1989) and more recently by Aguiló et al. (2005), Bramwell (2004) and Agarwal and Shaw (2007) the debate in general has focused on the structure, growth, marketing and impacts of the towns, cities and regions that offer a clearly defined beach centred coastal holiday experience. Examples include: Cyprus (Ioannides, 1992), Southeast Asia (Wong, 1998), Pattaya (Smith, 1992), British seaside resorts (Cooper, 1997; Agarwal, 1997, 2002; Soane, 1993); Malta Oglethorpe (1984), Costa Bravacc (Priestly and Mundet, 1998), the Balearic Island (Aguilo, 2005), Caribbean Islands (Wilkinson, 1987; Debbage, 1990), South Pacific Islands (Weaver, 1990, 1998), Isle of Man (Cooper and Jackson, 1989), Minorca (Williams, 1993), the Gold Coast Australia (Prideaux, 2000), Cairns Australia (Prideaux, 2004). Some of the many issues that have been examined include development (Butler, 1980), planning (Inskeep, 1991; Gunn, 1994), economic sustainability (Bramwell 2004), time (Moissec, 1974), locality

(Lavery, 1974), decline (Agarwal, 2002; Gale, 2007), modelling growth paths (Butler, 1980), visitor types (Cohen, 1972; Plog, 1973) and so on.

A number of researchers have also discussed the growth of coastal tourism in the context of the Fordist and Modernist models of economic growth (Gill and Welk, 2007; Torres, 2002; Prideaux, 2004; Aguilo *et al.*, 2005; Uriely *et al.*, 2002; Urry, 1990). From a Fordist perspective the development of modern mass tourism is described as the outcome of new patterns of production and consumption that experienced enormous growth after World War Two (Torres, 2002). Prior to the Fordist period, tourism was largely confined to the wealthy middle and upper classes who had both the time and money to engage in resort vacations in beach localities. The shift in industry production systems from the Fordist era based on manufacturing, to the Post-Fordist or Neo-Fordist-based era centred on the service sector, has been reflected in an increased demand for new forms of individualized, small-scale, specialized niche tourism experiences (Smeral, 1998; Torres, 2002). From an alternative perspective these forces, described by Urry (1990) as a move from Modernism to Post-modernism, have influenced recent coastal resort development as tourists seek less standardized experiences. Poon (1989, 1993) described this shift from the perspective of the 'old tourist', a person engaged in Fordist style mass tourism, to the 'new tourist' who seeks more differentiated Post-Fordist or Post-modernist experiences. Recent research indicates that the demand for differentiated tourism experiences of the type embodied in the Post-Fordist and Post-Modernist models has influenced the physical structure of resorts (Aguiló *et al.*, 2005; Reichel and Uriely, 2002).

Many coastal resorts developed in peripheral areas, creating a pleasure periphery. The mobility of the modern tourist, a consequence of new high-speed, high-capacity transport systems based on aircraft, fast trains, Cruise ships in some areas and the automobile have reduced the tyranny of distance previously experienced by the periphery and promoted both sunlust and wanderlust tourism resort development in coastal areas (Papatheodorou, 2004). As a result, the Caribbean, parts of South East Asia and the Mediterranean have emerged as growth poles for sunlust and wanderlust tourism. According to Papatheodorou (2004) a dualism has developed in the pattern of development where sunlust and wanderlust resorts have become the focus of mass tourism typified by budget package travel while also promoting the idiosyncratic elements of their built and natural environments that facilitate experiences more correctly classed as Post-modernist. Case Study 7.1 illustrates how one resort has been able to develop a suit of experiences and accommodation that fulfils the expectations of both types of tourists. This development is illustrated in Figure 7.1 with a continuum where mass industrial scale tourism occupies one end of the continuum and individual experiences occupy the other end. It is

Individual Tourism	**Mass Tourism**
Production System - Post-Fordist - Postmodernist - New Tourism	**Production System** - Fordist - Modernist - Old tourism

Characteristics
- Small scale eco friendly
  accommodation
- Individualised tours
- Low overall vistor numbers
	Characteristics
	- Large resort hotels
	- Commodified
	  attractions
	- Mass tours

	Examples - Phuket - Cancun - Honoulu

FIGURE 7.2 *The tourism activity continuum.*

possible to envisage a tourism continuum of this nature where Fordist style mass tourism is shown on the right and Post-Fordist, individual tourism is illustrated to the left of the continuum. In reality mass tourism on an industry scale (Leiper, 1979) continues to be a major form of tourism activity and it is unlikely that given the shear size of tourism demand the individual style tourism activity depicted in Figure 7.2 will ever constitute more than a small percentage of total tourism demand. As discussed in Case study 7.1, the reality is more likely to be positioning of many resorts somewhere between the two extremes of the continuum.

Case Study 7.1

Cairns, located in the tropical zone of northern Australia, attracts over 2 million visitors per year which would at first glance indicate its positioning as a mass tourism resort. Seaward of the city, the World Heritage listed Great Barrier Reef has emerged as one of the city's major tourism icons while landward, the World Heritage listed Wet Tropics Rainforests has also become a major tourism drawcard. Most tourists are accommodated in high-rise hotels and serviced apartments located on or adjacent to the shoreline and visit the region's major natural attractions in a manner that suggests mass tourism. The rainforest and its animals are usually experienced in a commodified form via a commercial rainforest tour or a visit to a commercial rainforest or animal attraction while the reef is visited via a reef cruise boat. Beyond the city core a small number of ecotourism lodges located in the tropical rainforest offer accommodation that falls in the Post-Fordist/Post-Modernist end of the activity continuum. Similarly, visitors are able to join a growing number of personalized guided tours to both the reef and the rainforest that may be placed towards the Post-Fordist/Post-Modernist end of the activity continuum. The structure of the industry in Cairns supports Papatheodorou's notion of dualism that incorporates features of both Modernism and Post-modernism. A resort of this nature illustrates the reality that mass tourism experiences will continue to form a significant part of the tourism experience in most destinations, while simultaneously providing opportunities for more individual and small-scale tourism experiences.

Planning

In the first wave of British seaside resort, development occurred within the framework of the contemporary understanding of planning and as a consequence, a zoning hierarchy emerged that may still be observed. This tradition of planning continues into the present in nations in the developed world although it is a more recent development in many other areas. In a number of the resorts that developed in Asia and elsewhere in the 1970s and 1980s development was rapid, almost spontaneous and often without the guidance of planning schemes. In many areas including Pattaya in Thailand the pursuit of profit by investors, the slow response of government combined with corruption and ignorance of the significance of potential physical and environment impacts, created a series of resorts that were substandard (Wong, 1998). In the case of Pattaya beachfront development and inadequate infrastructure resulted in pollution, coral reef destruction, depletion of fish stocks and severe beach erosion. This pattern was repeated in many areas. A common theme in resorts of this nature is the disregard of the need for buffer zones of the nature illustrated in Figure 7.3 with construction being allowed to occur almost to the beach front as illustrated in Figure 7.4 taken in early morning on the Copacabana Beach in Rio de Janeiro. In Figure 7.3 zoning laws require hotels to be low rise and built away from the beach. Behind the screen of trees at the top of the photo is a hotel zone over 2 km in length.

In contrast to the spontaneous and largely unplanned development of resorts typified by Pattaya, more recent resorts have been built with the guidance of integrated planning schemes. Examples include Nusa Dua in Bali, Laguna Phulet in Thailand and Cancun in Mexico. In these resorts, more attention has been paid to infrastructure development, transport corridors, waste disposal and development that is sympathetic to the natural environment. However, even where integrated planning has occurred, insufficient understanding of the coastal environment can still create significant problems including pollution, habitat loss, erosion and social problems for the resort's original residents. As Wong (1998) observed, the use of hard coastal protection measures, inadequate setback and destruction of mangrove forests suggests that developers have failed to understand the consequences of poor development.

Many governments have recognized that effective coastal planning requires: comprehensive environmental assessment of all development proposals; identification of carrying capacity levels prior to development being undertaken; enforcement of policies and regulations; and that increased attention is paid to conservation and long-term economic and biological sustainability. Corruption continues to pervade development in many

FIGURE 7.3 *Kewarra Beach, Cairns. This photo illustrates a coastal destination where low-rise accommodation has been constructed behind a screen of beach front trees. (See colour insert.)*
Source: Photo courtesy of Bruce Prideaux.

FIGURE 7.4 *Intrusive beach front development on the Copacabana in Rio de Janeiro.*
Source: Photo courtesy of Bruce Prideaux.

areas particularly, but not only, in the developing world leading to substandard development. Beyond specific instances of corruption is a more subtle form of mismanagement where collusion between developers and public officials results in legal yet substandard development. In their haste to promote development it is not uncommon for Local Government Authorities to soften planning laws allowing development to occur in places and forms that are less than desirable. After the development is sold, the developer is able to walk away from any responsibility leaving the owner and in some cases the approving Local Government Authority to rectify the problems. Development practices of this nature were responsible for some of the damage suffered at Phuket during the 2004 tsunami.

In a recent book on mass coastal tourism in Southern Europe Bramwell (2004:3) observed that *'surprisingly few books (have) ... focus(ed) on the development and planning of coastal tourism and that there has been only a limited critical assessment of strategies'*. Beyond Bramwell's comments it is even more surprising that the larger issue of coastal zone tourism that embraces non-tourist specific coastal cities and other forms of tourism activity in the coastal zone has been almost completely ignored by tourism scholars. In the near future, if not already, it will become increasingly important to understand how tourism operates within the Coastal Zone. The following discussion focuses on the new reality where tourism resorts are only part of a much larger tourism system that operated within the coastal zone.

New forms of coastal zone tourism

While it is unlikely that there will be a reduction in the scale of tourism in the traditional beach centred coastal resort sector, tourism in the emerging coastal cities will rapidly overtake beach resorts in visitor numbers and economic significance. The shift in focus can be explained by several parallel forces. The move from the mass tourism of the 'old tourist' paradigm described by Poon (1989, 1993) to the 'new tourist', or from another perspective, the shift from packaged tourism of the neo-Fordist sun and sand tourist to 'post-Fordist' tourism described by Urry (2002), is in part made possible by the greater range of activities available in cities in the coastal zone. Size is another factor. Globally, cities in the coastal zone are growing rapidly and are attracting visitors interested in the activities that are a by-product of city growth including entertainment, shopping and leisure activities as well as business, visiting friends and family, the MICE market and for services such as health, education and entertainment. While it is apparent that the major focus of tourism interest in the coastal zone is shifting to coastal zone cities there is no evidence to suggest that the traditional beach centric resorts sector will suffer a decline in interest.

FIGURE 7.5   *The Sydney Opera House. (See colour insert.)*
Source: Courtesy of Bruce Prideaux.

Figure 7.5 illustrates the seaside location of the Sydney Opera House which, while an iconic building and one visited by numerous visitors, was built primarily as a venue for a wide range of orchestral and theatrical performances for Sydney residents rather than as a tourism attraction. Within the cities of the coastal zone tourism activity is less obvious and tourism flows are often difficult to discern from the normal pattern of intracity travel for recreation, leisure, shopping and entertainment.

One significant outcome of rapid urbanization in the last 60 years has been the growth of coastal mega cities. According to Li (2003), about half of the world's population lives within 60 km of the shoreline and in the next 30 years coastal populations could double, spurred on by the development of coastal mega cities and even larger urban forms such as the megalopolis described in Chapter 6. In the rapidly growing coastal zone super cities, it is the attractions offered by the city rather than its location in the coastal zone that is emerging as the central focus of visitor interest. In the emerging megalopolis on the Pearl Delta in southern China comprising Hong Kong, Shenxeun, Macau, Zhongshan and Guangzhou, it is the urban space and its offer of interesting activities and places rather than the beach that has become the main focus of attention. In Macau for example, beaches are available but rarely visited by tourists who are more interested in the city's

FIGURE 7.6   *One of the 29 Casinos that typifies contemporary Macau.*
Source: Courtesy of Bruce Prideaux.

29 casinos (see Figure 7.6) and shopping opportunities. This trend is reflected in numerous other coastal cities.

It is apparent that a duality in coastal tourism is rapidly developing where the new coastal super city structures will emerge as the major centres for coastal tourism while the traditional sand and sun resorts will continue growing but become increasingly less important in overall visitor nights and revenue generated. In some areas traditional sand and sun attractions will come under pressure from encroachment by other industries seeking coastal land including developers converting resort hotels into residential apartments, a trend that is demonstrated by Atlantic City, USA where a number of the grand resort hotels built during the 1920s have been converted into apartment. From this perspective it will become increasingly important to understand the dynamics of these new coastal cities and the position they hold within the tourism system as both destinations and generating regions.

Hall (2001:602) described coastal tourism as embracing '... *the full range of tourism, leisure, and recreational activities that take part in the coastal zone and the offshore waters. These include coastal tourism development (accommodation, restaurants, food industry, and second homes), and the infrastructure supporting coastal development (e.g. retail businesses, marinas and activity suppliers). Also included are tourism activities such as recreational boating, coastal and marine-based ecotourism, cruises, swimming, recreational fishing, snorkelling and diving'*. While inclusive of the major forms of tourism activity that occur in the coastal zone the definition needs to be broadened to introduce the idea of coastal zone cities that may have a limited interest in promoting tourism. In this context coastal tourism can be described as embracing all forms of tourism activity that occurs within the coastal zone including intracity and intercity, day and overnight tourism-related activities.

The growth of coastal zone cities has created the need to broaden our understanding of coastal tourism to encompass not only the traditional view of the beachside resort but to now include holiday and other forms of travel within the coastal zone, particularly where this activity takes place in cities located in this zone. In this broader context a visit to the beach is now becoming no more than one of many opportunities available. These opportunities will most probably retain the S of sex but delete the other three S's of beach tourism and include the S of shopping, the E of entertainment and the P of participation in a range of activities including museums, heritage precincts, sporting activities, visits to natural areas and so on. Thus the four Ss might metamorphose into SESP or some similar acronym. It is also likely that operators in this new tourism zone will have to work harder for recognition and be more aggressive in developing their case for recognition by government and for an equitable share of resources. It is this point that is of particular importance given Hall's (2001) observation that there is often little or no coordination between programs that promote tourism and the managers of planning agencies that are responsible for overseeing development in the coastal zone.

In the past coastal resorts developed as a response to increased leisure time, increased income and a desire to engage in activities in an atmosphere that did not have to conform to the time and energy dictates of the work week. In the emerging coastal zone cities the same factors continue to apply but are supplemented by other factors including health, education, visiting friends and relatives, business, shopping and the myriad of other activities encapsulated in the activities typology described earlier in Figure 6.6.

The shift in emphasis from the beach to the more holistic view of coastal destinations is demonstrated in Sydney where the appeal of the city's magnificent surf beaches continues to attract visitors but increasingly the beaches have to compete with other attractions in the city, a trend now recognized by hoteliers who have sought central city locations over beach locations for almost all new hotel constructions in the past two decades. This shift has been aided by enhanced mobility via public and private transport and new information technologies that allow electronic pre-booking and greater and faster access to visitor information. Hotel location is a fascinating index of the attractiveness of one urban location over another. In the past hotels clustered around transport terminals, business districts and in the case of beach resorts adjacent to the beach. In the new coastal zone city, hotels have moved from the beach zone to locate in areas where visitors are attracted to including the business district, entertainment zones, airports and shopping districts.

The typology illustrated in Figure 7.7 seeks to encompass some of the types of coastal cities that have emerged as attractive tourism destinations. It should be noted that the location of a city in a coastal location presupposes some maritime activity as well as manufacturing and in many cases

Primary City Function	Activities	Example
Multi function	Port, manufacturing, administration, commerce, distribution etc and tourism	Hong Kong, New York, Boston (USA), London, Singapore
Port	Trade, maritime, activities and associated manufacturing	Rotterdam (Netherlands), Antwerp (Belguim), Osaka (Japan)
Administrative capital	Port industries, administration	Port Moresby (PNG), Port Villa (Vanuatu)
Manufacturing centre	Primarily concerned with manufacturing and distribution	Gladstone (Australia)
Traditional seaside town	Beach focus supplemented by a range of activities that might include shopping, theme parks and dinning	Brighton (UK), Blackpool (UK)
Service city	Recent in origin and includes finance, wholesaling, education	Shenxeun and Zhongshan in the Pearl Delta China
Historic city	Maritime heritage	Dubrovnik (Croatia), Malacca (Malaysia)
Transport hub	Often located within the coastal zone but not necessarily by the sea and acts as a transport interchange	Bristol (UK)
Military	Defensive role	Gibraltar, Aden
Integrated coastal resort	Designed specifically as a tourism resort	Nusa Due (Indonesia), Cancun (Mexico)
Transformed Fishing/Port Village	Original functions of fishing and/or cargo port transformed by tourism interest	Cabo San Lucas (Mexico), Padstow (Cornwell, UK)

FIGURE 7.7 *Typology of coastal tourism destinations.*

cities can more accurately be defined as multi-function entities. Many lack beaches because of geography or when they are present, may have limited use because of climatic factors. However, the lack of a beach has not prevented many coastal cities adopting strategies to develop tourism but within the context of existing industry structures. Hong Kong emerged primarily as a port to service the interest of British traders operating in southern China. Later it acquired other functions including manufacturing, education, service and more recently tourism. While Hong Kong does have a small number of beaches these have never been promoted as major tourism attractions. Figure 7.8 illustrates Hong Kong's spectacular waterfront vista where almost all of the building illustrated are concerned with the city's role as a financial and commercial centre. The coastal city types listed in Figure 7.7 reflect the range of functions that cities perform in the zone. To the functions listed in Figure 7.7 can be added finance, administration, military, education, entertainment and services industries, health and commodity trading. In each of these city types the importance of tourism as an industry sector may vary between minor to major.

Paralleling the influx of new residents into coastal cities are tourists seeking many of the opportunities sought by the residents of the city, though for a shorter period of time. It is this part of the tourism phenomenon that

FIGURE 7.8 *The finance and commerce dominated skyline of Hong Kong Island.*
(See colour insert.)
Source: Courtesy of Bruce Prideaux.

has been largely ignored in the literature on coastal tourism. As discussed in Chapter 6, Ashworth and Tunbridge (2000) differentiate between tourist use and resident use of a city's attractions by identifying four classes of visitors: *intentional users from outside* visiting the city region for excursions: *intentional users from inside* the city region making use of the city's recreation/ entertainment facilities (recreating residents): *incidental users from outside* the city region, which includes business and conference visitors and those on family visits (non-recreating visitors): and *incidental users from inside* the city region, the most numerous group being ordinary residents (non-recreating residents). Given the size of the emerging cities of the coastal zone where the distance from one side of the city to the other may be many tens of kilometres, it is not difficult to image situations where residents of the core of the city may regard a visit to an attraction on the edge of the city as a day trip or even as an overnight stay.

Tourism activity in the coastal zone can be grouped into four major categories and within each category it is possible to identify numerous specific activity types (Hall, 2001). The categories are described as:

- *Urban*. This refers to tourism activity in the large coastal zone cities that continue to emerge throughout the world. Tourism activity in these cities may have little to do with current concepts of coastal resort tourism and more to do with the activities that are city focused including shopping, entertainment, recreation, health, wellbeing and heritage.
- *Resort*. Traditional resort tourism usually defined by the four Ss of sand, sun, sea and sex will continue to form an important part of the global tourism industry. It is likely that new coastal resorts will continue to emerge both in the developing and in the developed world and provide both mass and Post-Fordist styles of holiday experiences.
- *Nature*. A growing number of locations that are included in this category are coral reefs, geo parks, marches, biological hot spot regions, rainforest, coniferous forests, marine parks and nature parks. Activities vary enormously and may include walking, canoeing, hunting, camping, fishing, boating and bird watching amongst others. It is likely that with increasing recognition of the value of natural areas for recreation, water catchment areas, as biological refuges, and their contribution to ecosystem services there will be pressure for the declaration of additional protected areas as well as increases in the size of existing protected areas.
- *Marine*. In the marine zone activities may overlap with the previous category including not only visiting coral reefs and fishing but also ocean fishing, sailing, boating, diving, snorkelling and ocean cruising.

Environmental impacts

In analysing the impact of tourism on the coastal zone consideration needs to be given to environmental concerns. New technologies have made the coastal zone more accessible and marine areas in particular have suffered through overfishing, clearing of mangrove forests, marina construction, foreshore development and poor management of coral reefs. Of particular concern is the overall lack of understanding of the interaction between tourism and the environment in coastal areas. All too often, discussion on the impact of tourism deals with generalities rather than the outcomes of scientific research on tourism impacts.

There is a pressing case for tourism researchers, planners and investors to make greater use of science as a tool for understanding the environment in which the industry operates. Failure to actively seek out and incorporate good science into all aspects of planning and management may result in suboptimal development, poor business returns, loss of long-term sustainability and create problems that will need future remediation. The need for science is most apparent in areas where tourism activity occurs in natural areas. Chapter 8, for example, comments on the need for a more rigorous science-based approach to planning ski resorts in sensitive mountain regions. Tourism activity on coral reefs provides a useful example of the need for science in coastal areas. Reefs are attractive but fragile ecosystems subject to damage by human activity. Where little attention has been paid to regulating their use for tourism-related activities the reef ecosystem is likely to suffer reducing their appeal. Burke and Maidens (2004), in a report on the worldwide state of coral reefs, noted that compared to the Great Barrier Reef, Caribbean reefs had suffered extensive damage from fishing and tourism-related activities, primarily because of poor management. In areas where active scientific investigation has underpinned management schemes the biological integrity of reefs has been retained and their appeal enhanced.

Management of the Great Barrier Reef (GBR) in Australia is actively guided by science resulting in a natural asset that continues to retain its biological integrity although it is visited by two million visitors per year. In the GBR, all reef tour operators undergo stringent licensing conditions and the reef, which contains approximately 40% of the world's coral, has been divided into a number of zones including no-go zones that act as a refuge for species under pressure. In a similar example, the declaration of Marine Protected Areas (MPA) commencing from 1982 in Belize has achieved considerable success in protecting the Belize Barrier Reef from a number of threats. Estimated to contribute up to 30% of the country's gross domestic product (Cho, 2005) through commercial fisheries and tourism, the protection afforded by the MPA system introduced by the Belize Government has been effective although major challenges remain including financial sustainability of the management authority.

In an analysis of coastal tourism development in southern India, Damodaran (2006) pointed out that increased interest in tourism development involves the challenge of balancing the objectives of conservation and social equity with economic development. Damodaran observed that coastal development has contributed to the disintegration of traditional seashore commons which, in turn, had led to the breakdown in the livelihoods of local communities that relied on these commons for grazing. In Mexico, Ortiz-Lozano *et al.* (2005) found that the coastal zone is the main source of foreign currency for the country, with petrochemical chemical industries and resort tourism being the largest contributors. Noting that the Mexican government had yet to coherently organize and collect data on the coastal zone the authors found that there were a number of serious social and ecological problems associated with tourism development in the coastal zone. These include pressure on natural resources from the large number of coastal resorts that had been built without proper consideration of their impact on the local environment, habitat destruction and problems with negative effects on water quality.

In Turkey Burak *et al.* (2004) highlight the impact that uncontrolled tourism development has had on coastal ecology. Disruption of the ecological balance that has resulted from pollution of coastal waters has generated local eutrophication while construction of marinas has had a major impact on coastal flora and fauna. On the land, excessive demands for groundwater reservoirs have lowered coastal watertables leading to seawater intrusion into coastal aquifers.

A summary of environmental and ecological impacts that arise from tourism activity (see Hall, 2001) includes:

■ Environmental degradation and pollution,
■ Destruction of habits and ecosystem damage,
■ Species loss,
■ Loss of coastal and marine resources,
■ Coastal pollution, and
■ Groundwater and surface water diversion.

To these environmental issues can be added a number of social and moral issues:

■ Loss of built heritage,
■ Loss of livelihood,
■ Displacement of original residents,
■ Decline in the resilience of the local community,
■ Cultural disruption, and
■ Increased crime.

Development opportunity model

While the preceding list of negative impacts is lengthy and at first glance so damming that coastal tourism development appears to be a poor development alternative, the reality is that with effective planning within the ICM process, many of the negatives can be mitigated. Moreover, tourism development creates employment and importantly generates wealth, some of which finds its way into government revenue that can then be redistributed through the social security system and government infrastructure schemes to improve the quality of life of coastal residents. For the tourism industry to make a positive contribution it is essential that the industry actively participates in ICM. Figure 7.9 seeks to encapsulate the position of the tourism industry within the much larger coastal zone economy.

The major factors influencing development in coastal zones include the structure of existing communities (including skill base), major industries and

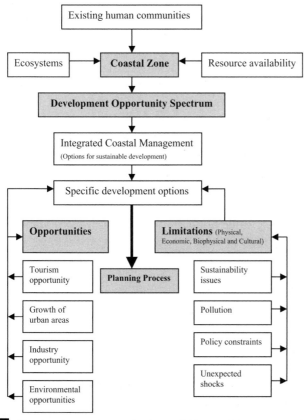

 FIGURE 7.9   *The development opportunity model in coastal zone areas.*

administrative roles, the structure and robustness/fragility of existing ecosystems and the availability of resources. In the sense used here resources include land, water, minerals, biological resources (forests for example), investment funds and weather (temperature, hours of sunlight, precipitation). Collectively, these factors indicate the capacity of a particular area to be developed and in Figure 7.9 is represented as a development opportunity model. The concept of a development opportunity recognizes that some forms of development may be complimentary while others may be exclusive. For example, a wetland can be preserved as a tourism resource or drained and used for urban development. The two forms of development are not complementary. In Figure 7.9 major limitations are shown as sustainability issues, pollution and policy constraints. Collectively, these define the particular development options that are available. Development opportunities include tourism opportunities, lifestyle options, public sector options, environmental options and industry options. Lifestyle options may be used to either determine the form of development to be encouraged or may be an outcome of the form of development adopted. In the form presented in Figure 7.9 the Development Opportunity model provides a useful conceptual model that illustrates the collective factors that exercise a significant influence on the scale of tourism development vis a vies other industry sectors that may be seeking locations in the coastal zone. Following a review of the resources available in the zone and the resilience of the zone's ecosystem, opportunities are able to be identified and integrated planning may be undertaken. Options will become apparent and trade-offs may be required if not all industries can be given the space they require. Options will be determined by limitations including physical, economic, biophysical and cultural.

Ideally the process outlined in the Development Opportunity model will allow policy makers and planners to identify options for future development and then assess the value of these options through consultation with stakeholders and the use of evaluative tools such as cost–benefit analysis. Once a specific policy direction has been identified planning can commence, ideally following the structure outlined in Figure 3.2. As an open system, the process of development is subject to many influences including shocks of the nature discussed in Chapter 5.

FUTURE THREATS TO THE COASTAL ZONE

This chapter has highlighted a number of threats that are faced by the tourism industry operating in the coastal zone. The management of these threats has proved difficult because growth has been rapid and driven by the forces of economic growth that have in the past preferred to ignore these threats particularly if profits are affected. Three recent disasters highlight the seriousness of the problems that confront contemporary trends in coastal development. In each case it appears that there has been an underlying assumption that nature can be dominated and therefore largely discounted as a force that needs to be taken into account as a primary determinant of the size, form and extent to which coastal systems can be modified. The 2004 Tsunami highlighted the dangers that coastal zones face from undersea earthquakes (Laws *et al.*, 2007). The Thai resort of Phuket suffered considerable damage during the tsunami. Defences against events of this nature are difficult to build leaving early detection and warning as the main strategy for preventing significant loss of life but not property. Prediction of events of this nature remains an illusive goal. The damage wrought by Hurricane Katrina on New Orleans (2005) was a further example of the difficulty of building coastal defences to protect low lying urban areas from massive wind storms (cyclones, hurricanes and typhoons) as well as an example of how the destruction of natural defences including reefs and mangrove forests can increase the severity of damage (Laws *et al.*, 2007). The final recent example of the dangers that coastal areas face was demonstrated by Cyclone Nargis which struck the delta area of the Irrawaddy River in Burma on 2 May 2008. Driven by strong winds generated by the category three cyclone a wall of water swept over the delta destroying villages and towns, killing an estimated 100,000 and leaving another estimated 1.7 million homeless. Initial assessments of the damage point to the removal of coastal mangroves forests as one of the factors that exacerbated the damage caused by the cyclone.

If the predictions of climate change generated sea level rises occur coastal cities will have to decide if they should defend their current low lying areas against rising sea levels in the manner that the Dutch protect vast areas with dykes or accept defeat and migrate inland. The prospect of defending vast areas of urban areas against rising sea levels should be measured against the cost of defences failing as in the case of New Orleans.

The magnitude of the impacts that may occur and the policy responses that will be required are daunting. During past glacial phases global sea levels have been up to 120 m, (or more) below present levels (CSIRO Sea Level Rises http://www.cmar.csiro.au/sealevel/sl_hist_intro.html#140). There are several schools of thought about global movements in seawater levels. One school has assumed a steady state of return of meltwaters from ice caps and sheet ice to the oceans resulting in a steady rise in sea levels. Another school advocates that sea level rises in the past have been episodic, that is periods of fast rises punctuated by short pauses. Geological evidence (CSIRO Sea Level Rises http://www.cmar.csiro.au/sealevel/sl_hist_intro.html#140) indicates that the last time the sea was at its current level was about 120,000 years ago during the last interglacial period and Greenland was about 3 °C warmer than today.

In recent decades coastal areas have become hotspots for urban growth and the areas occupied are often low and will be subject to inundation if sea levels rise. If Greenland's ice cap melts completely sea levels will rise by approximately 7 m (Hansen, 2007). Current IPPC (2007) predictions indicate a rise of between 18 and 59 cm this century depending on the success of global strategies to reduce CO_2; however as Hansen (2007) noted dynamic thinning and other wild cards may accelerate disintegration with resulting sea level changes in the order of metres.

To the catalogue of risks must be added threats posed by growing water scarcity, peak oil and food security. From the previous discussion it is obvious that future analysis of tourism activity in the coastal zone must occur within the context of the ICM and will need to be aware of competing demands for the resources required for tourism.

CONCLUSION

Previous research into coastal tourism has primarily focused on coastal towns and cities that had developed as resorts. Investigations included identification of the drivers of growth and their consequences, identification and analysis of threats and impacts and aspects of marketing. Given the accelerating growth of cities located in the coastal zone and the new roles many of these cities have in the post-industrial landscape it is apparent that research needs to be urgently refocused. As this chapter has highlighted, the direction that tourism is taking in the coastal zone is very different to the traditional interpretation of tourism activity in this area. The reality of the new phenomenon of coastal mega cities and other major coastal cities is that they represent the future of coastal tourism. The relationships between tourism, other land uses and industry sectors located in this zone are not well understood but are fundamental to the operation of the tourism industry.

This chapter has raised a number of issues that have been largely ignored in the tourism literature. Of particular importance is the need for a re-evaluation of the role of tourism within the coastal zone and the role that the tourism industry must play in ICM. Future research directions should include the application of urban tourism principles to cities in the coastal zone, the role of tourism in ICM and a deeper appreciation of environmental issues and the science that informs on these issues.

Of increasing concern are the long-term impacts of climate change. While there is considerable scientific debate on the possible impacts of climate change the tourism literature has been largely silent. It is essential that more attention be paid to this issue in the tourism literature if for no other reason than to gauge the impact that mitigation and adaptation policies will have on the scale and operation of tourism in the coastal zone. The possible impact of sea level rises above the level predicted by the IPCC (2007) also needs to be considered. If sea level rise is in the order of metres rather than centimetres coastal resorts are in considerable danger. Research challenges include examination of community resilience to the effects of climate change and investigation into how tourism operations will be affected and how they will respond.

KEY ISSUES

- Tourism researchers have largely ignored the importance of Integrated Coastal Management.
- The scale of growth of coastal cities is enormous and the role that tourism plays in these cities is not well understood.
- Traditional coastal resorts will continue to attract significant tourism flows, climate change impacts not withstanding.
- Mass tourism will continue to flourish alongside Post-Fordists/ Post-modernists forms of tourism demand.
- Major threats to coastal zone tourism include the pressures of urbanization and climate change.
- If sea levels rise significantly many coastal resorts will face the danger of inundation.

CHAPTER 8

Mountain Destinations

Created by isolation, celebrated for their uniqueness but endangered by their attractiveness

Mountains are dominating features of the landscape occupying approximately a quarter of the Earth's land surface, including 54% of the land area of Asia and 36% of the landmass of North American. In some European traditions mountains were viewed as places of isolation, of fascination and as fearsome places inhabited by trolls and dragons (Bernbaum, 1997). In other cultures mountains were thought to be the home of gods and were the objects of worship. In China and Korea mountains were viewed in a different light to those in Europe and were seen as places of retreat, Mt Gumgang in Korea being one of numerous examples, and as ideal locations for places of worship. The remoteness and isolation of mountains, a result of both location and difficulty of access in the era before the construction of modern high speed transport networks, resulted in the emergence of mountain communities where lifestyles and cultures differed from those of surrounding lowland communities leading to the popularization of a view of mountain communities as backward and places to be avoided.

In the contemporary era, mountains continue to be places of fascination with a growing range of tourism activities. Their re-invention as desirable places has facilitated the emergence of mountain enclaves that exhibit quite different features from most other destinations. The forms of tourism that have emerged in mountainous regions include eco-tourism, nature-based tourism, alternative tourism, winter tourism, rural tourism, adventure tourism and small-scale tourism (Weaver, 1998; Fennel, 1999). Recent interest in mountain tourism (Godde *et al.*, 2000) is also linked to an increasing concern for ecosystems considered to be 'fragile' or affected by human activities. The significance of mountain tourism development has also been recognized by a number of international organizations including UNCED (Godde *et al.*, 2000)

Resort Destinations: Evolution, Management and Development

and UNECSO's World Heritage Program. Of the 851 proprieties on UNESCO's world heritage list in 2006 approximately 25% were either mountain regions or build and natural sites located in mountain regions.

There is a small but growing body of research on tourism usage of mountains both within and outside of the tourism literature. Within the tourism literature research has examining issues that include sustainability (Miles and Couin, 2000), activities (Hudson, 2000), environmental stewardship (Hudson and Miller, 2005), community development (Gurung and De Coursey, 1999) and mountain culture (Pfisher, 2000). In other literatures the focus of research has centred on issues that included community development, cultural heritage disaster planning and recovery, sustainability (Barry, 2003) and planning. This chapter draws from this growing body of research to overview a range of issues that concern the development, operation, planning and sustainability of destinations within mountains settings. Given the large number of mountain landscapes, their diversity and the range of issues that affect their development as mountain destinations, coverage of this topic is necessarily broad.

Mountains are often dangerous places where bad weather, temperature extremes, rugged landscapes, avalanches and lack of shelter can mean injury or loss of life for the unprepared. Yet within this landscape a wide range of tourism-related activities have emerged, based on the unique resources found in mountainous regions. Touristic activities include those that rely on landforms, weather, the ecosystem and the cultural and heritage resources that have been developed by mountain communities. The development of tourism activities in these settings requires recognition of the sensitivity of mountains ecosystems, the desirability of achieving sustainability, accessibility issues, community issues, work force issues, political issues, cultural issues and in the near future the impact of climate change. Planning is therefore a significant issue and must be present in all aspects of mountain destination activity including management, investment in new facilities, rejuvenation of existing areas, community development, environmental management and in marketing. Unfortunately, in many mountainous regions the required level of planning and care for the environment has yet to be achieved.

Following a discussion on the distribution of mountainous destinations from a global perspective, this chapter examines the range of activities that take place in mountain destinations and comments on planning issues. This is followed by an examination of a range of issues that have particular impacts on mountain destinations including sustainability, assess, seasonality and climate change. This chapter uses a number of case studies to illustrate how many of these issues impact on the operation of mountain destinations.

GEOMORPHIC CHARACTERISTICS

Mountain terrains have higher elevation than surrounding areas and in many cases form component parts of mountain belts and ranges. Examples of mountain belts include the Andes in South America, the Rockies in North America and the Himalayas in Asia. Mountain belts and chains are the result of tectonic processes including volcanism, folding and elevation. Mountain ranges have both terrestrial and oceanic locations with the Hawaiian Islands forming the visible part of a much larger mid-oceanic belt of submerged extinct, dormant and active volcanoes. Folding of sedimentary rock to form long ridges and valleys is a common form of mountain building along with volcanism and elevation. In the case of elevation the resulting mountain systems may develop as mountain belts, chains or in small number of cases isolated ranges. A further form of mountain building occurs when plateaus or large uplifted areas are eroded away to form residual mountains. Examples of this form of mountain building which may occur over a period lasting in excess of one hundred million years are the Urals in Russia and the Appalachians in the USA.

DISTRIBUTION

Mountain landscapes may be examined from a number of perspectives including highland/lowlands, plateaus and a coastal mountain/interior mountain perspective. Because of their location mountain regions have climatic patterns that differ from surrounding lowlands. Endemic flora and fauna communities have evolved to create unique altitude and climate dependent ecosystems. Similarly, human communities that have migrated into mountainous regions have been forced to adapt to extreme climates and fragile ecosystems and through this process have created unique social, cultural and economic responses that set them apart from those in surrounding lowlands. The uniqueness of mountain societies is often expressed in material culture, dance, festivals and architecture. In some instances the rugged nature of the terrain has resulted in the emergence of localized cultures that differ from those even in nearby valleys. In New Guinea, the mountainous nature of much of the country has led to the development of nearly 800 different language groups and tribal cultures most with cultures that have developed in isolation even from nearby tribes because of the impenetrable nature of the terrain.

While there are mountainous regions in most countries, a small group of countries occupy positions almost entirely located within mountainous regions or highlands. Countries in this group are usually landlocked and include Bolivia, Nepal, Bhutan, Switzerland and Austria (see Table 8.1). These nations exhibit many differences including climate, ecosystems, cultural

TABLE 8.1 Landlocked Countries Which Have Extensive Mountainous or Plateau Areas			
Africa	**Asia**	**Europe**	**South America**
Swaziland	Mongolia	Austria	Bolivia
Uganda	Afghanistan	Switzerland	
Lesotho	Kazakhstan	Georgia	
Ethiopia	Kyrgyzstan	Andorra	
Central African Republic	Turkmenistan	Armenia	
Rwanda	Laos	Macedonia (F.Y.R.O.M.)	
Burundi	Nepal	Slovakia	
Central African Republic	Bhutan	Kosovo	
Chad	Azerbaijan	Liechtenstein	
Malawi	Tajikistan	San Marino	
Zambia	Uzbekistan		

heritage and stage of economic development. Switzerland and Austria are examples of first world economies that have long histories of human habitation and use of mountains for recreation and have progressive first world economies. In comparison, both Nepal and Bhutan typify third world economies that have long histories of human habitation but with a much shorter history of the use of mountains for domestic recreation and in more recent times for international tourism. Another group of nations including Japan, South Korea, Sweden and Norway have a very high percentage of their landmass occupied by mountains.

Many mountain-located countries in Asia, Africa, South America and even parts of Europe have only recently begun to develop a tourism sector. In Africa these include Rwanda (Grosspietsch, 2006), Uganda (Lepp, 2007), Swaziland (Harrison, 1994) and Lesotho (Harrison, 1995). In Asia, a number of countries including Mongolia (Yu and Goulden, 2006), and the former USSR Republics of Kyrgyzstan, Uzbekistan (Airey and Shackley, 1997; Kantarci, 2007), Armenia (Kantarci, 2007), Kyrgyzstan (Kantarci, 2007), Kazakhstan (Kantarci, 2007), Turkmenistan (Kantarci, 2007) have recently begun to focus on tourism. In Europe a number of countries that were previously incorporated in the Former USSR and Yugoslavia have also began to show interest in developing tourism, however in some cases including Moldavia (former USSR) and Macedonia (former Yugoslavia) recent political unrest has impeded progress.

Within nations that have substantial mountainous areas there is also a growing emphasis on mountain tourism particularly as national middle classes develop. In China for example, the Province of Yunnan (Prideaux and Tao, 2005) has experienced rapid growth in domestic and international tourism underpinned by the development of new destinations such as Zhongdian on the lower Tibetan Plateau and Lijang which was placed on the World Heritage Site list in 1999. Other Chinese mountain destinations that have recently emerged to service the rapidly growing domestic market include Mt Lushan in Jiangxi Province, Mt Huangshan in Anhui Province and Mt Wuji in Fujian Province.

From the mid-20th century the convergence of a number of global trends has opened almost every country to tourism development. These trends include: the growth in mass tourism commencing from the mid-20th century, rising GDP in many countries, the lack of major global conflicts since the conclusion of the Second World War, the introduction of new travel friendly technologies; and more lately the new opportunities made possible by the internet revolution. Decolonization which was largely completed by the collapse of the USSR in 1991 has also had a major impact on the tourism industry opening new regions for tourism development and providing new generating markets. Finally, the emergence of globalization as a new way of organizing economic activity within a global rather than a national context has created a vast number of opportunities for travel and development. Combined, these trends have made travel more accessible and affordable and reduced the barriers of periphery. A consequence of the reduction of the barriers of periphery has been a corresponding reduction in uniqueness as expressed through material culture. While these trends have provided new opportunities for tourism development they have also created situations where financial returns have been given a higher priority than sustainability. Mountain regions in particular are susceptible to unsustainable development either through poor planning, unsustainable development, corruption or ignorance.

HIGHLANDS/LOWLANDS

Most countries have landscapes that include both mountains and lowlands. In countries that have a coastal location it is usual to find a transition from a coastal plain to interior mountain ranges or highland regions. In the United States major mountain ranges are located inland from the coastal plains found on both the east and west coasts. On the west coast the Rocky Mountains have attracted considerable tourism development based primarily on domestic tourism generated by the growing urban populations of coastal cities that include San Francisco, Los Angles and Seattle in addition to other urban areas in the United States. The US mountain states of Montana, Colorado, Utah and Wyoming have emerged as popular ski destinations that include Aspen (Colorado), Snowbird (Utah), Big Mountain (Montana) and Jackson Hole Ski Resort (Wyoming). In the Canadian Rockies ski resorts have been built in many locations including Fernie (British Columbia) and Sunshine Village in Alberta. On the East Coast a similar pattern has emerged with a number of destinations including Killington Mountain Resort and Stowe, both of which are located in Vermont, providing mountain recreation for lowland cities including New York, Boston and Montréal. Similar patterns are found in many Asian nations, Australia, parts of Europe, and in South America.

A relatively common lowland/highland or plains/mountains relationship that has emerged occurs where the mountain hinterland counterpart of a lowland destination supplies a range of complementary attractions to the coastal or lowland destination. This pattern has emerged in many settings including islands, coastal plains flanked by a mountain range and even in landlocked and elevated countries where major cities have emerged as tourism destinations. In Brazil Rio de Janeiro, Latin America's best-known international destination, has a close relationship with its surrounding mountains as illustrated in Figure 8.1. In Australia there are a number of examples of this relationship. The Blue Mountains, west of Sydney, has emerged as a popular

FIGURE 8.1 *The relationship between Rio de Janerino and its surrounding mountains. (Note: Rio de Janerino's most famous landmark, the Statue of Christ is located on the highest feature in the photo illustrating the relationship between the city and its surrounding mountains.) (See colour insert.)*
Source: Photo courtesy of Bruce Prideaux.

day trip destination as well as an overnight destination. Further north, the small mountain village of Mt Tamborine located in the World Heritage listed Boarder Ranges has emerged as a mountain counterpart of the Gold Coast, a major international coastal destination. In Japan ski resorts including Gala-Yuzawa in the Japanese Alps are located in close proximity to Tokyo allowing day trips for skiing and snow boarding. In Thailand, the River Kwai region west of Bangkok and site of the infamous Burma Death Railway of World War Two has experienced rapid growth based on adventure activities designed to attract the youth market.

This form of complimentary development may result in the emergence of mountain destinations that are able to attract visitors from major lowland destinations, often for day tours but also in some cases for overnight stays (see Case Study 8.1 on the Blue Mountains). Generally overshadowed by the larger lowland market, complimentary destinations of this nature usually develop marketing strategies and attractions that complement rather than compete with the major destination they service. The complementary approach enables mountain destinations to engage in co-branding and cooperative marketing allowing them to leverage off the greater market power of the major destination while minimizing investment in the more extensive marketing and infrastructure development that is required to support a stand alone destination. An added benefit for destinations of this nature is their ability to develop a domestic day tourism or even overnight market in the adjoining city in addition to tapping into the citys' own visitor market.

Case Study 8.1 Blue Mountains – An Example of a City/Mountains Complimentary Relationship

The Blue Mountains west of Sydney, Australia is an example of the complimentary relationship that has emerged in many mountain destinations that are located in close proximity to a major lowland city. The Blue Mountains has a long history of attracting day-trippers and overnight visitors from Sydney supplemented in recent decades by a growing number of interstate and international tourists. The pulling power of the Blue Mountains has been recognized by Sydney's tourism industry and day trips to the Blue Mountains are widely featured in the city's promotional materials and marketing campaign. In this sense, the Blue Mountains has been able to develop a visitor market based on visitors to Sydney as well as Sydney residents.

Extending for a distance of approximately 200 km the Blue Mountains form part of the Great Dividing Ranges which runs parallel to the east coast. Erosion of the region's sandstone strata estimated to have been formed 250 million years ago has created a landscape of deep V shaped valleys, sheer exposed cliffs, spectacular limestone caves and deep narrow canyons. The relatively low altitude precludes the use of the region's infrequent snowfall for traditional winter sports. Tourism is one of the Blue Mountains' major industries and attracts in excess of 0.65 million overnight visitors annually.

In a recent guidebook on the mountains, Meredith (2000) described the region as an extraordinary amalgam of old town grandeur juxtaposed on unique natural settings. Early settlement focused on agriculture; however, the opening of a railway line to nearby Sydney in 1868 created significant interest in the region's natural beauty and a large number of second homes were built. Artists, Sydney commuters and retirees followed creating a number of sophisticated mountain townships, the largest of which is Katoomba. Paralleling this development a large number of hotels, guesthouses, chalets and self-catering rental homes were built commencing from the 1880s. During the late 1920s the region attracted 500,000 visitors annually and had about 100 guesthouses with the largest concentration in Katoomba. Visitor numbers declined during World War Two with the decline continuing in the post-war years as interest in mountain tourism waned (Davidson and Spearritt, 2000).

The opening of a cable car service in 1959 to carry tourists over Katoomba Falls provided an injection of investment in the region's tourism industry. Since then a number of new attractions have opened and the region's iconic hotels, including the Carrington and Hydro Majestic (Figure 8.2), have been refurbished. In summer and to a lesser extent in winter the major outdoor activities include walking, bushwalking, camping, mountain-biking, climbing,

FIGURE 8.2 *The recently renovated Hydro Majestic Hotel, Katoomba, an example of the grand hotels built in the 19th century and recently refurbished.*
Source: Photo Courtesy of Bruce Prideaux.

canyoning, abseiling, four wheel driving, hang-gliding and horse riding. Visitor numbers have increased in recent decades and by 2006 had climbed to 2.418 million per annum (http://corporate.tourism.nsw.gov.au/Sites/SiteID6/objLib18/Blue_Mountains_YE_Dec_06[1].pdf).

Meredith (2000:14) observed that '*If nature untamed is the Blue Mountain*'s *prime draw card, nature tamed offers its own grand spectacle*'. Building on the European origins of many of its early settlers, European-style gardens containing exotic scrubs, trees and flowers were planted in surrounds that emphasized the wilderness aspects of the region. Similarly, grand European style hotels and lodges surrounded by carefully manicured European gardens were built in locations that afforded the most spectacular views of the mountain vistas and vast native forests that cover the region. The creation of the Blue Mountains national park in 1956 recognized the uniqueness of the region's natural landscapes and cultural heritage including considerable evidence of Aboriginal settlement. Later expanded to 10,000 km^2 in size, the region's five national parks are the home to 26 mammal species, over 200 species of birds, 58 reptile and 32 amphibian species and a large number of rare species of flora. The most interesting plant is the Wollemi Pine, a species of the ancient *Araucariaceae* conifer family, which the fossil record indicates were present in the region up to 100 million years ago. In recognition of its significance the Blue Mountains were added to the World Heritage Register in 2000.

Aside from demonstrating the emergence of mountain destinations that compliment nearby lowland destinations, the Blue Mountains is an example of a destination that has recognized that sustainability is a major issue requiring public/private partnerships and that retention of cultural and natural heritage is an important element in destination planning. In recent years both the local municipal authorities and a number of departments of the state government (New South Wales) have worked together to develop urban communities and tourism infrastructure that promotes long-term sustainability.

DEVELOPMENT OF MOUNTAIN TOURISM

Long before modern forms of mountain tourism emerged, mountains were settled by agriculturalists as well as religious communities. Many agricultural communities developed in isolation from the nearby lowland communities, except where trade was an important component of the regional economy. Religious communities often selected mountain locations as sites for monasteries and other forms of religious community because of the isolation these sites gave from the everyday affairs of society (Berndaum, 1997). However, religious communities also fostered a steady flow of people, including pilgrims and members of religious orders, between the highlands and the lowlands. In some regions mountains not only provided sites for the construction of religious buildings but were also the object of worship.

In Korea, where Mountains comprise about three quarters of the country's landmass, mountain worship developed in isolated agrarian and aboriginal cultures millennia ago. In a small number of isolated areas remnants of this belief system continue to be practiced under the spiritual leadership of Shaman. The Korean concept of *San-shin* (Mountain spirit, Mountain God or Spirit of the Mountain) (Mason, 1999) symbolized the unique nature of the country's' mountains. Each mountain was believed to be inhabited by a spirit that exercised guardianship over the mountain and the people who lived there. In many parts of Asia, mountains have a long history of providing sites for temples and monasteries constructed by Buddhist, Animists and other faiths. One of the best known is the great Tibetan Buddhist Monasteries located in Lhasa. In Japan, Korea, India, Nepal and parts of China, temples constructed by the adherents of the Hindu, Buddhist, Taoist and Animist faiths continue to occupy sites high up in the mountains offering worshipers spectacular views as well as isolation and tranquillity – qualities that aid meditation. Figure 8.3 illustrates one of the many forms of monasteries that continue to service adherents of the Buddhist faith in Kyushu Japan. In Europe, Christian orders built monasteries in mountain regions as places for escape from everyday life and as training institutions. One of the largest concentrations of Monasteries of this nature

FIGURE 8.3 *A typical Japanese Buddhist temple located in the mountains of north west Kyushu, Japan. (See colour insert.)*
Source: Photo courtesy of Bruce Prideaux.

FIGURE 8.4 *Snow boarders at Gala-Yuzawa 90 minutes by rail from central Tokyo. (See colour insert.)*

is found in Greece at Mount Athos where 20 major monasteries and hundreds of smaller monasteries, sketes, and hesicaterons have been built in a region that can only be visited by men with special permission granted by both the Greek government and the government of the Holy Mountain.

Pilgrims, now as in the past, visiting these sites required food and shelter during their journey ensuring the growth of a hospitality sector in surrounding villages. In the past, the focus of the journey to these places was on spirituality. In the post-modern tourism landscape the focus has shifted from the religious to the secular and for many visitors, places of worship have now also become places of curiosity and in some cases of leisure. The village-based infrastructure that once supported the spirituality of pilgrims has metamorphosed into centres where secularism embodied by the notions of luxury, self-centred pursuit of pleasure and materialism, now dominate.

In Europe development of organized mountain tourism can be traced back to the mid-18th century when writers, poets, artists and members of the aristocracy began visiting mountains (Godde *et al.*, 2000). One of the first visitor groups were mountaineers (Beedie and Hudson, 2003) who engaged in what would now be defined as adventure tourism although they probably did not see themselves as tourists. Freed of earlier notions of mountains as forbidding places unsafe but for the most ardent adventurer, 19th century Europeans developed a romantic view of mountains where exploration, journey and adventure became important qualities. Reacting to the development of a growing interest in mountain tourism character-ized by Thomas Cooks' first package tour to Switzerland in 1863, cable-ways such as the one established in Rigi in 1873 were developed laying the foundation for the establishment of many other Swiss mountain resorts. In the 20th century, movies such as The *Sound of Music (1965)*, which centred on events in pre-World War Two Austria, conveyed a similar sense of mountain romanticism to moviegoers reinforcing the attractiveness of mountains as leisure destinations.

In the second half of the 19th century, Railways conquered the tyranny of distance through speed while their comfortable passenger cars replaced the travail of journeying by foot or by animals. Mountain regions thus became more accessible, paving the way for the development of mountain destinations in many countries. In Canada, as was the case in Europe several decades before, construction of railways opened the Rocky and Selkirk Mountains to tourism in the mid-1880. Eager to profit from its heavy investment in railway construction the Canadian Pacific Railway (CPR) became a keen advocate of tourism. Company hotels based loosely on European mountain architectural styles were built in a number of locations while the company's advertising painted the Rockies as a new Alps style destination location in the Americas (Marsh, 1985). To the east in Colorado, a cog railway to the summit of Pike's Peak was opened in 1891 and marked the emergence of Colorado as a winter destination.

In a number of countries, Hill Stations were built by colonial authorities as summer retreats for expatriate officials, settlers and members of the military. In the Indian subcontinent, British colonial authorities and the British Indian Army built as many as 50 of the approximately 80 hill stations found in the region; the remainder being built by Indian rulers as leisure retreats or in some cases as permanent capitals. Hill Stations built by the British colonial author-ities as well as those built by Indian rulers have experienced a revival in recent decades based on growing domestic middle class demand for travel. Examples of British Hill Stations include Horsley Hills (elevation 1265 m) located 160 km from Bangalore and now the site for many Bollywood movies and Darjeeling Hill Station located in the State of West Bengal. Darjeeling Hill Station is one of the best known of the Hill Stations and in 1999 the Darjeeling Himalayan Railway was listed as a World Heritage Site. The growing popularity of Hill Station tourism has created pressure on the fragile mountain ecosystems through increased visitor numbers and urbanization as new areas have been developed to house workers and the service industries that support tourism. Other colonial era Hill Stations include the Cameron Highlands in Malaysia, the French built Sa Po in Vietnam (Michaud and Turner, 2006) and Bokor in Cambodia. In a more recent development, modern versions of the colonial hill stations have emerged in parts of Asia. In the Lonely Plant guide to Malaysia, Singapore and Brunei, Richmand *et al.* (2004:110) described the Genting Highlands in Malaysia as a 'a garishly modern hill station designed as a kind of Asian Disneyland for the affluent citizens of KL (Kula Lumpa) just 50 km to the south. In contrast to the Old English style of other Malaysian hill stations, Genting's landscape is a forest of high-rise blocks . . . with high theme parks and extensive entertainment and activity programmes . . .'.

Specific examples of destinations within Mountain regions must commence with Europe which has the longest history of mountain resort development. Within the landlocked countries of Switzerland and Austria, Alpine resorts including Davos, St Moritz and Laax in Switzerland and St Anton and Kitzbuhel in Austria typify the forms of development that offer winter ski activities. In Germany ski resorts are generally quite small, in comparison to elsewhere in the European Alps. Two of the better known are Garmisch-Partenkirchen, which has access to Zugspitze, Germany's highest mountain and Oberstdorf which hosted the 2008 Ski Jump World Cup. In the former Warsaw Block of nations a number of new mountain resorts have been built while others have been rejuvenated including Poiana Braov in Romania (Turnock, 1990). In Asia, economic development has created demand for winter tourism activities leading to the development of mountain destinations such as Mt Kumgang (Kim and Prideaux, 2003) in North Korea, Mt Soruk in South Korea, Sapporo in Japan and the Shangri-La region of northern Yunnan, China.

Several other factors may affect the development of tourism in mountain regions. These include boundary disputes and security. The arbitrary division of Kashmir between India and Pakistan in 1947 is one example of how political boundaries create difficulties for whole-of-region planning and generate violence at sufficient levels to deter tourism. Divisions of this nature may generate conflict that precludes tourism development and implementation of sound sustainable planning. Tourism will only flourish if visitors feel safe from physical threat. At the time of writing regions where political boundaries have generated conflict and reduced the potential for sustainable tourism development include Assam (India) where Maoist insurgents have waged a low-level guerrilla campaign against the Indian government for many years, Afghanistan where Taliban insurgents continue to oppose the central government, Kurdish regions of Northern Iraq, Eastern Turkey and Western Iran, and Chechia located in the Caucasus Mountains region of the Russian Federation. In Nepal a long running Maoist rebellion (1996–2006) led to a steep decline in tourism arrivals with Nepal falling in iExplore's list of most popular destinations for adventure travellers from 10th to 27th by 2004 (http://www.iexplore. com/about/pr_2005-01-10.jhtml). Srinagar in Indian-controlled Kashmir also suffered a steep decline because of violence instigated by insurgents fighting for various objectives including independence from India. Where there is peace and cooperation, borders cease to be an irritant to tourism. For example in the border regions in the European Alps it is possible to book into a hotel on the French side of the border in the morning and ski on the Swiss side of the mountain in the afternoon.

The growth in interest in mountain tourism and the activities that have emerged may be traced through the observations of travel writers. In 1765 Thomas Gray (cited in Hooper, 2002), a traveller to the Scottish Highlands wrote *'The mountains were ecstatic, and ought to be visited in pilgrimage once a year. None but those monstrous creatures of God know how to join so much beauty with so much horror'*. Commenting on Gray's observations Hooper (2002:176) wrote that *'... physical hardship was expected routinely to accompany aesthetic experience was the Scottish highlands ...'*. In 1765, the year Gray wrote of his experiences in the Scottish Highlands, a visitor domicile in London would expect to undertake a 10-day coach journey to Edinburgh and a further week to the highlands. Contemporary writers, often publishing in travel magazines, see mountains as places for indulgence, of fascination, of recreation or as places for escape from the pressures of the working lifestyle of the modern 21st century city dweller. Middle class affluence, the quest for indulgence and escape and the ease of modern travel underlie many of the popular images of mountains in the contemporary era.

ACTIVITIES

Tourist-related activities include a wide range of winter sports, adventure sports, spas, mountain-climbing, hiking, camping, hunting, fishing and sight seeing. Of all the activities available, winter sports continue to be the dominant form of activity in many regions as illustrated in Figure 8.4 which depicts snowboarding in the Japanese Alps. In Norse Mythology, skiing was invented by Skadi, the snowshoe goddess and the Norwegian term 'ski' first appeared in the English language in 1890 (Crossley-Holland, 1980). The democratization of skiing through mass tourism laid the foundation for the emergence of a specialized mountain tourism industry to which has been added an increasing number of other mountain specific activities (Hudson, 2000). In recent decades winter sports have moved beyond skiing to include snow boarding and tobogganing, and have stimulated the emergence of a growing number of large multipurpose destinations such as Aspen in Colorado and Whistler in Canada. The urbanization of mountain resorts to support the growth in demand for tourism is a recent trend that has some dangers for mountain destinations which will be considered later in the chapter.

In a similar manner to skiing, mountaineering has also become fragmented and commodified with climbing relabelled as adventure climbing or sports climbing. Abseiling has emerged from mountaineering to become a sport in its own right as has canyoning. Hill walking has become trekking and mountain biking has moved off-road and into the mountains (Beedie and Hudson, 2003). In a further system of classification, mountain activities can be grouped into hard and soft adventure based on the level of physical exertion and technical skills required for participation. Thus mountaineering along with mountain biking and white water rafting may be classed as hard adventure while hiking, animal viewing, canoeing and camping are classed as soft adventure (Beedie and Hudson, 2003; Buckley, 2006).

During the 20th century the age old urge of humanity to engage in conquest found one manifestation in climbing the globe's most inaccessible mountains. Since the first conquest of Mt Everest by Sir Edmond Hillary and Sherpa Tenzing Norgay in 1953, 10% of the 2000 plus individuals who had climbed the mountain by the early 2000s have died though this high attrition rate has not been a deterrence to continued climbing of Mt Everest or other difficult mountains. However, even this experience has been commodified with the construction of cell phone repeaters by China Telecom to allow climbers to use cell phones during their climb and the inclusion of the summit of the mountain on the route for the 2008 Olympic torch relay.

In recent decades the range of activities has increased rapidly providing additional motivation for the growing interest in mountain tourism. The following, though not exhaustive, list highlights the variety of activities that are now available (Table 8.2).

Activities can be classified on a number of scales including: winter/summer activities, soft/hard adventure; high impact/low impact; expensive/low cost; safe/dangerous; high altitude/low altitude; eco friendly/non-eco friendly; river/

TABLE 8.2 The Expanding List of Mountain Sports and Recreational Activities

Snow/Ice-Centred	In the Air	Water-Based
Snow boarding	Paragliding	Kayaking
Skiing	Cliff jumping	Scuba diving
Snow shoeing	Gliding	Water skiing
Tobogganing	Hang-gliding	White water rafting
Down hill racing	Micro-lighting	Canyoning
Ice skating	Paragliding	Sailing
Cross county skiing	Parachuting	
Ski jumping	Skydiving	
Ice hockey	Bungee jumping	
Curling		
Nature Focus	**Motorized**	**Climbing**
Wild flower viewing	Motorcycling	Abseiling
Birding	Quad biking scrambling	Mountain climbing
Camping	Off road driving	
Wildlife viewing	Snow mobiling	
Hiking		
Other		
Hunting		
Caving		
Dog sledding		
Orienteering		
Via Ferrata wilderness experiences		

land activities; group/individual; and sustainable/non-sustainable. Participants may either be recreationist or professionals and activities can either be highly organized or unstructured, free or commercial. Most ski destinations offer skiing opportunities that include a mix of professional and amateur as well as hard and soft.

The modern Winter Olympic Games, first were held in Chamonix, France in 1924, became a key factor in generating interest in winter sports and mountain tourism. By fostering the development of semi professional athletics, promoting the concept of winter sports and featuring winter sports locations, the Winter Olympics has underpinned the growing popularity of winter sports and of the locations where these activities occur. For example, the 2002 Winter Olympics held in Salt Lake City, Utah in the USA attracted 250,000 visitors as well as millions more viewers of television coverage of the event.

DEVELOPING MOUNTAIN DESTINATIONS

A number of factors impact on the ability to build and maintain successful destinations in a mountain context. In developing mountain destinations a range of issues need to be considered by policy makers, planners, investors and residents. Collectively these factors which include visual impact, planning philosophy, urbanization, sustainability, climate change, accessibility, seasonality, community issues, political issues and cultural and heritage issues can be used to compare and contrast aspects of mountain destination. The remainder of this chapter will look at some of these elements of mountain destination development.

Visual impact

Mountains provide stunning visual experiences and in Urry's (1995) terminology are places to be consumed. Photos allow a sharing of that consumption. According to Sontag (1977:10) photography encourages users to become active participants *'having a camera transforms a person into something active, a voyeur, whilst at the same time creating an element of distance and separation'*. In the past capture of images of grandeur, uniqueness and differentness was the preserve of artists but the 20th century boom in cinematography has popularized the incorporation of mountain images in movies including *Gorillas in the Mist* (1988), *The Lord of the Rings Trilogy* (2001–2003) and *Legends of the Fall* (1994). Unfortunately the use of mountains as the sets for movies has not always been successful from an environmental perspective. The destruction of some sensitive scenic areas during the filming of a movie in Zhongdian China in 2006 led the authorities to restrict access to that and other sensitive sites to movie makers. The popularization of photography has also enhanced the appeal of mountains as places for recreation able to be shared via the medium of digital images with others particularly through the combined use of digital photography and cell phone communications as illustrated in Figure 8.2 of a tourist taking a picture of herself at the statue of Christ in Rio de Janerio (Figure 8.5).

Planning

As in any setting, planning is an important element in the continued success of tourism in mountain regions. Tourism by its nature can be an intrusive industry both on the landscape and its resources and on the people who live in the vicinity of tourism development. The scale of tourism development as well as the activities that are permitted are important measures of how the industry will impact on the environment and mountain communities and it is from

FIGURE 8.5 *A tourist taking a picture of herself at the statue of Christ in Rio de Janerio using a cell phone.*

this perspective that the need for planning is apparent. In the past the needs of the tourism developer and investor have often taken precedence over sustainability with planning often following Boosterism or Economic Development traditions. This situation is now changing as mounting evidence of the impact of unsustainable practices becomes apparent in declining tourist yields and increasing maintenance and restoration costs. Greater recognition has been given to adopting sustainable approaches to development and planning. The planning model outlined in Figure 3.2 provides an effective framework for ensuring that the needs of the community, the investor and the visitor are recognized. In the long term, the effectiveness of planning will remain an output of the planning approaches adopted in the Preplanning stage where decisions are made at a political level to follow a particular development path. Planning approaches may include an economic approach, a sustainable approach or a community development approach.

It is apparent that for a mountain destination to achieve sustainability, priority must be given to planning for the long-term use of the resource. To date, most of the academic commentary on sustainable planning has ignored the need to draw on the outputs of scientific research where it informs on mountain ecosystems and landscapes. Scientific research is essential to establish the geographic and biological boundaries that define the extent to which a specific area can be used for recreational activities, to identify the resilience of ecosystems and specific species to human activity and to measure the likely impacts of human habitation and recreational use. In the past it is apparent that little consideration was given to incorporating scientific investigation into issues as diverse as boundary planning of parks and other planning boundaries, construction of infrastructure in sensitive ecosystems and introduction of non-endemic species into domestic gardens. Ignoring science will ultimately result in degrading, ensuing loss of amenity for visitors and in some cases decline of the destination. In the future a much closer science-based approach is required for planning and where needed adjustment to the type and intensity of current use patterns. It is also apparent that with growing evidence of climate change a number of mountain destinations will lose part or all of their winter snow while others will experience a rapid change in their biological structure. In both cases the affected regions will be forced to adapt and respond with a range of new experiences or face rapid decline. Case Study 8.2 illustrates the importance of incorporating scientific research into planning in sensitive mountain environments.

Sustainability

Sustainability is an issue that has a centrality in this book and in mountains as elsewhere, is a major issue that needs to be addressed if successful tourism development is to continue. Moreover, because of their role in the global water cycle and as the site for the headwaters of all the world's major river systems the development of mountains and the impact that development has on the water cycle is a significant issue for inhabitants of lowland regions. In their book on mountain tourism Godde *et al.* (2000) argued that to the traditional three sets of interrelated factors of sustainability – ecological, economic and socio-cultural – must be added a political aspect. Arbitrary political boundaries often ignore geographic, cultural and biological boundaries creating management difficulties and increasing the potential for conflict as discussed earlier in this chapter.

It is apparent that the fragility of many mountain ecosystems must be a major consideration in development policies to ensure the long-term sustainability (Godde *et al.*, 2000). As Hudson and Miller (2005) reminded us, sustainable tourism emphasizes the importance of environmental stewardship. It is also apparent that sustainability has a wider stage than the environment and must also include economic sustainability of the firms operating in mountain resorts (Goeldner *et al.*, 2000) as well as the sustainability of the communities that have developed in these regions. A number of authors have commented on the tensions that have emerged between the need to reconcile environmental and economic sustainability (Hudson and Miller, 2005; Miles and Covin, 2000). A further group of authors (Williams and Gill, 1999; EU, 2001) have postulated mechanisms for determining the carrying capacity of sensitive environments. Without environmental sustainability, long-term economic sustainability becomes problematic. Unfortunately, the need for economic sustainability has at times taken precedent leading to development that is ultimately ecologically unsustainable. The centrality of sustainability is nowhere more apparent than in the issues that have arisen over climate change in mountainous regions. Rising global temperatures threaten many ski destinations.

Ski resorts are one of the most intrusive forms of tourism development in mountain regions (Buckley *et al.*, 2000). Requiring large areas for infrastructure including accommodation and ski runs as well as the development of supporting urban areas to house staff and other support workers, industry and transport, the construction and operation of ski resorts can have major environmental impacts. The development of the Cairngorm ski region in Scotland demonstrates the type of environmental impact that the construction of ski destinations may have on sensitive mountain environments. During the construction phase of that project the artic-alpine environment was damaged by heavy equipment, road construction and vegetation removal to build ski runs (Holden, 1998). Vegetation removal later led to flash flooding. After the opening of the destination litter left by skiers attracted competitor species to indigenous birds and animals upsetting the delicate balance of existing ecosystems. In Australia's Alpine region, the endangered Pygmy Possum (*Burramys parvus*) is facing a greater threat from the construction of ski runs than from forest fires. The fragmentation of habits caused by the development of ski runs, roads and continued grooming of snow-covered areas where they hibernate over winter has seen the population crash to as little as 1800. The impacts of skiing must also be viewed in the context of a number of ski destinations seeking to extend their season beyond the winter to include summer activities which bring with them another layer of activities that may potentially impact on long-term sustainability.

From an ecological perspective other impacts from development include deforestation, introduction of invasive species, loss of habitat and erosion. From the visitor's perspective, adverse impacts include loss of amenities such as pristine wilderness and mountain landscapes that remain uncluttered with the evidence of human occupation. In high altitude areas the damage inflicted on the environment by summer and winter sports including hiking may be considerable. At high altitudes flora is often rare, of high aesthetic value and fragile due to slow growth rates. Excessive use of these areas may lead to hardening, erosion, fragmentation of habitat, introduction of non-endemic species and fires. Monitoring and enforcement of regulations to maintain the ecological integrity of these areas is necessary and while achievable in developed countries such as Canada, Switzerland, the United States and New Zealand that have strong institutions, developing countries that have relatively weak institutions may experience difficulty in achieving long-term development able to ensure ecological sustainability. The growing accumulation of litter and human waste along parts of Nepal's trekking trails and in the base camps that service climbers in Mt Everest and other mountains illustrates the difficulty developing countries face in hosting large numbers of tourists.

In areas where cultural landscapes are an important component of the mountain destination experience, unrestricted development has resulted in the demolition of traditional buildings and their replacement with structures that are not in harmony with the architecture or scale of the original buildings. Even the replacement of a single traditional building with a more contemporary structure may dramatically alter the harmony of the original streetscape. In other areas, depopulation due to new agricultural technologies or loss of traditional agricultural markets has led to abandonment of buildings and in some cases of entire settlements. This is a growing trend in a number of countries including Japan, Korea and Greece (Valaoras, 2000). Deforestation, soil erosion, loss of markets for traditional agricultural markets and the growing attractiveness of urban life and the services that are available in these settings have had an adverse impact on some mountain communities. In many instances the children of farmers have left for the attractions of the cities leaving ageing populations and in some cases abandonment of mountain villages. Recognizing this trend the Japanese Government has instituted the *Furusato* policy (return to cultural roots in rural areas) aimed at using tourism to revitalize rural areas. The mountain spa resort town of Yufin, in Kyushu is one example of where this policy has been successful and resulted in substantial investment in tourism (see Figure 4.4). Unfortunately, in the process of Yufin many traditional buildings have been demolished and pseudo architectural styles substituted. Similarly, the area's agricultural landscape has been rapidly eroded as new settlers acquire former farms and redeveloping them for housing or for commercial purposes.

Yunnan China provides examples of the impacts that rapid development can have and how parts of the original cultural landscapes have been retained but modified. In the WTO World heritage listed city of Li Jang considerable efforts have been made to retain the original streetscapes of the old city. This has been successful however as the use for these buildings has changed from residential and light service industry to tourism many small changes have been made to individual buildings. Buildings that were once family residents have become shops and former shops have been extensively renovated completely removing the original interiors and replacing them with more contemporary styles. More importantly, considerable urban sprawl has occurred near the site as hotels have been built and homes for tourism workers constructed. Unfortunately, the post-Communist commercial architecture of these buildings is completely at odds with those in Li Jang creating an unpleasant vista of the juxtaposition of the old with the new.

The preceding discussion highlights the need for effective and proactive destination planning to ensure sustainability in sensitive mountain areas. Limited physical space creates conundrums for planners. Growth requires space for new structures and services but growth also destroys the amenity of the resource and the experience that underpins the attractiveness of the resource. Many mountain regions have a low tolerance for development. To achieve a high degree of ecological sustainability the extent and type of planning undertaken must be extensively and openly debated as recommended in the first two stages of the planning framework outlined in Figure 3.2. An important caveat here is that all aspects of planning must be underpinned by science. The natural self-correcting mechanisms of the past whereby excessive development of resource resulted in starvation of human and animal populations have been replaced by the global supply chain where resource deficiencies can be imported removing the previous balance that promoted sustainability.

The following case study illustrates the importance of having access to scientific research that is able to inform management authorities and planners of likely ecosystem changes as a result of climate change.

Case Study. 8.2 Possible Impact of Climate Change

The World Heritage listed (1988) Wet Tropics Rainforests located in North Queensland occupy 900,000 hectares of narrow coastal mountain range and are extremely sensitive to climate change. The mountain rainforests contain 3000 plant species and about a third of Australia's 315 mammal species including 13 mammal species found nowhere else. Research by Krockenberger, Kitching and Turton (2004) found that even the least extreme scenario of temperature change of just 1 °C will limit the range of endemic frogs (eight species), endemic mammals (six species), birds (three species) and skinks (three species) by 50%. Temperature change will also impact on the distribution of many species throughout the forests as illustrated in Figure 8.6 which shows the loss of species diversity as global temperatures rise. Because of the nature of the mountain system that contains the wet

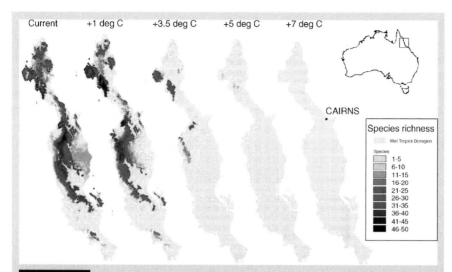

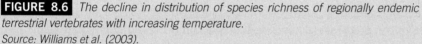

FIGURE 8.6 *The decline in distribution of species richness of regionally endemic terrestrial vertebrates with increasing temperature.*
Source: Williams et al. (2003).

tropics rainforests, species will not be able to migrate to higher latitudes and in many cases have limited scope to migrate up-mountain. At the ecosystem level some species redistribution will occur resulting in new ecosystems that will be derived from existing systems but will be different. Further impacts will occur at the ecosystem services level (the maintenance of air, soil and water quality), there will be an increased risk from invasive species and there will also be increased occurrences of extreme climatic events. Research by Prideaux and Falco-Mammone (2007) found that the Wet Tropics generated AUD$ 426 in million direct expenditure by tourists in 2006. Climate change is likely to impact on the attractiveness of the region and will have an impact on visitors though the extent is unknown. The use of the Wet Tropics Rainforests as a key selling point for tourism in the region will also need to be reviewed as will the current use of some sensitive areas of the forest for tourism purposes. In the future, the management authority (Wet Tropics Management Authority) will increasingly need to rely on scientific research to understand the extent of the changes that will occur as well as employing social science methods to understand how these changes will impact on visitor numbers and effect the economic contribution of the rainforest to the local economy (Prideaux and Falco-Mammone, 2007).

Climate change

Many mountain destinations will be severely effected by global climate change and will be forced to adapt by offering new experiences or face decline. As global temperatures rise (IPCC, 2007) glaciers will continue to melt at an increasing rate and the snow line will retreat. Evidence of these changes is already apparent as glaciers in New Zealand, Iceland and the USA. In Africa glaciers on

Mt Kenya and Mt Uganda may entirely disappear by the 2020s (Taylor *et al.*, 2006). As the snow line retreats the areas available for snow-based activity will decline with a number of possible outcomes (Koenig and Abegg, 1997; Elasser and Burki, 2002; Scott *et al.*, 2003; Becken and Hay, 2007). Where snowfields are located in mountains with low altitudes the ski season will be at first reduced in length followed later by an absence of snow. Destinations facing this situation have little option but to switch to other forms of mountain experiences or decline. Where mountains have sufficient elevation, ski fields will move up mountain if suitable areas can be developed. This will be paralleled by the opportunity for mountain regions located in higher latitudes to expand their ski fields. One likely impact is that as the number of ski opportunities diminishes the price is likely to escalate.

A further impact of climate change will be rapid ecosystem change as highlighted previously in the case study on the Wet Tropics Rainforests. As temperatures increase invasive species of flora and fauna will migrate into mountain regions creating significant pressure on ecosystems that will already be in the process of decline and adaptation. Fire and erosion are likely to be companion threats as ecosystems change. As plant communities are modified and some plant species lost animals adapted to feeding on those species are likely to perish.

Climate change will not signal the end of winter sports although the opportunities for participation are likely to be reduced. In the longer term it may have an impact on events such as the Winter Olympics. There is also the possibility that additional purpose built indoor ski fields of the nature of the snowdome developed in Dubai will emerge although the sustainability of such facilities in a society that will become increasingly aware of its carbon footprint and the scarcity of non-renewable energy sources is questionable.

Urbanization

Edensor (1988) observed that while heterogeneous space, typified by mountains, is concerned with the freedom to move and the need to find space for self-expression, urbanization creates enclaves that bring with them constraints and convention. The symbolic values of freedom and adventure that were synonymous with early forms of tourism development in the mountains of Europe and even the United States have in more recent times been replaced with conformity and commodification. This is to be expected because the mass tourism industry of the contemporary era demands certainty of enjoyment and value for money packaged into a 5–7-day time frame within a setting that is both exotic but at the same time familiar and unthreatening.

The urbanized spaces that support tourism include both the enclaves where visitors are accommodated and the much larger enclaves that support the tourism industry and its employees. Roads have replaced walking tracks, signs inform, advertising promotes the pristine nature of the space beyond the enclave, and uniformity replaces the chaos of nature. Perhaps the juxtaposition of conformity ensuring certainty in a space that is attractive because of its non-conformity and uncertainty is a metaphor for the impact of mass tourism and its accompanying standardization on a formally pristine landscape.

Paralleling the development of mass mountain tourism there remains a demand for Edensor's heterogeneous space where forest views remain uncompromised by creeping urbanization. In a number of areas small parts of these spaces have been filled by small highly priced accommodation that market exclusivity as a major selling point. However, even these locations face change as the demand for more development of this type increases.

In a number of countries the growth of mountain tourism destinations has fuelled substantial in-migration from surrounding areas leading to pollution, loss of ecosystems through clearing and deforestation and loss of identity for the original community. In an analysis of the impact of tourism development in the Kathmandu Valley in Nepal, Shah and Nagpal (1997) noted how the quality of air in the Valley had declined in parallel with urbanization. One impact of this form of development is creeping urbanization of hill slopes as shown in Figure 8.7.

FIGURE 8.7 *Creeping urbanization in the foothills surrounding Poços de Caldas in Brazil.*
Source: Photo courtesy of Bruce Prideaux.

The down valley expansion of urbanized areas to support Aspen (Colorado) is an example of the impact that tourism can have on mountain regions. Commercial development along highways and uncontrolled home construction has occurred in Gelnwood Springs and Carbondale and has the potential to erode the amenity of the mountain experience and increase pressure on the region's sensitive ecosystem. In these circumstances planning regimes that cover the entire region and are multi-municipality in nature are required.

The development of Whistler, first to service the nearby Vancouver market and later the international market, demonstrates the impact that ski resort development can have on mountain regions. In 1973, 2400 acres of forest were deleted from the surrounding Garibaldi National Park to build ski facilities followed by an additional 780 acres in 1978 and 1520 acres in 1987 (Saremba and Gill, 1991). Continued expansion of ski runs and urban sprawl into sensitive ecosystems are dangers that must be taken into account by planners if long-term sustainability is to be achieved. Part of the urban sprawl can be attributed to the construction of second homes and accommodation for resort workers.

Accessibility

The development of transport technologies in the 19th and 20th centuries was one of the major factors, along with growing national and individual prosperity, that facilitated the opening of mountain areas for tourism development, particularly those in peripheral locations. The 19th century development of rail allowed new mountain resorts to open in Europe particularly in the Alps region while a similar trend in North America facilitated parallel development in the Rockies, Colorado and elsewhere. In the first half of the 20th century construction of all weather roads to connect mountain communities with large lowland urban centres further stimulated development. In the second half of the 20th century the rapid development of commercial aviation completed the opening of mountains to tourism. On a global scale, the ability of air transport to carry tourists over long distances in safety and at a relatively low cost has greatly expanded the number of generating regions that supply mountains with visitors, while at the same time greatly expanding the number of competitors, both mountain and non-mountain. On a smaller scale, roads, tunnels, cable cars and ski lifts have opened formally inaccessible mountain areas to tourism development. While improved accessibility has opened up many mountains areas for development it has also created a number of problems including destruction of sensitive ecosystems, erosion, providing corridors for the introduction of invasive species and facilitating urban sprawl. The emergence of Machu Picchu in Peru as a major tourism attraction illustrates the role played by transport in developing remote mountain regions to tourism. The remoteness of the site precluded its development for touristic purposes until a railway line could be built into the region opening it for tourism development.

Seasonality

Seasonality is a major issue, particularly for destinations that rely on winter tourism. Within mountain regions seasons are divided into winter and summer. Each season can expect to attract very different visitor segments. In winter the emphasis on winter sports predominates while in summer a different and often less extensive suite of activities become available. Employment, the need for businesses to generate cash flow during low seasons and returns on investments are major issues. Underlying these issues is the role of visitor motivations which are subject to frequent change and often do not match those of the host community. As Godde *et al.* (2000) noted, tourists are short-term visitors who seek high service standards and value for money over a short period of time while the host community is looking for long-term financial and environmental sustainability. The expectations of either party may not always be met with the result that destinations suffer. In Europe some mountain destinations reverted to agriculture due to a decline in interest in mountain tourism and increased competition from other destinations in the period between the First and Second World Wars (Kroener, 1968 cited in Godde *et al.*, 2000). Similarly, despite the long tradition of summer tourism activity, a number of European mountain destinations have experienced declining interest in this form of tourism particularly in recent years (Godde *et al.*, 2000). One reason for this decline in interest may be the result of increased competition from other destinations outside of Europe.

To overcome some of the problems created by the seasonal nature of winter sports many winter resorts have encouraged the development of summer programs based on activities such as trekking, climbing and adventure. Where summer programmes have been established multi-season employment can be offered to staff greatly reducing the problems of recruiting staff for short period of time and also assisting mountain communities achieve greater stability with assured all year round employment. In Canada, Whistler has developed as a four-season destination overcoming many of the problems that arise when employment is seasonal. In areas where multi-season employment remains a problem a form of complimentarily labour migration has emerged where mountain workers migrate to summer resorts for the summer season. In Spain, tourism and hospitality workers migrate between the winter destinations in the Pyrenees and summer destinations along the coast.

From their genesis as the start points for mountaineering expeditions, mountain destinations such as Queenstown in New Zealand have grown to encompass a much wider range of visitors for whom the mountains provided an attractive backdrop but are not the major reason for their visit. Shopping, cultural tourism and other non-mountain activities are major attractions in many mountain destinations. To overcome the fluctuations in occupancy levels caused by seasonality an increasing number of destinations have developed summer activities. In winter destinations new activities have emerged below the snow line and during the summer these activities become the focus of tourism interest.

CONCLUSION

From the preceding discussion it is apparent that the long-term sustainability of mountain areas and the destinations they support is an important issue and one that cannot be left to the market place. New forms of joint public–private sector partnerships embedded in and supported by strong community support are required. Planning in its broadest sense is a key ingredient to the successful long-term survival of mountain destinations. The fragility of mountain environments, their susceptibility to a range of disasters, the pressures caused by tourism development and in the future, the changes that will occur due to global climate change, require that all levels of government, the community and the private sector are engaged in meaningful planning and on-going dialogue.

From a public policy perspective the issues that face planners include: maintaining ecological sustainability; achieving institutional coordination within and between each national and international level of administration represented in mountain regions; ensuring that the growth of tourism and other industries is sustainable; provision of essential services; maintaining sustainable communities and; ensuring political stability. Achieving these sometimes conflicting objectives will not be easy but failure will result in economic decline. While many developed countries with strong institutions are able to provide planning of the required standard the task is much more difficult for developing countries where there are substantial calls on public resources for a large range of issues such as health, national infrastructure, education and so on. In countries such as Nepal, where the value of tourism is understood, planners face considerable difficulties because of skills shortages, lack of funds for infrastructure, poor enforcement of regulations, corruption and development that is regulated but often unsupervised. In nations where communities are poor and/or disenfranchised and where tourism has yet to be elevated in the list of national priorities, the problems are greater.

Despite the shadow cast by climate change the future for mountain tourism is bright, particularly if the global economy continues to expand. Demand is likely to increase but as pointed out in the beginning of this chapter, growth will create new pressures on managers and planners to first define sustainability and second develop strategies that will achieve and maintain sustainability. It is likely that new destinations will emerge particularly in countries where tourism has only started to be developed. Demand will also increase in China and India as rapid economic growth occurs and the newly enriched middle and later working classes look for new domestic tourism opportunities.

KEY ISSUE FOR THE FUTURE

The discussion in this chapter has identified a number of significant issues that require additional research to enhance understanding of mountains as a class of tourism destination and a form of tourism activity. These include:

- The form of planning required. Given the fragility of many mountain ecosystems planning approaches used in the Boosterism and Economic Planning traditions are not appropriate and a more sensitive science-based approach based on ecological sustainability is more appropriate.
- Seasonality is an important issue and in many destinations is being addressed by adding summer activities to give mountain destination a four-season market.
- In the near future climate change will become an increasingly important issue.
- Given the sensitivity of mountain ecosystems there is an urgent need to incorporate science into the planning and management processes that occur in mountain destinations.

CHAPTER 9

Island Destinations

Delighting in differentness, escaping to fantasy

INTRODUCTION

In a recent travel magazine specializing in island vacations readers were informed by Hawaiian Airlines that '*Our home will set you free*' (Islands, Special Issue: How to Run Away to Paradise, 2007:21) while an advertisement for Aruba promised '*Always find the perfect something, or nothing, to do*' (Islands, Special Issue: How to Run Away to Paradise, 2007:15). A few pages on and past the article on Hawaii that promised that the destination would allow you to '*Experience the ultimate escape*' (Steutermann Rodgers, 2007) an article titled *The last nomads, on A Thai island, Moken sea gypsies live as they have lived for centuries* (Skolinick, 2007) extolled the life style of the Moken Sea Gypsies of Thailand. The article ended with the following observations 'His (one of the sea gypsies) is a look of connection with the earth, and at this moment I'm feeling it too. This may be why the Moken have no word for goodbye. It makes moments like this never end'. The evocative messages in this publication are directly aimed at the readers' dreams of a holiday that promises a world that is different, exotic and where the frame of modern urban life can be swapped for a different world that is rustic, slower more organic perhaps, where the subject of the gaze becomes the new reality if only for a short time. Musing on this I wondered if I should pack up my laptop and join the queue for the next flight to an island paradise (but I remembered, I have a tourism planning class to teach).

Islands are intriguing tourism destinations. In one sense their location confers upon them a range of often unique attractions including landscapes, heritage, climate, flora, fauna and indigenous culture. In another sense their

231

Resort Destinations: Evolution, Management and Development

location may also be a major inhibitor to their development as isolation, a feature that may in some cases also be a major attraction, leads to increased access costs for both visitors and freight. Many of the images used to promote islands focus on themes that include: sand, sun, surf and in some cases sex; heritage; culture; isolation; slow pace of life; landscapes; and the environment. Many of these images fit easily into the postmodern urban dweller tourists 'bubble' experience where commodified and artificially constructed experiences are consumed as mass tourism or even individual products. Other images portray culture and heritage themes that appeal to MacCannell's (1975) quest for authenticity. Island experiences are consumed by an increasing number of tourists and it is timely to consider a range of issues that must be faced by island destinations when developing products and experiences that are marketed in the global market place.

The issues surrounding the development of tourism in island settings have attracted considerable interest amongst tourism scholars who have sought to identify the characteristics that differentiate island tourism from other forms of tourism as well as explore strategies for enhancing tourism development (see collected essays on islands by Lockhart and Drakakis-Smith, 1997; Conlin and Baum, 1995; Briguglio et al., 1996 for example). Islands have also attracted the interest of a range of international bodies and have been the subject to discussions at a number of international conferences including the Earth Summit in Rio (1992), the United Nations Global Summit on Small Island Developing States (SIDS) in Barbados in 1994, the International Conference on Sustainable Tourism in Small Island Developing States and Other Islands in Spain in 1998, and the World Summit on Sustainable Development in Johannesburg in 2002. The significance of tourism in many Small Island Developing States is apparent when the ratio of visitors to residents is observed. The WTO (2002:17) found that in 24 SIDS the annual number of tourists exceeded the number of residents. Norfolk Island in the Pacific, for example, has a ratio of 18 tourist to each resident in 2007.

Islands can be categorized in many ways including size, their gross domestic product (GDP) per capita, environment, location relative to major tourism generating centres (Weaver, 1998) culture and the impacts of tourism. In a chapter of this nature it is not possible to cover the full spectrum of issues that have been examined in the literature or the entire range of island destinations. To illustrate the major issues that impact on the development of island tourism destinations this chapter will focus on small islands with a particular emphasis on Small Island Developing States although issues concerning larger islands are also discussed.

The selection of these islands as the key focus of this chapter was based, in part, on the range of problems they face, their diversity and their natural

TABLE 9.1 Small Island Colonies, Trust Territories and Dependencies

United Kingdom

Anguilla, Ascension Island, Cayman Islands, Falklands Islands, Bermuda, Guernsey, Isle of Man, Jersey, Alderney, Montserrat, Pitcairn Islands, St Helena, Tristan de Cunha (dependency of St Helena), Ascension island (dependency of St Helena), Turks and Caicos Islands, Virgin Islands, British Indian Ocean Territory

France

French Southern and Antarctica Lands, Guadeloupe, St Martin (Dependency of Guadeloupe), St-Barthelemy (Dependency of Guadeloupe), St Martin (Dependency of Guadeloupe), Martinique, Mayotte, New Caledonia, St Pierre and Miquelon, Wallis and Futuna Islands, Reunion

United States of America

American Samoa, Guam, Northern Mariana Islands, Puerto Rico, Virgin Islands

Netherlands

Aruba, Netherlands Antilles, St Maarten (part of Netherlands Antilles), Saint Eustatius (part of Netherlands Antilles)

Norway

Cocos Keeling Island, Christmas Island, Norfolk Island

Australia

Cocos Keeling, Christmas, Norfolk Is

New Zealand

Cook Islands, Niue, Tokelau

Denmark

Greenland, Faroe Islands

attractiveness. Surprisingly, in the post-colonial era the last remaining vestiges of former Empires are still to be found in a small number of island colonies and dependencies scattered around the globe. Perhaps because of their lack of economic progress, or a nostalgic yearning for the past glories of empire, island colonies and dependencies continue to dot the world's oceans as outlined in Table 9.1.

Small islands demonstrate most if not all the major issues facing the development of tourism destinations located in island settings. In this chapter each small island is treated as a single destination. On larger islands including the islands of Indonesia and the Philippines, there may be two or even more separate destinations. While this chapter will have a particular focus on Small Island Developing States, the discussion will also include references to other islands such as Hawaii which are parts of much larger political units. The chapter will conclude with a case study that illustrates many of the difficulties that island destinations face.

Tourism is seen by many SIDS and development agencies as one of the few industries that can offer the potential to achieve economic growth. Most SIDS have limited natural resources and where resources do exist they are often limited to timber, agriculture, fishing, mining and in some instances remittances from island residents who are guest workers in other countries. For islands with resources that are attractive to the tourism industry including unique ecosystems, a pleasant climate, indigenous culture, and attractive beach areas, tourism offers the opportunity to develop an alternative stream of export income. However, to develop a tourism industry that can compete in the global market place SIDS, as well as larger islands, must overcome many hurdles including access to finance, development of a work force with an appropriate skills set, establishment of infrastructure that meets international standards and legal and administrative systems that can integrate into the international market place. While many islands find these hurdles are difficult to surmount others have developed successful tourism industries including Fiji, Aruba, the Bahamas, Guam, Bermuda and the Maldives. Other islands that have sought to develop tourism as a major national economic sector, and which are still classed as low-income, least-developed states include Cape Verde, Haiti, Cuba, Kiribati, Samoa, Tuvalu and many of the island states found in the Caribbean. Larger island nations such as Japan, New Zealand and Ireland are less dependent on tourism because of their size and relatively greater endowment of other resources.

The problems of small island development were recognized by the United Nations General Assembly in February 1993 (United Nations, 1993) which saw that there was a need for specific measures to assist developing island countries. The resolution recognized that aside from the general range of issues facing developing nations, SIDS also face issues that arise from their small size, susceptibility to natural disasters, geographical dispersion and remoteness. Collectively, these factors plus the often fragile nature of their ecosystems, may conspire to limit economic growth and hamper social development (Abeyrantne, 1999). In the resolution, an appeal was made to the international community to increase the level of concessional finance and technical assistance provided to these states and assist them achieve economic growth through increased export earnings. In the following year, the 1994 Global Conference on Sustainable Development in Small Island Developing States (United Nations, 1994) described tourism as one of the few options small island states have for achieving economic development. Commenting on this resolution, Meheux and Parker (2006) stated that this recognition can be attributed to the potential income-multiplying effect of tourism and the ability of many SIDS to use their resources of natural beauty, warm climate and beaches to underpin tourism development. The significance of tourism for many SIDS is apparent when the percentage of GDP derived from tourism is calculated. According to Scheyvens and Momsen (2008) nine of the 10 most tourism-dependent countries, based on tourism as a percentage of GDP, are

Small Island Developing States with six located in the Caribbean, two in the Indian Ocean and Sao Tome and Principe off the west coast of Africa.

In the tourism literature the dominant research themes pertaining to the development of island tourism destinations include management and planning issues, marketing, their location on a periphery (Weaver, 1998), stage of development, issues of sustainability, their cultural resources and concerns with commodification. A number of researchers including Harrison (2001), Milne (1992), Craig-Smith *et al.* (1994), Craig Smith (1996), Wilkerson (1987) Fagence (1997), Carlsen (1999) and Tisdell and McKnee (1988) have investigated issues that confront island nations. Fagence (1997), for example, stated that Nauru, a microstate located in the South Pacific faced an uncertain future unless new industries including tourism were developed. Milne (1992) noted that in a number of Pacific microstates such as Kiribati, Cook Islands, Niue, and Tonga, tourism was one of the very few industries able to make a substantial contribution to economic growth. Environmental impacts of tourism were discussed by Carlsen (1991), while King and McVey (1997) identified infrastructure deficiencies as a major problem. Tisdell and McKee (1988) observed that social problems may arise from the uneven distribution of wages paid to tourism workers while Cassidy (2002) noted that there was often a lack of political and administrative leadership as well as a lack of destination knowledge by potential visitors. Elliott and Neirotti's (2008) analysis of recent developments in Cuba highlighted the role that the governments of some developing island nations have assumed in tourism planning and infrastructure provision. Weaver (1998) observed that domestic core-periphery problems may also inhibit tourism development. A number of authors have cited examples where remote island countries have overcome these problems by implementing strategies that have enabled them to build substantial tourism industries. For example, Mistilis and Tolar (2000) observed that Bali and Fiji had developed successful tourism industries. Other examples include Hawaii (Craig-Smith, 1996), the Maldives (Sathiendrakumar and Tisdell, 1988) and Saipan (Craig-Smith, 1996).

THE APPEAL OF SMALL ISLANDS

The consumption of touristic experiences, often through the lens of Ury's tourism gaze (1990, 1995), lies at the heart of the attractiveness of many small islands destinations. Islands offer differentness, another world remote from the stage of ordinary life. A cascade of evocative terms may be used to describe the experiences of differentness and uniqueness that provide a rich well for the creative marketing campaigns that are used to promote island escapes.

Islands have strong images that have attracted travellers for centuries. In the European tradition many of the first visitors to islands beyond Europe were explorers, scientists and sailors. Their descriptions laid the foundations for later travel writers whose accounts were widely read by people who while interested in travel were not in the position to undertake the journey, a parallel to the popular travel programmes of network television and pay TV channels such as National Geographic that appeal to current cohorts of armchair travellers.

Edmond (2002) pointed to the power of island imagery in his essay on Tahiti. While not visited by Europeans until the 1767 the idea of the fantasy tropical island had been invented long before. Islands of plenty where the prohibitions of guilt of Europe's Judeo-Christian cultures did not apply found a wide audience in the popular literature of the time. If known islands were not seen as suitable settings, islands were invented, a tradition that has extended to the present. Crab Key, the hideout Dr No in the first James Bond movie is a recent example of this tradition that can be traced back to Plato's story of Atlantis. To its first European visitors Tahiti must have appeared to be the embodiment of these fantasies. Bouganville's (cited in Edmond, 2002:140) encounter with a young Tahitian woman who swam out to his boat was described as '... *(she) carelessly dropt a cloth, which covered her, and appeared to the eyes of all beholders, such as Venus showed herself to the Phryian shepherd, having indeed the celestial form of that goddess*'. This evocative image of guilt free sexual freedom established, according to Edmond, the terms in which Tahiti has been viewed ever since. The vivid images of a tropical playground have become a dominant image that continues to the present and continues to be reinforced in advertising in the contemporary era. The image of an exotic paradise is also a theme that has been used by film-makers and writers as the backdrops to their craft. In *Gulliver's Travels* written by Jonathan Swift and first published in 1726 we read about the make-believe islands of Blefuscu and Lilliput while in the popular Harry Potter books (written by J.K. Rowling) and movies the mythical prison island of Azkaban casts a dark shadow over the lives of the book's principal characters.

Translating the innate appeal of islands into a tourism product is a difficult process for many of the reasons outlined in the literature above. This difficulty was highlighted in a discussion by Cameron and Gatewood (2008) on the potential to develop heritage in many of the Caribbean islands. Despite some islands having a built heritage stretching back over 500 years many islands had failed to move past sand, surf and sun. For the residents of islands the benefits of tourism may be lost unless careful planning and policy implementation is placed in the foremost position of development agendas.

MAJOR ISSUES

Major issues that are confronted by island communities wishing to develop a tourism industry include:

- Physical characteristics including size,
- Structure of the economy,
- Resource availability,
- Political structure and governance issues,
- Distance from markets,
- Access issues including airlines,
- Marketing,
- Level of infrastructure development,
- Issues of sustainability including economic and ecological dimensions,
- Community participation,
- Uniqueness factors expressed as a combination of landforms, flora, fauna and human cultural heritage,
- Investment issues including the level of foreign ownership as well as the level of government ownership.

Together, these factors create the tourism-specific structures that shape, and limit, the ability of islands to develop a tourism industry. Collectively, these factors provide a basis for classification, analysis and comparison of islands. In the following discussion these factors are described in general terms and are not used as a framework for comparison leaving that task for a later publication.

Size

While aspects of size are a major issue for small islands, size cannot be divorced from other interrelated elements such as distance to origin markets, natural resource endowment and political structures. Size includes elements such as landmass, population and economic measures. Politically, as well as physically, islands range in size from micro to macro. Size and political status are important discriminators. Although there are a small number of independent or self-governing island states, most islands are incorporated in much larger political entities. Examples of micro islands belonging to the latter class of islands include Kelly's Island located in the United States part of Lake Erie, Gabriel Island which belongs to Mauritius and Double Island located just offshore of Cairns in Australia. Illustrated in Figure 9.1, Double Island is a near shore protected area that is 2 km^2 in size and supports a 20 apartment five-star resort property available only for whole of resort bookings usually by celebrates.

FIGURE 9.1   *Double Island a micro-offshore island hosts a small five-star resort although most of the island is a protected area.*
Source: Photo courtesy Bruce Prideaux.

Examples of self-governing or independent small islands include:

- Niue, an independent state located in the Pacific, has a population of 1490 persons (2001 figure) and a landmass of 260 km². Tourism is a major industry.
- Pitcairn Islands, an overseas territory of the United Kingdom located in the Pacific has an area of 47 km² and about 48 residents (www.cia/library/publications, 2008).
- St Pierre and Miquelon, a territorial Overseas collectivity of France, has an area of 242 km², approximately 7000 residents and is located south of Newfoundland (Timothy, 2001; www.cia/library/publications 2008).
- St Helena, an overseas territory of the United Kingdom, is located in the South Atlantic and has an area of 413 km² with a population of 7543. (www.cia/library/publications 2008).
- Bermuda, located in the north Atlantic is an overseas territory of the UK with an area of 53 km² and supports a population of 66,000. Tourism is the island's major industry (www.cia/library/publications 2008).

A further group of islands can be described as mid-sized and include:

- Malta, an independent nation located in Mediterranean Sea, has an area of 316 km^2 and a population of 403,000. Tourism is a major industry (www.cia/library/publications 2008).
- The Faeroes, a self-governing overseas administrative division of Denmark located in the Atlantic, has an area of 1399 km^2 and a population of about 49,000 (www.cia/library/publications 2008). Tourism is a minor industry.
- The Falkland Islands, an overseas territory of the United Kingdom and also claimed by Argentina, is located in the south Atlantic, has an area of 12,173 km^2 and a population of 3140 (www.cia/library/publications 2008).
- Comoros located in the Indian ocean has an area of 2173 km^2 has a population of 731,000 (www.cia/library/publications 2008).
- Hawaii, located in Pacific Ocean, is a state of the United States of America and has a landmass of 10,931 km^2 and a population of 1.28 million persons.

At the other end of the geographic size scale there are a number of politically independent large islands including Taiwan, Ireland, Iceland, and Madagascar as well as large islands that form part of nations. This latter group include Newfoundland (Canada), Greenland (Denmark), Tasmania (Australia) and Sicily (Italy). Archipelagos constitute another class of islands and include Japan, the Philippines and Indonesia. In most cases these island groups are independent countries and do not face the same range of problems faced by SIDS, although within the archipelago there will often be a number of small and remote islands that face a similar range of problems to those encountered by SIDS. The final island grouping is the islands of the Caribbean which can be described as an archipelago of independent as well as colonial island states ranging in size, economic status and population.

Another element of size is per capita GDP, a measure used by development agencies when classifying islands for receipt of development assistance. Where islands form part of a larger political unit this measure will have less relevance. For example, in the Mediterranean, Corsica is part of France and while the island does share a range of development difficulties common to other islands, its per capita GDP is much higher because it is part of a larger and in this case wealthier country. Malta on the other hand is also located in the Mediterranean, but is independent and must rely on its own resources and abilities to generate economic wealth.

Geological structure

Islands are generally grouped into two major classes: continental islands and oceanic islands. Continental islands are located on continental shelves and include Greenland, Great Britain, Ireland, Sumatra and Tasmania. Micro-continental islands are a subclass of continental islands that form when a continent is rifted. Examples include Madagascar and the Kerguelen Islands (French Southern and Antarctica Lands). Oceanic islands do not sit on continental shelves and are either volcanic in origin or the result of uplift caused by tectonic forces. Examples of volcanic islands include the Hawaiian chain, the Aleutian Islands (USA) and Mauritius. Examples of uplift include Iceland and Jan Mayen (Norway), both in the Atlantic Ocean. Geographically related islands are described as archipelagos.

Geological structures of islands can also differ considerably. The Hawaiian Islands are the visible sections of a large oceanic chain of volcanic mountains some of which continue to be active. Other islands such as the Solomon Islands in the Pacific are also the visible top of a large under ocean mountain chain but in their case the volcanic activity has largely subsided. Atolls are another form of island and include the Marshall Islands, the island groups of Kiribati, Tuvalu, The Chagos Archipelago, a number of islands in the Solomon Islands and the Maldives. Atolls are interesting geological formations that also owe their existence to undersea volcanoes. At some time in the past the top of the volcano was above sea level and surrounded by a fringing coral reef (Coghlan, 2008). Over time the volcanic island subsided and corals grew upward forming a barrier reef around the island. Provided the growth of coral growth keeps pace with the rate of volcanic subsidence the atoll is formed with a central lagoon where the volcanic island was once located. Because of their low level above sea level, atolls are very susceptible to global climate change. If sea levels rise considerably in the future, caused by substantial melting of the Antarctic and Greenland ice caps and an expansion of the volume of the ocean as it warms, the drowning of coastal regions on a global scale will create a new group of near shore continental islands.

Another class of islands are those that have formed at the mouths of large rivers to create delta islands. Examples include Llha de Marajo at the mouth of the Amazon River, islands that have formed at the mouth of the Nile River in Africa and the group of islands that have formed at the mouth of the Ganges River in Bangladesh. These islands are also at risk from inundation from global warming.

Location

Location is a significant factor and can be considered from several perspectives. Geographically, islands occupy freshwater as well as oceanic positions. Freshwater islands include those located in lakes (for example, Tana Cherkoc, one of

37 islands located in Lake Tana, Ethiopia contains many heritage sites of Ethiopia's Coptic Christian Church) and in rivers. Oceanic islands range from near-shore to off-shore and mid-oceanic. For example, Singapore is located close enough to the Malaysian peninsula to allow a causeway to be constructed while Sardinia is connected to nearby Europe by ferry and air services. The Canary Islands in the Atlantic can be described as off-shore islands as can the Faroes (Atlantic Ocean) and Cocos Island (Indian Ocean). Pitcairn and Hawaii in the Pacific Ocean and Ascension Island in the Atlantic Ocean occupy a mid-oceanic location.

Aside from physical location, islands also in occupy locations in a periphery that may be based on a combination of physical distance and difficulty of access from potential generating countries. Hawaii has a reputation as being one of the most isolated island groups by virtue of its mid-oceanic location in the Pacific Ocean. In terms of its physical periphery, Hawaii has a very distant location relative to generating markets but in terms of access suffers little because of the volume of air passenger travel it attracts and its location near the major trans Pacific air route from the USA to Australia. Pitcairn Island in the Pacific also occupies a distant peripheral location from the perspectives of access and distance but because of its small physical size and small population it is unlikely to ever have an airport.

Case Study 10.1 St Helena

St Helena, a volcanic island located in the South Atlantic 2000 km west of Namibia, is the United Kingdom's second oldest colony and best known as the location where the French Emperor Napoleon Bonaparte was exiled between 1815 and 1821. The island has no airfield and relies on a regular passenger shipping service operated by the last Royal Mail Ship the RMS *St Helena*. Stopovers in St Helena range from 1 to 3 days making it difficult to support an island-based tourism industry. The island's economy is weak and aside from revenue generated by postage stamps and some agriculture the economy is propped up by aid funds from the United Kingdom. St Helena occupies a distant periphery position in both distance and ease of access to European markets including France where the status of the Island as Bonaparte's place of exile offers some scope for tourism development. The opening of an airport scheduled for 2012 will dramatically change St Helena's status from a distant periphery to a near periphery and will most probably facilitate an increase in tourism. Given that the island has limited experience with tourism developing a tourism industry will require extensive planning including community participation in decision making about the type of experiences to be offered, how the industry will be financed and target markets.

A further dimension of peripherality that is evident in many SIDS as well as in more mature island destinations are peripheries that can be seen within a national context. In Vanuatu, for example, Cassidy (2002) found that the lack of tourism development on the outer islands such as Espiritu Santo was largely due to their peripheral location at the national level. In effect they were the peripheries of the periphery or from another perspective, a national periphery. Tourism development in Vanuatu has in the past focused on the capital of Port Villa because of its ready access to international markets via air and its position as the national capital while development in the outer islands including Espiritu Santo has been limited even though they arguably have more interesting cultural resources.

Difficulties imposed by distance and position in the periphery have in the past been referred to as the 'tyranny of distance'. While the physical aspects of this form of tyranny have been spectacularly eroded by the introduction of jet airliners and the emergence of the Low Cost Carrier airline model, it is the 'death of distance', described by Cairnscross (1997) as the closing of distance by cyberspace, that has brought SIDS closer to the core via new high-speed information systems. The feeling of remoteness caused by physical distance and information isolation in countries on the periphery has been replaced by the feeling of connectiveness that comes through access to 24 h media services, the growing range of web-based information tools and jet air services. Taking advantage of these distance-shrinking technologies, however, is difficult and requires a level of investment in infrastructure and human resources that many SIDS struggle to achieve.

Development of tourism in SIDS, as in other settings, may also create situations where tourist-orientated economic development can lead to unequal socio-economic development across all regions of the country. The development of economic hot spots based on a successful tourism venture may act as a stimulus to internal migration from less-developed areas of the country (Karkazis and Thanassoulis, 1998; Nash and Martin, 2003). In a study of the development gap between the hinterland and the coast on Crete, Andriotis (2006) noted that tourism had produced a significant regional imbalance between the coastal tourism destination and its mountain hinterland. A similar development gap exists in parts of Bali where coastal communities have been able to benefit from tourism developments in beach areas such as Kuta, Nusa Dua and Legian. In the Island's interior the economic impact of tourism has been restricted to a small number of locations such as Udub.

Political dimensions

The ability of islands to develop a tourism industry has a significant political dimension. As discussed previously, islands that lie within a larger national identify share many of problems faced by similarly sized islands that have political autonomy or independency but with the advantage that they have access to central government funds and a larger domestic capital market. The island of Sardinia, an autonomous region of Italy, has access to supplementary funding from the National Government to compensate it for problems that arise from its size and location. Moreover, the smoothing effect of subsidies from the national government and access to domestic sources of investment as well as domestic generating regions largely offsets the problems that have arisen from its status as an island. In the case of Fiji located in the Pacific Ocean, the government has to look to foreign capital markets for investment and foreign aid to supplement shortfalls in internal revenue raising to provide essential social and physical capital. In many SIDS political stability and governance pose major problems for the development of tourism. Tourists demand safety and investors require institutional and economic stability. Where dangers arise that threaten the physical safety of tourists and the financial safety of investment funds, tourism does not thrive. Threats of this nature often arise through internal political problems such as political instability including coups, terrorism and corruption.

Fiji, which is heavily dependent on Australia for inbound tourists and investment funds, has a growing history of political instability which has affected the island's tourism sector. While tourists have not been physically threatened, the effect of foreign governments issuing travel advisories to their nationals advising them not to travel to Fiji has had a detrimental effect on arrivals. Also in the Pacific, ongoing internal unrest in the Solomons has prevented growth in the island's tourism industry while politically incited rioting in Tonga in 2006 caused a steep decline in tourism arrivals. In other island nations such as Sri Lanka and the Philippines, political unrest is a recurrent problem but its containment to specific areas away from those localities frequented by tourists has to some extent negated concerns about safety and failed to cause a substantial decline in inbound numbers.

Economic factors

Economic factors are key elements in any discussion of small island destination development. In the economics of international trade small islands are often price takers rather than price makers (Croes, 2006). As a consequence of their size, many SIDS lack reliable institutional frameworks, do not have advanced capital markets that can hedge against macroeconomic shocks, are prone to experience considerable dislocation when affected by natural disasters such as wind storms and earthquakes and in the future are likely to face severe problems that will arise from global warming (Shareef and Hoti, 2005). Moreover, some economists (Palmer and Riera, 2003) consider that the environmental impacts of tourism development, particularly at the mass end of the scale, are a negative externality. In some cases excessive deterioration of the environment has been caused by tourism services that have been priced too low and the total cost (including social and environmental third-party costs) exceeds the income received. Structurally, many SIDS have Migration, Aid, Remittances and Bureaucracy (MIRAB) economies that support large public sectors and rely on aid and remittances from nationals working off-shore as guest workers or who constitute a Diaspora in a host country. van der Velde *et al.* (2007) described the Pacific nation of Tonga as an aid and remittance dependent country that has significant but as yet underdeveloped tourism potential. Similar comments can be made about Samoa and the Philippines.

Shareef and Hoti (2005) identified a number of economic characteristics that exercise significance influence over the economic success of small tourism-dependent islands. Because of their small economic base and heavy reliance on tourism as a key export they face a higher risk of experiencing volatility in economic growth. The level of volatility is often a combination of their susceptibility to natural disasters, narrowness of their export base and the impact of swings in the global economy. Second, because most small islands do not receive preferential treatment and must import a wide range of goods and services to support their tourism industry, their proportion of trade relative to GDP is relatively high exposing them to possible adverse impacts from trade liberalization. A major limitation facing small tourism-dependent islands is their ability to finance development. Many of these islands are aid dependent and lack a consistent inflow of overseas capital. Access to investment capital for private and public investment is often a major hurdle for tourism development. Other economic problems faced by these nations include the prevalence of poverty in many though not all small islands, governance and the structure and maturity of the public sector which often plays a dominant role in economic activates including investment.

Political maturity is a major factor and if policy is inconsistent issues such as investor confidence and levels of corruption may become significant issues. In addition to these issues performance may be hampered by domestic demand which for many products may fall below the minimum scale required to support efficient manufacturing. The inherent diseconomies of scale have a further impact in an international trade environment that is shifting rapidly towards the globalizing economy. In the global economy those elements of domestic production that have higher unit costs than imports may be phased out, potentially adding to balance of trade deficits.

According to Croes (2006) tourism may assist small islands overcome some of the economic problems they face. By providing a larger volume of customers for goods and services that are also demanded by locals, including banking, basic services such as water and telecommunications and construction, economies of scale can be achieved that will allow for decreases in the unit costs of imports, local manufacturing and distribution. Profits then become available for limited capital mobilization, upgrading through reinvestment and acquisition of new technologies (Armstrong and Read, 1998). Tourism also encourages increased competition by encouraging new entrants that will often seek to increase their market share by reducing prices and/or enhancing service or quality levels. By providing greater consumer choice as well as providing larger markets and increased competition, living standards can be raised. For example, Maloney and Montes Rojes (2001) found that in the Caribbean, revenue from tourism was between two and five times as stable as revenue from other exports suggesting that in many cases tourism revenues are less susceptible to volatility than commodities.

Community attitudes

In many nations, tourism destinations are the product of an idea developed by an entrepreneur, firm or government and formulated around the need to build a venture that is competitive in the market places it operates in (Mitchell and Reid, 2001). Initial reactions to investment opportunities by resident communities are often influenced by pressing social and economic concerns and the desire to improve individual and community wellbeing. Doxey (1975) proposed the Irridex model which postulated that after an initial wave of euphoria community reactions may change as outsiders begin to make demands on the community that force them to change traditional ways of life. Doxey's Irridex model, although subject to some criticism particularly in relation to its failure to consider the complexity of factors that either positively or negatively impact on residents attitudes (Lankford and Howard, 1994), is an interesting concept that should be noted by planning authorities as well as investors. To date, the evidence does not conclusively support Doxey's model in small islands states.

It is evident that tourism can be a two-edged sword: while creating employment and funding investment in community social and physical capital, control may shift from local residents to government officials in distant capital cities and to investors who may reside off-shore. As Mitchell and Reid (2001) noted, shifts in power of this nature have led to deterioration of the environment and left local communities relatively worse off. This has led to calls by some commentators (Friedmann, 1992; Mitchell, 1998; Mitchell and Reid, 2001), for policies that enable local communities to reassert control over their resources. In reality however this may prove difficult because of the level of technical expertise, managerial skills and access to finance that is required to enable contemporary globally orientated development to take place. Many local communities, even in developed countries, simply lack and cannot afford to acquire the technical, financial and administrative expertise required to effectively manage large internationally focused tourism developments. In SIDS, as in many developed nations, control is often centralized at levels of power where the requisite range of skills and knowledge resides. The previously discussed example of the development gulf between the outer islands of Vanuatu and the capital of Port Villa illustrates this pattern of development which in many SIDS is exacerbated by the disparity of service standards and availability between the core and the periphery. This will of course create tensions that must be managed through a political process that gives local communities opportunities, the ability to express their opinions and enables them to meaningfully participate in ways that are not seen as tokenism.

It should also be noted that calls by commentators for strong community input and even ownership must be tempered by the fact that communities do not have the skills base or marketing networks to successful partner large projects. An alternative strategy may be to allow foreign investment on a large scale while fostering the development of a local entrepreneurial class who over time will amass the skills and capital to fund new development and in some cases buy back infrastructure that was originally financed by overseas investors.

Several other issues that are evident in tourism development funded by outside enterprises include the impacts that arise when outsiders are employed in the tourism industry and its associated support services, dislocation of locals from areas where traditionally they have had exclusive access to and social dislocation when populations are moved to make way for tourism developments. Shield (1975:265) states that social impacts are '... *responses of social systems to the physical restructuring of their environment*'. Further, Shields (1975) identified six general types of social impacts: displacement, relocations, demographic, institutional, economic impacts and disruption to community cohesion and lifestyles. In small islands, impacts of this nature may be magnified if large numbers of outsiders are employed in the tourism industry and as a consequence of their own cultural requirements and preferences seek to restructure local cultures and economies to a state where they feel less alienated. A recent example of this form of cultural modification occurred when a number of prostitutes were flown into East Timor to work in the commercial sex industry that emerged after United Nations peace keepers were posted to East Timor in the transition period between Indonesian rule and independence (1999–2002). This introduced a new element to the traditional society that may be difficult to eliminate in the post-independence period. Similarly, Green (2005) observed that growth of the tourism sector on the Thai island of Koh Samui was paralleled by the growth in prostitution and massage parlours.

Green (2005), commentating on the social impacts of tourism on Koh Samui, observed that locals lost access to the beach areas that they had traditionally used for fishing, gathering firewood, socializing and other activities. Other locals were forced to move to make way for new roads and hotels. While those directly affected may be compensated, many other community members will experience indirect effects such as local price inflation but are not compensated.

At a practical level activate participation in planning is one mechanism that allows local communities to voice their concerns over tourism development. While this is the ideal situation the reality is often the opposite. In island communities where political structures are either controlled or heavily influenced by political elites, the voice of the community may be subservient to the needs of the elite. Prior to the resignation of President Suharto of Indonesia in 1999, a powerful non-elected elite including Suharto family members exercised extraordinary influence over the development of the economy including investments in tourism. The ability of Bali to generate foreign income ensured that the island's tourism industry was given privileged access to government decision makers. In the post-Suharto era, participatory democracy and a strengthening of the rule of justice has reduced the power of the elite and given some voice to local communities which now have some ability to make their views known. The strength of communities to exercise influence is still limited however, reflecting the situation found in many other island nations.

Infrastructure

Infrastructure development is a major issue that must be addressed by islands aspiring to develop internationally competitive tourism destinations. The increasingly sophisticated nature of life in the 21st century has created a cohort of international tourists who demand high standards of service in the destinations they visit. Beginning with the need to develop aviation services that support contemporary jet aircraft, islands need to develop a range of infrastructure that in effect cocoons visitors in an environment that is able to offer safe drinking water, a consistent supply of electricity, deliver high standards of public health, ensure the personal security and safety of visitors, provide staff that offer high standards of service and who can operate the various support services found in the global tourism system and increasingly provide access to the entire spectrum of the world wide web and mobile communications technologies. The private sector also has an important role through its investments in hotels, shopping precincts, attractions and purchase of inputs such as food, construction and maintenance services. Where standards do not match international standards the tourism industry will suffer. In Papua New Guinea, tourists visiting the capital of Port Moresby have access to services that are generally of international standard except for personal security. Away from Port Moresby however the standards of many services are lower inhibiting the potential for tourism growth. Similarly, the spectre of further terrorist attacks on tourists in Bali following the Bali bombings of 2002 and 2005 has inhibited recovery of the island's tourism industry and postponed plans for further growth.

A further issue that has a significant impact on development is the transport system that has evolved within the country. The tourism transport system has at least seven elements: the journey from home to the terminal where the trip to the destination will commence; the combination of modes used during all stages of the holiday; the journey to the destination; travel within the destination; travel to attractions in the surrounding hinterland; control and governance of transport within the national setting as well as the international setting; and the range of technologies used. While the rapid development of the international aviation system has allowed many remote destinations to gain access to global aviation services the ability of islands to build suitable transport systems to distribute tourists around the destination remains a problem. In many instances public transport systems are not suitable for tourist use forcing visitors to either hire cars or use tour buses. In some cases transport between islands and along the coast is by boat sometimes with problematic safety standards.

Aviation

Aviation has a central role in strategies to develop tourism, however many SIDS have experienced substantial difficulty in developing and sustaining international aviation services. A number of nations have unsuccessfully attempted to develop national airlines and in the process have incurred substantial financial losses and importantly failed to develop access to significant international markets because of limitations of equipment, high overheads and limited marketing budgets. In the Pacific, small nationally owned airlines have struggled for decades and a number of them have collapsed. Air Nauru, the state-owned operator servicing the Republic of Nauru, had its only aircraft, a B737, reposed in 2005 because it could not meet repayments. The airline was subsequently able to lease another B737 to resume flights to the island. The 2005 collapse of Norfolk Jet Express which flew between Norfolk Island, Australia and New Zealand created significant problems for the destination that were eventually resolved by the Island's government establishing its own airline, Norfolk Air (see Figure 9.2).

FIGURE 9.2   *Passengers boarding a Norfolk Air flight at Norfolk island. (See colour insert.)*
Source: Photo courtesy of Bruce Prideaux.

Realizing that national ownership is largely impractical a number of Pacific nations have opened their aviation markets to foreign-owned airlines such as Australia's Virgin Pacific and benefited from the lower ticket prices that are able to be achieved though the economies of scale that are available to large airlines. A number of small islands operate government-owned airlines with varying success including Singapore (Singapore Airlines) and the Bahamas (Bahamasir). Many other islands are also serviced by private-owned national carriers including Antigua and Barbuda (LIAT), Hong Kong (Cathy), Cayman Islands (Cayman Airways), Dominican Republic (Dominicana) and Haiti (Tortug' Air).

Marketing

In one sense Islands have an ability to sell themselves as potential destinations but translating the desire into reality is the task of marketers and the owners of the hotels and attractions that collectively constitute the product that is on offer. This chapter commenced with references to the evocative language used by marketers of small island products. As Chacko (1997) reminded us, images are a set of mental ideas and impressions that people have about an object or place. These mental images must be used by marketers to convert interest and preference into a sale. As part of this process, destinations must be positioned in such a way that mental images are enhanced or if needed recreated to create the desire for travel. The task of marketing is important and is a role that is usually shared between the private and public sectors. Many small island administrations find it difficult to fund destination marketing and rely on the private sector to undertake a major share of this task. Where the private sector has external links such as the global networks of major hotel chains and airline affiliations it can undertake some of this task quite effectively. Major hotel chains such as Hilton and Sheraton have links to the global distribution system not readily available to independent properties. The role of international airlines is also paramount. In a parallel to the difference between global and independent hotel brands, small airlines lack the marketing clout of major international carriers that are members of global alliances and which have large international route networks and code-sharing arrangements. When Australian owned Virgin Pacific began to operate from Australia to near Pacific destinations such as Samoa and Tonga the larger marketing budget and distribution system of parent airline Virgin Blue was used to tap into a much wider distribution system and importantly achieve significant economies of scale that were used to reduce prices. Endorsement of these destinations by a respected national carrier has added to consumer confidence and made islands serviced by Virgin Pacific more attractive to Australian consumers. This has translated into larger inbound numbers in these Pacific nations.

Another strategy adopted by islands has been to combine some of their resources to create regional marketing organizations to increase their visibility and impact. For example, the South Pacific Tourism Organisation representing the Cook Islands, Kiribati, Fiji, New Caledonia, Niue, Solomons, Vanuatu, Samoa, Tahiti (French Polynesia), and Papua New Guinea provides members with research, some cooperative marketing and policy development.

Other strategies adopted by small islands include Internet advertising, advertising in specialist travel magazines (*Islands* for example) and sponsorship of the increasingly popular lifestyle network television programmes that focus on exotic holiday opportunities. The Internet, in particular, has provided small islands with the opportunity to develop independent distribution systems in a manner that is not possible using the traditional distribution system and intermediaries.

Sustainability

Defining and then achieving sustainability is a major issue for all destinations. As previously suggested, SIDS have particular problems in the area of sustainability. At some point the adoption of a pro-tourism development strategy is likely to lead to the classic 'contradiction' between economic progress and environmental degradation described by van der Velde *et al.* (2007) as the intersection between limited resources such as land and water and the demands placed on these resources by industries including tourism. Overuse of land and other resources may create a comparative disadvantage if the natural resources that confer a natural advantage are degraded.

In the past considerable efforts have been made to develop indicators that measure impacts such as sustainability, income, education and employment. While useful, indicators are often viewed on an individual basis rather than in a holistic manner. The adopting of the concept of the ecological footprint (EF) suggested by Hunter and Shaw (2007) is one measure that may assist SIDS develop more effective monitoring tools for assessing the long-term sustainability of tourism development. EF informs planners and politicians of the consequences of various alternatives in a more holistic manner than other indicators. In an era when the dangers of global climate change are becoming apparent and the economic viability of many SIDS remains a major issue, the use of EF or similar assessment tools, for measuring and management has considerable appeal. As in other destinations, many SIDS face a classic contradiction between economic progress and environmental degradation. Understanding the trade-offs thus becomes an important issue.

STRUCTURE OF ISLAND DESTINATIONS

There is a spectrum of spatial forms that tourism development at the destination level may follow. At one end of the spectrum are core areas around which clusters of tourism development occur including shopping, accommodation, attractions and entertainment zones. It is normal to also find service industry zones near core areas. Bali is a good example of this form of development. Major resort properties, shopping districts and restaurant precincts have been developed around a limited number of locations including Kuta, Legian and Nusa Dua. At the other end of the spectrum, scattered self-contained integrated resorts have developed beyond the main point of entry. Fiji is an example of the latter. Integrated resorts, where tourists spend most of their time, comprise a large part of the nation's accommodation inventory. As a consequence, most tourist consumption takes place at the resort level. This form of development poses a number of problems for planning authorities including the delivery of water and electricity, overdevelopment of foreshores, local pollution from effluent discharge that may not be treated to tertiary stage, deforestation, loss of mangroves and damage to other fragile coastal ecosystems and uncontrolled exploitation of adjacent reefs. An even more extreme example of this form of development is the Maldives where tourists are dispersed amongst the country's coral atolls and discouraged from visiting the capital except during transit to or from the

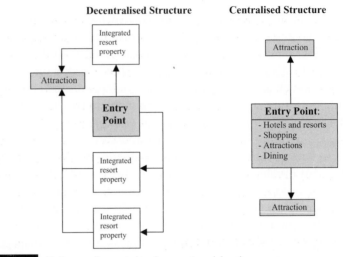

Decentralised Structure   Centralised Structure

FIGURE 9.3 *Patterns of resort development on islands.*

outlying resorts. Figure 9.3 illustrates the two extremes of island spatial development patterns with the decentralized structure model representing the spatial system observed in the Maldives. Vanuatu is an example of the centralized model. In reality, the structure adopted by many islands lies somewhere between the two extremes particularly on larger islands such as New Zealand which has multiple entry points.

In large island nations including the United Kingdom and Japan entirely different patterns of development have emerged with the range of spatial structures that reflect the size and level of development. Many UK and Japanese destinations have been developed to service the domestic tourism industry and only recently have turned their attention to the international market.

PLANNING ISSUES

Planning is a major issue given that the outcome of planning often leads to changes in land use, urban and rural environments, lifestyle and local economic opportunities. In an island setting, as in many other tourism settings, effective planning is important if the opportunities for sustainable tourism development are to be realized. In many SIDS tourism plans have been sponsored by aid agencies and handed to island administrations to implement sometimes without the additional financial resources and skilled experts required to implement the plan. Many small island communities experience difficulties translating planning objectives into practice because of conflicting governance issues, lack of finance, resistance to change or corruption. Moreover, if there is a shortage of domestic capital, foreign investment is often seen as a viable alternation.

In island settings the primary issue associated with tourism planning is the capacity of the island community to implement recommended strategies. In the planning process issues that should be addressed in the initial stage of planning include impacts on communities, impacts on heritage sites and cultural traditions, issues relating to sustainability, peripherally, transport, employment and importantly, external threats. As suggested in Chapter 3, the use of futures scenarios is an effective method of informing island administrations of the possibilities for future development. Where climate change is likely to adversely effect islands as may occur with the Maldives and Kiribati, planning should include options for relocation of the population. The next most pressing need is to identify sources of capital that are able to be regularly used to underwrite development.

FUTURE ISSUES AND DANGERS

It is apparent that long-term sustainability and adaptation to climate change standout as the two of the more significant issues that will confront islands in coming decades. In an island context, sustainability has been viewed as maintenance of island ecosystems, cultural and heritage asserts and land use patterns within a global system that has a stable climate. It is apparent that in the future even the best managed ecosystems and those that now have remained untouched will suffer from some degree of change. Traditional measurements of sustainability become problematic in such conditions. In the future, the meaning of sustainability will change as islands struggle to adapt to climate change and the changes that this process will cause to ecosystems. Management of adaptation will become one of the key benchmarks of success. For this to occur, there will need to be the adoption of national levels of integrated planning to comprehensively manage development and where necessary the adaptation of all resources including the shoreline, marine resources and the terrestrial ecosystem.

The coastal resources management policy adopted by the Indian Ocean Tourism Organisation (IOTO) (Dowling, 1998) illustrates how some of the issues discussed in this chapter need to be addressed by SIDS as well as other islands within the overall context of island tourism development. Planning processes recommended by the IOTO include recognition of the need to adopt integrated national plans for the shoreline and marine resources, the need to review individual coastal tourism developments to ensure that they proceed within coastal zone management plans, the need to protect natural scenic and cultural resources along the coast, community involvement in the planning process, clear and manageable targets in the CZM program, continual monitoring and evaluation of impacts and appropriate education programmes for employees, resort operators and resort operators. To these there is a need to add a new emphasis on the impact of climate change and other forces including globalization, peak oil and consideration of how the tourism industry can be used as a lead sector to improve social conditions as well as per capital GDP.

KEY ISSUE FOR THE FUTURE

The foregoing discussion has highlighted a number of issues that will contribute to the future success of island tourism and which require further attention by researchers. In the past many of the issues identified in the literature were structural and as such must be taken as given. Distance from generating markets is one example. Because of their nature it is unlikely that a great deal can be done to overcome the impact of factors such as distance. However, there are a further group of factors identified in this discussion that can be addressed as a matter of policy by island communities and their governments.

Implicit in many of the following points is the source of funds required for both private and public sector investment in tourism infrastructure. Ownership either by the public sector, local investors or off-shore interests is an associated issue that has been central to debates about tourism industry development in many SIDS. Limited capital formation and high external borrowings are major issues. Because of the limited scope for economic development some islands have become aid dependent while others have sought foreign investment with associated claims that profits have been remitted off-shore. In summary, the major issues for SIDS and many other island communities include:

- Identifying investment needs and sources where funds may be obtained;
- Identifying strategies for encouraging local skills development and capital formulation;
- Infrastructure enhancement to promote tourism development;
- Enhancing education, public health and public security;
- Enhancing environmental and economic sustainability in a time of global change;
- Impacts of globalization, in addition to tourism, on national culture;
- Identification of appropriate market sectors and developing appropriate products and services;
- Funding for marketing campaigns;
- Preparing for crises;
- More effective planning that includes community participation;
- Research that more effectively integrates science and social science to provide a more holistic view of issues.

CHAPTER 10

Sustainability, Change and Drivers – Shaping Future Destinations

Caring for the future today by facing the challenge of adapting to change

Preceding chapters identified a range of factors that may affect the manner in which destinations will develop and function in the future. In Chapter 3, planning was identified as a major factor in successful destination development and operation while in Chapter 5, the need to plan for crises was discussed. To these were added the future role of technology and peak oil (Chapter 4), sustainability (principally in Chapters 8 and 9), climate change in most chapters and the role of innovation in Chapter 1. Besides these factors there are a large and diverse range of factors that will exercise varying degrees of influence on the shape of destinations in the future. The difficulty of planning for the future, given the uncertainty about the impact of these and other factors, is a problem that has occupied the attention of humanity since the dawn of time. Despite our best efforts at forecasting, scenario construction and other techniques, the future remains as elusive as it did to the priestess' who occupied the position of Oracle of Delphi, a site in Greece that was concerned with foretelling the future between about 800 BC and 395 AD. In the contemporary era no one forecast the Global Financial Crisis that gripped the world from September 2008. In hindsight the warning signs were obvious but ignored. Yet in the contemporary world planning for the future has become increasingly important particularly where substantial investment is required to fund infrastructure and decisions have to be made on policy directions that will effect not only current generations but also unborn generations. Our response to climate change is

255

one such issue that is now being increasingly recognized as a factor that will have enormous ramifications for the future.

This chapter builds on the discussion that commenced in Chapter 3 to examine a range of factors that at the time of writing appear likely to either shape, inhibit or nurture future destination development. Understanding the potential of these factors to influence tourism demand and assessment of how destinations might respond is essential. Moving from a state of understanding to a state of action requires planning of the nature discussed in Chapter 3, the selection and application of guiding models of the nature discussed in Chapter 2 with the added ability to effectively respond to crises as discussed in Chapter 5. But first there is a need to conceptualize aspects of the future including how actions in the present can influence the shape of the future.

The range of possible factors that affect destinations is vast and beyond the scope of a single chapter. The approach taken in this chapter is to first examine a number of conceptual issues (Figure 10.1) into which the various factors may be nested. In particular, the chapter will examine the concept of change and the various factors that create change. The aim is to build a conceptual framework around which individual factors may be grouped and variables including cause and effect identified. The chapter then examines several key issues and how these may exercise some influence over the path of destination development in the future. The first of these issues is climate change which is emerging as a significant driver that will influence many aspects of the lives of people in the future including how and where they travel for holidays. The second key issue examined is sustainability.

GAZING INTO THE FUTURE

It is apparent that the tourism industry will face numerous challenges in the near future. While some of these challenges have been predicted by researchers and specialist futurologists including Silver (1998), Maddox (1998), Cocks (1999), Huntington (1996) and Coates et al. (1997) there will be other challenges that will only be revealed in the course of time. To date speculation on the courses open to the tourism industry of the future has been limited to forecasters and a small number of other researchers (e.g. Hall, 2000; Prideaux, 2002; Prideaux et al., 2003; Cetron, 2001; Faulkner and Russell, 2000; Yeoman, 2007; Becken, 2008). This is a weakness that needs to be urgently addressed given the magnitude of change that may occur through climate change and other events. Gazing into the future is now more urgent than exercises of this nature have been in the past.

The future, broadly defined as the time-space that contains all events that are yet to occur, is an alluring though frustrating concept. Science fiction writers and movie makers revel in the freedom to create new worlds, social orders, new species and technologies in their versions of the future, which at times has an uncanny ability to transform from science fiction into science fact. Jules Verne's stories of submarines (*Twenty thousand Leagues Under the Sea* published in 1869) and flights to the Moon (*From the Earth to the Moon* published in 1865) became reality in the following century. At this point in the discussion it is worth contemplating the relationship between the present and the future. Futureology, described as the art, science and methods used to postulate possible futures that may be plural and alternative rather than singular and predictable (see Figure 3.5), has developed a range of tools for undertaking this task (Bell, 1997). However, even with these techniques and methods the future remains largely a mystery. Of the future and our desire to know more about the world as it will be Prideaux (2002:318) wrote '*The future is just that, a different world, not yet made, but currently in the process of being created. This 'brave new world' will have its own dynamics and directions where today is tomorrow's yesterday and where the things that are valued, the places that are visited and the people who are revered (today) will be the subject of interpretative displays, weighty academic discourse and historical theses. Yet the keys of tomorrow are held in the present, even though people usually fail to see this reality without the benefit of hindsight*'. Again looking at the future Prideaux (2002:318) observed that '*In the future, which in a sense is being ... (developed) ... on the drawing boards of today, many of the accepted norms of the past and present will fall away creating new social, economic and cultural structures that will radically alter current concepts of travel*'.

Future destinations will be the product of the decisions we make in our contemporary time-space, just as our present destinations are the product of the actions of the past. The term 'time-space' is used in this context to describe relationships that include spatial elements, the economy, social trends, nature and consumer demand patterns, all of which change over time. The term should not be confused with the concept of 'space-time' used by physicists and others to describe space as three-dimensional with time occupying the fourth dimension. For this reason understanding the relationships between the present and the future, at least in respect to destinations, is critical. Building on the relationships described in Figure 1.2, Figure 10.1 illustrates the relationship between time-space (past/present/future) and the factors that shape, inhibit or nurture destinations. As illustrated in Figure 10.1 the structure and operation of the present time-space has been influenced by two sets of processes in the past. The effect of crises, trends and drivers as well as inhibitors, nature and random events (explained later in the chapter) create

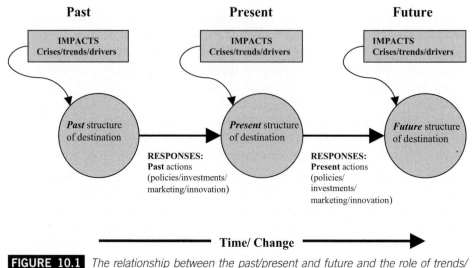

FIGURE 10.1 *The relationship between the past/present and future and the role of trends/ drivers/policy/marketing and investment in destination development.*

impacts that must be met with *responses* that can be broadly bundled into policies, investments, innovation and marketing. Combined, the elements of *impacts* (cause) and *responses* (effects) shape the future. As illustrated in Figure 10.1, the present is the sum of the impacts and subsequent responses of the past in the manner that the future will be the sum of the impacts and responses of the present.

While difficult, there remains the need to attempt to understand how the future will unfold based on the elements of change that can be identified in the present. The future is too important to be left to the future alone, and where the opportunity exists efforts need to be made to create a future that given the current state of knowledge appears to offer the best hope for the desirable version of the future identified in Figure 3.5 rather than the undesirable version that may otherwise occur. The following discussion reviews a number of issues that are likely to be confronted in the future and that will exert pressures on destination development and growth. From the perspective of the present, the list appears to be comprehensive but in all probability a reader in the future will identify issues that will be important in their time-space but that were missed in this discussion and find issues that appeared to be significant in the present time-space that had little impact in the future. The discussion in the remainder of this chapter picks up where Chapter 3 left off and commences with a brief discussion of the concept of change before reviewing the role of various types of impacts and responses and how destinations may respond.

CHANGE

Change refers to a *fundamental long-term shift* and is a key force in the continuing process of reshaping and reordering of the global society we live in. Change is manifest in every aspect of our lives. By understanding the forces that create and propel change, destinations are able to innovate and adapt their products and services to tomorrow's market place. In tourism, examples of change include the shift from mass tourism to more individual forms of tourism and the shift from sea to air travel for intercontinental travel. If destinations fail to recognize change and its implications they are more likely to continue to sell yesterday's products and services in today's market often leading to a decline in popularity, demand and income (see Case Study 10.1) of the nature predicted by Butler (1980) and Prideaux (2002, 2004). The main agents that create change include:

- Trends
- Disasters and Crises (refer to Chapter 5 for a full discussion)
- Chance or random events
- Innovation
- New technology
- Nature, and
- Policy which describes the responses made to the previous agents of change.

In almost all societies, cultural, social, economic, political and technological environments are changing at rates that far exceeded the rate of change in the past. Just as these aspects of society have combined, or repelled, to create history and shape the present they will continue to interact to create the future. Recognizing change is important as is the parallel action of response. Change is such a continuous process that we almost fail to recognize it. Change occurs through drivers that push society and its many elements into new directions and must first be recognized and then responded to by innovation and adaptation. Change can be incremental, rapid or revolutionary. Incremental change is a process of gradual change which may be either positive or negative. At the destination level incremental change entailing small losses of natural areas to development that may not appear to be significant at first but over time may become significant. Alternatively, change can be rapid and occur over short time frames or revolutionary where change may include over-turning existing policy frameworks or even social or political structures. In tourism, change has a propensity to be incremental because of the nature of the investments that are required to implement change but in some circumstance may be either rapid or revolutionary if external shocks affect the system.

An obvious outcome of change in recent decades has been the explosion of domestic and international travel options centred on place and activity types. In a global sense, destinations can no longer remain static and have been forced to embark on a constant process of reinvention to respond to changing demand. Destination managers and marketers must therefore continually monitor shifts in short-term trends and be cognizant of the more fundamental drivers of change if they are to successfully identify where change is occurring and what response strategies are required. The success of response strategies will usually be a function of how well the private and public sectors are aware of their responsibilities for destination management and development and how well the two sectors work together. The private sector has the lead role in responding to change with the introduction of new products and rejuvenation of existing products and services. The public sector is responsible for updating polices that reflect contemporary views and beliefs and for providing guidance that facilitates rather than hinders rejuvenation.

Research is the key mechanism for understanding change and must occur at many levels including at the enterprise level, the destination level and the national level. The types of research undertaken also vary, ranging from formal academic studies through to private consultancy and publically funded 'public good' research. Research may also be explorative or confirmative and tactical or strategic. Moreover, research should strive to be innovative and forward looking not retrospective. Without exploratory research destinations operate in a vacuum unsure about who their visitors are and what experiences and quality they are seeking. Confirmative research may be used to verify the findings of explorative research creating knowledge that can be diffused to both the public and private sectors in the destination. Similarly, tactical research provides information about the present while strategic research has more to do with the future.

It is a sad reflection on the current state of tourism research that the majority of research is reflective, lacking in interdisciplinary focus and is concerned with small-scale issues that fail to provide insight or guidance on the major issues that will affect the industry in the future. There is a need for tourism researchers to look forward and outwards and embrace the challenges of the future. A proactive strategy by journal editors to encourage research of this nature is one strategy that might assist a favourable resolution to this problem.

In recent decades destinations have undergone significant change driven by a number of impacts (crises/trends/drivers) that include:

- Changing patterns of consumer demand and preferences for leisure.
- An increased emphasis on a range of security issues following terrorist attacks and natural disasters.

- Rising crude oil prices.
- New regional and political structures and agreements that made cross border travel easier, promoted world peace and encouraged travel beyond national borders.
- A lack of prolonged multinational conflicts.
- Technology including web-based marketing and distribution.
- Reduction in international tensions since the collapse of the USSR.
- Increasing global wealth and a globalizing economy.
- Increasing ease of long distance transport.
- Increasing personal wealth in many countries, and
- Transformation of travel from a luxury to a consumer good.

Responses (policies/investments/marketing innovation) to these changes by the tourism industry can be measured through spatial changes, new products and responses to new consumer segments and include:

- Mass tourism fuelled by world economic growth, enhanced security and cheap air travel.
- Emergence of new forms of tourism including ecotourism, adventure tourism and heritage tourism.
- Emergence of a global travel network of hotels, tour operators, transport companies and attractions that actively promote travel as one of life's necessities rather than a luxury.
- Emergence of numerous new destinations.
- Realization by government that tourism has a special case for government assistance in funding promotional activities.

Collectively, impacts of the type outlined and the responses to these impacts have shaped the current structure of travel and destinations while current impacts and the manner in which they are responded to will shape the future structure of travel and destinations.

IMPACTS: THE ROLE OF TRENDS, CRISES, DRIVERS, INHIBITORS, NATURE, AND RANDOM EVENTS

Collectively, the most significant factors that cause change are trends, crises drivers, inhibitors, policy, random events, technology and nature. The role of each of these forces within the destination is at times confusing and overlapping. While this discussion treats trends and drivers as separate though related forces, there is an equally strong case for viewing them as different aspects of the same group of factors that cause change.

Trends

Trends are those sequences of events that can be identified in the present and which, unless remedial action is taken, will cause some magnitude of disruption, or progress, in the future. Several types of trends effect tourism:

- Short-term trends that include places and activities that are currently in demand or fashionable.
- Long-term trends where there has been a fundamental shift such as the emergence of new forms of tourism demand, a prolonged period of economic growth or a prolonged period of economic decline.

Falling birth rates in many developed economies will generate significant shifts in future travel patterns. In Japan the population is projected to decline by 17.9 million between 2000 and 2050 at current fertility rates, while the number of persons aged 60 years or more will climb to 42% of the population (Cooper and Eades, 2007). Trends of this nature can be identified in the present and responded to by the tourism industry as it adjusts its products. From a political perspective, trends of this type are amenable to change through policy adjustments including incentives for women to increase fertility rates. From the perspective of the tourism industry it is necessary to identify trends that will impact on future demand and incorporate this knowledge into investment and policy decisions.

Drivers

Drivers are defined as those *factors that underpin change* and cause it to occur. There are numerous drivers which operate at international, national, regional and personal levels. The following examples of global drivers highlight their diversity. Global drivers include:

- *Technology.* Technological change was the driving force behind the European industrial revolution that reordered European society and its economy in the late 18th to mid-19th centuries and laid the foundation for the contemporary era. New transport technologies facilitated the creation of mass tourism by reducing the time and cost of travel. Numerous other technologies had important roles in transforming society and the economy. In the present era the impact of a fundamental shift in industrial technology may be observed in China and to a lesser degree in India. Both countries are undergoing a modern day version of the European Industrial Revolution with similar results being observed in the growing demand for tourism in both countries.
- *The growth of the service economy.* The ability to produce the necessities of life with an increasingly smaller percentage of the

workforce has generated an expansion of the service economy and the ability of consumers to spend on services that include travel.

- *World economic growth.* In the decade or so prior to 2008 global economic growth was underpinned by growth in China and to a lesser extent in India as well as growth in the United States and in parts of the developing world. In the long run the probability that growth will slow, decline or halt should be seriously considered.
- *Increasing number and variety of destinations.* The increasing demand for travel and novelty has created opportunities for the emergence of many new destinations.
- *Climate change.* This driver will be examined in more detail later in the chapter.
- *Peak oil.* Peak oil is defined as the point at which the rate of global oil extraction reaches its maximum rate after which the rate of extraction enters terminal decline. Currently, there is considerable dispute over when this point will be reached. Sharp increases in the price of crude oil in 2008 point to the future where the demand for oil will be greater than supply forcing further price rises. As the price rises, new technologies will become viable and substitutes, including fuel cells, battery powered cars and third generation biofuels, will become affordable reducing the demand for oil.

Personal drivers which influence decisions about travel include:

- *Rising travel by baby boomers and younger generations who are more interested in travel than their forbears.* Baby boomers, in general, have greater access to wealth than any previous generation and have become history's most travelled generation. The substantial fall in wealth caused by the 2008–2009 Global Financial Crisis may affect baby boomer's propensity to travel for some time.
- *Acceptance that change is a normal condition of life.* In the past change was often resisted. Today people embrace change which for the tourism industry has both positive and negative elements. Consumers are now more willing to try new destinations, products and methods of travel and in the process, are showing a declining level of loyalty to once favoured destinations.
- *Travel is fashionable.* Travel is now an ordinary consumer good not a luxury.
- *Increased post-cold war global security.* In spite of wars, terrorism etc there continues to be an increasing number of secure destinations open for business.
- Demand for travel visa a vies other forms of consumer spending.

- *Ethical travel.* In the future will consumers view carbon-producing travel within in an ethical decision-making framework of personal values?
- Demand for flat screen TVs and other consumer goods and services limits consumer's ability to undertake travel.

Inhibitors

Inhibitor is a general term that describes factors of any type (including trends, drivers, random events, policy) and from any source that place restrictions on growth and also on change. In this sense inhibitors may be negative in that they prevent desirable change or positive in the sense that they stop growth that has negative impacts. In identifying inhibitors there is also overlap with trends, policies and drivers. Some trends, for example, may inhibit change. Similarly, policies that quarantine some natural areas from redevelopment may be classed as inhibitors.

Prideaux (2000d) suggested that in the near future the following may inhibit tourism:

- The impact of AIDS – particularly in Sub-Saharan Africa, and potentially in the Indian subcontinent and the Russian Federation;
- Terrorism employed to achieve political or religious objectives;
- Unexpected natural disasters;
- Unanticipated wars; and,
- Militant religious fundamentalism.

To these factors can be added insurance. If the risk of building on coastlines that are exposed to rising sea levels or more violent weather events is regarded as substantial insurance companies will either increase premiums or simply refuse to accept the risk forcing investors to consider other sites for tourism activity.

Beyond the proximate future Prideaux (2000b) has speculated that a spectrum of possible factors may disrupt tourism including:

- The future direction that is taken by capitalism following the demise of socialism;
- Technological innovation, particularly as it impacts on leisure and transport;
- Demographic change, in terms of ageing populations in developed economies, as well as growing populations in many developing countries;
- A continuing search for political identity by ethnic and religious groups causing further fragmentation in a number of nations;

- Overuse and abuse of natural resources, particularly of farming lands, water, marine resources and non-renewable energy;
- Environmentalism, especially if global warming continues;
- Public health scares such as pandemic diseases;
- Warfare that could be triggered by many of the preceding factors or as new power blocks emerge to challenge the existing international order; and
- A possible clash between Westernism (roughly defined as the projection of the West's contemporary and dominant social, economic and cultural structures through globalization) and radical Islam. The apparently widely supported rejection of Westernism's aggressively secular libertarianism by Islam's world-view of a theocratic state centred on the teachings of the Koran may shape international relations, and tourism, for some time.

Nature

Nature works in cycles and time frames that are beyond human control and are not adequately understood. As a consequence, long-term prediction is difficult if not impossible and even short-term forecasting has yet to demonstrate a satisfactory level of reliability. Observation and response is the only recourse open, at least within our present understanding of nature. In the past the world has been dramatically and regularly reshaped by events that include glaciation, volcanism, changes in weather cycles, magnetic poles have reversed, and meteors that have dramatically altered global ecosystems leading to mass species extinctions. There is every reason to believe that nature will continue to act in the future as it has in the past and in time frames that we cannot predict. Our inability to tame or better still dominates these forces of nature leaves adaptation, whatever the cost, as the only acceptable response. In previous chapters numerous references have been made to climate change but in any discussion of nature, and accepting our lack of knowledge of the causes of major long-term climate shifts, it would be remiss not to consider the topic of Ice Ages. During the late Pliocene ice sheets advanced across the Northern hemisphere in a cycle of glaciation where ice sheets advanced and retreated on 40,000–100,000 year time scales. The last period of glaciation ended about 11,000 years ago and the Earth is currently in the Holocene interglacial period. When and if a new period of glaciation will occur and how conditions associated with climate change will affect the cycle of advance and retreat of glaciers is unknown. One recent paper (EPICA community members, 2004) based on analysis of ice cores in the Antarctic postulated that the next ice age may be some way off, a position supported by Berger and Loute (2002).

Chance or random events

While many of the previous forces of change allow some scope for prediction, the notion of chance, defined as an opportunity, possibility or probability that a random event will occur, defies predictability. Randomness can be described as a lack of a defined plan or pre-arranged order and follows no describable deterministic pattern but does follow a probability distribution. A recent movie titled *Sliding Doors* (1998) staring Gwyneth Paltrow encapsulated the notion of chance in a very theatrical manner. The movie explores alternative futures for the principle character using two scenarios. In the first she just manages to catch a London Underground train and on arriving home finds her boyfriend with an ex-girlfriend and in the second misses the train and has no idea of the relationship. One way of viewing the concept of chance is to consider possible histories that never happened because of a random event. For example, we will never know what the world of 2008 could have been if the September 11 terrorist attack had not occurred. That alternative future was possible before the events of September 11th but impossible after the events of that day. Further back in time, how would the world be different if the assassin who killed Archduke Franz Ferdinand (the heir to the Austro-Hungarian throne) and set in train the events that culminated in the outbreak of World War One, had missed or the shot that killed US President John F. Kennedy had not been fatal?

The impact of events that occur by chance (the concept of either *being in the right place at the right time* or the converse idea of *being in the wrong place at the wrong time* or variations on this theme) is unpredictable but must be anticipated and able to be dealt with by appropriate response mechanisms.

RESPONSES – POLICY, INVESTMENT AND MARKETING

The previous discussion centred on a range of impacts that can affect destinations and tourism in general. Once an impact occurs some order of change can be expected and will generate a response by key destination stakeholders in the public and private sectors as well as from consumers.

Policy

Policy can be described as a position, strategy, action or product adopted by government and arising from contests between different ideas, values and interests (Hall, 2008). Government policy provides the framework around which businesses respond to the drivers of change. In a period of change policy makers need to be adaptive and forward looking rather than reflective and defensive. Policy can create change as well as respond to change.

Investment

The private sector may respond to change with new investment if there is an opportunity to improve profits or disinvestment if the policy is seen as negative. Without investment destinations are unable to respond to pressures to change and face the prospect of decline.

Marketing

Marketing is a key element in communicating positive messages about the destination's response to impacts. In circumstances where some form of crisis has occurred marketing is used to reassure. Where the response of the destination to impacts is less obvious and occurs over a long time period the aim of marketing should be to promote the destination and increase its market share.

Innovation

Innovation is a key strategy for responding to change. A number of destinations have been able to build significant tourism markets by developing nature-based experiences. Similar comments may be made about other destinations that have developed their available resources to capture new markets. In the future destinations that are able to rapidly respond to changing consumer demand, peak oil, climate change and so on will remain successful.

FUTURE DIRECTIONS OF TOURISM

A number of issues appear to be influencing the shape of future tourism flows including: emerging source markets; new technologies; concern about climate change; improving health standards; and a largely peaceful world where few off-limit borders remain to impede the global traveller in their quest for new places to gaze upon and experience. Identifying the impact of these issues and deciding how the destination should respond is a significant exercise. Looking at source markets for example it appears that in the future the primary opportunities for growth will come from:

- Increasing numbers of tourists from the newly industrializing Asian economies particularly China and India. On a smaller scale new cohorts of travellers will emerge from Latin America, Eastern Europe and, in a more distant time frame, possibly from sub-Saharan Africa;
- Longer annual holidays in developing countries will boost domestic bed nights first, followed by international bed nights.

- As life expectancy increases additional post-retirement travel will be possible, subject to retirees having sufficient funds to provide for normal living expenses incurred during their expected post-retirement life span.
- New technologies will assist these new tourist cohorts, as well as existing cohorts to travel further, cheaper and faster with the caveat that rising fuel prices in the absence of new fuel technologies may create rises in the price of transport to the extent that global demand falls. One example of a new technology is the Maglev train previously discussed in Chapter 4.

RESPONDING TO CHANGE

It is apparent that change must be recognized and then responded to. This process is often neglected because change may be difficult to detect, difficult to quantify and it is often difficult to predict how successful responses will be. Failure to change is also a function of the desire to accept the status quo, a desire to reap the benefits of past experiences, a tiredness that emerges after a period of innovation or growth, or just plain bad management. Whatever the reason, failure to change often results, in the case of destinations, in a loss of markets. Case Study 10.1 illustrates a situation of this nature where the tourism industry as well as the government of Norfolk Island, a small Australian dependency located in the South Pacific, grew complacent with its product, comfortable with its visitor market, and failed to reinvest. The inevitable downturn forced the Island community to re-evaluate its tourism industry, which is the island's major industry and employer, and implement a new long-term strategy that addressed the major causes of decline.

Case Study 10.1 Norfolk Island

Located just over 2 h by passenger jet from the major Australian generating regions of Brisbane and Sydney, Norfolk Island has become increasingly dependent on tourism as its major source of external revenue and of employment. The island is a self-governing territory of Australia and elects its own Legislative Assembly. The Island was first used by British Colonial authorities as a penal colony to house the very worst convicts that had been sent to the Australian colonies at the end of the 18th century and early 19th century. After the penal institution was closed the island was settled by the descendents of the mutinous crew of the HMS Bounty. Its main attractions are its penal heritage (illustrated in Figure 10.2) and nature. As with many other small islands in the Pacific and elsewhere, Norfolk Island is confronted with a range of problems including over-dependency on

FIGURE 10.2   *The Kingston heritage reserve on Norfolk Island. The buildings in this illustration were constructed prior to 1850 and form part of a larger penal settlement out of view in the photo.*
Source: Photo courtesy of Jacquie Cox.

tourism, lack of viable economic alternatives, limited tourism research, a peripheral location, carrying capacity limitations, a market follower rather than a market leader, and tourism infrastructure that has fallen behind contemporary standards in its main generating markets of Australia and New Zealand.

Research undertaken by Prideaux *et al.* (2007) found that while the island had a strong positive image as a heritage destination, had high levels of visitor satisfaction, was competitively priced and offered high service standards, it had failed to recognize that the characteristics of its main market, the seniors market, had undergone a generational shift. The pre-war generation (people born prior to 1946) had been the mainstay of the Island's tourism industry for some time, however this generation is now being replaced by the baby boomer generation (born between 1946 and 1965) as the new seniors. Baby boomers require a destination that offers a range of experiences and services that are significantly different to the experiences and services expected by the previous generation. Glover and Prideaux (2009) noted that failure to change tourism products and services to reflect the consumption patterns of non-senior travellers could result in a slow decline in visitor numbers. The danger of a decline of this nature is that it would reduce the capacity of the government and private sector to refurbish existing infrastructure and undertake new investment. In the case of Norfolk Island, the result was a decline in visitor numbers in the

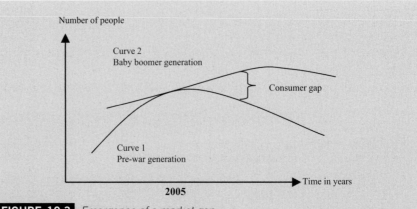

FIGURE 10.3 *Emergence of a market gap.*
Source: Modified version of model developed by Singer and Prideaux (2009).

five-year period 2000–2005 by 15% to 34,000 visitors after which numbers stabilized. A report (Acumen Alliance, 2005) into the Island's financial sustainability predicted that if 2005 visitor levels were maintained the Norfolk Island Government would have insufficient operating funds by mid-2007.

The failure to react to changing demand patterns may lead to the emergence of a consumer gap of the type illustrated in Figure 10.3. Using Norfolk Island as an example two demand curves were developed to illustrate potential demand based on generation membership. These curves could also represent other factors including age, income and motives. As they pertain to Norfolk Island, Curve 1 represents the pre-war generation while Curve 2 represents the potential growth of visitor numbers based on the size of the baby boomer cohort. As the number of pre-war seniors declines over time demand generated by this segment will decline. If pre-war seniors are not replaced by another group, baby boomers for example, a market gap will emerge. In a sense tourism demand is following a classic product life-cycle trajectory that will enter decline unless a new range of products are developed to meet the demands of the new group of seniors.

To close this gap the Island's tourism industry must develop a new range of products while still retaining the services and products favoured by the pre-war seniors market. If new or re-imaged products are not developed to fill the gap, baby boomers will seek other destinations leading to a sharp decline in tourism arrivals. The Norfolk Island Five Year Tourism Strategy 2007/08–2011/12 (Global Tourism and Leisure, 2007) recognized the emergence of the product gap and recommended a rejuvenation of the destination through a 5-year recovery and development strategy that shifted the focus of marketing onto the baby boomer generation. The destination accepted that it needed to change, adopted the report and at the time of writing was embarking on a series of reforms to develop new products and services geared to the baby boomer market.

Climate change

In the past decade concern over the long-term impact of increasing CO_2 and other 'Greenhouse' gasses (including methane and ozone) has occupied the attention of policy makers and more recently consumers. Concerns about climate change date back several decades with the first major report on climate change being issued by the Inter Parliamentary Committee on Climate Change in 1990. The report later formed the basis for the United Nations Framework Convention on Climate Change (UNFCCC) held in Rio de Janeiro in 1992.

As a general concept climate change describes a long-term change in 'average weather' patterns where average weather refers to the day-to-day state of the atmosphere and is measured through average temperature, wind patterns and precipitation. Climate change of this nature is long-term and has in the past been caused by dynamic processes that include volcanism, variations in sunlight activity, orbital variations and plate tectonics (Pittock, 2005). In the past, global temperatures have shown considerable variation. In its more recent context the term climate change has been used to describe the shift in weather patterns and associated ecosystem responses that are caused by increasing emissions of greenhouse gasses through human action.

As previously outlined in this chapter the most recent and significant climate process to affect global weather patterns was glaciation, a process that is continuing to occur with the Earth presently in the Holcene inter-glacial period. At the height of its cycle during the last period of glaciation average global temperatures were much lower than current global average temperatures, ice caps had advanced from the polar regions and mountain systems to cover large tracts of land, sea levels were up to 120 m lower than today and the mosaic of global ecosystems was vastly different from those of today.

The current concern about climate change is based on fears that rapidly rising atmospheric carbon dioxide concentrations in addition to rising levels of other gasses including methane will cause an increase in global average temperatures leading to a range of adverse impacts (IPCC, 2007). The impacts that are of most concern include changes in global weather patterns that will disrupt ecosystem distribution and health, and the potential for increasing sea levels. The 2007 IPCC Report estimated that on average a temperature rise of 3.5 °C could cause extinctions of between 40% and 70% of species assessed. Concerns have also been voiced about the possible impact of increasing acidity of the Earth's oceans in a process known as acidification.

The world's scientific community has responded relatively quickly to these concerns and supported substantial investment in research into mitigation (defined as strategies to reduce the emission of CO_2 and other gasses) and adaption (defined as adjustment strategies to cope with climate-induced change) to climate change. Case Study 8.2 which examined possible impacts of Climate Change on the Wet Tropics Rainforests of North Queensland, is just one example of the type of investigations being undertaken in the natural sciences. The global community has also responded through international protocols including the 1997 Kyoto Protocol and more recently through legislative measures that will lead to mandatory carbon trading. Surprisingly, the tourism industry which has much to lose and less to gain from climate change has been slow to respond to the concerns expressed by the scientific community. The tourism literature reflects this apparent lack of concern. Only a small number of papers and even fewer books (see Becken and Hay, 2007; Hall and Higham, 2005 for example) have been published and there seems to be a lack of concern about possible impacts. Recent research by Prideaux *et al.* (2009) highlights the continuing gap between individual awareness and action in responses to climate change issues.

The series of reports issued by the IPPC Fourth Assessment Report (2007:1) written by a team of over 600 scientists warns that warming of the climate system is unequivocal and is '. . . is now evident from observations of increases in global average air and ocean temperatures, widespread melting of snow and ice and rising global average sea level'. Further, the report noted that 'Observational evidence from all continents and most oceans shows that many natural systems are being affected by regional climate changes, particularly temperature increases'. Expected impacts of climate change noted by the IPPC (2007) included shifts in the range of some species, increasing acidification of the oceans, flooding, retreating glaciers, rises in global sea levels, reduced snow fall in some areas, longer and more sever drought, reduced summer flows of snow feed rivers in many areas, coral bleaching, more intense fire events and so on.

The IPPC has been criticised as being conservative and that its climate models may have underestimated the severity of climate change. For example, the 2007 Report estimated that sea levels could rise between 18 and 59 cm but in this estimation excluded any possible increase due to melting of the Greenland ice sheet because of a lack of published research on this topic. While the causes of changes of this nature are not altogether clear there is concern about unpredicted 'surprises' or tipping points (defined as a slow or gradual change that may accelerate and become irreversible) that accelerate predicted or unpredicted changes. In the human domain McKercher *et al.* (2008) identified the importance of a future 'tipping point' where consumers will realize that change is not an issue for others to worry about, but is an issue requiring the acceptance of personal responsibility and action.

It is apparent that the tourism industry will not escape policies that are aimed at both mitigation and adaption with the impacts likely to grow as the extent of mitigation and adaption required becomes evident. According to Matzarakis (2002) and Braun *et al.* (1999) the impacts of climate change will be severe, long lasting and expensive. There is every likelihood that large-scale disturbances are possible in some tourism markets if the tourism industry fails to respond in a timely manner (Hamilton *et al.*, 2005). Destinations and individual businesses that recognize the need for adaption and assume the role of innovators will in all probability experience fewer negative impacts than destinations and individual operators that are less willing to innovate or are inclined to adopt a 'wait and see' attitude will endure. Surprisingly, there has been little work undertaken into how either destinations or consumers will respond or how destinations may innovate.

It is highly likely that tourism will become a target for climate change policy given its reliance on fossil fuel, its transport-dependent nature and the carbon foot-print which this entails. This situation is compounded by the failure of the collective tourism industry to organize on an industrial basis to gain the recognition that other industry sectors enjoy, including perversely' major polluters such as power generation and cattle producers. Given that tourism is estimated to contribute 5% of global greenhouse emissions (Becken and Hay, 2007) the industry faces threats from policy makers wishing to reduce carbon emissions particularly if tourism is seen as a non-essential consumer good. The initial threat is likely to be the added costs imposed through carbon trading schemes followed soon after by consumer concerns about the amount of carbon they are responsible for. As the distance of travel increases there is a parallel rise in the tourist's carbon footprint. Already there are signs emerging that European consumers are becoming more aware and concerned about their carbon footprint. If concern is translated into action, long haul and carbon expensive destinations may lose popularity.

Issues of this nature are of critical importance to destinations that rely on long haul tourists but have yet to be addressed in depth in the tourism literature and aside from a small though growing number of publications (see for example Becken, 2004, 2007; Koeing and Abegg, 1997; Hall and Highman, 2005) the debate has been left to other literatures (see for example specialist journals such as *Climate Change*). This is surprising given the prominence of the issue in the debates arising from the Kyoto Protocol, carbon trading and the publicity surrounding the publication of the IPPC Report of 2007, the Stern Review Report (2006) and Al Gore's (2006) film *An Inconvenient Truth*. It is apparent that additional research needs to be focused on the ethical dimensions of travel in a climate change context, the manner in which consumers will respond when they are faced with the external costs of their travel decisions, the severity of mitigation impacts such as carbon trading, the cost of adaptation, possible crises that may arise from unexpected tipping points being reached and the changing nature of the conservation debate and what this means for current ideas of sustainability. Additional research into carbon footprints of the type undertaken by Simmons and Becken (2004) as well as the possible impact of carbon trading is urgently required to guide policy makers and investors. Dwyer and Forsythe (2008) argued that long-haul travel will be subject to additional costs from carbon trading schemes and negative media images. The translation of research of this nature into predictions or forecasts that are able to be used by policy makers and planners has yet to occur. Other research into specific environments of the nature undertaken in alpine and skiing destinations (Koenig and Abegg, 1997; Elasser and Burki, 2002; Scott *et al.*, 2003; Becken and Hay, 2007) and in marine and coastal tourism destinations (Gable, 1997; Hoegh-Guldberg, 1999; Becken and Hay, 2007) is also required.

As Prideaux *et al.* (2009) point out climate change is likely to affect tourist behaviour and demand in two ways. The most obvious effect is the impact of climate change on the resource base of affected destinations. Severe impacts will reduce the appeal of these destinations. Coral bleaching and the absence of snow are two examples. Secondly, tourism behaviour is likely to be affected by moral, ethical and economic issues. Concern over the carbon cost of travel as well as carbon trading price increases may force consumers to re-evaluate their travel plans.

Recent research by the author (Prideaux *et al.*, 2009) found that most consumers have yet to view their travel plans through the lens of climate change mitigation. However, within this seeming lack of concern there is some evidence of change (Prideaux *et al.*, 2009). There is increasing consumer interest in finding out about the size of personal travel carbon footprint (Prideaux *et al.*, 2009). The same survey identified a number of indicators that could be used to identify shifts in consumer sentiment towards climate change. The indicators identified included: changes in the number of people who currently measure their carbon footprint; the number who were interested in finding out the size of their carbon footprint; willingness to pay a carbon offset; percentage of respondents who fly less; purchasing carbon offsets from airlines; percentage of respondents who participate in conservation programmes; consumer behaviour in regard to buying green electricity; shopping at stores that offer carbon offsets; and purchasing products that include carbon offset schemes. Further research of this type is required to confirm the strength of these indicators which may be useful variables for predicting future consumer decision-making patterns where climate change issues are seen as important.

As serious as these concerns are, not all destinations will suffer significant challenges directly from climate change although all will probably suffer from indirect effects caused by mitigation and adaptation policies such as carbon trading. The type of disruptions likely to be suffered will include coral bleaching that will impact on destinations that rely on access to reefs as a major component of their tourism industry, ski destinations particularly in lower altitudes, coastal areas if sea levels rise significantly and regions where ecosystems will be substantially modified due to changes in weather factors.

Sustainability

Sustainability has been a buzzword in tourism research for some time but it is apparent that the concept and its underlying premises are poorly understood (Cooper *et al.*, 2005). Sometimes ago Murcott (1996 in Cooper *et al.*, 2005) listed 57 definitions of sustainability. Cooper *et al.* (2005) identified two schools of thought about sustainability: strong or fully sustainable proponents: and weak or partial sustainable supporters. The supporters of the strong sustainability school view growth as reducing sustainability while the weak supporters maintain there is some scope for development. From an ecological perspective sustainability refers to the ability of ecosystems to maintain ecological processes, functions, productively and biodiversity into the future. Sustainability in practical terms refers an ability to use resources in a manner that can be continued indefinitely in the future (Krebs, 2008). As Krebs (2008:128), an eminent ecologist, observed *'like all populations, human populations are subject to the rule that critical resources limit population growth sooner or later. The carrying capacity of Earth for humans may have already been exceeded, and the transition from a growing human population to a stable one is one of the most important problems of the century'*.

In a global sense sustainability is possible when the consumption of resources occurs at a rate that allows resources to be replaced. There is mounting evidence that the global community is consuming resources at a rate that exceeds nature's ability to replace them. In the tourism literature little of the current discussion on sustainability acknowledges the science on which the concept rests. Much of the current thinking about sustainability appears to assume that ecosystems are stable and able to retain their biological integrity over the long-term. Views of this nature fail to understand that biological communities are not restricted by temporal measures such as park boarders and respond to changes in climate (both natural and human induced) by adaption, migration or extinction. Global climate patterns are constantly changing in a series of short- and long-term cycles which have been documented but remain an area of debate amongst climatologists. As a consequence biological communities are constantly changing. Human-induced climate change is a new factor in this long-term cycle of climate change and is forcing plant and animal communities to respond at rates that are more rapid than in the past.

In the past the central agenda of most conservation ecologists was to establish protected habits that were viable based on the premise that climates are stable. Increasingly, conservation ecologists are recognizing that the premise of stable biological boundaries protected by imposed administrative boundaries is no longer valid. As weather conditions change and variables including temperature, rainfall and humidity fluctuate some species will migrate in search of more favourable weather conditions. Previous boundaries no long become sustainable as ecosystems respond in this manner. As Oosthoek (2008:33) observes that 'there is a growing chorus of scientists who are recommending a radical shift in thinking about the role of conservation'. Rather than trying to preserve nature in the state we found it there is a case for reassembling ... damaged ecosystems to improve them'. Choi (2007:351) states that it is not realistic to replicate pre-disturbance ecosystems because of the irreversible nature of the damage that has occurred. Instead, a more logical approach is to rehabilitate essential ecological functions.

In a long but inclusive definition of sustainable tourism development the World Tourism Organisation (in Welford, 1999:165) states 'Sustainable tourism development meets the needs of present tourists and host regions while protecting and enhancing opportunities for the future. It is envisaged as leading to management of all resources in such a way that economic, social, and aesthetic needs can be fulfilled while maintaining cultural integrity, essential ecological processes, and biological diversity, and life support systems'. The sentiment expressed in this definition leans towards the weak sustainability school of thought. Whether further economic development of the nature we have witnessed in the past is possible or desirable needs to be measured against the views of Kerbs and others who state that the Earth has already exceeded the limits of its ecological footprint. Perhaps a more logical approach to sustainability is to shift the emphasis from the tourist and host community to the environment, recognizing that in the near future many ecosystems will change. A revised definition might read: sustainable tourism firstly protects and enhances the environment while secondly recognizing the needs of present tourists and host communities, provided that their presence does not degrade ecological processes, biodiversity or interfere with the ecosystem's ability to respond to climate change.

If the impact of the drivers discussed in this chapter is as dramatic and far-reaching as predicted the case for no-growth will be compelling. How destinations will react cannot be ascertained at this point in time but there are grounds for contemplating a future where long distance air travel will be on a scale below that of today and leisure travel will be more local in nature.

CONCLUSION

In future debates on sustainability and the ability of humanity in general to negotiate the threats posed by peak oil and climate change, the tourism industry must have its views recognized if the industry is not to suffer unduly from policy frameworks imposed to combat the effects of climate change and declining sustainability. To find its voice and to be heard in the chorus of other actors seeking recognition of their own claims the tourism industry must become more sensitized to the possible effects outlined preciously and draw on science and other disciplines to vigorously argue its case. It is all to easy to cite the unrealized fears of the Y2K bug as an excuse to label the concerns outlined in this chapter as of little real consequence. It has, it seems, been difficult for the academic community to accept leadership on these issues and for destinations to accept that these issues are important and need urgent responses. Hopefully this will change in the near future.

At the outset of this book reference was made to the role of innovation as a strategy for navigating the problems of the future. The way forward lies in innovation or early adoption on new ideas. Destinations that choose to ignore the changing reality of the market place, the wider economy nature will be left behind, those that listen and respond are more likely to be at the forefront.

KEY ISSUE

- Change must be recognized and acted upon.
- There are a number of drivers that underpin change and in the tourism context which are poorly understood.
- While climate change will pose a large number of problems for destinations there are opportunities for growth.
- Innovation is a key strategy for successfully negotiating change.
- The tourism industry will need to organize on an industrial scale to ensure its voice is heard and concerns are accorded legitimacy.

REFERENCES

Abd-Alah, A. M.A. (1999). Coastal zone management in Egypt. *Coastal Zone Management*, 42, 835–848.

Abeyrantne, R. (1999). Management of the environmental impact of tourism and air transport on small island developing states. *Journal of Air Transport Management*, 5, 31–37.

Abeyratne, R. I.R. (1993). Air Transport Tax and its Consequences on Tourism. *Annals of Tourism Research*, 20, 450–460.

Adam-Smith, P. (1983). *When We Rode the Rails*. Lansdowne.

Agarwal, S. (1994). The resort cycle revisited: implications for resort. *Progress in Tourism, Recreation and Hospitality Management*, Cooper, C. P., and Lockwood, A., (eds.). Belhaven, Vol. 5, pp. 191–208.

Agarwal, S. (1997). The resort cycle and seaside tourism: an assessment of its applicability and validity. *Tourism Management*, 18, 65–73.

Agarwal, S. (2002). Restructuring seaside tourism, the resort lifecycle. *Annals of Tourism Research*, 29(1), 25–55.

Aguiló, E., Alegre, J., and Sard, M. (2005). The persistence of the *sun and sand* tourism model. *Tourism Management*, 26, 219–231.

Agyei-Mensah, S. (2006). Marketing its colonial heritage: a new lease of life for Cape Coast, Ghana? *International Journal of Urban and Regional Research*, 30, 705–716.

Airbus Industries. (2007). Flying by nature: global market forecast 2006–2025. Retrieved from, http://airbus.com/fileadmin/documents/gmf/PDF_d1/00-all-gmf-2007.pdf. p. 140.

Airey, D., and Shackley, M. (1997). Tourism development in Uzbekistan. *Tourism Management*, 18, 199–208.

Allchin, C. (2008, August). Architecture's hotspots. *Qantas Australian Airways In-flight Magazine*, pp. 150–157.

Andriotis, K. (2006). Researching the development gap between the hinterland and the coast—evidence from the island of Crete. *Tourism Management*, 27, 629–639.

Anker, H., Nellemann, V., and Sverdrup-Jensen, S. (2004). Coastal zone management in Denmark: ways and means for further integration. *Ocean and Coastal Management*, 47, 495–513.

Ankomah, P. K., and Crompton, J. L. (1992). Tourism cognitive distance: a set of research propositions. *Annals of Tourism Research*, 19, 323–342.

Armstrong, H., and Read, R. (1998). Trade and growth in small states: the impact of global trade liberalisation. *World Economy*, 21(4), 563–583.

Aruba (advert). (2007). Advert. *Islands, Special Issue: How to Run Away to Paradise*, 27 (7), 15.

Ashworth, G., and Hartmann, R. (2005). *Horror and Human Tragedy Revisited: The Management of Sites of Atrocities for Tourism*, Cognizant Communication Corporation, New York.

Ashworth, G. J., and Tunbridge, J. E. (2000). *The Tourist-Historic City: Retrospect and Prospect of Managing the Heritage City*, Elsevier Science Ltd.

279

Ayres, R. U. (2000). On forecasting discontinuities. *Technological Forecasting and Social Change*, 65, 81–97.

Bairoch, P. (1993). *Economics and World History*, University of Chicago Press.

Barff, R., Mackay, D., and Olshavsky, R. W. (1982). A selective review of travel-mode choice models. *Journal of Consumer Research*, 8, 370–380.

Barrett, J. A. (1958). *The Seaside Resort Towns of England and Wales*. Unpublished PhD thesis. University of London.

Barry, R. (2003). Mountain cryospheric studies and the WCRP climate and cryosphere (CIiC) project. *Journal of Hydrology*, 282, 177–181.

Barton, L. (1994). Crisis management: preparing for and managing disasters. *The Cornell Hotel and Restaurant Association Quarterly* 59–65.

Basu, P. (2000). Conflicts and paradoxes in economic development tourism in Papua New Guinea. *International Journal of Social Economics*, 27, 907–916.

Baum, T. (1998). Taking the exit route: extending the tourism area life cycle model. *Current Issues in Tourism*, 1(2), 167–175.

Beamann, J., Hegmann, S., and DuWora, R. (1991). Price elasticity of demand: a campground example. *Journal of travel Research*, 30(1), 22–29.

Becken, S. (2004). How tourists and tourism experts perceive climate change and carbon-offsetting schemes. *Journal of Sustainable Tourism*, 12, 332–347.

Becken, S. (2008). Developing indicators for managing tourism in the face of peak oil. *Tourism Management*, 29, 695–705.

Becken, S., and Hay, J. E. (2007). *Tourism and Climate Change: Risks and Opportunities*, Channel View Publications.

Beeedie, P., and Hudson, S. (2003). Emergence of mountain-based adventure tourism. *Annals of Tourism Research*, 30, 625–643.

Beirman, D. (2003). *Restoring Tourism Destinations in Crisis: A Strategic Marketing Approach*, CABI International.

Bell, W. (1997). *Foundations of Futures Studies*, Transaction Publishers, Vol. 1.

Benson, G. (1911). *York*. Blackie and Sons Limited.

Bentley, R. (2002). Global oil and gas depletion: an overview. *Viewpoint Energy Policy*, 30, 189–205.

Berger, and Loute. (2002). Climate: an exceptionally long interglacial ahead? *Science* 1287.

Berndaum, E. (1997). *Sacred Mountains of the World*, University of California Press, London.

Bernstein, W. (2008). *A Splendid Exchange How Trade Shaped the World*, Atlantic Monthly Press.

Bianchi, R. (1994). Tourism development in resort dynamics: an alternative approach. *Progress in Tourism, Recreation and Hospitality Management*, Cooper, C. P., and Lockwood, A., (eds.). John Wiley and Sons, Vol. 5, pp. 181–193.

Blake, A., and Sinclair, T. (2003). Tourism crisis management: UK response to September 11. *Annals of Tourism Research*, 30(4), 813–832.

Bood, R., and Postma, T. (1997). Strategic learning with scenarios. *European Management Journal*, 15(6), 633–647.

Borthwick, J. (2008). *Fables of a Spice Island. Vacations & Travel* (Apr/May/June 2008 Issue), Global Publishing, Balmain, Sydney, pp. 43–46.

Bramwell, B. (2004). The policy context for tourism and sustainability in Southern Europe's coastal regions. *Coastal Mass Tourism Diversification and Sustainable Development in Southern Europe*, Bramwell, B. (ed.). Channel View Publications, pp. 32–47.

Braun, O., Lohmann, M., Maksimovic, O., Meyer, M., Merkovic, A., Messerschmidt, E., Riedel, A., and Turner, M. (1999). Potential impact of climate change effects on preferences for tourism destinations: a psychological pilot study. *Climate Research*, 11, 247–254.

Briguglio, L., Archer, B., Jafari, J., and Wall, G. (1996). *Sustainable Tourism in Islands and Small States: Issues and Policies*, Pinter.

Buckley, R. C. (2006). *Adventure Tourism*, CAB International.

Buckley, R., Pickering, C., and Warnken, J. (2000). Environmental Management for Alpine Tourism and resorts in Australia. *Tourism and Development in Mountain Regions*, Godde, P., Price, M., and Zimmermann, F. (eds.). CABI, pp. 27–46.

Burak, S., Dogan, E., and Gazioglu, C. (2004). Impact of urbanisation and tourism on coastal environment. *Ocean and Coastal Management*, 47, 515–527.

Burke, L., and Maidens, J. (2004). *Reefs at Risk in the Caribbean*, World Resources Institute.

Burton, R. (1994). *Travel Geography*, (2nd edition). Pitman Publishing.

Busby, J. (2006). Climate change and collective action: troubles in transition to a post-oil economy. *St Antony's International Review*, 2(1), 35–55.

Butler, R. (1980). The concept of a tourist area resort cycle of evolution: implications for management of resources. *Canadian Geographer*, 14(1), 5–12.

Buzard, J. (2002) The grand tour and after (1660–1840). *The Cambridge Companion to Travel Writing*, Cambridge.

Cairncross, F. (1997). *The Death of Distance: How the Communication Revolution Will Change our Lives*, Harvard Businees School Press, Harvard.

Callegari, F. (2003). Sustainable development prospects for Italian coastal heritage: a Ligurian case study. *Journal of Cultural Heritage*, 4, 49–56.

Cameron, C., and Gatewood, J. (2008). Beyond sun, sand and sea: the emergent tourism programme in the Turks and Caicos Islands. *Journal of Heritage Tourism*, 3, 55–73.

Capra, F. (1996). *The Web of Life*, Harpers Collins Publishers.

Carlsen, J. (1999). 'Tourism impacts on small islands: a longitudinal study of community attitudes to tourism on the Cocos (Keeling Islands)'. *Pacific Tourism Review*, 3(1), 25–35.

Carson, D., and Jacobsen, D. (2005). Knowledge matters: harnessing innovation for regional tourism development. *Regional Tourism Cases: Innovation in Regional Tourism*, Carson, D., and Macbeth, J. (eds.). Common Ground, pp. 7–27.

Cassidy, F. (2002). Espiritu Santo, an event. *Journal of Sport & Tourism*, 7(3), 26–28.

Casson, L. (1994). *Travel in the Ancient World*, John Hopkins, London, UK.

Cetron, M. (2001). The world of today and tomorrow: the global view. *Tourism and Hospitality in the 21st Century*, Lockwood, A., and Meldik, S. (eds.). Butterworth-Heinemann, Oxford, pp. 18–28.

Chacko, H. (1997). Positioning a destination to gain a competitive edge. *Asia Pacific Journal of Tourism Research*, 1(2), 69–75.

Chang, Y., Hsu, C., Williams, G., and Pan, M. (2008). Low cost carrier's destination selection using a Delphi method. *Tourism Management*, 29, 898–908.

Chapman, K. (1979). *People, Pattern and Process: An Introduction to Human Geography*, Edward Arnold.

Cherlow, J. R. (1981). Measuring values of travel time savings. *Journal of Consumer Research*, 7, 360–371.

Chevs, J. R., Stoll, J., and Sellar, C. (1989). On the commodity value of time travel in recreational activities. *Applied Economics*, 21, 711–722.

Chew, J. (1987). Transport and tourism in the Year 2000. *Tourism Management*, 8(2), 83–85.

Cho, L. (2005). Marine protected areas: a tool for integrated coastal management in Belize. *Ocean and Coastal Tourism*, 48, 932–947.

Cho, L. (2005). Marine protected areas: a tool for integrated coastal management in Belize. *Ocean & Coastal Management*, 48(11–12), 932–947.

Choi, Y. (2007). Restoration ecology to the future: a call for a new paradigm. *Restoration Ecology*, 15, 351–353.

Choy, D. J.L. (1992). Life cycle models for Pacific Island destinations. *Journal of Travel Research*, 30(3), 26–31.

Christaller, W. (1963). Some considerations of tourism location in Europe: the peripheral regions in underdeveloped Countries recreation areas, *Regional Science Association: Papers XII*, Lund Congress, pp. 95–105.

Christie, P. (2005). Is integrated coastal management sustainable? *Ocean and Coastal Management*, 48, 208–232.

Coastal Zone Policy. (2008). European Commission. Retrieved 5 June 2008, http://ec.europa.eu/environment/iczm/home.htm.

Coates, J. F., Mahaffie, J. B., and Hines, A. (1997). *2050: Scenarios of US and Global Society Reshaped by Science and Technology*, Oak Hill Press, Greenboro, NC.

Cocks, D. (1999). *Future Makers, Future Takers: Life in Australia 2050*, University of New South Wales Press, Sydney.

Coghlan, A. (2008). Atoll. *The Encyclopaedia of Tourism and Recreation in Marien Environments*, Luck, M. (ed.). CABI.

Cohen, E. (1972). Toward a sociology of international tourism. *Social Research*, 39, 164–184.

Cohen, J. (2005). *Human Population: History, Status, Trends*, Scientific American Earth Institute at Columbus University, 20 October 2005. Accessible at www.earth.columbia.edu.

Collins, J. (2007). Ethnic precincts as contradictory tourist spaces. *Tourism, Ethnic Diversity and the City*, Rath, J. (ed.). Routledge.

Conlin, M., and Baum, T. (1995). *Island tourism: Management Principles and Practices*, Wiley.

Cooper, C. (1992). The life cycle concept and strategic planning for coastal resorts. *Built Environment*, 18(1), 57–66.

Cooper, C. (1997). Parameters and indicators of the decline of the British Seaside Resort. *The Rise and Fall of British Coastal Resorts: Cultural and Economic Perspectives*, Shaw, G., and Williams, A. (eds.). Cassell, London.

Cooper, M., and Eades, J. (2007). Landscape as Theme Park: demographic change, tourism, urbanization and the fate of communities in 21st century Japan. *Tourism Research International*, 11(1), 9–18.

Cooper, C. P., and Jackson, S. (1989). Destination life cycle: the Isle of man case study. *Annals of Tourism Research*, 16(3), 377–398.

Cooper, C., Fletcher, J., Fyall, A., Gilbert, D., and Wanhill, S. (2005). *Tourism Principles and Practise*, (3rd edition). Pearson Education.

Coto-Millan, Banos-Pino, J., and Inglanda, V. (1997). Marshallian demands of intercity passenger transport in Spain: 1980–1992. An economic analysis. *Transportation Research Part E: Logistics and Transportation Review*, 33E(2), 79–96.

Craig-Smith, S., and Fagence, M. (1994). *Learning to Live with Tourism*, Pitman.

Craig-Smtih, S. (1996). Tourism in the Pacific: issues and cases. *Economic Impact of Tourism in the Pacific*, Hall, C.M., and Page, S.J. (eds.). International Thomson Business Press, London, pp. 36–48.

Craik, J. (1991). *Resorting to Tourism Cultural Policies for Tourism Development in Australia*, Allen & Unwin, Sydney.

Croes, R. (2006). A paradigm shift to a new strategy for small island economies: embracing demand side economics for value enhancement and long term economic stability. *Tourism Management*, 27, 453–465.

Crompton, J. (1979). Motivations for pleasure vacation. *Annals of Tourism Research*, 6(4), 408–424.

Crossley-Holland, K. (1980). *The Norse Myths*, Pantheon Books.

Crouch, G. I. (1992). Effect of income and price on international tourism. *Annals of Tourism Research*, 19, 643–664.

Crouch, G. I. (1994). Demand elasticities for short-haul verses long-haul tourism. *Journal of Travel Research*, 33(2), 2–7.

Damodaran, A. (2006). Coastal resource complexes of South India: options for sustainable management. *Journal of Environmental Management*, 79, 64–73.

Dann, G. (1977). Anomie, ego–enhancement and tourism. *Annals of Tourism Research*, 4(4), 184–194.

Dann, G. M.S. (1994). Travel by train: keeping nostalgia on track. *Tourism: The State of the Art*, Seaton, A.U. (ed.). Wiley and Sons.

Davey, S., and Schlossman, M. (2007). *Unforgettable Islands to Escape to Before You Die*, BBC Books.

Davidson, J., and Spearritt, P. (2000). *Holiday Business: Tourism in Australia since 1870*, University of Melbourne Press.

Davis, M. (2003). The results are in … and now it's time to party. *New Scientist*, 178(2389), 22–23.

Department of Civil Aviation, Tourism and Culture. (1987). Five Year Tourism Development Plan, 1987–1992. Government of Papua New Guinea.

Dear, M., and Flusty, S. (1998). Postmodern urbanism. *Annals of the Association of American Geographers*, 88(1), 50–72.

Debbage, K. (1990). Oligopoly and the resort cycle in the Bahamas. *Annals of Tourism Research*, 17(5), 513–527.

di Benedetto, C. A., and Bojanic, D. C. (1993). Tourism area life cycle extensions. *Annals of Tourism Research*, 20(3), 557–570.

Digance, J. (1997). Life cycle model. *Annals of Tourism Research*, 24(2), 452–454.

Dimanche, F., and Lepetic, A. (1999). New Orleans tourism and crime: a case study. *Journal of Travel Research*, 38, 19.

Dowling, R. (1998). Indian Ocean Tourism Organisation (IOTO) Coastal Zone Management Workshop. *Tourism Management*, 19(3), 293–299.

Downton (1997) cited in Prideaux, B. (2005), Tourism Transport in Ecocities, *The City Limits: Rethinking the Significance of the City in a Globalizing Age*, APU International Symposium, Beppu, Japan, January 29–30 2005.

Doxey, G. (1975). A causation theory of visitor-residents irritants: methodological and research inferences, In: *Sixth Annual Research Conference*, San Diego, CA, 8–11 September, pp. 195–198.

Drabek, T. E. (1995). Disaster planning and response by tourist business executives. *Cornell Hotel and Restaurant Administration Quarterly*, 36(3), 86–96.

Dunn, N. W. (1981). *An Introduction to Public Policy Analysis*, Prentice-Hall, New York.

Dunne, G., Buckley, J., and Flanagan, S. (2007). City break motivation: the case of Dublin – A successful national capital. *Journal of Travel & Tourism Marketing*, 22, 95–107.

Duval, T. (2007). *Tourism and Transport Modes, Networks and Flows*, Channel View.

Dwyer, L., and Forsythe, P. (2008). Climate change policies, long-haul air travel and tourism. In *CAUTHE, Proceedings of the 18th Annual CAUTHE Conference*, Griffith University, Gold Coast, 11–14 February.

Edensor. (1988). *Tourists of the Raj*, Routledge.

Edmond, R. (2002). The Pacific/Tahati: queen of the South Seas. *Travel Writings*, Hulme, P., and Youngs, T. (eds.). Cambridge University Press, pp. 139–155.

Elliott, S., and Neirotti, L. (2008). Challenges of tourism in a dynamic island destination: the case of Cuba. *Tourism Geographies*, 10(3), 375–402 p. 28.

Elsasser, H., and Bürki, R. (2002). Climate change as a threat to tourism in the Alps. *Climate Research*, 20, 253–257.

EPICA Community Members. (2004). Eight glacial cycles from an Antarctic core. *Nature*, 429–623.

European Commission. (2001a). EC Focus on Coastal Zones: Turning the Tide for Europe's Coastal Zones. European Commission.

European Commission. (2001b). Defining, measuring and Evaluating Carrying Capacity in European Tourism Destinations Final Report (B43040/200/2945/MAR/D2). European Commission.

European Union, (2004), http://www.ecosyn.us/ecocity/Proposal/proposal1.html.

Fact Monster, Pearson Education. (2000–2007). Retrieved 6 September 2008, http://www.factmonster.com/ipka/A0762524.html.

Fagence, M. (1997). An uncertain future for tourism in microstates: the case of Nauru. *Journal of Tourism Management*, 18(6), 385–392.

Falco-Mammone, F., Coghlan, A., and Prideaux, B. (2006). *The Impacts of Cyclone Larry on Tourism in the Mission Beach, Tully and the Atherton Tablelands Region*, James Cook University.

Faulkner, B. (2001). Towards a framework for tourism disaster management. *Tourism Management*, 22, 135–147.

Faulkner, B. (2002). Rejuvenating a maturing tourist destination: the case of the Gold Coast. *Current Issues in Tourism*, 5(6), 472–520.

Faulkner, B., and Russell, R. (2000). Turbulence, chaos and complexity in tourism systems: a research direction for the new millennium. *Tourism in the Twenty First Century: Lessons from Experience*, Laws, E., and Faulkner, B. (eds.). Continuum, London, pp. 328–349.

Faulkner, B., and Vikulov, S. (2001). Katherine, washed out one day, back on track on the next: a post-mortem of a tourism disaster. *Tourism Management*, 22(4), 331–344.

Feldman, L. P., and Hornik, J. (1981). The use of time: an integrated conceptual model. *Journal of Consumer Research*, 7(4), 407–419.

Fennel, D. (1999). *Ecotourism: An Introduction*, Routledge.

Fink, S. (1986). *Crisis Management*, American Association of Management.

Fleischer, A., and Pizam, A. (2002). Tourism constraints among Israeli seniors. *Annals of Tourism Research*, 29(1), 106–123.

Frawley, G. (2004). *Jetstar – Lined up for Takeoff*, Australian Aviation.

Future Foundation. (2004). FutureScoping.

Forum on Vision and Strategy of an Ecocity, Ceju Island, Korea, Koran Federation for Environmental Movements, 29–30 October: pp.49–69.

Gable, F. J. (1997). Climate change impacts on Caribbean coastal areas and tourism. *Journal of Coastal Research*, 27, 49–70.

Gale, T. (2007). The problems and dilemmas of northern european post-mature coastal resorts. *Managing Coastal Tourism Resorts: A Global Perspective*, Agarwal, S., and Shaw, G. (eds.). Channel View, pp. 21–39.

Garrett, L. (2005). The next pandemic? *Foreign Affairs*, 84(4), 3–23.

Gates, C. (2003). *Near Eastern, Egyptian, and Aegean Cities, Ancient Cities: The Archaeology of Urban Life in the Ancient Near East and Egypt, Greece and Rome*, Routledge.

Gee, C., and Gain, C. (1986). Coping with crisis. *Travel and Tourism Analyst* 3–12.

GESAMP Joint Group of Experts on the Scientific Aspects of Marine Environmental Protection. (1996). *The Contributions of Science to integrated Coastal Management*. GESAMP Reports and Studies No. 61.

Getz, D. (1986). Models in tourism planning: towards integration of theory and practice. *Tourism Management*, 7(1), 21–32.

Getz, D. (1992). Tourism planning and destination life cycle. *Annals of Tourism Research*, 19(4), 752–770.

Gilbert, E. W. (1939). The growth of inland and seaside health resorts in England. *The Scottish Geographical Magazine*, 55(1), 16–35.

Gill, A., and Welk, E. (2007). Natural heritage as place identity: Tofino, Canada, a coastal resort on the periphery. *Managing Coastal Tourism Resorts: A Global Perspective*, Agarwal, S., and Shaw, G. (eds.). Channel View, pp. 169–183.

Glaesser, D. (2003). *Crisis Management in the Tourism Industry*, Butterworth-Heinemann.

Global Tourism and Leisure (Norfolk Island tourism 5 Year Strategy 2007/2008 to 2011/2121, 2008). Global Tourism and Leisure.

Gloster, M. (1997). *The Shaping of Noosa*, Noosa Blue Publishing Company.

Glover, P., and Prideaux, B. (2008). Using population projections to identify aspects of future tourism demand. *Advances in Hospitality and Leisure 4*, Chen, J. (ed.)., pp. 185–212.

Glover, P., and Prideaux, B. (2009). Implications of population ageing for the development of tourism products and destinations. *Journal of Vacation Marketing*, 15, 25–37.

Godde, P., Price, M., and Zimmermann, F. (eds.). (2000). Tourism and development in mountain regions: moving forward into the new millennium. In: *Tourism and Development in Mountain Regions* (pp. 1–26). CABI.

Godet, M. (2000). The art of scenarios and strategic planning: tools and pitfalls. *Technological Forecasting and Social Change*, 65, 3–22.

Goeldner, C., Ritchie, B. J.R., and McIntosh, R. (2000). *Tourism Principle, Practices, Philosophies*, Wiley.

Goncalves, V. F.D. C., and Aguas, P. M.R. (1997). The concept of life cycle: an application to the tourist product. *Journal of Travel Research*, 36(2), 12–22.

Gordon, S. (2008). *When Asia was the World*, Yale University Press.

Gordon, I., and Goodall, B. (1992). Resort cycles and development processes. *Built Environment*, 18(1), 5–11.

Gormsen, E. (1981). The spatio-temporal development of international tourism: attempt at a centre-periphery model, *La Consommation d'Espace par le Tourisme et sa Preservation* (pp. 150–170), C.H.E.T.: Aix-En-Provence.

Gossling, S., Ceron, J., Dubois, G., Patterson, T., and Richardson, R. (2005). The eco-efficiency of tourism. *Ecological Economics*, 54, 417–434.

Gotham, K. (2007). Destination New Orleans: commodification, rationalisation, and the rise of urban tourism. *Journal of Consumer Culture*, 7(3), 305–334.

Gottmann, J. (1961). *Megalopolis: The Urbanised Northeastern Seaboard of the United States*, Twentieth Century Fund, New York.

Government of Papua New Guinea. (1987). Five Year Tourism Development Plan, 1987–1992, Boroko; Department of Civil Aviation, Tourism and Culture.

Graedel, T. E. (1999, Winter). *The Bridge* 29(4).

Green, R. (2005). Community perceptions of environmental and social change and tourism development on the island of Koh Samui, Thailand. *Journal of Environmental Psychology*, 25, 37–56.

Grey, P., Williamson, J., Karp, D., and Dalphin, J. (2007). *The Research Imagination*, Cambridge University Press.

Griffin, T., and Hayllar, B. (2007). Historic waterfronts as tourism precincts: an experiential perspective. *Tourism and Hospitality Research*, 7, 3–16.

Grosspietsch, M. (2006). Perceived and projected images of Rwanda: visitor and international tour operators perspectives. *Tourism Management*, 27, 225–234.

Gunn, C. (1988). *Tourism Planning*, (2nd edition). Taylor and Francis.

Gunn, C. A. (1994). *Tourism Planning Basics Concepts Cases*, Taylor and Francis.

Gurtner, Y. (2007). Phuket: Tsunami and tourism – a preliminary investigation. *Crisis Management in Tourism*, Laws, E., Prideaux, B., and Chon, K. (eds.). CABI, pp. 217–233.

Gurtner, Y. (2007). Crisis in Bali: lessons in tourism recovery. *Crisis Management in Tourism*, Laws, E., Prideaux, B., and Chon, K. (eds.). CABI, pp. 81–97.

Gurung, C., and De Coursey, M. (1999). Too much too fast: lessons from Nepal's lost kingdom of Mustang. *Tourism Development in Critical Areas*, Singh, T.V., and Singh, S. (eds.). Cognizant, pp. 239–254.

Haimes, Y., Kaplan, S., and Lambert, J. H. (2002). Risk filtering, ranking, and management framework using hierarchical holographic modelling. *Risk Analysis*, 22(2), 383–397.

Hall, P. (2000). The Changing role of capital cities. *Plan Canada*, 40(3), 8–12.

Hall, C. M. (2001). Trends in ocean and coastal tourism: the end of the last frontier? *Ocean & Coastal Management*, 44(9), 601–618.

Hall, D. (2007). Policy response to rural dangers: managing educational visits in the wake of the foot and mouth and *E. coli* crisis. *Crisis Management in Tourism*, Laws, E., and Chon, K. (eds.). CABI, pp. 32–42.

Hall, M. (2008). *Tourism Planning Policies, Processes and Relationships*, (2nd edition). Pearson.

Hall, M., and Higham, J. (2005). *Tourism, Recreation and Climate Change*, Channel View Publications.

Hall, C. M., Timothy, D. J., and Duval, D. T. (2003). *Safety and Security in Tourism: Relationships, Management and Marketing*, The Haworth Hospitality Press.

Hamilton, J., Maddison, D., and Tol, R. (2005). Effects of climate change on international tourism. *Climate Research*, 29, 245–254.

Hansen, J. (2006). Dangerous human-made interference with climate: a GISS Model 1E study. *Atmospheric Chemistry and Physics Discussion*, 6, 12549–12610.

Hansen, J. (2007). Science reticence and sea level rise. *Environmental Research Letters*, 2, 6 Retrieved stacks.iop.org?ERL/2/024002.

Hardy, A. (2003). An investigation into the key factors necessary for the development of iconic touring routes. *Journal of Vacation Marketing*, 9(4), 314–330.

Harrison, D. (1994). Tourism and prostitution: sleeping with the enemy? The case of Swaziland *Tourism Management*, 15, 435–443.

Harrison, D. (1995). Development of tourism in Swaziland. *Annals of Tourism Research*, 22(1), 135–156.

Harrison, D. (2001). Tourism in small islands and microstates. *Tourism Recreation Research*, 26, 3–8.

Hart, C. W., Casserly, G., and Lawless, M. J. (1984). The product life cycle: how useful? *The Cornell Quarterly*, 24(4), 54–63.

Harvey, D. (1989). *The Condition of Post-Modernity*, Blackwell.

Hawaiian Airlines Advert. (2007). *Islands, Special Issue: How to Run Away to Paradise*, 27(7), p. 21.

Hay, I., and Yoeman, (2007). The Role of Scenario Planning in Destination Marketing: A Road Map for Scotland to 2025, Tourism – Past Achievements, Future Challenges, Council of Australian University Tourism and Hospitality Educators Annual Conference, 11–14 February 2007, Sydney (available on CD-ROM).

Haywood, M. T. (1986). Can the tourist area life cycle be made operational? *Tourism Management*, 7(3), 154–167.

Henderson, J. (2007). International tourism and infectious disease: managing the SARS crisis in Singapore. *Crisis Management in Tourism*, Laws, E., Prideaux, B., and Chon, K. (eds.). CABI, pp. 186–200.

Hensher, D. (1993). The transportation sector in Australia: economic issues and challenges. *Transportation Policy*, 1(1), 49–67.

Henson, R. (2008). *Can we Live with Climate Change? Extreme Weather Astronomy Special Issue*, Kalmbach Publishing, Waukesha WI pp. 26–33.

Hodgson, A. (1992). Hexagons for systems thinking. *European Journal of Operational Research*, 59, 220–230.

Hoegh-Guldberg, O. (1999). Climate change, coral bleaching and the future of the world's coral reefs. *Marine Freshwater Research*, 50, 839–866.

Holden, A. (1998). The use of visitor understanding in skiing management and development decisions at the Cairngorm Mountains, Scotland. *Tourism Management*, 19(2), 145–152.

Holden, P., Bale, M., and Holden, S. (2003). *Papua New Guinea — A Private Sector Assessment The Realities of Crisis*, The Enterprise Research Institute, for the Asian Development Bank.

Hollister, C., and Bennett, M. (2006). *Medieval Europe: A Short History*, McGraw-Hill.

Hooper, G. (2002). The Isles/Ireland: the Wilder Shore. *Travel Writing*, Hulme, P., and Youngs, T. (eds.). Cambridge University Press, pp. 174–190.

Hovinon, G. (2002). Revisiting the destination lifecycle model. *Annals of Tourism Research*, 29, 209–230.

Howard, P., and Pinder, D. (2003). Cultural heritage and sustainability in the coastal zone: experiences in South West England. *Journal of Cultural Heritage*, 4, 57–68.

http://www.context.org/ICLIB/IC08/Register.htm, visited 12 September 2004.

Huan, T., Beaman, J., and Shelby, L. (2004). No-escape natural disaster: mitigating impacts on tourism. *Annals of Tourism Research*, 31(2), 255–273.

Hudson, S. (2000). *Snow Business: A Study of the International Ski Industry*, Cassell.

Hudson, S., and Miller, G. (2005). The responsible marketing of tourism: the case of Canadian Mountain holidays. *Tourism Management*, 26, 133–142.

Hunter, M. (2007). Climate change and moving species: furthering the debate on assisted colonisation. *Conservation Biology*, 21, 1356–1358.

Hunter, C., and Shaw, J. (2007). The ecological footprint as a key indicator of sustainable tourism. *Tourism Management*, 28, 46–57.

Huntington, S. (1996). *The Clash of Civilizations and the Remaking of World Order*, Simon & Schuster, New York.

Inskeep, E. (1991). *Tourism Planning, An Integrated and Sustainable Development Approach*, Van Nostrand Reinhold.

Ioannides, D. (1992). Tourism development agents: the Cypriot Resort Cycle. *Annals of Tourism Research*, 19, 711–731.

Intergovernmental Panel on Climate Change. (2007). Summary for Policy Makers. In: Solomon, S., Qin, M., Manning, Z. Chen, M., Marquia, K., Averyt, M., Tignor, M. and Miller, H. (eds.). *Climate Change 2007: The Physical Science Basis*. Contribution of Working Group 1 to the Fourth Assessment Report of the Intergovernmental Panel on Climate Change, Cambridge University Press.

Jacobsen, D. (2005). Processes influencing innovation in the tourism system in Woodburn, New South Wales. *Regional Tourism Cases: Innovation in Regional Tourism*, Carson, D., and Macbeth, J. (eds.). Common Ground, pp. 131–136.

Jafari, J., and Ritchie, B. (1981). Towards a framework of tourism education: problems and perspectives. *Annals of Tourism Research*, 8, 13–34.

Jang, S., and Cai, L. (2002). Travel motivations and destination choice: a study of British outbound markets. *Journal of Travel and Tourism Marketing*, 13(3), 111–131.

Johnson, R. J. (1991). *Geography and Geographers*, Edward Arnold, London.

Johnson, D. *The Geology of Australia*. Cambridge University Press.

Judd, D. (1999). Constructing the Tourist Bubble. *The Tourist City*, Judd, D., and Fainstein, S. (eds.). Yale University press, New Haven.

Judd, D. R., and Fainstein, S. S. (1999). Cities as Places to Play. *The Tourist City*, Judd, D.R., and Fainstein, S.S. (eds.). Yale University Press.

Kaiser, C., and Helber, L. E. (1978). *Tourism Planning and Development*, CBI Publishing, Boston p. 144.

Kantarci, K. (2007). Perceptions of foreign investors on the tourism market in central Asia including Kyrgyzstan, Kazakhstan, Uzbekistan, Turkmenistan. *Tourism Management*, 28, 820–829.

Karkazis, J., and Thanassoulis, E. (1998). Assessing the effectiveness of regional development policies in Northern Greece using data envelopment analysis. *Socioeconomic Planning Science*, 32(2), 123–137.

Kaul, R. N. (1985). *Dynamics of Tourism: A Trilogy, Vol. 111 Transportation and Marketing*, Sterling Publishers.

Krebs, C. (2008). *The Ecological World View*, CSIRO Publishing.

Keller, C. P. (1987). Stages of peripheral tourism development – Canada's North West territories. *Tourism Management*, 8, 20–32.

Kenworthy, J. R. and Laube, F. B. (2001) The millennium cities database for sustainable transport. *International Union (Association) of Public Transport*, Brussels, Belgium and ISTP, Perth, Western Australia (CD-ROM publication).

Keown-McMullan, C. (1997). Crisis: when does a molehill become a mountain? *Disaster Prevention and Management*, 6(1), 4–10.

Kermath, B. M., and Thomas, R. N. (1992). Spatial dynamics of resorts, Sosua, Dominican Republic. *Annals of Tourism Research*, 19, 173–190.

Kilsby, D. (2004). Energy Futures for Australian Transport. Retrieved July 30 2008. http://www.nctr.org.DiscussionPapers/Enargy_Futres.pdf.

Kim, S., and Prideaux, B. (2003). Tourism, peace, politics and ideology: impacts of the Mt. Gumgang Tour Project in the Korean Peninsula. *Tourism Management*, 24(6), 675–685.

King, B. (1994). Research on resorts: A review. *Progress in Tourism, Recreation and Hospitality Management*, Cooper, C. P., and Lockwood, A., (eds.). John Wiley & Sons, Chichester, Vol. 5, pp. 165–180.

King, B. (2001). Resort-based tourism on the pleasure-periphery. *Tourism and the Less Developed World: Issues and Case Studies*, Harrison, D. (ed.). CABI International, Wallingford, pp. 175–190.

King, B., and McVey, M. (1997). Hotel investment in the South Pacific. *Travel and Tourism Analyst*, 5, 63–87.

Knabb, R. D., Rhome, J. R., and Brown, D. P. (December 20, 2005; updated August 10, 2006). ''Tropical Cyclone Report: Hurricane Katrina: 23-30 August 2005'' (PDF). National Hurricane Center. http://www.nhc.noaa.gov/pdf/TCR-AL122005_Katrina.pdf. Retrieved on 22-07-2008.

Koczberski, G., Curry, G., and Connell, J. (2001). Full circle or spiralling out of control? State Violence and the control of urbanisation in Papua New Guinea *Urban Studies*, 38(11), 2017–2036.

Koenig, U., and Abegg, B. (1997). Impacts of climate change on winter tourism in the Swiss Alps. *Journal of Sustainable Tourism*, 5(1), 46–58.

Kolb, B. M. (2006). *Tourism Marketing for cities and towns*, Butterworth-Heinemann.

Kosters, M. J. (1992). Tourism train: its role in alternative tourism. *Tourism Alternatives: Potential and Problems in the Development of Tourism*, Smith, V.L., and Eadingten, W.R. (eds.). International Academy for the Study of Tourism, USA.

Kotler, P. (1988). *Marketing Management: Analysis, Planning, Implementation and Control*, (6th edition). Prentice Hall, Englewood Cliffs, New Jersey.

Krebs, C. (2008). *The Ecological World View*, CSIRO Publishing, Collingwood.

Krockenberger, A., Kitching, R., and Turton, S., (eds.). (2004). *Environmental Crisis: Climate Change and Terrestrial Biodiversity in Queensland*, Rainforest CRC at James Cook University.

Laaksonen, P., Laaksonen, M., Borisov, P., and Halkoaho, J. (2006). Measuring image of a city: a qualitative approach with case example. *Place Branding*, 2, 210–219.

Lankford, S., and Howard, D. (1994). Developing a tourism impact attitude scale. *Annals of Tourism Research*, 20, 121–139.

Larner, J. (1999). *Marco Polo and the discovery of the World*, Yale University Press.

Lavery, P. (1974). The Demand for Recreation. *Recreational Geography*, Lavery, P. (ed.). David and Charles, Newton Abbot.

Law, C. (1993). *Urban Tourism: Attracting Visitors to Large Cities*, Mansell.

⚓ Law, C. M. (2002). *Urban Tourism: The Visitor Economy and the Growth of Large Cities*, Continuum.

Laws, E. (1995). *Tourism Destination Management: Issues, Analysis and Policies*, Routledge.

Laws, L., and Prideaux, B. (2005). Crisis management: a suggested typology. *Journal of Tourism and Travel Marketing*, 19(2–3), 1–8.

Laws, L., and Prideaux, B. (2005). Special issue on crisis. *Journal of Tourism and Travel Marketing*, 19(2–3), 1–8.

Laws, L., and Prideaux, B. (2005). Crisis management: a suggested typology. *Journal of Tourism and Travel Marketing*, 19(2/3), 1–8.

Laws, E., and Scott, N. (2007). *Journal of Travel and Tourism Marketing*, 21(3), [Special Issue on the theme of Tourism Crisis and Marketing Recovery Strategies].

Laws, E., Prideaux, B., and Chon, K. (2007a). Crisis management in tourism: challenges for managers and researchers. *Crisis Management in Tourism*, Laws, E., Prideaux, B., and Chon, K. (eds.). CABI, pp. 1–12.

Laws, E., Prideaux, B., and Chon, K. (2007b). Crisis management in tourism: challenges for managers and researchers. *Crisis Management in Tourism*, Laws, E., Prideaux, B., and Chon, K. (eds.). CABI, pp. 1–13.

Leaper, N. (2004). *Tourism Management*, (3rd edition). Pearson Education Press.

Lee, D., and Chok, S. (2005). Developing a Tourism System: A Tapestry of Knowledge. *Regional Tourism Cases: Innovation in Regional Tourism*, Carson, D., and Macbeth, J. (eds.). Common Ground, Melbourne, pp. 41–51 (change).

Leiper, N. (1979). The framework of tourism: towards a definition of tourism and the tourism industry. *Annals of Tourism Research*, 6, 390–407 90–407.

Leiper, N. (1990). *Tourism Systems An Interdisciplinary Perspective*, Department of Management Systems, Massey University, New Zealand.

Leiper, N. (2004). *Tourism Management*, (3rd edition). Pearson Education: Frenchs Forest.

Lennon, J., and Foley, M. (2000). *Dark Tourism: The Attraction of Death and Disaster*, Continuum.

Lepp, A. (2007). Residents' attitudes towards tourism in Bigodi village. *Uganda. Tourism Management*, 28, 876–885.

Li, H. (2003). Management of coastal mega-cities – a new challenge in the 21st century. *Marine Policy*, 27, 333–337.

Li, G. (2008). The nature of leisure travel and demand. *Aviation and Tourism Implications for leisure travel*, Graham, A., Papatheodorou, A., and Forsyth, P. (eds.). Aldershot, Ashgate, pp. 2–21.

Lim, C. (1997). An econometric classification and review of international tourism demand models. *Tourism Economics*, 3(1), 69–81.

Lindgren, M., and Bandhold, H. (2003). *Scenario Planning: The Link Between Future And Strategy*, Macmillan, Palgrave.

Litvin, S., and Crotts, J. (2007). A comparison of pre- and post-9/11 traveller profiles: post-crisis marketing implication. *Crisis Management in Tourism*, Laws, E., Prideaux, B., and Chon, K. (eds.). CABI, pp. 298–309.

Lockhart, G., and Drakakis-Smith, D. (1997). *Island Tourism, Trends and Prospects*, Pinter.

Lowych, E., Van Langenhave, L., and Bollaert, L. (1992). Typologies of Tourist Roles. *Choice and Demand in Tourism*, Johnson, P.A.D., and Thomas, B. (eds.). Mansell Publishing, London.

Lue, C. C., Crompton, J. L., and Fesenmaier, D. R. (1993). Conceptualization of multi-destination pleasure trips. *Annals of Tourism Research*, 20, 289–301.

Lundtrop, S., and Wanhill, S. (2001). The resort lifecycle theory; generating processes and estimation. *Annals of Tourism Research*, 28, 947–964.

Lyon, A., and Worton, A. (2007). Proposed model for tourism crisis management. *Crisis Management in Tourism*, Laws, E., Prideaux, B., and Chon, K. (eds.). CABI, pp. 200–216.

MacCannell, D. (1975). *The Tourist: A New Theory of the Leisure Class*, Schocken.

Mackintosh-Smith, T., (ed.). (2003). *The Travels of Ibn Battutah*, Picador.

Maddison, D. (2001). In search of warmer climates? The impact of climate change on flows of British tourists *Climatic Change*, 49, 193–208.

Maddox, J. (1998). *What Remains to be Discovered*, The free Press, New York.

Malaysian Airlines. (2008). *Vacations & Travel* (Apr/May/June 2008 Issue). Global Publishing, Balmain, Sydney.

Malaysian Airlines (2008) Shop till you drop in Kuala Lumps (advertisement), *Vacations and Travel* p. 154.

Malaysian Airlines, (2008), *Vacations & Travel*, Apr/May/June 2008 Issue, Global Publishing, Balmain, Sydney.

Maloney, W., and Montes Rojes, G. (2001). *Demand for Tourism*, The World Bank.

Mansfeld, J. (1999). Consuming spaces. *Explorations in Human Geography: Encountering Place*, Le Heron, R., Murphy, L., Foster, P., and Goldstone, M. (eds.). Oxford University Press, pp. 318–343.

Marsh, J. (1985). The Rocky and Selkirk Mountains and the Swiss Connection 1885–1914. *Annals of Tourism Research*, 12, 417–433.

Martin, C. A., and Witt, S. F. (1988). Substitute prices in models of tourism demand. *Annals of Tourism Research*, 15, 255–268.

Masini, E. B., and Medina Vasquez, J. (2000). Scenarios as seen from a human and social perspective. *Technological Forecasting and Social Change*, 65(1), 49–66.

Mason, D. (1999). *Spirit of the Mountains Korea's SAN-SHIN and Traditions of Mountain-Worship*, Hollym.

Matzarakis, A. (2002). Examples of climate change research for tourism demands. 15th Conference on Biometerology and Aerobiology joint with International Congress on Biometerology, 27th October–1 November 2002, Kansas City, Missouri, pp. 391–392.

Mayeres, I., Ochelen, S., and Proost, P. (1996). The marginal external cost of public transport. *Transportation Research Part D: Transport and Environment*, 1D(2), 79–96.

McDonald, J. (2005) Bird Flue to savage economies, *The Courier Mail* 5 November, p. 20.

Mckee, D. L., and Tisdell, C. (1988). The developmental implications of migration from and between small island nations. *International migration*, 26(4), 417–426.

McKercher, B. (1999). A chaos approach to tourism. *Tourism Management* 424–434.

McKercher, B., and Pine, R. (2005). Privation as a stimulus to travel demand? *Journal of Tourism and Travel Marketing*, 19(2–3), 107–116.

McKercher, B., Chan, A., and Lam, C. (2008). The impact of distance on international tourist movements. *Journal of Travel Research*, 47(2), 208–224.

McKercher, B., Prideaux, B., Cheung, C., and Law, R. (2002). *The Uphill Battle to Reduce Tourism's Carbon Footprint*.

McKinsey and Company. (2008). Preparing for China's Urban Billion. Retrieved www.mckinsey.com/mgi/publicatiosn/china_urban_summary_of_findings.asp.

Meethan, K. (1996). Consuming (in) the civilized city. *Annals of Tourism Research*, 23, 322–340.

Meheux, K., and Parker, E. (2006). Tourist sector perceptions of natural hazards in Vanuatu and the implications for a Small Island Developing State. *Tourism Management*, 27, 69–85.

Meredith, P. (2000). *The Australian Geographic Glovebox Guide to the Blue Mountains*, Australian Geographic.

Meyer-Arendt, K. (1985). The Grand Isle Louisiana resort cycle. *Annals of Tourism Research*, 12, 449–465.

Michaud, J., and Turner, S. (2006). Contending visions of a hill-station in Vietnam. *Annals of Tourism Research*, 33, 785–808.

Miles, M., and Covin, J. (2000). Environmental marketing: a sources of reputational, competitive and financial advantage. *Journal of Business Ethics*, 23(3), 299–311.

Mill, R. C., and Morrison, A. M. (1985). *The Tourism System: An Introductory Text*, Prentice Hall, New Jersey.

Milne, S. (1991). Tourism development in Papua New Guinea. *Annals of Tourism Research*, 18(3), 508–510.

Milne, S. (1992). Tourism and development in South Pacific Microstates. *Annals of Tourism Research*, 19(2), 191–212.

Miossec, J. M. (1976). *Elements pour une Theorie de l'Espace Tourisque*, Les Cahiers du Tourisme, C-36, C.H.E.T., Aix-en-Provence.

Mistilis, N., and Tolar, M. (2000). 'Impact of Macroeconomic Issues on Fiji's Hidden Paradise', paper presented to Council for Australian University Tourism and Hospitality Education (CAUTHE), Mt. Buller Victoria Australia, 2–5 February 20000.

Mitchell, R., and Reid, D. (2001). Community integration island tourism in Peru. *Annals of Tourism Research*, 28, 113–139.

Mitroff, I., Pearson, C., and Pauchant, T. (1992). Crisis management and strategic management: similarities, differences and challenges. *Advances in Strategic Management*, Shrivastava, P., Huff, A., and Dutton, J., (eds.). JAI Press Inc, Vol. 8.

Mo, C., Howard, D. R., and Havitz, M. E. (1993). Testing an International Tourist Role Typology. *Annals of Tourism Research*, 20, 319–335.

Moissec (1974).

Morgan, M. (1991). Dressing up to Survive Marketing Majorca Anew. *Tourism Management*, 12(1), 15–20.

Morrison, S. A., and Winston, C. (1985). An Economic Analysis of the Demand for Intercity Passenger Transportation. *Research in Transportation Economics: A Research Annual*, Keeler, T. E., (ed.). JAI Press, Greenwich, CT, Vol. 2, pp. 213–237.

Mules, T., Pforr, C., and Ritchie, B. W. (2007). The impact of domestic tourism on perceptions of Australia's National Capital. *Journal of Travel & Tourism Marketing*, 22, 35–53.

Nash, R., and Martin, A. (2003). Tourism in peripheral areas – the challenges for Northeast Scotland. *Tourism Research*, 5, 161–181.

New Zealand Ministry of Tourism. (2007). *Draft New Zealand Tourism Strategy 2015*. Ministry of Tourism.

Niiniluoto, I. (2001). Futures studies: science or art? *Futures*, 33(5), 371–377.

Norfolk Island Government. (2005). Department of Transport and Regional Services Norfolk Island Government Financial Report. Acumen Alliance.

Noronha, L. (2004). Coastal management policy: observations form an Indian case. *Ocean and Coastal Management*, 47, 63–77.

O'Flaherty, B. (2005). *City Economics*, Harvard University Press.

Oglethorpe, M. (1984). Tourism in Malta, A crisis of dependence. *Leisure Studies*, 3, 147–162.

Olsen, M. (2002). Keeping track of the self-drive market. *Drive Tourism: Up the Wall and Around the Bend*, Carson, D., Waller, I., and Scott, N. (eds.). Common Ground Publishing.

Oosthoek, S. (2008). Nature 2.0. *New Scientist*, 2663, 3235.

Oppermann, M. (1993). Tourism space in developing countries. *Annals of Tourism Research*, 20, 535–556.

Oppermann, M., and Chon, K. (1997). *Tourism in Developing Countries*, International Thompson Business Press, London.

Ortiz-Lozano, L., Granados-Barba, A., Solis-Weiss, V., and Garcia-Salgado, M. (2005). Environmental evaluation and development problems of the Mexican Coastal Zone. *Ocean and Coastal Management*, 48, 161–176.

Pacific Asia Travel Association. (1991). *Crisis Management Planning in the Travel and Tourism Industry*, PATA: Bangkok.

Page, S. (1995). *Urban Tourism*, Routledge.

Page, S. (1999). *Transport and Tourism: 'Themes in Tourism' Series*, Addison Wesley Longman, London.

Page, S. (2005). *Tourism and Transport Global Perspectives*, (2nd edition). Pearson.

Page, S., and Hall, M. (2003). *Managing Urban Tourism*, Prenctice Hall.

Page, S. J., and Hall, C. M. (2003). *Managing Urban Tourism*. Pearson Education Limited.

Palmer, T., and Riera, A. (2003). Tourism and environmental taxes, with special reference to the "Balearic ecotax". *Tourism Management*, 24, 665–674.

Papatheodorou, A. (2004). Exploring the evolution of tourism resorts. *Annals of Tourism Research*, 31, 219–237.

Papua New Guinea Tourism Promotion Authority. (2007). *Growing PNG Tourism As A Sustainable Industry*. Final Report.

Parkhe, A. (1993). Messy research, methodology predispositions and theory development in International Joint Ventures. *Academy of Management Review*, 18(2), 227–268.

Parr, M.-V. (2008). *10 Best Golf Courses by the Sea, Coast, March*, The National Magazine Company, London pp. 20–22.

Patton, M. (2002). *Qualitative Research and Evaluation Methods*, Sage Publications.

Pearce, P. (1981). *Tourism Development*, Longmans, London.

Pearce, F. (2006). *When the Rivers Run Dry; What Happens When Our Water Runs Out?*, Transworld Publishers.

Pearce, D. (2007). Capital city tourism: perspectives from Wellington. *Journal of Travel & Tourism Marketing*, 22, 7–200.

Peasley, A. (2008). *Qantas the Australian Way (August)*, Qantas Airways, Sydney pp. 144–147.

Peck, T. G., and Lepie, A. S. (1977). Tourism Development in Three North Carolina Coastal Towns. *Hosts and Guests: An Anthropology of Tourism*, Smith, V. (ed.). University of Pennsylvania Press, Pennsylvania, pp. 159–172.

Peng, B., Hong, H., Xue, X., and Jin, D. (2006). On the measurement of socioeconomic benefits of integrated coastal management (ICM): applications to Xiamen, China. *Ocean and Coastal Management*, 49, 93–109.

Peters, M., and Pikkemaat, B. (2005). Crisis management in Alpine winter sports resorts – the 1999 Avalanche disaster in Tyrol. *Journal of Tourism and Travel Marketing*, 19(2–3), 9–20.

Pfisher, R. (2000). Mountain cultures as a tourism resource: aboriginal views on the privileges of story telling. *Tourism and Development in Mountain Regions*, Godde, P., and Zimmermann, F. (eds.). CABI.

Pittock, A. B. (2005). *Climate Change Turning up the Heat*, CSIRO Publishing.

Pizam, A. (1999). A comprehensive approach to classifying acts of crime and violence at tourism destinations. *Journal of Travel Research*, 38(1), 5–12.

Pizam, A., and Fleischer, A. (2002). Severity versus frequency of acts of terrorism: which has a larger impact on tourism demand? *Journal of Travel Research*, 40, 337–339.

Pizam, A., Tarlow, P., and Bloom, J. (1997). Making tourists feel safe: whose responsibility is it? *Journal of Travel Research*, 36(1), 23–28.

Plog, S. (1973). Why destination areas rise and fall in popularity. *Cornell Hotel and Restaurant Association Quarterly*, 14(4), 55–58.

PNGTPA (2007). PNGTPA Monthly newsletter Issue 01 January. Retrieved 12 April 2008, http://www.pngtourism.org.pg/png/export/sites/TPA/news/newsletters/NewsLetter_Jan_2007_01.html.

Poon, A. (1989). Consumer strategies for a new tourism. *Progress in Tourism, Recreation and Hospitality Management*, Cooper, C., (ed.). Vol. 1, pp. 91–102.

Poon, A. (1993). *Tourism, Technology and Competitive Strategies*, CAB International, Wallingford.

Prideaux, B. (1998). The resort development spectrum: an examination of the role of the market in resort development. In: Faulkner, B., Tidswell, C., and Weaver, D. (eds). *Progress in Tourism and Hospitality Research, Proceedings of the Eight Australian Tourism and Hospitality Research Conference* (pp. 670–690). Gold Coast. Bureau of Tourism Research.

Prideaux, B. (1999a). The millennium bug: harmless insect or contagious business killer. Molloy, J., and Davies, J. (eds.). *Tourism and Hospitality: Delighting the Senses*, Proceedings of the Ninth Australian Tourism and Hospitality Research Conference, Bureau of Tourism Research, Canberra, p. 80.

Prideaux, B. (1999b). Tracks to tourism – Queensland rail joins the Tourism Industry. *International Journal of Travel Research*, 1(2), 73–86.

Prideaux, B. (2000a). The resort development spectrum. *Tourism Management*, 21(3), 225–241.

Prideaux, B. (2000b). The role of transport in destination development. *Tourism Management*, 21(1), 53–64.

Prideaux, B. (2000c). The role of the transport system in the growth of coastal resorts – an examination of resort development in South East Queensland. Unpublished PhD Thesis, The Department of Tourism and Leisure Management, The University of Queensland, pp. 1–309.

Prideaux, B. (2000d). The Asian Financial Crisis and the Tourism Industry – Lessons for the Future. *Current Issues in Tourism*, 2(4), 279–293.

Prideaux, B. (2002). The Cybertourist. *The Tourist as a Metaphor of the Social World*, Dann, G. (ed.). CAB International, Wallingford (Oxon), pp. 317–339.

Prideaux, B. (2003). The need to use disaster planning frameworks to respond to major tourism disasters: analysis of Australia's response to tourism disasters in 2001. *Journal of Travel and Tourism Marketing*, 15(4), 281–298.

Prideaux, B. (2004). The resort development spectrum: the case of the Gold Coast Australia. *Tourism Geographies*, 6(1), 26–59.

Prideaux, B. (2006). Responding to climate change: a case study using scenarios to explore options for destination response, 2006 ATLAS Conference, 5-6 December 2006, University of Otago (available on CD ROM).

Prideaux, B. (2008). The role of visitor attractions in peripheral areas. In: Fyall, A., Garrod, B., Leask, A., and Wanhill, S. (eds.). Managing Visitor Attractions (pp. 80–94). Heinemann: Butterworth.

Prideaux, B., Croswell, M., and Ng, W. Y. (2007). *Norfolk Island Visitor Survey 2002*, James Cook University, Cairns.

Prideaux, B., Coghlan, A., and McKercher, B. (2009, Februaury). Identifying indicators measure the tourists' views on climate change. *CAUTHE 2009: See Change: Tourism and Hospitality in a Dynamic World*, Carlsen, J., Hughes, M., Holmes, K., and Jones, R. (eds.). Promaco Conventions PTY ltd, Fremantle.

Prideaux, B., and Falco-Mammone, F. (2007). *Economic Values of Tourism in the Wet Tropics World Heritage Area*, Cooperative Research Centre for Tropical Rainforest Ecology and Management, James Cook University pp. 1–64.

Prideaux, B., and Laws, E. (2007). Reflections and Future Research Priorities. *Crisis Management in Tourism*, Laws, E., Prideaux, B., and Chon, K. (eds.). CABI, Wallingford, pp. 375–388.

Prideaux, B., and Master, H. (2001). Health and safety issues effecting international tourists in Australia. *Asia Pacific Journal of Tourism*, 6(2), 24–32.

Prideaux, B., and Tao, Y. (2005). Developing ecotourism in Yunnan: the key role of education in achieving long-term sustainability. *ASEAN Journal on Hospitality and Tourism*, 4(1), 39–50.

Prideaux, B., Wei, S., and Ruys, H. (2001). The senior drive tour market in Australia. *Journal of Vacation Marketing*, 7(3), 209–219.

Prideaux, B., Laws, E., and Faulkner, B. (2003a). Events in Indonesia: exploring the limits to formal tourism trends forecasting methods in complex crisis situations. *Tourism Management*, 24(6), 475–487.

Prideaux, B., Laws, E., and Faulkner, B. (2003b). Events in Indonesia: exploring the limits to formal tourism trends forecasting methods in complex crisis situations. *Tourism Management*, 24(4), 511–520.

Prideaux, B., Laws, E., and Faulkner, B. (2003). Events in Indonesia: exploring the limits to formal tourism trends forecasting methods in complex crisis situations. *Tourism Management*, 24(4), 475–487.

Priestly, G., and Mundet, L. (1998). The post-stagnation phase of the resort cycle. *Annals of Tourism Research*, 25, 85–111.

Prosser, G. (1995). Tourist destination life cycles: progress, problems and prospects. *Proceedings of the National Tourism and Hospitality Conference 1995*, Shaw, R. (ed.). Bureau of Tourism Research, Canberra.

Quade, E. S. (1979). *Analysis for Public Decisions*, Elsevier, New York.

Quinn, B. (2005). Arts festivals and the city. *Urban Studies*, 42, 927–943.

Register, R. (1997), EcoCities Making Cities Sustainable is a Crucial Challenge.

Richardson, B. (1994). Crisis Management and the management strategy: time to ''loop the loop''. *Disaster Prevention and Management*, 3(3), 59–80.

Richmand, S., Cambon, M., Harper, D., and Watkins, R. (2004). Malaysia, Singapore and Brunei. Lonely Planet.

Ringland, G. (1998). *Scenario planning: managing for the future*, John Wiley.

Ritchie, B. W. (2004). Chaos, crises and disasters: a strategic approach to crisis management in the tourism industry. *Tourism Management*, 25, 669–683.

Robson, C. (1993). *The Qualitative Story*. Survey, Spring, 13–14.

Rogers, E. (1983). *Diffusion of Innovations*, (3rd edition). The Free Press.

Rogers, E. (1995). *Diffusion of Innovations*, (4th edition). The Free Press, New York.

Rolle, J. D. (1997). Estimation of Swiss railway demand with computation of elasticites. *Transportation Research Part E: Logistics and Transportation Review*, 33E(2), 117–128.

Rostow, W. W. (1960). *The Stages of Economic Growth: A Non Communist Manifesto*, Cambridge University Press, Cambridge.

Rovos Rail. (1996). Royos Rail Steam Safaris. Brochure produced by Rovos Rail, Pretoria, Republic of South Africa.

Russell, R., and Faulkner, B. (1998). Reliving the destination life cycle in Coolangatta. *Embracing and Managing Change in Tourism: International Case Studies*, Laws, E., Faulkner, B., and Moscardo, G. (eds.). Routledge.

Russell, R., and Faulkner, B. (1999). Movers and shakers: chaos makers in tourism development. *Tourism Management*, 20(4), 411–423.

Russo, A. (2002). The 'Vicious circle' of tourism development in heritage cities. *Annals of Tourism Research*, 29(1), 165–182.

Ryan, C. (2003). *Recreational Tourism: Demand and Impacts*, Channel View.

Samuelson, P. (1992). *Economics 3rd Australian Edition*, Mc Graw-Hill, Sydney.

Santana, G. (2003). Crisis management and tourism: beyond the rhetoric. *Journal of Travel and Tourism Marketing*, 15(4), 299–321.

Santana, G. (2007). *Tourism and Crisis Management*, Tauris and Co Ltd.

Santos, C., Belhassen, Y., and Caton, K. (2008). Reimagining Chinatown: an analysis of tourism discourse. *Tourism Management*, 29, 1002–1012.

Saremba, J., and Gill, A. (1991). Value conflicts in mountain park settings. *Annals of Tourism*, 18, 455–472.

Sathiendrakumar, R., and Tisdell, C. (1989). Tourism and the economic development of the Maldives. *Annals of Tourism Research*, 16(2), 254–269.

Scheyvens, R., and Momsen, J. (2008). Tourism and poverty reduction: Issues for Small Island States. *Tourism Geographies*, 10, 22–41.

Schmidt, P., and Berrell, M. (2007). Western and Eastern approaches to crisis management: some differences. *Crisis Management in Tourism*, Laws, E., Prideaux, B., and Chon, K. (eds.). CAB International, pp. 66–80.

Schultz, P. (2003). *1000 Places to See Before you Die: A Travelers' Life*, Workman Publication Company.

Schwartz, B. (1988). Forecasting and scenarios. *Handbook of Systems Analysis*, Miser, H.J., and Quade, E.S. (eds.). Wiley.

Schwartz, P. (1998). *The art of the long view: planning for the future in an uncertain world*, Wiley, Chichester.

Scott, D., McBoyle, G., and Mills, B. (2003). Climate change and the skiing industry in southern Ontario (Canada): exploring the importance of snowmaking as a technical adaptation. *Climate Change*, 23, 171–181.

Shaalan, I. (2005). Sustainable tourism development in the Red Sea of Egypt threats and opportunities. *Journal of Cleaner Production*, 13, 83–87.

Shah, J., and Nagpal, T. (1997). *Urban Air Quality Management Strategy in Asia: Kathmandu Valley Report*, World Bank Technical Paper, No. 378.

Shareef, R., and Hoti, S. (2005). Small Island tourism economies and country risk ratings. *Mathematics and Computers in Simulation*, 68, 557–570.

Shaw, G., and Agarwal, S. (2007). Introduction: the development and management of coastal resorts: a global perspective. *Managing Coastal Tourism Resorts: A Global Perspective*, Agarwal, S., and Shaw, G. (eds.). Channel View, pp. 1–21.

Shaw, G., and Williams, A. (1994). *Critical Issues on Tourism: A Geographical Perspective*. Oxford.

Shaw, G., and Williams, A., M. (2002). *Critical Issues in Tourism: A Geographical Perspective*. Blackwell Publishers Ltd.

Shields, M. (1975). Social impact studies. *Environment and Behaviour*, 7(3), 265–284.

Silver, B. L. (1998). *The Ascent of Science*, Oxford University Press, New York.

Simmons, D., and Becken, S. (2004). Ecotourism: the cost of getting there. *Case Studies in Ecotourism*, Buckley, R. (ed.). CAB International, pp. 15–23.

Singer, P., and Prideaux, B. (2004). Implications of demographic change for the development of tourism products and destinations. In European Academy of Bolzano (ed.) Shaping the Future of the Tourism and Leisure Industry – Proceedings of the 2nd Leisure Futures Conference, Bolzano, Italy, 10–12 November 2004, European Academy of Bolzano, Bolzano.

Singer, P., and Prideaux, B. (2005). Scenarios as a tool for identifying future tourism demand, 15th CAUTHE Conference, Alice Springs, 2–5 February, available on CD Rom.

Skolnick. A. (2007). The last nomads, on A Thai island, Moken Sea Gypsies live as they have lived for Centuries. *Islands, Special Issue: How to Run Away to Paradise*, 27(7), 37–40.

Smeral, E. (1998). The impact of globalisation on small and medium enterprises: new challenges for tourism policies in European countries. *Tourism Management*, 19(4), 371–380.

Smith, V. (1977). Introduction. *Hosts and Guests, The Anthropology of Tourism*, Smith, V.L. (ed.). University of Pennsylvania Press, Pennsylvania.

Smith, R. A. (1992). Beach resort evolution. *Annals of Tourism Research*, 19, 304–322.

Snoussi, M., and Aoul, E. H.T. (2000). Integrated coastal zone management program Northwest African Region case. *Ocean and Coastal Management*, 43, 1033–1045.

Soane, J. (1993). *Fashionable Resort Region: Their Evolution and Transformation*, AB International.

Soanne, J. (1992). The origin, growth and transformation of maritime resorts since 1840. *Built Environment*, 18, 12–26.

Soja, E. (1989). *Postmodern Geographies: The Reassertion of Sapce in Critical Social Theory*, Verso.

Somnez, S., Apostopoulos, Y., and Tarlow, P. (1999). Tourism in Crisis: managing the effects of terrorism. *Journal of Travel Research*, 38, 13–18.

Sontag, S. (1977). *On Photography*, Penguin Books, London.

Stabler, M. J. (1991). Modelling the tourist industry: a new approach. *The Tourism Industry an International Analysis*, Sinclair, M.T., and Stabler, M.J. (eds.). CAB International, Wellingford, pp. 15–44.

Stansfield, C. (1978). Atlantic City and the resort cycle: background to the legalisation of gambling. *Annals of Tourism Research*, 5, 238–251.

Steene, A. (1999). Risk management within tourism and travel – suggestions for research programs. *Tourizam*, 47(1), 13–18.

Stern, N. (2006). *The Economics of Climate Change The Stern Review*, Cambridge University Press.

Steutermann Rodgers, K. (2007). Discover experience the ultimate escape. *Islands, Special Issue: How to Run Away to Paradise*, 27(7), 18–20.

Stewart, G. (2008). *When Asia was the World*, Yale University Press, New Haven and London.

Stix, G. (2008). Traces of a distant past. *Scientific America*, July, 299, 38.

Stone, A., Chow, C., and Ho, R. (2008). *Hong Kong and Macau City Guide*, Lonely Planet Publications.

Stoppford, J., and Strange, S. (1991). *Rival States, Rival Firms: Competition for World Market Share*, Cambridge University Press.

Strapp, J. (1988). The resort cycle and second homes. *Annals of Tourism Research*, 15, 504–516.

Taplin, J. H.E. (1980). A coherence approach to estimates of elasticities in the vacation travel market. *Journal of Transport Economics and Policy*, 14, 19–35.

Taylor, C. J. (1983). Rail Passenger Transport in Australia; A Critical Analysis of the Network and Services. Unpublished PhD Thesis, Department of Regional and Town Planning: The University of Queensland.

Taylor, R., Mileham, L., Tindimugaya, C., Majugu, A., Muwanga, A., and Nakileza, B. (2006). Recent Glacial Recession in the Rwenzori Mountains of East Africa Due to Rising Air Temperature, *Geophysical Research Letters*, 33, L10402, doi: 10.1029/2006GL025962.(Mt Kenya glacier gone in 20 years).

Teye, V. B. (1992). Land Transportation and Tourism in Bermuda. *Tourism Management*, 13(4), 395–405.

The Macau Daily. (2008). 'I need a break' (advert), 3 April 2008, p. 3.

The Sunday Times Travel. (2008). Hip Cities 2008. *The Sunday Times Travel*. April.

Theobald, W. F. (1994). The Context, Meaning and Scope of Tourism. *Global Tourism: The Next Decade*, Theobald, W.F. (ed.). Butterworth-Heinemann.

Thurot, J. M. (1973). *Le Tourisme Tropical Balneaire:le modele caraibe et ses extensions*, Thesis, Centre d'Etudes du Tourisme, Aix-en-Provence.

Timothy, D. J. (2001). Benefits and costs of smallness and peripheral location in tourism: Saint-Pierre et Miquelon (France). *Tourism Recreation Research*, 26(3), 61–70.

Timothy, D. (2002). *Journal of Travel Research*, 41, 107–113.

Tol, R. (2007). The impact of a carbon tax on International tourism. *Transportation Research Part D: Transport and the Environment*, 12, 129–142.

Tooman, L. A. (1997). Applications of the life in cycle models in tourism. *Annals of Tourism Research*, 24(1), 214–234.

Torres, R. (2001). Toward a better understanding of tourism and agriculture linkages in the Yucatan: tourist food consumption and preferences. *Tourism Geographies*, 4(3), 282–306.

Torres, R. (2002). Cancun's tourism development from a Fordist spectrum of analysis. *Tourism Studies*, 2, 8–116.

Tourism Queensland. (2004b). *Developing & Marketing Tourism Drive Routes*. Tourism Queensland.

Tribe, J. (1997). The indiscipline of tourism. *Annals of Tourism Research*, 24(3), 638–657.

Turner, L., and Ash, J. (1975). *The Golden Hordes: International Tourism and the Pleasure Periphery*. Constable.

Turnock, D. (1990). Tourism in Romania rural planning in the Carpathians. *Annals of Tourism Research*, 17, 79–102.

United Nations (1994) Report of the Global Conference on the Sustainable Development of Small Island Developing States, United Nations. Retrieved http://www.un.org/documents/ga/conf167/aconfl67-9.htm.

United Nations General Assembly Resolution 47/186(A/RES/47/186, 25 February 1993.

UNWTO (2003). *Tourism 2020 Vision Vol. 7 Global Forecasts and Profiles of Market Segments*, UNWTO: Madrid.

Unwin, T. (1992). *The Place of Geography*, Longman, London.

Uriely, A., Aviad, A., and Reichel, A. (2002). Heritage proximity and resident attitudes toward tourism development. *Annals of Tourism Research*, 29, 859–861.

Urry, J. (1987). Some social and spatial aspects of services. *Environment and Planning: Society and Space*, 5, 5–26.

Urry, J. (1990). *The Tourist Gaze*, Sage.

Urry, J. (1995). *Consuming Places*, Routledge.

Urry, J. (2002). *The Tourist Gaze*, (2nd edition). Sage.

Usal, M., and Jurowski, C. (1994). Test the push and pull factors. *Annals of Tourism Research*, 21(4), 844–846.

Valaoras, G. (2000). Conservation and development in Greek Mountain Areas. *Tourism and Development in Mountain Regions*, Godde, P., Price, M., and Zimmermann, F. (eds.). CABI, Wallingford.

Vallega, A. (2003). The Coasta; cultural heritage facing coastal management. *Journal of Cultural Heritage*, 4, 5–24.

van der Heijden, K. (1996). *Scenarios: The Art of Strategic Conversation*, John Wiley & Sons.

van der Velde, M., Green, S., Vanclooster, M., and Clothier, B. (2007). Sustainable development in small island developing states: agriculture intensification, economic development, and freshwater resources management on the coral atoll of Tongatapu. *Ecological Economics*, 61, 456–468.

van Doorn, J. W.M. (1986). Scenario writing – a method for long-term tourism forecasting? *Tourism Management*, 7(1), 33–49.

Wack, P. (1985). Scenarios: shooting the rapids. *Harvard Business Review* 139–150.

Wall, G. (1982). Cycles and capacity. Incipient theory a conceptual contradiction? *Tourism Management*, 3(3), 188–192.

Wall. G. (1993). Towards a tourism typology. In: Nelson, J. G., Butler, R. N., and Wall, G. (eds.). *Tourism and Sustainable Development: Monitoring, Planning, Managing*, Department of Geography Publication Series Number 37, University of Waterloo.

Wall, G. (2000). Centre-periphery. *Encyclopaedia of Tourism*, Jafari, J. (ed.). Routledge, pp. 76.

Walsh, R. G., Sanders, L. D., and McKean, J. R. (1990). The consumption value of travel time on recreation trips. *Journal of Travel Research*, 24(1), 17–24.

Watkins, S., and Jones, C. (2006). *Unforgettable Journeys to take Before you Die*, BBC Books.

Weaver (1990).

Weaver, D. B. (1993). Grand Cayman island and the resort cycle concept. *Journal of Travel Research*, 29(2), 9–15.

Weaver, D. (1998a). Peripheries of the periphery tourism in Tobago and Barbuda. *Annals of Tourism Research*, 25, 292–313.

Weaver, D. (1998b). *Ecotourism in the Less Developed World*, CAB International.

Weaver, D. (2000). The exploratory war-distorted destination life cycle. *The International Journal of Tourism Research*, 2, 151–161.

Weiner, A. J., and Kahn, H. (1972). Crisis and Arms Control. *International Crises: Insights from Behaviour Research*, Hermann, C.F. (ed.). The Free Press, pp. 21.

Welford, R. (1999). Tourism and sustainable development: an analysis of policy and guidelines for managing provision and consumption. *Sustainable development*, 7(4), 165.

Wheatley, A. (2008). China Urged to Shift Urban Growth to Supercities, Reuters. Retrieved 28 March 2008. www.planetark.com/dailynewstory.cfm/newsid/47623/story.htm.

Whyte, and Prideaux. (2008). The growth in low-cost carrier services in Queensland: implications for regional tourism destinations. *Tourism Recreation Research*, 33, 59–66.

Wilkerson, P. F. (1987). Tourism in small island nations: a fragile dependence. *Leisure Studies*, 6, 127–146.

Williams, M. (1993). An expansion of the tourist site cycle model: the case of Minorea (Spain). *Journal of Tourism Studies*, 4(2), 24–32.

Williams, P., and Gill, A. (1999). A workable alternative to the concept of carrying capacity: growth management planning. *Tourism Development in Critical Areas*, Singh, T.V., and Singh, S. (eds.). Cognizant, pp. 51–64.

Williams, S., Bolitho, E., and Fox, S. (2003). Climate change in Australian tropical rainforests: an impending environmental catastrophe. *Proceedings of the Royal Society of London Series B*, 270, 1887–1893.

Wilson, I. (2000). From scenario thinking to strategic action. *Technological and Social Change*, 65, 23–29.

Windybank, S., and Manning, M. (2003). Papua New Guinea on the Brink, Issue Analysis, The Centre for Independent Studies, Vol. 30, 12 March 2003.

Witt, S. F. (1980). An Econometric Comparison of U.K. and German Foreign Holiday Behaviour. *Managerial and Decision Economics*, 1(3), 123–131.

Wong, P. P. (1986). Tourism development and resorts on the east coast of Peninsular Malaysia. *Singapore Journal of Tropical Geography*, 7, 152–162.

Wong, P. (1998). Coastal tourism development in Southeast Asia: relevance and lessons for coastal zone management. *Ocean and Coastal Management*, 38, 89–109.

WTO. (2002). *The Economic Impact of Tourism on the Islands of Asia and the Pacific: A Report on the WTO International Conference on Tourism and Island Economies*. Madrid: WTO.

WTO. (1996). *Tourist Safety and Security: Practical Measures for Destinations*. Madrid: World Tourism Organisation.

WTO (1998) *Handbook on Natural Disaster Reduction in Tourist Areas*. Madrid: World Tourism Organisation.

Yang, B-E. (2004). A Vision of Ecological Cities in South Korea, *In International*.

Yeoman, I. (2007). *Tomorrow's Tourist Scenarios and trends*, Elsevier, Oxford.

Yeoman, I., and McMahon-Beattie, U. (2005). Developing a scenario planning process using a blank piece of paper. *Journal of Vacation Marketing*, 5(3), 273–285.

Yeoman, I., Lennon, J., Blake, A., Galt, M., and Greenwood, U. (2007). Oil depletion: what does it mean for Scottish tourism? *Tourism Management*, 28, 1354–1365.

Yin, R. K. (1989). *Case Study Research-Design and Methods. Applied Science Research Series*, (5th revised edition). Sage Publications.

Yin, R. K. (1993). Applications of Case Study Research. Applied Social Research Methods Series. Vol. 34, Sage Publications.

Yin, R. K. (1994). *Case Study Research*, Sage Publications.

Yoon, A. (2007). GE Aviation. Virgin Atlantic 747 to test Biofuel in Early 2008. Retrieved 15 August 2008 www.planetrack.com/dailynewsstory.

Young, B. (1983). Touristization of traditional Maltese fishing-farming villages: a general model. *Tourism Management*, 4(1), 35–41.

Yu, L., and Goulden, M. (2006). A comparative analysis of international tourists' satisfaction in Mongolia. *Tourism Management*, 27, 1331–1342.

Yuan, S., and McDonald, C. (1990). Motivational determinates of International pleasure time. *Journal of Travel Research*, 24(1), 42–44.

Zillinger, M. (2007). Tourist routes: German car-tourists in Sweden. *Tourism Geographies*, 9, 64–83.

Index